Racing & Foot

JUMPS RACING GUIDE 2017-18

Interviews • Statistics • Results
Previews • Training centre reports

DOUBLE e
5/6 (83p)
10/11 (90p)
-£2.50

Contributors: Richard Birch, James Burn,
Graham Dench, Jack Haynes, Dylan Hill, Tony Jakobson,
Andrew King, Ed Quigley, Stuart Riley, Colin Russell,
Alan Sweetman, Nick Watts

Designed and edited by Nick Watts and Dylan Hill

Published in 2017 by Raceform Ltd
27 Kingfisher Court, Hambridge Road, Newbury RG14 5SJ

A catalogue record for this book is available from the British Library.

ISBN 978-1-910497-25-8

Printed by CPI Group (UK) Ltd, Croydon, CRO 4YY

Est. 1909
RACING & FOOTBALL OUTLOOK

Contents

Est. 1909
RACING & FOOTBALL OUTLOOK

Editor's introduction

TO paraphrase something our columnist Richard Birch wrote in September, "Racing can provide the most enormous highs; equally it can produce the biggest lows imaginable."

Birchy, of course, was writing about the life of a punter, but few people could ever testify to the truth of his words more than some of the top trainers in Britain and Ireland last season.

Nicky Henderson suffered one of the most desperate weekends of his long career last November, kicking off when he was forced to admit defeat in his attempts to get Sprinter Sacre back on the racecourse. At least Sprinter Sacre had the opportunity to fulfil his potential and could enjoy a well-deserved retirement. Not so Simonsig, the 2014 Racing Post Arkle winner who had barely run since due to injury and lost his life at Cheltenham that Sunday afternoon.

But Henderson hit back in the most memorable fashion, storming to his fourth trainers' championship largely on the back of a phenomenal week back at Cheltenham in March when Buveur D'Air provided the highlight by giving him a sixth Champion Hurdle – as remarkably predicted by Downsman in this annual 12 months ago.

For Irish champion Willie Mullins, who clung on to his crown by the narrowest of margins from Gordon Elliott, the emotional rollercoaster was condensed into just three days at the Cheltenham Festival.

Mullins suffered a catastrophic first two days at the meeting, coming to a head with the stunning 2-9 defeat of Douvan in the Champion Chase, and all the talk on Wednesday evening at Prestbury Park was that the Mullins horses, supposedly the most fearsome team ever assembled for Cheltenham, were wrong. Fast-forward 24 hours and how silly we all looked as Yorkhill, Un De Sceaux, Nichols Canyon and Let's Dance gave him a four-timer that must have been all the sweeter for all that had gone before it.

For poor Oliver Sherwood, the agony and the ecstasy of this great sport was experienced over a matter of seconds as his former Grand National winner Many Clouds topped even that achievement with the most gutsy and courageous of victories over Thistlecrack in January only to collapse and die just after the line.

Compared to the likes of Henderson, Mullins and Sherwood, last season was relatively sedate for Paul Nicholls. Lots of winners, including lots of big Saturday winners, but no superstar who could have helped him to fend off Henderson in the race for the trainers' title.

Nicholls now finds himself at a crossroads in his career and has publicly given up on fighting for the championship, instead packing his yard full of exciting youngsters in the hope one or two could develop into the next Kauto Star or Denman. It's a fascinating time at Ditcheat and it seemed the only place to start the annual, so we sent Graham Dench to speak to Nicholls for a fantastic stable tour.

Another trainer who can boast a sure touch with young horses is Tom Lacey, the subject of our other stable tour after a breakthrough campaign which saw him

NICKY HENDERSON: from the depths of despair to the trainers' championship

send out 21 winners, while our regional reporters have also been speaking to all the trainers in their area to bring you all the latest news on fresh arrivals and horses to follow from the rest of the leading names in the training ranks.

As well as all that, Nick Watts has picked out his 30 horses to follow from either side of the Irish Sea, while we have an ante-post guide to the big four races at the Cheltenham plus the King George and Grand National, the views of Richard Birch and Ed Quigley, a comprehensive guide to last season's big races by Dylan Hill and a rundown of the leading speed figures.

Then there are reams of statistics that should help your punting, including figures for last season's top ten trainers broken down by month, jockey, race type and course plus lists of the leading trainers and jockeys for every course in Britain.

We have every angle covered to make it a profitable season, although to keep up to date make sure you also buy your copy of the RFO every Tuesday.

Profiles for punters

Paul Nicholls

PAUL NICHOLLS: has loads of youngsters who "could be anything"

Profile by Graham Dench

TEN-TIMES champion trainer Paul Nicholls had to give best to Nicky Henderson last season for the second time in the last five years and, without a Kauto Star, Denman, Master Minded or Silviniaco Conti in the team, he is already pretty much resigned to coming up short once again.

Surprise packages such as Cliffs Of Dover, Frodon and San Benedeto kept him in the race last season, but he accepts that it's the Grade 1 winners who win titles and he would be hard pressed to nominate a single serious candidate for the principal championship races.

However, you would be mistaken if you thought the mood at Manor Farm Stables was anything but upbeat as Nicholls has a stable brimming with potential – literally dozens and dozens of youngsters who "could be anything".

He says: "We've got as strong a team as we had last season and we'll have a good season again, but we don't have as many at the Graded end, so we'll need a miracle to win the trainers' championship.

"I'm not going to lose sleep over it, though. We had 171 winners last season, which was more than we'd ever had before, and if we could get near that and top £2m in prize-money again we'll be happy. And you never know."

He adds: "I think Nicky will be champion again and the biggest danger to him might be Dan [Skelton, his former assistant] rather than Colin [Tizzard], although Dan won't be champion by winning all those races around the smaller tracks."

One can sense the anticipation as Nicholls casts his eye down the 130-plus names on his most up-to-date list. Underneath an outwardly more relaxed demeanour, the ambition still burns bright and he is clearly loving his job as much as ever, his enthusiasm invigorated by getting back in the saddle to ride our regularly for the first time in years.

Nicholls has focused on buying younger horses in recent years and with good reason.

He says: "We can't buy horses like Kauto Star or Neptune Collonges any more – horses who'd already won three or four and you know they're Graded horses. We might have to buy them after they've won a maiden, or just been placed in one, and then try to make them into Graded winners, which is a brave man's route.

"But we've got some lovely young horses and we've got to be patient and not rush them as they're our future. There's so much to look forward to."

The policy now means Nicholls has packed full of exciting novice chasers – no fewer than 25 who already have hurdle or chase ratings of 130 or more, any one of whom could be in line for championship honours by the end of the season.

Describing them as "an awesome bunch", Nicholls nominates Modus, Movewiththetimes, El Bandit and Capitaine as among the more likely members of the team to make it to the top, but he can't stop himself from adding Coastal Tiep, Dolos, Topofthegame, Copain De Classe and half a dozen others to that list before concluding that he has "an awful lot of horses who are going to win novice chases".

The list of potential novice hurdle and bumper stars is even longer and, while Nicholls picked out a dozen to discuss individually below, he could easily have selected another two dozen had space allowed, among them Captain Cattistock,

DENMAN: you never know when the next one will come along

Casko D'Airy, Cereal Killer, Dan McGrue, Dynamite Dollars, Get Out The Gate, If You Say Run, Kapcorse, Mont Des Avaloirs, Posh Trish, Stradivarius Davis, The Dellercheckout, Western Honour and Worthy Farm. Many of them are already the winners of either point-to-points or bumpers, some of them both.

Nicholls points out: "You just don't know what you might have with these novice hurdlers and bumper horses. If we'd been going through the team years ago you'd never have known at the same stage what Denman might be. He'd won an Irish point-to-point, like a lot of these, but he showed nothing at home. It's only when you get going with them on the track that you really find out."

And then there are the juveniles. Malaya, Sao and Tommy Hallinan are all discussed below, but Grand Sancy and Risk And Roll also get favourable mentions, as does Chief Craftsman, a former Luca Cumani maiden from the Flat. Could he be another Cliffs Of Dover?

The horses

Adrien Du Pont 5yo gelding
Califet – Santarkiya

He won a Grade 1 at Chepstow as a juvenile and then last season he had the sort of season that's typical of that sort of horse. He ran well but just struggled a little bit. He's always been a chaser in the making and he'll leave his mark of 143 well behind when he goes over fences.

Antartica De Thaix 7yo gelding
Dom Alco – Nouca De Thaix

I've always liked her a lot and she found her niche last season, winning three in a row including a Listed chase for mares at Huntingdon. She'll be running in all of those mares' Listed races and should do well again.

As De Mee 7yo gelding
Kapgarde – Koeur De Mee

He's a superb jumper who enjoyed his finest hour when he won the Grand Sefton at Aintree. That will be his target again and he'll get an entry in the Grand National. I think he might stay.

Binge Drinker 8yo gelding
Spadoun – Our Honey

He's new to us this season and is a really interesting one as he beat Might Bite at Ffos Las on his only start over fences. I've got it in mind that he might be a Welsh National horse and he could run first in the 3m trial they have there early in December. Ultimately I see him as a Grand National horse, but he'd need five or six runs before

ADRIEN DU PONT: *should leave his hurdles mark behind now he goes chasing*

CLIFFS OF DOVER: "will definitely win a big handicap" according to Nicholls

then. He's obviously an exciting horse.

Capitaine 5yo gelding
Montmartre – Patte De Velour

He won a Grade 2 over hurdles at Ascot last season and had his first run over fences at Newton Abbot in May when he won well. He's a really exciting novice chaser.

Chameron 4yo gelding
Laveron – Chamanka

I think he was rated 150 or so as a juvenile having won both his hurdle races at Auteuil. He was right up there with the best in France and, although he'll be short on experience, he's one I like a lot.

Clan Des Obeaux 5yo gelding
Kapgarde – Nausicaa Des Obeaux

He started off brilliantly over fences last season, but he lost his way and became a bit disappointing, developing a tendency to jump right. He had a little breathing issue, which was a factor, so he had a little wind operation in the summer. He's only five and I think there's a lot of improvement in him, so he could have a good season – there's a decent race in him. He might start with a prep over hurdles in something like the Silver Trophy.

Cliffs Of Dover 4yo gelding
Canford Cliffs – Basanti

What he did last season as a juvenile was amazing. He couldn't win a race on the Flat and came here rated 64, so I certainly wasn't expecting him to win six races over hurdles, including a Grade 2 at Doncaster. He jarred a tendon and, although it was only minor, he'd also had a fair bit of stick on the Flat so we left him alone in the second half of the season. He'll have a steady preparation for his return and might have one run on the Flat as he's obviously well handicapped. I'm aiming to have him ready for something nice around Christmas and he'll definitely win a big handicap and possibly another Graded race.

Copain De Classe 5yo gelding
Enrique – Toque Rouge

He's a massive horse who won two novice hurdles last season and just needed time.

DOLOS (right): could be another Nicholls four-year-old to thrive over fences

He's built like a chaser and is one I'm really looking forward to. He's a work in progress but worth waiting for.

Coup De Pinceau 5yo gelding
Buck's Boum – Castagnette III

He won both his bumpers, doing well to carry a penalty at Ascot. He then ran a lovely race when second to Lough Derg Spirit on his only start over hurdles at Kempton and that's good form. We decided to keep him a maiden after that and he'll stay novice hurdling.

Darling Maltaix 4yo gelding
Voix Du Nord – Rosalie Malta

He's one I like. He won his only bumper in France at Vichy but was a bit keen on his debut for us at Newton Abbot in September. He'd been doing things nicely at home, though, and he should make a nice novice hurdler.

Diamond Guy 4yo gelding
Konig Turf – Unique Chance

It was only a four-runner race when he won his bumper at Wincanton last season, but he won by half the track and he's a horse we like. He jumps well and has a bright future.

Diego Du Charmil 5yo gelding
Ballingarry – Daramour

He won the Fred Winter two seasons ago when we really fancied him and won twice last season, including a £50,000 handicap at Musselburgh. He's reached his limit over hurdles now so we've sent him over fences and he won at Newton Abbot in September. He's a lovely big horse and is going to be a really nice novice chaser.

Dolos 4yo gelding
Kapgarde – Redowa

He's a 135-rated hurdler who goes novice chasing now. He's tough and professional and is one of those who might end up being a Frodon or a San Benedeto, who excelled despite their age.

El Bandit 6yo gelding
Milan – Bonnie Parker

He won six over hurdles, including the Persian War at Chepstow, and started this season well when absolutely bolting up in a valuable novice chase at Warwick in May. He wants three miles and will be a grand novice chaser. I don't think I have a Hennessy horse this year, although Le Mercurey and Present Man will probably get entries, but if I did have one it might be a novice like him. It's a long shot, but Strong Flow won it as a novice.

Emerging Talent 8yo gelding
Golan – Elvira

He's a good horse who won three of his last four over hurdles two seasons ago and was second to Native River the season before. He got a leg injury and has had 18 months off, but he's come back in good shape and I've been riding him myself, so he'll be fit, that's for sure.

Frodon 5yo gelding
Nickname – Miss Country

He was a revelation last season and won the Caspian Caviar Gold Cup when still a four-year-old. He's a joy to train but life is going to be tough for him now off 152, although he's still only five and so could go on improving a little. He'll probably go for some of those conditions races, but he'll definitely have an entry in some of the better handicaps.

Give Me A Copper 7yo gelding
Presenting – Copper Supreme

He's a really exciting horse who has won a bumper and a point-to-point in Ireland and two novice hurdles. He's been beaten only once in his life and he was wrong that day. He's a model chaser who stays very well and has a great attitude. He could be a Hennessy type next season.

Ibis Du Rheu 6yo gelding
Blue Bresil – Dona Du Rheu

He paid the price for his win in the Martin Pipe two seasons ago and it was hard to find races for him last season, so he ended carrying top-weight in a couple of races and running okay. He needed to mature and we've not seen the best of him by a long way.

Irving 9yo gelding
Singspiel – Indigo Girl

He has problems with his joints and is difficult to train, but he always wins first time out and last season it was the Fighting Fifth, which he also won in 2014. After Christmas it can be a waste of time, but if he can win a Grade 1 again first time out everyone will be happy. He'll go straight to Newcastle, but it's probably going to be a tougher race this time as that hurdle race at Haydock which used to dilute it has been discontinued.

Le Prezien 6yo gelding
Blue Bresil – Abu Dhabi

He was a good novice chaser last season and won the Grade 2 at Cheltenham in November. He's a good horse and very solid, so he'll be going for some of those better handicaps.

Malaya 3yo filly
Martaline – Clarte D'Or

She's a lovely three-year-old and could be

MODUS: has schooled well over fences and could be one to look forward to

as good as anything we've got. She had decent Flat form in France and very quickly translated it to hurdles – she two of her three races there and maybe should have won all three. She's a very exciting filly.

Modus 7yo gelding
Motivator – Alessandra

He could be a really good novice chaser. Having won the Lanzarote last season, he is rated 156 over hurdles and we like to think that hurdlers like him often end up 10lb or 20lb higher when they go over fences if they can jump, which makes him really interesting. He's schooled really well and we're all looking forward to seeing him.

Movewiththetimes 6yo gelding
Presenting – Dare To Venture

He won a bumper and two novice hurdles and was then only just beaten by Ballyandy in the Betfair Hurdle, running very well. He had a minor setback afterwards, which is why he didn't run at Cheltenham. Whether we give him a run over hurdles to see where we are with him will be up to his owner, but ultimately he's going to be a very smart chaser.

Old Guard 6yo gelding
Notnowcato – Dolma

He's had a wind operation and will probably mix hurdling and chasing. He's won only one chase and didn't jump well, but if I can get him jumping well he'll probably go for a graduation chase.

Politologue 6yo gelding
Poliglote – Scarlet Row

He won three novice chases last season and was desperately unlucky not to win a Grade 1 at Aintree, where he came down at the last and left San Benedeto to benefit from it. We'd been riding him patiently to get home over two and a half miles, but Aintree showed me he can make a top-class two-miler this season. He's going for the Haldon Gold Cup first and we'll get plenty of graft into him before that. After that we'll know if he's good enough to go the Graded route.

Present Man 7yo gelding
Presenting – Glen's Gale

He came good in no uncertain terms last season, racking up a four-timer. He loves going right-handed and attacking his fences, so we're aiming him first at the Badger Ales Chase at Wincanton in November.

Ptit Zig 8yo gelding
Great Pretender – Red Rym

He couldn't quite win again after landing the French Champion Hurdle last summer, but he ran some honest races in defeat and picked up plenty of place money. He could go for the Wetherby Grade 2 that Silsol won last year and we might have another go over fences with him one day.

Romain De Senam 5yo gelding
Saint Des Saints – Salvatrixe

He was trained specifically for the novice handicap chase at Cheltenham last season and it was sickening when he missed the cut by one. I'm convinced he wants a strongly run two and a half miles and I'm sure he's well handicapped off 133, so he'll be going straight for the BetVictor Gold Cup at Cheltenham off a light weight. He's getting better as he matures.

San Benedeto 6yo gelding
Layman – Cinco Baidy

He kept on improving last season, winning

ROMAIN DE SENAM: being laid out for the BetVictor Gold Cup at Cheltenham

six times including the Grade 1 at Aintree in which Politologue fell at the last. He'll probably start off in the Haldon Gold Cup and then go for the £100,000 handicap at Ascot at the end of November.

Sao 3yo gelding
Great Pretender – Miss Country

He's another very nice juvenile who won at Compiegne in May for Guillaume Macaire, who also had his half-brother Frodon at the same stage. He's an elegant-looking horse and goes nicely.

Secret Investor 5yo gelding
Kayf Tara – Silver Charmer

He won his only point-to-point in Ireland and then ran very well to be second to Kimberlite Candy at Ascot in November on his only start over hurdles. We've given him lots of time and he's a ready-made winner.

Silsol 8yo gelding
Soldier Hollow – Silveria

He won the Grade 2 West Yorkshire Hurdle at Wetherby last autumn but then had a minor injury. He's back again and will be running in good staying hurdles again. He'll be ready for Wetherby again, but he'd want cut in the ground to be running there.

Some Man 4yo gelding
Beat Hollow – Miss Denman

He won his only point-to-point in Ireland, fairly bolting up, and his dam was a sister to Denman, so he's one to look forward to in novice hurdles.

Tommy Hallinan 3yo gelding
Intense Focus – Bowstring

He showed a nice level of form on the Flat in Ireland and we bought him and gelded him after he won at Cork in May. He'll be a nice juvenile.

Tommy Silver 5yo gelding
Silver Cross – Sainte Mante

He's a 146-rated hurdler who won at Taunton and Plumpton last season and loves decent ground. He's going over fences

SILSOL: back from injury and will run in top staying hurdles

TOPOFTHEGAME (left): will improve into a serious horse one day

and will be a nice 2m-2m4f novice chaser.

Topofthegame 5yo gelding
Flemensfirth – Derry Vale

He's a giant of a horse who has chaser written all over him. He won his only point-to-point and then, in three runs over hurdles, he won at Ascot first time, when he surprised us a little, and ended up only just beaten there on his last start. He might not go to the top as a novice, but he'll go on improving for a season or two and will be a serious horse one day.

Vicente 8yo gelding
Dom Alco – Ireland

He just seems to blossom in the spring and he'll have a lightish campaign geared towards a bid to win the Scottish National for a third year in a row. He'll have an entry in the National, but I honestly don't think his jumping is good enough. It was probably a blessing that he fell at the first there in April as it meant he didn't have a race and was fresh for Ayr two weeks later.

Zarkandar 10yo gelding
Azamor – Zarkasha

He's won ten races for us, all of them Graded races and four of them Grade 1. We were thinking of retiring him, but he's too young for that. He'll probably have just four races and we'll keep him below the very top level now in small-field conditions races, possibly in France or Ireland. The race at Aintree in November he would have won last year is an obvious target.

Zubayr 5yo gelding
Authorized – Zaziya

Things didn't quite fall into place for him last season, but he was only just touched off in the Scottish Champion Hurdle and would have won if he had jumped the last. He's been running well on the Flat since then and he'll always be remembered here for giving us our first winner in a maiden at Kempton. There's a good handicap in him on the Flat one day, but in the short term he could be one for the Elite Hurdle.

Profiles for punters
Tom Lacey

TOM LACEY: pre-training yard has evolved into an up-and-coming win machine

Profile by Dylan Hill

TOM LACEY probably entered the consciousness of most racing fans only last season when he sent out 21 winners from his Herefordshire yard, a clear personal best that promises much for the future.

However, Lacey, 47, is no young buck just starting to make his way in the sport but a man with many years of experience in preparing horses for the racecourse – just not at the sharp end.

Lacey's background lies in pre-training horses, whereby he would be sent young horses by owners or trainers to learn the ropes before entering full training at a racing yard.

He learned his trade at the pre-training yard of Captain Charles Radclyffe, who was a big influence on him.

Lacey recalls: "I was shocking at school and when I was 16 the headmaster called me into the office and said there was a job going at a yard down the road and I should take it. I didn't really have a racing background, although I'd done hunting and pony racing – there were ponies around from as young as I can remember."

Radclyffe was responsible for the pre-training of horses belonging to the Aga Khan and the Queen Mother among others and Lacey credits Radclyffe for teaching him everything.

"He had a typical army mentality. It was attention to detail as much as everything, getting the job done properly. What he put us through, you wouldn't be able to do to people now – you'd be locked up! But it was a hell of a grounding."

From there Lacey went on to become head lad at Brian Meehan's yard for a couple of years, but he admits becoming a trainer in his own right is something that has simply evolved over time and was never an ambition.

Instead it was back to pre-training and the buying and selling of horses, something with which Lacey has always had a knack, with last season's Cheltenham Festival runner-up Singlefarmpayment – bought as an unbroken three-year-old before leaving him for Tom George last year – among the latest big names to pass through his hands.

"It got to the point where I stopped being able to sell them for what I thought they were worth," he says. "I had to start running them myself just so they'd proved themselves outside the point-to-point arena."

Around that time, in the 2014-15 campaign, Lacey sent out five winners from 38 runners. The following season there were nine from 81 and then last term his numbers shot up to 21 winners from just 102 runners at a terrific strike-rate of 21 per cent. Anyone backing all his horses would have ended up £87 in front to £1 level stakes.

That strike-rate would be the envy of many, but Lacey isn't one to pore over the form book trying to find his horses the best opportunity.

"I don't worry about other people's horses," he says, "just my own. It's a case of running them when they're fit, healthy and ready to run to the best of their ability. It costs a lot to send a horse to the races so there's no point doing it if they're wrong – and if you do, it takes them forever to get over it. It's about sending them to a race when they're spot on and after that everything falls into place."

A key part of Lacey's success has also been the move to a yard in Herefordshire three years ago.

SINGLEFARMPAYMENT: bought by Lacey, who trained him until last year

"The farm where I was pre-training was sold and we couldn't afford to stay in the Cotswolds. Here we were able to get 206 acres in the most beautiful countryside, although it was a derelict fruit farm when we bought it. There were no facilities at all, just a new-build house. The farm building was dilapidated, there were no gallops or fencing around the paddocks or anything at all.

"We were able to create it exactly as we wanted. We did all the ventilation through the barns properly and put in a two-furlong deep sand gallop which I think has been hugely beneficial and gets the horses fit without them really realising it – we don't overgallop them or pound them up a hill."

Still, Lacey refuses to be drawn on pinpointing the reasons for his success.

"It's a results-based industry," he says. "I had a few horses, did well with them and that means you get more. It's just natural growth and I'd like to think I've got a good reputation. I'm not a people person but I am a horseman."

Perhaps inevitably, young horses remain Lacey's stock in trade and he has a yard full of three-year-olds, but there are still several others ready to peak and potentially take their trainer on to the big stage this term, not least Kimberlite Candy, bought by JP McManus after winning at Ascot last season, and the hugely exciting Equus Amadeus.

The horses

Equus Amadeus 4yo gelding
Beat Hollow – Charade

We got him as an unbroken three-year-old and we always thought he was a very nice horse. He's big, strong and powerful and will make a great chaser one day. I think he could win a nice race this season first, though, as he won well on his hurdling debut at Uttoxeter in September. I'm looking at the Persian War Novices' Hurdle at Chepstow for him next and he'll have a live chance. He'll also stay further.

Flashing Glance 4yo gelding
Passing Glance – Don And Gerry

He's very much a project. He has plenty of ability, but we could hardly ride him when he first came here in the new year as he was so fractious. The wheels came off on his hurdling debut at Bangor in September, but he was much better at Stratford later in the month and won by 20 lengths before a good second at Newton Abbot. He'll be a good horse one day over fences, but we're in no rush with him as he needs to grow up in handicaps this season and then have another summer on his back.

Isle Of Ewe 6yo mare
Kayf Tara – Apple Town

She was second in a couple of bumpers and then hacked up on her hurdling debut at Southwell last year, but unfortunately she got a leg injury and it's been very slow to heal. We have to take things day by day with her, but she's back in work and it would be great to get her out in the second half of the season.

Jester Jet 7yo mare
Overbury – Hendre Hotshot

We got her earlier this year and she must have been well handicapped because she won her first three for us before a good third at Aintree last time. We decided to give her a break after that, but she injured herself out in the field and won't run again until after Christmas. She'll go chasing and I think she could improve for fences.

Kimberlite Candy 5yo gelding
Flemensfirth – Mandys Native

He's a real chasing type. He won twice over hurdles last season before being pulled up when we stepped him up in class for the Classic Novices' Hurdle at Cheltenham, but anything he achieved over hurdles was always going to be a bonus. He'll go straight over fences and will be out when we get some genuine ease in the ground. He's summered well and really strengthened up, but we'll tip away quietly with him before any big plans.

Mary Eleanor 5yo mare
Midnight Native – Lady Rebecca

She was a good bumper horse last year. She was beaten a neck at Huntingdon and then third in a better race at Newbury, while her last race at Bangor came too quickly for her. She'll go novice hurdling this season and jumps nicely.

Polydora 5yo gelding
Milan – Mandysway

I've always liked this horse, but I don't think I've ever had him right. He's had major problems with his feet and he's hypersensitive with allergies. He ran in a couple of bumpers last season and was well beaten, but he's extremely talented.

Sir Egbert 4yo gelding
Kayf Tara – Little Miss Flora

He showed some promise in a couple of

KIMBERLITE CANDY (left): a real chasing type now set to go over fences

bumpers last season and will go novice hurdling this season. He'll need extremely soft ground as he has a very high knee action, although he seems to get from A to B fine.

Snapdragon Fire 4yo gelding
Getaway – Global Diamond

We went to £32,000 to get him at the Goffs sale last year and he ran a nice race on his debut in a bumper at Southwell in September, staying on to finish second. He jumps well and is one to look forward to over hurdles.

Sword Of Fate 4yo gelding
Beneficial – Beann Ard

He did really well to win his only bumper at Exeter in April by ten lengths. He'll go novice hurdling this season and we have high hopes for him. He's summered well and jumps nicely.

Unnamed 5yo gelding
Kayf Tara – Marello

We've had to take our time with this horse as he's had a lot of problems – nothing major, just niggly issues because of his size as he's a big, fine horse. We should get him out in a bumper just before Christmas, though, and he's a nice prospect.

Vado Forte 4yo gelding
Walk In The Park – Gloire

I think he could be exceptional. He made his debut at Kempton in March and was sent off favourite, but he tore a hamstring. Then he was much too keen on his hurdling debut in September and finished a well-beaten eighth. He's hugely talented and some of his work at home would take your breath away, but he's hot-headed and we just have to keep a lid on him and teach him how to race.

Nick Watts' 30 horses to follow

AMI DESBOIS 7 b g

Dream Well – Baroya (Garde Royale)

1123151-

Ami Desbois was a very consistent performer in staying hurdles last season and placed at the highest level behind Messire Des Obeaux in the Challow Hurdle at Newbury. He ran a superb race in his big target race of the season – the Albert Bartlett – finishing fifth behind Penhill on ground that was a touch quick for him. Now he embarks on a new venture – novice chasing – and it's a discipline he should do well in over distances of two and a half miles or more.

Graeme McPherson, Gloucestershire

AUVERGNAT 7 b g

Della Francesca – Hesmeralda (Royal Charter)

3U14-12

Auvergnat hasn't quite made the big breakthrough in banks races yet, but this young horse is in the right yard to do so before too long. He did manage to win the PP Hogan Chase at Punchestown in February, which was encouraging, and wasn't disgraced behind the classy Cause Of Causes when fourth at the Cheltenham Festival. In good form over the summer, he could take a big leap forward this season and challenge for all the top cross-country races.

Enda Bolger, Co Limerick

BACARDYS 6 b g

0/1

Coastal Path – Oasice (Robin Des Champs)

3F11P1-

Having won the Deloitte at Leopardstown, Bacardys was unlucky in the Neptune at the Cheltenham Festival – hampered early and ultimately pulled up – but then made handsome amends at Punchestown, taking the prized scalp of Finian's Oscar over 2m4f to claim his second Grade 1. That was a great performance and one that bodes well for his future this season. It seems likely that he will spearhead Willie Mullins' team of novice chasers and, as a point-to-point winner, he ought to go far in that sphere as well.

Willie Mullins, Co Carlow

BLAKLION 8 b g

Kayf Tara – Franciscaine (Legend Of France)

45324-

Although winless last season, Blaklion couldn't have caught the eye much more than he did, particularly on his final start of the campaign when fourth in the National. If Noel Fehily had his time again I'm sure he would have held on to him for longer, but having looked an almost certain winner three out he weakened at the last and was overhauled by One For Arthur and two others. With more patience, he could easily go back to Aintree next April and make amends for what could be construed as an unlucky defeat.

Nigel Twiston-Davies, Naunton

BLOW BY BLOW 6 ch g

Robin Des Champs – Shean Rose (Roselier)

211/1-

Blow By Blow missed last season having been transferred out of the Willie Mullins stable. The form of his Grade 1 bumper win at Punchestown in April 2016 when last seen has lost a bit of sheen after runner-up Moon Racer's disappointing spring, but this is still a high-class prospect and one who is likely to do well this season now he is back in training. He predictably has quotes for most races at the Cheltenham Festival next year, but it is surely over staying trips he is going to excel and maybe the Albert Bartlett will be the race for him.

Gordon Elliott, Co Meath

BRISTOL DE MAI 6 gr g

Saddler Maker – La Bole Night (April Night)

221375-

Last season was mostly one of disappointment for Bristol De Mai. Twice beaten at odds-on and well beaten in the Gold Cup and Betfair Bowl, with just one solitary win to his name. However, it was the nature of that win in the Peter Marsh Chase that makes him worthy of inclusion in this list. He absolutely pulverised a load of high-class chasers, defeating Otago Trail by 22 lengths. As he is still only six, it's very much worth excusing subsequent disappointments and he can easily be a force at the highest level this season when the mud is flying.

Nigel Twiston-Davies, Naunton

CAPTAIN FOREZ 5 b g

Network – Pourkoipa Du Forez (Robin Des Champs)

322-

Three defeats from three starts last season means Captain Forez retains his novice status and that could be a bonus. He accrued some very useful experience in good races, particularly on his last start at Aintree in a Grade 1 hurdle over 2m4f. Finian's Oscar won the race but next best was Captain Forez, upwards of three lengths ahead of the third, Messire Des Obeaux. With La Bague Au Roi, Brio Conti and Le Breuil all well beaten, it is a race that will almost definitely work out and this horse should do his bit for the form.

Dan Skelton, Alcester

CHARBEL 6 b g

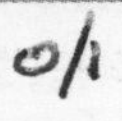

Iffraaj – Eoz (Sadler's Wells)
512F3-

So what would have happened had Charbel stood up in the Arkle? The probability is that Altior would have won anyway, but Charbel was in the process of giving Nicky Henderson's latest superstar an almighty race and had him stretched in a way we didn't see either before or afterwards. Forget his run at Aintree afterwards – he hit a few fences and was not himself, probably still feeling the effects of his Cheltenham endeavours. Charbel is normally very sure-footed, so put it down to a one-off. He is still a very good prospect.

Kim Bailey, Andoversford

CLAN DES OBEAUX 5 bb g

Kapgarde – Nausicaa Des Obeaux (April Night)
412514-

Three times a beaten favourite last season, Clan Des Obeaux's chase mark of 148 might prove to be a lenient one as he enters his second year of chasing. A defeat by Whisper at Cheltenham on New Year's Day doesn't read too badly now, but it was his Newbury display prior to that, when winning a Grade 2 by ten lengths, that marked him out as a potential future star. It will be interesting to see what Nicholls does with him this season, but maybe a return to Newbury for what used to be the Hennessy could be an option.

Paul Nicholls, Ditcheat

COME TO ME 5 b g

Spanish Moon – Hasta Manana (Useful)
1-

A dark horse, even for the Irish champion trainer. Come To Me made it to the racecourse only once last season, but it was a winning run as he took apart a field of bumper horses at Punchestown in December. The form of the race hasn't worked out, with the second and third not mustering a win between them afterwards. However, there was something in the style of the win that impressed me. Obviously things haven't gone to plan since, hence the fact we never saw him after that win, but he could do well hurdling this season if back to his best.

Willie Mullins, Co Carlow

CONSTANTINE BAY 6 b g

Kayf Tara – Alina Rheinberg (Waky Nao)
11144-

Constantine Bay looks a perfect candidate for staying chases this season and is possibly up to a Scottish National bid next spring if things go the right way. He was a classy novice hurdler last season, kicking off with three wins in a row, including a Grade 2 event at Doncaster. Although beaten on his last two starts, he still finished fourth in the Albert Bartlett and a Grade 1 hurdle at Aintree which looked a very hot race. A point-to-point winner, he has the size and scope for chasing and he looks a natural candidate for the four-miler at Cheltenham.

Nicky Henderson, Lambourn

DEBECE 6 b g

Kayf Tara – Dalamine (Sillery)

123313-

A few years ago Tim Vaughan changed his strategy, buying in more store horses with the future in mind. It took a while for the policy to pay off, but it is starting to bear fruit and Debece is evidence of that. This half-brother to Don Poli was given a very quiet campaign over hurdles, gradually going up in trip as the season wore on. His final start was his best one as, running over three miles for the first time, he finished third, beaten just half a length, by The Worlds End in a Grade 1 at Aintree. All roads lead to fences now and he should do well over them.

Tim Vaughan, Glamorgan

DEFI DU SEUIL 4 b g

Voix Du Nord – Quarvine Du Seuil (Lavirco)

11111111-

Putting in a horse like Defi Du Seuil is risky – if he doesn't come up to scratch as a Champion Hurdle candidate then he might find himself in a bit of a twilight zone, as many do out of their juvenile season. However, the memory of him having the Triumph Hurdle won turning into the straight lingers long in the memory and he may well prove up to the task. He was apparently vulnerable at the festival, racing on quicker ground than he was used to, but if anything it improved him and he won easily. I expect him to continue where he left off.

Philip Hobbs, Somerset

DISKO 6 gr g

Martaline – Nikos Royale (Nikos)

6133131-

Rarely have I seen a novice jump as well as Disko did last season and that great asset will always give him a chance of landing some big prizes. He won two Grade 1 races last season, including when stepped up in trip to three miles at Punchestown on his final start, thereby increasing his options enormously for this season. Prior to that he had looked best at intermediate trips, but with another year on his back he could develop into a proper stayer. He may be hard to beat in the Grade 1 at Down Royal in November.

Noel Meade, Co Meath

DJAKADAM 8 b g

Saint Des Saints – Rainbow Crest (Baryshnikov)

21342-

The perennial bridesmaid. Ruby Walsh couldn't have done much more to get Djakadam to win this year's Gold Cup, but after a blunder two out he was swept aside once again, surely ending any hopes of him ever winning the big one. However, his season did include another with in the Grade 1 John Durkan Chase and he must now be dropped in trip in order to realise his potential. He travels like a top-class horse and the Ryanair Chase, over 2m5f, should suit him down to the ground. Don't write him off yet.

Willie Mullins, Co Carlow

FOX NORTON 7 b g

Lando – Natt Musik (Kendor)

112211-

A revelation, pure and simple. Fox Norton was good with Neil Mulholland but took a major leap forward after joining Colin Tizzard. Almost successful in the Champion Chase, he then stepped up in trip at Aintree and thrashed a good horse in Sub Lieutenant before beating Un De Sceaux over the minimum trip at Punchestown. A bid for the King George has been shelved with the owners already having Sizing John for that, so anything from 2m-2m4f comes into the equation for him and he will take plenty of beating wherever he heads.

Colin Tizzard, Dorset

GREAT FIELD 6 b g

Great Pretender – Eaton Lass (Definite Article)

1111-

Watching horses running and jumping quickly is a great sight, if a little worrying at times if they happen to meet one wrong. Great Field did that a couple of times last season, almost ending in disaster, but he always managed to find a leg, winning every race he contested and progressing to a chase mark of 161 in the process. He formed a formidable alliance with Jody McGarvey and, encouragingly, he was safe enough when winning in Grade 1 company at Punchestown in April. He looks top-class.

Willie Mullins, Co Carlow

L'AMI SERGE 7 b g

King's Theatre – La Zingerella (Phardante)

2233251-21

Having looked frustrating for the most part of the season, have connections finally found the key to this horse? L'Ami Serge went to Auteuil this summer for the Grade 1 Grande Course de Haies d'Auteuil over 3m1½f – best known as the French Champion Hurdle – and won by a length and a half. Wearing a hood to help him concentrate and running over an extreme trip that he appeared to relish made all the difference. Now races such as the Long Walk, Cleeve and Stayers' Hurdle all come into the equation and rightly so. He could be a force in any of them.

Nicky Henderson, Lambourn

LET'S DANCE 5 b m

Poliglote – Baraka Du Berlais (Bonnet Rouge)

21111124-

Let's Dance finished the season on a slightly disappointing note, but it was the end of a long season and Willie Mullins was desperate to win the trainers' championship so maybe went to the well once too often. Up until her Fairyhouse defeat in April, this mare had carried all before her, winning five races in succession, culminating with an impressive victory in the mares' novice event at the Cheltenham Festival. She has pace and stamina so it will be interesting to see where she slots into the mix this year, but she could be good enough for the Champion Hurdle.

Willie Mullins, Co Carlow

MELON 5 ch g

Medicean – Night Teeny (Platini)

122-

Melon was made favourite for the Supreme after an impressive win in a maiden hurdle at Leopardstown. However, the race was a very moderate one and I felt he had it all to do at Cheltenham – lacking experience and with nobody really sure what he was capable of. Therefore, to run as well as he did behind the mercurial Labaik, was a most promising effort. Perhaps he was committed too early at Punchestown afterwards, leaving Cilaos Emery to pick up the pieces, but he is still a very classy prospect.

Willie Mullins, Co Carlow

MONTALBANO 5 ch g

Monsieur Bond – Alpen Glen (Halling)

1531-

Montalbano won impressively on his debut at Leopardstown's Christmas meeting, but the wheels came off on his next two starts and he was well beaten both times. However, he came back to his best at Punchestown in April when beating the classy Riven Light by a head. He did well to battle back and score that day having been headed at the last and the key to him this season will be to get him settled. Occasionally he pulled too hard, to his detriment, but if that side of his game can be fixed then he can still do very well.

Willie Mullins, Co Carlow

NICHOLS CANYON 7 b g

Authorized – Zam Zoom (Dalakhani)

312F12-

Having previously been campaigned at around two miles and as a Champion Hurdle candidate, there was no guarantee Nichols Canyon would stay prior to him running in the Stayers' Hurdle in March. Stay he did, however, as he ground out a courageous win over Lil Rockefeller. A subsequent defeat by Unowhatimeanharry at Punchestown was slightly disappointing, if understandable, but he should be back for more this season and can hoover up the staying races in Ireland before attempting to retain his crown.

Willie Mullins, Co Carlow

OUR DUKE 7 b g

Oscar – Good Thyne Jenny (Good Thyne)

1121-

For a horse who was a capable but not brilliant hurdler, Our Duke made enormous strides as a novice chaser last season and should be on everyone's shortlist for the Gold Cup. He looked good when winning a 3m Grade 1 novice chase at Leopardstown last Christmas, but he was positively frightening when running away with the Irish National on his final start. That is traditionally one of the toughest races in the calendar, but he made it look very, very easy. Stamina, class, sound jumping – he has it all.

Jessica Harrington, Co Kildare

RATHER BE 6 b g

Oscar – Irish Wedding (Bob Back)

112U18-

Rather Be wasn't always the easiest as a bumper horse and wore a hood on occasions. However, his temperament seemed to improve last season and he enjoyed a very consistent and winning campaign as a result. The highlight of his season was a gutsy win in a handicap hurdle at Aintree's Grand National meeting, where he beat Dream Berry by half a length. Although below-par on his final start of the campaign at Sandown, he can be forgiven that and if he goes chasing now then he has the potential to do well.

Nicky Henderson, Lambourn

RED JACK 4 b g

Mahler – Hollygrove Bonnie (Lord Americo)

11-

Considering he has Grand National winner Numbersixvalverde in his pedigree, Red Jack did incredibly well to win two bumpers and show a high level of form to boot. The bumper he won at Naas in January was one of the hottest of the season and he was 10-1 to win it, but he managed to beat Debuchet and Le Richebourg, who have both advertised the form repeatedly since. He then followed up at Fairyhouse and will now go hurdling. He looks an obvious type for the Neptune as he should stay well.

Noel Meade, Co Meath

SAMCRO 5 ch g

Germany – Dun Dun (Saddlers' Hall)

111-

Trainers are well known for being creatures of habit, so the fact that this horse won the same Navan bumper as Gordon Elliott's Don Cossack and Death Duty has to bode well for his future. That win wasn't overly impressive, but his last one at Fairyhouse in April when winning by 17 lengths certainly was. Predictably he has been priced up for everything this season, but my guess is he will head over staying trips and the Albert Bartlett. Connections have had expensive failures in that race recently – No More Heroes and Death Duty – but will be keen to make amends.

Gordon Elliott, Co Meath

SHANTOU VILLAGE 7 b g

Shantou – Village Queen (King's Theatre)

11F11-

A fall at Wincanton in November prevented a perfect campaign, but either side of that Shantou Village won four times, showing considerable aplomb for jumping fences. He saved his best for last as he was sent to Sandown in April and got the better of a thrilling duel with Brother Tedd to win by a neck. A feature of his victory that day was some fast and fluent jumping and that will help him as he joins the handicap ranks this season. Although he was favourite for the 2016 Albert Bartlett, he now looks best at distances short of three miles.

Neil Mulholland, Wiltshire

SIZING CODELCO 8 b g

Flemensfirth – La Zingerella (Phardante)

38P24011-

Early on last season things didn't look great for Sizing Codelco, but at Christmas they took a turn for the better as he ran Top Notch to a length and a quarter at Ascot and in the spring they really took off. In the midst of what was a golden spell for trainer Colin Tizzard, he won the 3m1f handicap at Aintree on Grand National day with ridiculous ease. As if that wasn't enough, he then repated the trick at Punchestown and is now up to a mark of 160. That might be tricky, but if he drops a few pounds in the interim he looks every inch a 2018 Grand National contender.

Colin Tizzard, Dorset

SLOWMOTION 5 bb m

Soldier Of Fortune – Second Emotion (Medaaly)

52F211212-3

For one so young, Slowmotion has proved herself to be a high-class, tough and progressive chaser. She won her first chase at Naas in January and since then it has been onwards and upwards, with a further two wins and three places. One of those placed runs came in the Galway Plate – a stiff ask for any horse, but she did really well to finish third, not far behind the more experienced Balko Des Flos. Similar handicaps will be the way forward for her and she may be one to race in Britain at some stage.

Joseph O'Brien, Co Kilkenny

WILLIAM HENRY 7 b g

King's Theatre – Cincuenta (Bob Back)

2121-

It was a real shame that William Henry was forced to miss the Cheltenham Festival last season due to inury as he had looked an intriguing outsider for the Neptune. In January he had finished second behind the solid yardstick Wholestone at Cheltenham on unsuitably soft ground and he later returned there in April to win again. His form figures at Cheltenham now read 221 – the other defeat came behind Aintree Grade 1 winner Pingshou – so it is encouraging he likes it so much there. Fences now surely beckon for the Dai Walters-owned beast.

Nicky Henderson, Lambourn

Top ten horses

Debece	Red Jack
Fox Norton	Samcro
Let's Dance	Sizing Codelco
Montalbano	Slowmotion
Our Duke	William Henry

Est. 1909
RACING & FOOTBALL OUTLOOK

Ante-post preview Dylan Hill & Nick Watts

King George

IF a bookmaker had offered 4-1 about **THISTLECRACK** for this season's King George in the immediate aftermath of last year's race, you'd surely have gone straight to the nearest bank thinking of ways to persuade them into giving the biggest loan you could possibly get.

Of course, plenty has gone wrong for the horse since to lead to a price that would have been unimaginable back then, but even so it's worth thinking back to Thistlecrack's devastating performance and backing him for a repeat.

Sure, it wasn't the strongest King George ever run with just five runners, one of whom, Silviniaco Conti, was past his best.

But the way Thistlecrack jumped them into the ground was stunning and Cue Card simply couldn't match him when the pair locked horns down the far side, which led to his rather legless capitulation in the straight. In contrast, Thistlecrack was still going strong at that point and was eased down close home, value for a far greater margin of victory.

King George — Kempton, December 26

	Bet365	*Betfred*	*Boyles*	*Coral*	*Hills*	*Lads*	*P Power*	*Skybet*
Thistlecrack	3	11-4	5-2	3	3	3	**4**	3
Might Bite	3	4	7-2	3	4	3	**9-2**	4
Sizing John	4	**5**	**5**	3	4	7-2	7-2	4
Douvan	6	8	8	8	5	8	**10**	7
Fox Norton	12	8	12	**14**	12	12	8	**14**
Un De Sceaux	12	-	-	-	-	-	12	**16**
Djakadam	**20**	10	16	14	16	-	10	16
Tea For Two	**20**	16	16	16	12	14	16	**20**
Native River	14	10	16	**20**	14	**20**	**20**	**20**
Coneygree	**20**	14	**20**	-	16	-	**20**	**20**
Cue Card	**20**	-	16	**20**	16	**20**	**20**	**20**
Yorkhill	12	10	-	14	-	14	20	**25**
Bristol De Mai	**25**	-	**25**	16	-	20	**25**	**25**
Josses Hill	**33**	-	-	**33**	**33**	**33**	**33**	**33**

each-way 1/4 odds, 1-2-3

Others on application, prices correct at time of going to press

HISTLECRACK: in no danger as Tom Scudamore looks back at Kempton

Although beaten next time, he went own fighting against a top-class oppo-ent in Many Clouds and it just seemed o be the extra distance on a more testing ack that caught him out. At his best, three iles around Kempton looks ideal.

Thistlecrack will be turning ten soon fter the King George, but age has never een the barrier to success in this race hat it is in the Gold Cup, with the second-eason chasers who tend to dominate at heltenham often spending the first half of he season playing catch-up.

Thistlecrack winning the King George s a novice therefore stands out as even nore of an anomaly than a novice like oneygree winning the Gold Cup, but hat's a testament to this special horse's bility. Indeed, it's hard to think of such an outstanding hurdler ever taking so well to fences.

His absence since January is an obvious concern and means the fact he retains all his ability has to be taken on trust, but so it does with many of the contenders at this stage.

Sizing John, for example, endured a tough end to the season. Most Gold Cup winners have been packed off for a well-deserved summer break at the time he was being pushed to the limit by Djakadam at Punchestown and plenty of them already struggled to repeat their Cheltenham heroics the following season.

Might Bite, clearly well suited by the course and distance given he was winning the Kauto Star Novices' Chase so easily last year until falling at the last, could be

DJAKADAM (left): could come over for the King George but doesn't often win

a more solid choice, but as mentioned above it might not be until Cheltenham that he catches up with the more established chasers.

That's what happened with **Tea For Two** last season when well beaten in this race but a Grade 1 winner at Aintree in the spring. He could do better at a big price and loves Kempton, but it was probably a weak race for the grade when he struck at Liverpool and the suspicion is that he would have to drop lucky again.

Thistlecrack's trainer Colin Tizzard has plenty more options and is never afraid to throw them all in against each other.

However, Alan and Ann Potts appear to have had something to say about that regarding **Fox Norton**, who will probably run only if something happens to Sizing John – in the same ownership – in the Betfai That's a shame because he looked bes when stepped up in trip at Aintree an would be really interesting here.

Cue Card may again run well but hi time has surely passed, while the othe Tizzard possible, **Native River**, lacks th pace for this race.

Willie Mullins could really spice thing up by running **Douvan** or **Un De Sceaux** but I can't see Douvan stepping up thi sharply in trip so early in the season anc while Un De Sceaux would be feared, Mu lins doesn't seem keen on the idea wit him either.

Mullins is more likely to rely on **Djakad am**, who could go off a lot shorter than hi current price but doesn't win often enoug for my liking. (DH)

Champion Hurdle

IT IS normal for Willie Mullins horses to confuse ante-post markets and nowhere is this more apparent this season than in the Champion Hurdle.

Yorkhill could win this, could win a Gold Cup, could win a Ryanair Chase, Stayers' Hurdle and most other things if Mullins wanted him to.

But what does Mullins want him to do? That is the question and it may not be resolved for some time yet.

Therefore a safer option at this stage would be to back **DEFI DU SEUIL** at 8-1, safe in the knowledge that he is staying over hurdles this season and this will be his aim should he prove up to it.

That's the big question, of course, and everyone knows it is not an easy transition from champion juvenile to champion hurdler, but if any horse has the tools for the job it is this one.

He was exceptional when it mattered in the Triumph Hurdle, having the race won turning for home, and it was a performance that made people who had been sceptical of his talent previously sit up and take notice.

Having begun his campaign at Ffos Las. Defi Du Seuil had won Chepstow's Finale Hurdle in deep ground and that resulted in doubts as to how he would handle quicker ground at the festival. But his jumping was more solid than ever and conditions didn't bother him one iota.

A subsequent Grade 1 win at Aintree was rather less inspiring, but that was understandable coming at the end of an eight-race campaign.

Pre-Christmas, the International Hurdle looks the ideal race for him to go for and, given his Cheltenham record, it would be no surprise if a win there saw him shorten considerably for this race.

There is already only one horse ahead of him in the market, underlining the fact there are few standout contenders at this stage, and while the favourite, **Buveur D'Air**, is a very good horse, he isn't necessarily one to be running scared of.

Buveur D'Air made an impressive return to hurdling during the second half of the season and proved himself more adaptable ground-wise than he had been in his novice season, when soft going appeared to be what he needed, as his last two wins at Cheltenham and Aintree encouragingly

Champion Hurdle

Cheltenham, March 14

	Bet365	*Betfred*	*Boyles*	*Coral*	*Hills*	*Lads*	*P Power*	*Skybet*
Buveur D'Air	**4**	7-2	3	5-2	3	3	7-2	7-2
Faugheen	6	**8**	6	**8**	6	**8**	**8**	7
Defi Du Seuil	**8**	**8**	6	**8**	**8**	**8**	7	7
Yorkhill	10	10	10	8	10	8	**12**	8
Apple's Jade	14	10	10	16	-	16	**20**	**20**
Limini	16	-	**20**	**20**	-	**20**	**20**	**20**
Min	12	12	-	8	16	10	**20**	**20**
Melon	16	**25**	16	12	16	14	20	20
Petit Mouchoir	20	**25**	**25**	20	16	**25**	20	**25**
Wicklow Brave	**25**	20	**25**	20	20	**25**	-	**25**
Charli Parcs	**33**	-	-	25	-	25	**33**	**33**
Cilaos Emery	**33**	25	-	25	25	25	-	25
Let's Dance	25	-	-	20	-	16	**33**	25
My Tent Or Yours	33	**40**	-	33	-	25	**40**	33

each-way 1/4 odds, 1-2-3

Others on application, prices correct at time of going to press

came on good to soft and good ground.

However, while he may well improve again, he will almost certainly need to given he was only beating the ten-year-old **My Tent Or Yours** last spring.

I'm also interested in **LET'S DANCE**, although I realise I'm being quite contradictory in doing so.

The Mullins mare has at least as many options this season as Yorkhill does and could easily stay in the mares' division.

However, owner Rich Ricci also has **Limini** and **Vroum Vroum Mag** to play with there and a couple of easy wins might see Let's Dance start being given a mention or two.

First of all, you can forget her defeats at Fairyhouse and Punchestown late last season when Mullins was chasing the Irish trainers' title. Everything was being wheeled out at that stage when plenty had done enough for the season.

Let's Dance had been impressive prior to that, putting together a five-race unbeaten run that culminated in a victory at Cheltenham in the Grade 2 Trull House Mares' Novices' Hurdle.

Admittedly the form of that win doesn't make her an obvious contender for this, but there was something about the way she sluiced through the pack to win going away that was seriously impressive.

She certainly didn't look slow despite being dropped in trip from 2m4f and having the stamina for that longer distance can be a big help in this race.

She improved throughout the main chunk of last season and there's no reason why she shouldn't do so again.

Stablemate **Faugheen** is harder to fancy as the 2015 winner has had a long time off the track and will be ten next year.

The last horse to win at that age was Sea Pigeon in 1980, which highlights the enormity of his task, and it would make more sense for him to go up in trip for the Stayers Hurdle – assuming injuries haven't robbed him of his talent completely. (NW)

LET'S DANCE: wins easily at the Cheltenham Festival last season

MIN: made a big impact chasing last season and can do so again

Champion Chase

THIS race looked a done deal last season with **Douvan** seemingly impregnable in a division shorn of Sprinter Sacre and featuring mostly ageing stars.

However, an injury sustained early in the Champion Chase ruined Douvan's bid and the race went to **Special Tiara** – something I still have trouble believing.

Willie Mullins does appear to have a bit of a jinx in this race and has yet to win it, but surely he will do so sooner rather than later and I fancy him to crack it in 2018 with a Rich Ricci-owned gelding who isn't Douvan.

The horse's name is **MIN**, who is available at 12-1 in places.

A good novice hurdler who found only Altior too strong in the 2016 Supreme, he made a stunning transition to fences last season and it was a great pity that injury robbed him of a crack at the Arkle – and therefore another go at beating Altior.

Before the injury happened, he'd won two out of two over fences, landing a novice event at Navan before taking the leap up to Grade 1 level in his stride to win at Leopardstown's Christmas meeting.

He thrashed his field, jumping fast and fluently throughout, and unlike some Irish races this one did have depth to it. Arkle third Ordinary World chased him home, nine lengths adrift, and further behind were future Cheltenham Festival winners Road To Respect and Tully East.

All were made to look distinctly ordinary and it appeared, on this display, that Min had taken a considerable step forward from his novice hurdle form.

Likely to be kept around the minimum trip, he makes plenty of appeal as long as he makes a full recovery from the injury he sustained.

He certainly makes more appeal now than his stablemate Douvan, who is more cut out for longer trips than Min and may go for the Ryanair, with Ricci and Mullins having already shown they are prepared to split their stars in an unpopular way.

Altior is the most likely winner but that is reflected in his short quotes.

It's hard to pick holes in his form and the way he thrashed Special Tiara at Sandown last April suggests he would have won this race last season had connections gone for it.

That said, his most workmanlike performance came in the Arkle when Charbel was giving him a very good race until falling two out.

Min has seven lengths to make up with him from their Supreme Novices' running and may well have wiped out some of that by now.

Yorkhill gets his standard quote, even though this race would appear unlikely, and the same applies to **Fox Norton**, who would be an excellent Ryanair candidate.

If there is a leftfield winner then **Great Field** could be the one. He looked exciting at Punchestown last season, but his jumping can be a little hair-raising at times and he was lucky on a few occasions to get away with it. He has the ability, but I do wonder whether his suspect jumping will get found out at the highest level. (NW)

ALTIOR: only workmanlike at Cheltenham and looks too short

Champion Chase

Cheltenham, March 15

	Bet365	*Betfred*	*Boyles*	*Coral*	*Hills*	*Lads*	*P Power*	*Skybet*
Altior	5-4	**6-4**	5-4	5-4	**6-4**	11-8	**6-4**	5-4
Douvan	11-4	3	3	3	3	3	3	**10-3**
Min	**12**	10	**12**	10	8	10	8	9
Great Field	**12**	8	10	**12**	10	**12**	10	10
Fox Norton	7	8	8	12	**14**	12	12	12
Yorkhill	6	8	6	5	7	6	**14**	**14**
Un De Sceaux	16	-	-	-	-	-	16	**20**
Special Tiara	14	16	16	20	16	20	20	**25**
Charbel	16	**25**	**25**	14	12	16	20	20
Top Notch	16	-	20	16	-	16	-	**25**
Politologue	**25**	-	-	-	-	-	20	20
Ar Mad	20	-	-	-	-	-	-	**25**
Cloudy Dream	20	-	-	**33**	-	**33**	**33**	**33**
Sir Valentino	25	-	-	33	-	33	**50**	**50**

each-way 1/4 odds, 1-2-3

Others on application, prices correct at time of going to press

›tayers' Hurdle

F Willie Mullins has a hoodoo in the Champion Chase, then he also had one in this race until last season.

However, **NICHOLS CANYON** won him his first Stayers' Hurdle and this ardy little horse seems certain to have ıother crack this season.

For much of his career Nichols Canyon ad seemed to fall between two stools – ɔt quite good enough to win anything :her than domestic 2m Graded hurdles ıd with stamina for further (one run in the S aside) not completely assured.

His latest campaign appeared to have ɔnfirmed that. He won the Morgiana but as then well beaten by Petit Mouchoir Christmas before falling (beaten at the ne) behind the same horse in the Irish hampion Hurdle.

Mullins then made the inspired deci- on to hike him up a whole mile in trip for e Stayers' Hurdle and it paid off as he ound out a narrow victory over Lil Rock- eller and **Unowhatimeanharry**.

He was unable to confirm the form with e latter at Punchestown, but there was ɜry little in it and I would expect Nichols anyon to come out on top again if the two locked horns again next March.

NICHOLS CANYON: a real fighter ideally suited to these demands

Unowhatimeanharry had swept all before him prior to Cheltenham, but he will be ten next year and the last horse to win this race at a double-figure age was Crimson Embers way back in 1986. It will be a tall order for him.

Stayers' Hurdle — Cheltenham, March 16

	Bet365	*Betfred*	*Boyles*	*Coral*	*Hills*	*Lads*	*P Power*	*Skybet*
ichols Canyon	5	6	6	6	6	5	**7**	5
nowhatimeanharry	6	6	6	6	6	6	**8**	6
ıe Worlds End	**12**	**12**	**12**	8	**12**	10	10	10
anworth	7	-	8	6	10	7	12	**14**
pple's Jade	10	10	8	10	12	12	**14**	**14**
enhill	**14**	10	10	10	10	8	12	**14**
upasundae	12	-	-	-	**16**	-	-	**16**
acardys	**16**	-	-	14	12	**16**	-	**16**
'holestone	-	-	-	16	16	14	-	**20**
Ami Serge	16	**20**	-	-	-	-	16	**20**
ıe New One	20	-	-	16	-	16	-	**25**
'illoughby Court	16	-	16	20	-	20	16	**25**
l Rockerfeller	20	**25**	16	**25**	16	20	**25**	20
ugusta Kate	25	-	-	16	25	16	**33**	25

each-way 1/4 odds, 1-2-3

Others on application, prices correct at time of going to press

THE WORLDS END: likely to stay over hurdles for a Stayers' Hurdle bid

Bearing in mind this is almost certain to be the race Nichols Canyon runs in at the festival, best prices of 7-1 seem quite generous as it seems inconceivable he won't at least be in the three. I think he will win again.

I fancy him even more when looking through the market at potential opponents.

The young pretender is **The Worlds End** from Tom George's stable.

He really sprung to prominence when taking a Grade 2 event at Haydock in February and was well fancied for the Albert Bartlett on the back of that. It's possible he may have obliged, too, but for falling two out when in contention.

He didn't let that affect him as he then went on to Aintree to grind out a victory in the Grade 1 Sefton Novices' Hurdle, a race won by Thistlecrack in 2015 before he went on to take this.

After that win George intimated that The Worlds End will stay over hurdles and has more improvement in him, but he has plenty to find with a proven stayer as good as Nichols Canyon.

I'd still prefer him to **Penhill**, who took advantage of The Worlds End's fall to win the Albert Bartlett. That seemed to come as a surprise to connections given he was a 16-1 shot and plans to run him on the Flat haven't materialised, so I'd like to see how he's campaigned first.

Things get more confused the furth down the market you travel.

Yanworth ranges from 7-1 to 14-1 price and that's largely down to the fa that he is meant to be going chasing th season.

If he doesn't take to fences then th would be a very realistic option as his w at Aintree in April showed that he had bee crying out for the longer trip, but if thing go according to plan then he is surely a RSA horse.

Buveur D'Air made the switch back su cessfully last season and Yanworth cou easily do likewise, but it's not somethin you can really bet on at fairly stingy odds

The same applies to **Apple's Jad** albeit for different reasons.

She had a funny season, thrice being beaten favourite but winning three Grac 1 events. They all came over 2m4f an she will most probably stay much furthe but connections have intimated she w stay within her own sex again this seaso which means a similar campaign to la year and no Stayers' Hurdle challenge.

L'Ami Serge is more interesting nc connections have worked out he is a sta er. He has the class to figure, having som good form in the book, and while he ha never been the easiest to win with, his vi tory in France over the summer suggeste he has turned over a new leaf. (NW)

Gold Cup

SURELY this is the race **YORKHILL** should be running in – in which case I'd be very keen on backing him.

Willie Mullins seemed to be very downbeat after his loss at the Punchestown Festival – you can understand why in a way as his horse had just thrown away victory in a Grade 1 chase with a wayward performance that almost saw him refuse at the last – but it was ridiculous to then suggest he might return to hurdles.

Why? Just a look at his form figures shows that he took to fences very well and he won the JLT, which was his big target of the season.

I think there are two things to bear in mind about Yorkhill. The first is that he must now go left-handed. He was very professional at Cheltenham, showed no kinks and had plenty left in the tank when beating Top Notch.

The second thing, and something not picked up on by most pundits, is that Cheltenham perhaps takes a lot out of him as he is never as good afterwards.

Rewind to his hurdling season and, after thashing Yanworth in the Neptune, he looked barely rideable at Aintree when struggling home against Le Prezien and then came nowhere at Punchestown. This time he didn't go to Aintree but was still just as wayward at Punchestown.

I don't think that mentally he can cope with many races, so just run him once or twice before March, go to Cheltenham and

HOW NOT TO DO IT: Yorkhill comes to a halt and almost falls at the last

OUR DUKE: seen here winning the Irish National, he is a big Gold Cup player

then stop. Are you reading, Willie?

If Yorkhill does go elsewhere then we need a cover shot in this race and Jessica Harrington's **OUR DUKE** can provide it.

He was a good hurdler but was simply stunning as a novice chaser last season and his win in the Irish National had to be seen to be believed.

In what is always one of the toughest races in the calendar, he made a mockery of it. He travelled well, jumped really well and never looked like losing at any stage.

A 14-length winning margin didn't flatter him at all and, although it was only the veteran Bless The Wings chasing him home, that shouldn't be held against him in what was a thrilling display.

Things will be harder this season, but the Gold Cup is all about stamina, which Our Duke possesses plenty of, and he is also a Grade 1 winner over 3m so he ticks the class box as well.

Thistlecrack is the favourite, but I'm not sure about him.

He will be ten next year, which is older than ideal so his injury last season may well have robbed him of his best chance of winning this race. I was also disappointed he couldn't beat the gallant Many Clouds in the Cotswold Chase in January.

Might Bite is another to consider. He has the label of being quirky, but is that really true?

He looked very resolute when winning at Aintree and a fall at the last when the Kauto Star Novces' Chase at Kempton was won can happen to any horse.

The only time he looked tricky was at Cheltenham, but then he had set a strong pace and not seen another horse for a long time, so he was entitled to idle. Once he caught sight of Whisper, he ran on again, so don't think that just because he is by Scorpion he is difficult.

He could easily get involved in this and t a much shorter price if he can land the ing George in the meantime. Bearing in nind how effective he looked at Kempton ast Christmas, that must be a distinct possibility.

With last year's novices so strong, this ould well be a stronger race than last ear, so **Sizing John** faces a tall order retain his crown. **Djakadam** has had nough chances, while **Minella Rocco** nd **Native River** also just came up short.

The one to take from last year's race ould be **Bristol De Mai** at a huge price if nly he could find some consistency.

He was brilliant in the Peter Marsh, howing his true colours, and was wrong t Newbury next time, but he was only verage in the Gold Cup and disappointng again at Aintree on his final start.

Bearing in mind he is only young, it's vorth giving him the benefit of the doubt nd maybe a few more small-field events t Haydock can come his way – I wouldn't ut anyone off him landing a Betfair Chase n deep ground.

But he may really need an attritional ear to prosper at Cheltenham and that ould also suit the likes of Minella Rocco nd Our Duke. Maybe one day. (NW)

MIGHT BITE: not so quirky after all

Cheltenham Gold Cup

Cheltenham, March 17

	Bet365	*Betfred*	*Boyles*	*Coral*	*Hills*	*Lads*	*P Power*	*Skybet*
histlecrack	5	5	5	5	5	5	**11-2**	5
izing John	5	4	5	**6**	5	**6**	5	5
orkhill	**8**	7	7	6	**8**	6	6	7
light Bite	8	**10**	**10**	8	**10**	**10**	8	**10**
ur Duke	**10**	**10**	8	8	8	8	8	**10**
ouvan	**12**	-	-	-	7	-	10	**12**
lative River	**12**	**12**	**12**	**12**	**12**	**12**	**12**	**12**
linella Rocco	12	**16**	12	**16**	12	**16**	12	14
jakadam	**16**	12	14	**16**	12	**16**	14	**16**
oneygree	14	16	16	16	**20**	16	16	16
isko	25	20	25	25	20	25	**33**	25
Vhisper	25	-	25	25	25	25	20	**33**
mpire Of Dirt	20	-	25	25	-	25	20	**33**
merican	**40**	33	33	25	-	33	33	33

each-way 1/4 odds, 1-2-3

Others on application, prices correct at time of going to press

BLAKLION (second right): on his way to winning the RSA Chase in 2016

Grand National

I CAN'T remember seeing a more eye-catching run in the Grand National with an eye to the following year since Hedgehunter fell at the last in 2004 before returning to run away with the big one 12 months later.

The horse in question was **BLAKLION**, who jumped for fun over the National fences last April and was going so well three from home that he had even the normally unflappable Noel Fehily getting overexcited.

Fehily committed Blaklion for home at that point and he had opened up a clear lead at one stage, but the horse had done too much too soon and he had no answer in the straight as One For Arthur and Cause Of Causes swept past.

Still, he kept on well enough to finish fourth, suggesting this marathon trip is well within his compass under a more patient ride, and crucially he finished far enough back not to ruin his handicap mark.

Running off 152 that day, Blaklion was well in having gone up for a fine effort i Haydock's Grand National Trial after th publication of the weights, but he star this season on a mark of 155 and th would do nicely if connections can min him through to the weights launch again.

That run at Haydock, when he was bea en by handicap snip **Vieux Lion Roug** – a blatant non-stayer in this race – bu pulled miles clear of the rest, was one c a couple of other occasions when Blaklio looked like he had a major staying hand cap in him.

The first time came in the Henness when he was again travelled notably we to the straight only to find little, but co nections gave him a breathing operatic after that and he certainly saw out his ra es well enough at Haydock and Aintree i the circumstances.

It will be a source of frustration that h didn't win one last term, but all that will b forgotten if he can win the National and a 25-1 he looks a cracking bet.

The top of the market is packed wi

orses who may all be handicapped out
f contention.

Last year's first and second, **One For**
rthur and **Cause Of Causes**, will be sig-
ificantly higher in the weights this year,
while **Minella Rocco** and **Our Duke** may
vell have Grade 1 targets in mind and if
ll goes well on that front they could end
p giving lumps away. The same goes for
lative River and **Definitly Red** may have
nissed his chance given he was 10lb well
n last year.

Gordon Elliott, who won this race with
ilver Birch and went close to following up
en years on with Cause Of Causes, also
aces a race against time to get **Don Poli**
o the race after he suffered a setback this
ummer.

However, the trainer may still have
right prospects on several fronts, with
IGER ROLL perhaps the best of his team.
his horse has an enticing combination of
lass and stamina given he has a Triumph
lurdle and a National Hunt Chase in his
ocker, while he also seems well suited to
ig fields.

Ucello Conti, who caught the eye with
good run in the Becher over these fenc-
s and was going well in the big one when
eparting, and **Noble Endeavor**, who
ooks just the type to be laid out for the
ace, are others who give Elliott a particu-
arly strong hand. (DH)

Betting advice

King George

Thistlecrack 1pt 4-1
(Paddy Power)

Champion Hurdle

Defi Du Seuil 1pt 8-1
(generally available)

Let's Dance 1pt 33-1
(Paddy Power)

Champion Chase

Min 1pt 12-1
(Bet365, Boyles)

World Hurdle

Nichols Canyon 1pt 7-1
(Paddy Power)

Gold Cup

Yorkhill 1pt 8-1
(Bet365, Hills)

Our Duke 1pt 10-1
(Bet365, Betfred, Sky Bet)

Grand National

Blaklion 1pt 25-1
(Boyles, Coral, Hills)

Tiger Roll 0.5pt 50-1
(Coral, Paddy Power)

Grand National

Aintree, April 8

	Bet365	*Betfred*	*Boyles*	*Coral*	*Hills*	*Lads*	*P Power*	*Skybet*
)ne For Arthur	**16**	**16**	**16**	**16**	**16**	-	**16**	14
laklion	20	20	**25**	**25**	**25**	-	16	20
linella Rocco	20	**25**	20	20	-	-	20	**25**
)ur Duke	**25**	16	**25**	**25**	-	-	**25**	20
lative River	16	20	-	20	**33**	-	20	20
;ause Of Causes	20	**33**	25	25	25	-	20	25
)efinitly Red	25	**33**	25	**33**	-	-	20	20
'icente	**33**	25	-	-	**33**	-	**33**	20
loble Endeavor	**33**	**33**	-	**33**	-	-	**33**	**33**
Jcello Conti	**40**	33	33	-	-	-	33	33
izing Codelco	33	-	-	-	**40**	-	-	33
'iger Roll	20	-	33	**50**	-	-	**50**	40

each-way 1/4 odds, 1-2-3-4

Others on application, prices correct at time of going to press

FAUGHEEN: on the comeback trail and how he fares may affect Yorkhill plans

Ireland
by Jerry M

A MASSIVE gulf between six elite stables and the remainder is the most significant feature of an Irish jump racing scene which was formerly much more diverse.

The big story of last season was the intensity of competition between Willie Mullins, champion trainer in every season since 2008, and Gordon Elliott, whose powerful challenge was spearheaded by a sequence of big-value handicap wins.

Under pressure through the winter months, Mullins rallied to take the title, around €200,000 clear in the crucial earn-ings category, despite Elliott's numerica advantage of 193 to 180.

The title race had been opened up earl in the season when Michael O'Leary's Gig-ginstown House Stud operation split wit Mullins and this realignment, which wi continue to have an impact this seasor was not the only major owner-trainer rift.

The exit of horses owned by Alan Pott from Henry de Bromhead cost the C Waterford trainer several good horses including the subsequent Gold Cup wir-ner Sizing John and another Cheltenhar scorer Supasundae, both transferred to Jessica Harrington.

Yet De Bromhead overcame that reverse to record his best seasonal tally, ahead of eight-time former champion Noel Meade, Harrington and Joseph O'Brien, who has quickly made his presence felt in the premier league. Outside this group no other trainer surpassed the 20-winner mark.

This sextet dominates in terms of quantity as well as quality and, when it comes to assessing big-race prospects for this season, this powerful concentration of talent supplies the essential focus, a view supported by a breakdown of Ireland's record-breaking haul of 19 winners at the 2017 Cheltenham Festival. Both Elliott and Mullins supplied six, Harrington contributed three, Meade and De Bromhead one each. Handicap winners trained by Alan Fleming and Pat Kelly completed the list.

WILLIE MULLINS is still the only place to start and it will be fascinating to see what he does with **Yorkhill**, a rare and versatile talent, this season.

The dual Cheltenham Festival winner is good enough to embark on a Champion Hurdle campaign and that might become a tempting option for Mullins should anything more happen to **Faugheen**, his 2015 winner who is currently on the comeback trail from injury.

However, Yorkhill would also be a prime candidate for the Cheltenham Gold Cup, which is the significant omission on his trainer's illustrious career record, despite the fact he squandered another Grade 1 opportunity when his erratic jumping tendencies recurred at Fairyhouse in the Ryanair Gold Cup.

Djakadam, second to Coneygree and Don Cossack in the 2015 and 2016 runnings of the Gold Cup, could manage only fourth behind Sizing John last March before running a gallant race in losing out by only a short-head to the same horse at Punchestown.

He is only an eight-year-old and still has time on his side, but there is a suspicion he does not truly stay the Gold Cup trip and a campaign targeting the King George, the Irish Gold Cup and Punchestown might make more sense.

Mullins has won the Champion Hurdle in four of the last seven seasons and, in addition to Faugheen, his squad for the top 2m hurdles will include several graduates from last year's strong novice team, notably the Supreme Novices' runner-up **Melon** and his subsequent Punchestown conqueror **Cilaos Emery**.

Limini could also join them given the stable has immense back-up in the mares' division from the likes of **Let's Dance**, **Vroum Vroum Mag** and **Augusta Kate**.

Stayers' Hurdle winner **Nichols Canyon** has the potential to dominate in a category in which last season's Albert Bartlett winner **Penhill** could also shine.

After losing his aura of invincibility in last season's Champion Chase, **Douvan** will bid to assert dominance over Arkle winner Altior in the 2m chase division, while **Un De Sceaux** could also take in top 2m events before returning for the defence of his Ryanair Chase title at Cheltenham.

The crop of novice chasers at Closutton will be led by the talented **Bacardys**, who bounced back from a reverse at Cheltenham to beat Finian's Oscar in a 2m4f Grade 1 novice hurdle at Punchestown.

It will be surprising if Mullins does not exert a strong influence over the novice hurdling scene, with every chance his policy of buying French-bred youngsters will reap the same dividends as in recent years.

Among last season's bumper horses, **Getabird**, who suffered a setback which forced him to miss Cheltenham, will be very interesting and Cheltenham fourth **Next Destination** is another likely sort.

GORDON ELLIOTT, already with one major prize in the bag courtesy of Potters Point in the Kerry National, has a strong team of novices, headed by the brilliant mare **Fayonagh**, winner of the Grade 1 bumpers at Cheltenham and Punchestown last season.

She can be rated an exceptional novice hurdling prospect, probably the best in Ireland, though that may be disputed by fans of stablemate **Samcro**, unbeaten in a point-to-point and three bumpers.

Blow By Blow, a smart bumper horse for Mullins in the Gigginstown colours the

BALKO DES FLOS: the Galway Plate hero can continue to progress

season before last, did not appear last term but could make up for lost time.

Elliott's powerful novice chase team will include **Death Duty**, **Sutton Place** and **Monbeg Notorious**, all of whom are likely to make a significant impression.

Outstanding mare **Apple's Jade** is to stay over hurdles. She broke a long-running Mullins monopoly in the Mares' Hurdle at Cheltenham and rounded off the season with a commanding performance at Punchestown. She will be hard to beat in similar races.

HENRY DE BROMHEAD was at the centre of a swings-and-roundabouts theme last season given he inherited a couple of top performers in the Gigginstown switch having lost the Potts horses.

Petit Mouchoir, who won two Grade 1 events at Leopardstown and was best of the Irish contingent in the Champion Hurdle, could be a serious contender for the Racing Post Arkle if taking to fences as well as expected.

Another ex-Mullins horse, **Balko Des Flos**, has already played a part this term in winning the Galway Plate and looks set to make further progress, possibly giving the stable another contender for the Ryanair Chase as back-up for **Sub Lieutenant**, runner-up to Un De Sceaux last March.

Special Tiara, who took advantage of Douvan's eclipse to win the Queen Mother Champion Chase, will find it hard to retain his crown as an 11-year-old, though Moscow Flyer accomplished that feat in 2005 so it is not out of the question.

The yard's best young prospect is **Paloma Blue**, who won a bumper first time out at Naas and chased home Fayonagh at Punchestown on his only other outing, while **Monalee** should make a top-notch novice chaser.

In deciding to move **Sizing John** up in trip after his forlorn struggles against Douvan, *JESSICA HARRINGTON* made perhaps the most inspired decision of her career.

As a rising eight-year-old, Sizing John may still have some way to go before reaching the peak of his powers and has a strong chance of becoming the first horse since Best Mate to record back-to-back Cheltenham Gold Cup victories.

Harrington's brilliant campaign was crowned by victory for **Our Duke** in the Irish Grand National and this progressive staying chaser has the potential to challenge for top honours as well.

NOEL MEADE long ruled the roost on the Irish jumping scene before Mullins asserted supremacy. The trainer was hit badly by the recession, but he has staged a strong rally and celebrated another Cheltenham success last season with **Road To Respect**.

That one could be back for the Ryanair, which might also be the aim for **Disko**, who claimed two Grade 1 novice chase prizes on either side of a third placing behind Yorkhill in the JLT.

Meade has some good young horses on his hands, notably **Red Jack**, unbeaten in two bumpers runs last season. This one beat the Elliott-trained Dinons in a valuable Fairyhouse event and could be a prime candidate for owner JP McManus on the novice hurdling scene.

JOSEPH O'BRIEN has made his name with young hurdlers and, with McManus in support, it is only a matter of time before he manages to unearth a real star.

The one most likely to make the grade from his current crop is **Le Richebourg**, who completed a hat-trick of wins in novice hurdles at Galway in July and looks really exciting.

If there is a star in the making outside the powerhouse stables, it may be **Debuchet**, an outstanding jumping prospect for *MARGARET MULLINS*.

Winner of two of his four bumper starts, he ran up against the very promising Red Jack on his debut at Naas. He emerged with tremendous credit from his other defeat behind Fayonagh at Cheltenham.

PAT KELLY has helped to keep the Cheltenham dream alive for small-scale trainers by getting on the scoreboard at the last two festivals and his 2017 Pertemps winner **Presenting Percy** looks a smart sort for staying novice chases.

ALAN FLEMING saddled **Massey's Wood** to make an impressive debut in a bumper at the Listowel festival. This one appeals as a likely contender for good novice hurdles at up to 2m4f.

ENDA BOLGER has **Josies Orders** coming back from injury and the 2016 Cheltenham Festival should again be a force in cross-country races.

Invincible Irish

Fayonagh

Petit Mouchoir

Yorkhill

PRESENTING PERCY: the Pertemps Final winner is a smart chasing prospect

Berkshire by Downsman

ON the November weekend that saw Sprinter Sacre retired and Simonsig fatally injured, it took a mighty leap of faith to suggest *NICKY HENDERSON* would end the campaign on a high.

However, the master of Seven Barrows regrouped and rebounded in style, enjoying a fine Cheltenham Festival in the spring that helped him seal a fourth trainers' championship.

The good news for him is that the stars of last term have youth on their side.

At the top of the pecking order is **Altior**, the 2016 Supreme Novices' Hurdle winner who enjoyed an unblemished debut campaign over fences last season, culminating in wins in the Racing Post Arkle at Cheltenham and Sandown's Celebration Chase.

The prolific gelding should be hard to stop in the top 2m chases and a fifth Champion Chase triumph for Henderson must be within reach.

The RSA Chase winner **Might Bite** will be treated as a Cheltenham Gold Cup horse, although the King George VI Chase at Kempton, where he was in the process of perhaps his best performance last season until falling at the last in the Kauto Star Novices' Chase, will be his main aim for the first half of the season.

Whisper, second to Might Bite in the RSA, could develop into a Grand National candidate for Henderson, who would love to get that Aintree monkey off his back, although the Ladbrokes Trophy – the Hennessy Gold Cup in old money – may come first.

Over hurdles there is no reason why **Buveur D'Air**, who gave the trainer a record-breaking sixth Champion Hurdle victory in March, cannot retain his title, while it would be premature to write off **Charli**

MIGHT BITE: leads stablemate Whisper en route to success at Aintree

Parcs, who proved slightly disappointing as a juvenile after an impressive debut but is still held in very high regard by the trainer.

Brain Power, behind Buveur D'Air in the Champion Hurdle, heads Henderson's team of novice chasers and is an exciting prospect in that sphere.

Like Henderson, *ALAN KING* enjoyed a fine season, breaking through the 100-winner barrier for the first time since 2008-09.

His top hurdler **Yanworth** should be a force over fences and King has identified a race at Exeter for the Christmas Hurdle winner, while Champion Hurdle sixth **Sceau Royal** is another who could thrive chasing.

Label Des Obeaux is another for the Ladbrokes Trophy, with King hoping he could develop into a Scottish Grand National contender.

The trainer has not lost faith in **Winter Escape**, who promised to be anything 12 months ago and has returned looking "marvellous", while **Elgin**, who had some good Graded novice form, will be aimed at the top 2m handicap hurdles.

King's great pal *OLIVER SHERWOOD* had to endure the devastating loss of stable star Many Clouds in January and reckons his string were not right after that, but no-one would begrudge the popular trainer bouncing back.

There may well be more to come from **The Fresh Prince**, who runs in the Many Clouds colours of Trevor Hemmings and could easily improve on his mark of 123, especially on a sound surface, while Sherwood also thinks there are still races to be won with **Puffin Billy** in testing conditions.

Sherwood has a handy team of mares, including **The Organist**, who has summered fantastically. Useful over hurdles, she did not take to fences last term but could have another crack at chasing.

The trainer is also keen on fences for **Hitherjacques Lady**, who will be suited by winter ground, as will **Surtee Du Berlais**, another mare inked in for chasing.

The loss of Many Clouds and departure of some yard stalwarts mean the summer has been a transitional one for Sherwood, who hopes younger names **Book Of Gold**, **The Groovy Hoovy**, **Jersey Bean** and **Monkey Puzzle** can step up.

LA BAGUE AU ROI: in great nick

WARREN GREATREX, Sherwood's former assistant, is coming off his best season in terms of winners and is delighted with the team he has assembled for 2017-18.

Champion Bumper fifth **Western Ryder**, who was also third in Aintree's edition, is likely to be the leading light and has summered brilliantly before going novice hurdling. He will start over 2m but will easily get 2m4f and Greatrex hopes he can take high rank.

La Bague Au Roi is another to have returned in great nick from her break. She could run over hurdles at Wetherby in October before going novice chasing, which is what the trainer has in mind for **The Nipper**. Both are both big, scopey mares "made to jump fences".

Petticoat Tails, who goes novice hurdling, is another promising mare. She looks great and has improvement in her.

Greatrex has the biggest jumps prize of all in mind for **Missed Approach**. The National Hunt Chase second will be aimed at the Grand National but could be another to start in what was the Hennessy.

Hurdles will be the route for Grade 1 winner **One Track Mind**, who has had a wind

ALOOMOMO: had a fractured shoulder but has now fully recovered

operation as well as a spell schooling with three-time Cheltenham Gold Cup-winning trainer Henrietta Knight. Newbury's Long Distance Hurdle in December is his likely starting point.

Another not to forget is **Aloomomo**, who fractured a shoulder at Cheltenham in December but is back cantering and retains potential.

Of the new arrivals, **The Butcher Said** could be worth noting for novice hurdles, while **Peculiar Places** – the first horse Greatrex will train for Highclere Thoroughbred Racing - is related to 2009 Champion Bumper winner Dunguib and could be smart.

Greatrex is excited by point-to-point winner **Article Fifty** and is also purring about **Invisible Clouds**, who is by Many Clouds's sire Cloudings and one of two youngsters he has been sent by Hemmings.

JAMIE SNOWDEN, like Greatrex, had his most prolific innings last term and **Dans Le Vent**, sixth in the Champion Bumper, carries his hope. He is a lovely prospect for novice hurdles.

Double Treasure has had a wind operation and could be a handicap chaser to follow along with **Fact Of The Matter**, **Future Gilded** and **Champagne James**, who returns from a spell on the sidelines.

Three Ways could come into his own over fences, while **Kalahari Queen**, described as "a smashing mare with size and scope", and **Scorpion Sid**, a proper winter horse with a fine future over fences, are new recruits from the pointing sphere.

CHARLIE MANN was another who had a productive 2016-17 and reckons his team is quite forward. **Pickamix** and **Some Kinda Lama** are 3m novice chasers who could do well on decent ground, while **Like The Sound** will join them in that sphere.

Maid Of Milan and **Wishicould** are nice mares bound for fences and **Zen Master** is a well-regarded five-year-old, as is strapping point winner **The Ogle Gogle Man**.

Last season was not one to remember fondly for *HARRY WHITTINGTON*, whose new barn caused complications with the health of his yard.

However, Whittington is much happier now and as a result of the problems he may have a few well-handicapped horses.

The Grand National is the dream for **Emerging Force**, who could have a crack at the Becher and possibly the Grimthorpe Chase in the lead-up the big one.

Bigmartre has schooled brilliantly as he heads over fences, while **Affaire D'Honneur** has strengthened up and will also go chasing off a particularly nice mark.

Charlemar, who has had a cataract removed during the off season and now has full vision in both eyes, has also returned a stronger horse. He may begin over 2m4f, but Whittington is confident the five-year-old will get 3m.

Promising mare **Woolstone One** never made the track last season after throwing a splint and being caught up in the stable's health problems, but she is in good order and has schooled well.

Simply The Betts has a decent reputation having won two schooling hurdles in Ireland. A brother to the 134-rated Crimson Ark, he has a big engine and Whittington has already pencilled in Ascot for his hurdling debut under rules in November.

Just down the road from Whittington's Sparsholt yard *MARK BRADSTOCK* has had another frustrating summer with **Coneygree**, who had to miss a planned tilt at the Kerry National as rain turned the ground into a bog. He still seems to retain plenty of talent if conditions suit.

Bradstock is no one-horse operation and Coneygree's younger half-brother **Flintham**, who came agonisingly close to winning the Reynoldstown, must have a decent race in him, especially as he remains a novice over fences.

Delicate, he will be kept on soft ground and may be aimed at the Kauto Star Novices' Chase at Kempton, which Coneygree won in 2014.

Step Back is another inmate who should not be ignored and has the makings of a fine, staying chaser, but **Jaisalmer**, who unseated with a race all but in the bag at Kempton in the spring, will stay over hurdles.

SAM THOMAS enters his first full season in Lambourn and **Dancing Doug**, a Kalanisi half-brother to the high-class Sound Investment, could be a horse to help him make headlines.

He goes nicely and was in full training last season. A bumper before Christmas – to make the most of his four-year-old allowance – is the plan.

Mere Ironmonger, a smart bumper performer for Brendan Powell, has been off since April 2016, but he has been cantering since the start of August and looks great.

Best of Berkshire
Label Des Obeaux
Might Bite
Petticoat Tails

EMERGING FORCE (centre): could be a Grand National candidate next year

POLITOLOGUE: has definite similarities to the great Kauto Star

The West by Hastings

YOU'LL already have read that *PAUL NICHOLLS* has given up on wrestling his trainers' crown back from Nicky Henderson, but that's not to say there won't be a hatful of winners coming from his Ditcheat base this season.

Indeed, Nicholls may be downplaying his chances of having a serious contender for one of the championship races at the Cheltenham Festival because **Politologue** could scale the heights for the ten-time champion.

Politologue certainly showed he has a very bright future over fences last term and was desperately unlucky not to end the season with a victory in Grade 1 company at Aintree in the spring as he was clear and would have hacked up but for stumbling and unseating his rider a few strides after jumping the final fence cleanly.

Before that the striking-looking six-year-old had racked up impressive successes at Haydock, Ascot and Kempton and, while he was slightly disappointing in the JLT at Cheltenham, that came over a trip that was perhaps just beyond him at that stage.

Nicholls is set to campaign him as a two-miler this year, kicking off with the Haldon Gold Cup, and then it could be the Tingle Creek and ultimately the Champion Chase. There are definite similarlties to Kauto Star and it would be no surprise if he ended up one of the highest-rated chasers in Britain come April.

Nicholls has mentioned his exciting crop of novice chasers and **Movewiththetimes** may prove the standout among them.

He did everything but win the Betfair Hurdle at Newbury last February, going down in a driving finish to Ballyandy when it could be argued a more fluent jump at the final flight would have secured the prize.

A minor problem with a muscle in a hind leg put an end to his season afterwards, but he was always likely to come into his own over fences this term anyway as he has lots of size and scope.

Although all options are open for Movewiththetimes distance-wise, he can make up into a live candidate for the Racing Post Arkle at Cheltenham over the minimum trip.

Modus, who also runs in the colours of JP McManus, is another high-class hurdler going chasing and fences could prove the making of him.

Among the youngsters, **Malaya** and **Sao** are exciting prospects in the juvenile hurdling ranks while **Some Man** and **Western Honour**, who both signed off in Ireland with decent point-to-point victories, are two other nice imports for novice hurdles.

If Nicholls does not believe he can be champion trainer this time around, what about *COLIN TIZZARD*?

His rise to fame from milking 350 cows to handling Cheltenham and Aintree winners is little short of amazing and there is more than a chance he can build on last season's gains.

It's no coincidence that Tizzard's ascendency in the training ranks has tied in with his son, former jockey Joe, playing a bigger role in the entire operation and the pair certainly hit it off last season with high-profile successes for Native River, Thistlecrack, Finian's Oscar and Fox Norton.

Native River will have the Cheltenham Gold Cup in his sights again this campaign having progressed at such a rate of knots last term. He ended up finishing third in the race last March after winning the Hennessy Gold Cup and the Welsh Grand National and he should improve further with age.

The team at Venn Farm Stables are more than hopeful he clinch the Gold Cup this time around and he will be trained with that race very much in mind.

Fox Norton could be another force for Tizzard in the season's big chases.

Narrowly beaten in the Champion Chase, he gained compensation by winning at Aintree and Punchestown. Tizzard was initially keen to step him up again in trip, but his owners want to avoid a clash with Sizing John and he is now being aimed at the Tingle Creek, in which he will take plenty of beating.

A watching brief is advised on **Thistlecrack**, however. Last year's King George winner was on course for the Gold Cup when his season was cut short by a minor tendon problem and, while he is over that setback and on course to go back at Kempton, it should be remembered that he will already be approaching ten.

Finian's Oscar was Tizzard's other big

FOX NORTON: going up in trip

star last season, winning twice at Grade 1 level in the Tolworth at Sandown and the Mersey at Aintree when stepped up in trip. He is set to go novice chasing and should be a major force.

PHILIP HOBBS always targets 100 winners and £1 million in prize-money each season and rarely fails on both counts.

His obvious stable star is the unbeaten **Defi Du Seuil** as the four-year-old proved a revelation when winning all seven of his starts for the trainer last season.

The icing on the cake was probably his Triumph Hurdle success as many had doubted whether he would prove as good on a faster surface, many of his previous wins having come when the ground was testing.

However, he answered the doubters in very much the best way possible and gave the impression he was actually better suited by good ground at Cheltenham.

Many Triumph Hurdle winners fail to progress, but Defi Du Seuil looks absolutely exceptional and might very well be the exception.

Hobbs and the JP McManus team have resisted the temptation to go chasing as they believe Defi Du Seuil can end up a live Champion Hurdle candidate and that is definitely not out of the question.

Hobbs could still have a smart novice chaser in **Wait For Me**, who has a big engine if he ever manages to put it all together in the jumping department, while he also has another exciting prospect for McManus in the unbeaten **Jerrysback** (two from two in novice hurdles last season).

Last autumn *DAVID PIPE* was confident French import **King's Socks** would make his presence felt in the top races and a tilt at the BetVictor Gold Cup was being considered, but a training setback unfortunately saw him ruled out for the season.

But Pipe, like his legendary father Martin before him, is a dab-hand at getting this type of horse back on track and there is every chance he will be on racecourse duty later this season. He was bought with big festivals – Cheltenham and Aintree – in mind and that remains the aim.

Pipe reports that **Moon Racer** has had

JERRYSBACK (right): won both novice hurdles for Philip Hobbs last season

AMERICAN: fragile but could be Gold Cup class on soft or heavy ground

a colic operation and may be back only for the second half of the season, if at all, but dual Cheltenham Festival winner **Un Temps Pour Tout** and Grand National favourite **Vieux Lion Rouge**, who just doesn't seem to get home at Aintree, will be other big-race contenders.

Of the dark horses at Pond House, the mare **Timeforben** is worth keeping on your side as she looked good when winning an Irish point-to-point and will make her debut for Pipe this autumn. There is now a valuable programme for mares over hurdles and fences and she has all the right credentials for that division.

The sad loss of the very smart Neon Wolf, who finished second at the Cheltenham Festival in the Neptune behind Willoughby Court, over the summer proved a massive blow for *HARRY FRY*. Losing any horse is bad enough but one as classy as him is hard to bounce back from for anybody

However, trainers have to be resilient creatures and Fry may still have an ace in the pack in **American**.

The fragile seven-year-old looks entirely dependent on soft or heavy ground and Fry has to train him with kid-gloves, but he was unbeaten in three chases last season and could be up to Gold Cup standard if he were to ever get his conditions at Cheltenham in March.

It's more likely he will be one for something like the Welsh National at Chepstow, where underfoot conditions are invariably deep.

Western wonders

American
Defi Du Seuil
Politologue 1/1

The North by Borderer

FOR the third year in a row there were no northern-trained winners at the Cheltenham Festival last season and on the morning of the Grand National it seemed it would be another poor spring for the north at the big festivals.

But **One For Arthur** changed all that in the space of just nine minutes at Aintree, becoming the first Scottish-trained Grand National winner since Rubstic in 1979 and proving that, for all the firepower down south, the north can still punch above its weight.

Typically, One For Arthur wasn't expensive compared to many other top jumps prospects, costing £60,000 when bought by Tom Malone and his trainer *LUCINDA RUSSELL* at the Brightwells sale at Cheltenham in December 2013.

Just as typically, though, the northern jumps circuit has rallied together now he's proved a real star, with Kelso changing the conditions of their staying chase at the end of October to smooth One For Arthur's path towards a second National.

The Kelso race, for many years a 0-140 handicap, was the eight-year-old's starting point last season when he won off 127, but he would have been ineligible this year having rocketed up the handicap to a mark of 156.

However, One For Arthur will now be able to return for the same race before

ONE FOR ARTHUR: rescues the season for northern jumping

moving on to the Betfred Becher Chase back at Aintree in December, the Classic Chase at Warwick in January and then the National again.

Connections are aware things will be much tougher, especially with many National winners having struggled to win another race until Many Clouds came along, but like that horse One For Arthur was still young when successful at Aintree and is still maturing and improving.

Although he once had the reputation of being a real mudlark, One For Arthur also proved in the National that he doesn't need heavy ground to excel, with quicker conditions absolutely fine provided he has a real test of stamina, and he could well make a bold bid to emulate Red Rum and win the great race for a second successive season.

Big River is another Russell-trained horse to watch out for this winter.

Second in an Irish point-to-point in November 2014, he was sent to the Brightwells Cheltenham sales the following month and again bought by Malone and Russell for £50,000.

He has also proved a sound buy having won four of his eight starts, two of those in bumpers and the other two in handicap hurdles last season.

Chasing is likely to be his game and he should do well in staying novice events having produced his best run on his final start last season when breezing home by ten lengths over 3m2f on testing ground at Kelso.

The home-bred **Sammy B**, who also progressed well in staying hurdles last season, and the second-season chaser **Newtown Lad** are two other Russell-trained horses likely to pay their way this time.

As last year, Malton trainer *MALCOLM JEFFERSON* has probably the best team of jumpers in the north overall and once again the star is **Cloudy Dream**.

As his trainer predicted, he proved a smart novice chaser last season, winning three of his seven races and finishing second in the other four. When you consider the horses he failed to beat were Buveur D'Air, Forest Bihan, Altior and Flying Angel, it was a pretty impressive record.

Now that he settles better, Jefferson feels that two and a half miles will suit him well and his first likely target is the BetVictor Gold Cup at Cheltenham in November. How he performs there will determine where he will go for the rest of the season, though he wouldn't be the sort to excel ploughing through heavy ground in mid winter.

The other top-class prospect in the Jefferson yard is **Cyrus Darius**, who was impressive when winning the Top Novices' Hurdle at Aintree back in 2015 but has unfortunately proved tricky to both train and place since then.

Off the track for 16 months after winning on his sole run over fences in September 2015, he ran just three times last season, all over hurdles, and managed to win a fairly weak Morebattle Hurdle at Kelso.

Jefferson hasn't lost faith in him, though, and he is going to send him back over fences this time, probably stepping him up to two and a half miles.

One of the most improved horses in Jefferson's yard last season was **Double W's**, who won three times in his first season over fences, most notably in the Red Rum Handicap Chase at Aintree in April.

He is a fine jumper who is best on decent ground and will be contesting the good 2m handicap chases this term

Jefferson's best youngster of last season was **Mount Mews**, who followed up his two bumper wins with three over hurdles before running a career-best when second to Pingshou in the Top Novices' Hurdle at Aintree. He will stay over hurdles this season with Newcastle's Fighting Fifth a likely target.

The other Malton yard with a strong team of jumpers is that of *BRIAN ELLISON*, whose big star is **Definitly Red**.

He was one of the market leaders for last season's Grand National but was pulled up before halfway with a slipped saddle after being hampered at Becher's.

Although he had jumped the National-type fences really well at home, neither his trainer nor his owner Phil Martin were convinced that he was an Aintree sort but were rather forced into running him as

SMART TALK: Brian Ellison's high-class mare is back from injury

he was so well handicapped, with a 10lb rise for his runaway win in the BetBright Grimthorpe Chase at Doncaster yet to take effect.

That lofty mark might not matter now, though, as conditions races are likely to be on his agenda, probably kicking off with the Charlie Hall Chase at Wetherby.

Make no mistake, Ellison has always held him in very high regard and it will be no surprise were he to develop into a top-class chaser this time.

Another Ellison horse worth noting this season is **Forest Bihan**.

He beat Cloudy Dream in rather muddling race at Doncaster in January but proved that was no fluke by finishing a close second to San Benedeto in the Maghull Novices' Chase at Aintree.

Like Cloudy Dream, he should stay two and a half miles and has the option of conditions events or handicaps.

With the mare **Smart Talk** returning to go chasing after a year off, it promises to be another interesting jumps season for Ellison.

SANDY THOMSON trains at Greenlaw in the Scottish borders and his attempts to make a real breakthrough have been frustrated by injury setbacks for his stable star **Seeyouatmidnight**, who is out again and will miss the first half of the season.

Hopefully he could be back for a tilt at the Scottish National in the spring – he was third in that race in 2016 – and, given he's very lightly raced for his age, Thomson still thinks there is a big race in him off 154.

The Ladbrokes Trophy at Newbury – formerly the Hennessy – would have been a potential target, but fortunately Thomson has another likely contender for that race in **Seldom Inn**.

He put up a career-best performance when winning a competitive handicap chase at Kelso in March and is ideally suited by soft ground and three miles-plus.

Another Thomson horse to follow this season is **The Dutchman**.

He started last season by winning a novice chase at Wetherby over a trip just shy of 2m, which his trainer considered far too short for him, but he didn't progress quite as well as expected from there.

However, he ran several fair races and could be better than his mark, so he is worth noting in 2m4f handicap chases.

Greystoke trainer *NICKY RICHARDS* is renowned for his patience and he has two young chasers who look ready to peak this season.

Ballyboker Breeze has missed quite a lot of time through injury and had run only once in more than 18 months prior to returning last season, but that outing had seen him win on his chasing debut at Perth and he scored again at Bangor last December.

Richards was disappointed to see him go up 10lb for that win as it forced him into stronger company before the trainer felt he was ready and he duly managed only seventh in the Sky Bet Chase.

However, he may well prove competitive in that sort of big staying handicap as he gains experience.

Even greater tests of stamina will be on the cards for **Baywing**, a thorough stayer who pulled off a 33-1 upset when winning the Towton Novices' Chase at Wetherby last term.

Seriously progressive over hurdles the previous season, he ran only three times over fences last term and should have more to offer when stamina is at a premium.

REBECCA MENZIES' fourth season as a trainer proved to be her best by far last season as she sent out 17 winners and her Durham yard has also done well over the summer.

Acquiring a horse of the quality of **Pain Au Chocolat** epitomises the way Menzies is looking to strengthen her yard and the former 145-rated hurdler, who had lost his way for Dan Skelton, made a winning start for her in a 2m handicap chase at Perth in April.

He is still 6lb below his peak mark and can fly the flag for Menzies in style.

Angels of the north

Cloudy Dream
Definitly Red
One For Arthur

SELDOM INN: suited by soft ground and long distances

Midlands by John Bull

DAN SKELTON has enjoyed another terrific year as he heads towards the top of the tree as a trainer and is just waiting for a genuine superstar to cement his credentials as a future champion.

Skelton still hopes that horse could be **Superb Story**, who won the County Hurdle for him in 2016 but picked up an injury when being trained for a crack at the Champion Hurdle back at Cheltenham in March.

He had confirmed he was still going the right way when defying a big weight to win another handicap at Musselburgh on New Year's Day and will be back to compete in top 2m hurdles this term.

North Hill Harvey, another big Cheltenham handicap winner for Skelton when taking last season's Greatwood Hurdle, and **Long House Hall**, back from injury after winning the 2016 Summer Plate, are other potential stars in the Skelton ranks.

However, it is the abundance of young talent that is most striking, particularly among the novice hurdlers.

The pick of them may well be **Captain Forez**, who confirmed himself a horse for the future with three extremely promising runs last year, culminating in his runner-up finish behind Finian's Oscar in the Mersey Novices' Hurdle at Aintree in April.

Captain Forez, owned by John Hales, remains a novice for this season and should be among the leading lights of the division, with the Persian War at Chepstow and Challow Hurdle at Newbury among possible targets this side of the new year.

Momello is another novice who heads into the campaign armed with valuable experience. She beat Listed winner Brillare Momento on her hurdling debut at Newton

SUPERB STORY (in front): all the top 2m hurdles are open to him

SNOW LEOPARDESS: did well last season, culminating in this Newbury victory

Abbot in May and may well prove to be a leading novice in the mares' division.

Whiskey In The Jar, **Cause Toujours** and **Not That Fuisse**, three bumper winners heading over timber, should also be worth following.

Skelton has been busy replenishing his stock during the spring and summer and pinpointed two point-to-point winners to keep on side.

He said: "We've got plenty of new recruits in. We bought a very nice horse at the Cheltenham sales called **Brewin'upastorm**, who won a maiden point-to-point at Quakerstown in good fashion in April.

"**Maire Banrigh** is a nice mare – she looked very good when winning at Lingstown in March."

CHARLIE LONGSDON has assembled a strong team for the winter, with Grade 2 winner **Snow Leopardess**, **Forth Bridge** and **Monbeg Charmer** all worth keeping on your side in their second season over jumps.

Snow Leopardess improved with each run last season, culminating with victory in the mares' novice hurdle final at Newbury in March, and may well prove a Mares' Hurdle candidate in March, while Forth Bridge, who is likely to benefit from a step up in trip, and dual novice hurdle winner Monbeg Charmer appear fairly treated off their marks.

Our Kaempfer pulled up at Cheltenham and Aintree in the spring, but he had previously routed a competitive handicap chase at Kempton and has the ability to win a big handicap.

The same owners, the Swanee River Partnership, also have a nice youngster in **Searching For Gold**, who will be worth following in novice hurdles.

Hammersly Lake has run well on each start for Longsdon since joining from Nicky Henderson in the summer and is one to note on better ground.

OLLY MURPHY enjoyed a fantastic start to his training career in the summer and can make his mark during the winter with two exciting recruits.

Rio Quinto jointly topped the Tattersalls Ireland Cheltenham Sale in June when purchased by Murphy's father and prominent bloodstock agent Aiden for £130,000 and the promising four-year-old heads the rookie trainer's jumps team.

The son of Loup Breton ran with considerable promise when placed at Broughshane and Dromahane in the spring and

CHIEFTAIN'S CHOICE (centre): likes the better ground and a good gallop

Murphy is excited by his high-profile purchase.

Murphy said: "It's great to have only just started training and to have already been sent a sale-topper, especially as he's such a lovely horse. Both of the maidens he contested look well above average and I'm really looking forward to seeing him in action. The plan is to start him off in a bumper in the autumn."

Mon Port routed three rivals when winning a bumper at Warwick by 55 lengths in May and has since joined Murphy ahead of a novice hurdle campaign.

The trainer said: "Mon Port has come from Ben De Haan's having won his bumper in very impressive fashion – he's very exciting."

KEVIN FROST hopes to be at Cheltenham in March with the promising **Redemption Song**, who is a potential candidate for one of the mares' hurdles.

The imposing daughter of Mastercraftsman caught the eye on several occasions last season, most notably finishing fifth in the Grade 2 mares' bumper at the Grand National meeting at Aintree.

Frost said: "She's a great big mare and stands at 17 hands, so bumpers were never really her job, but we didn't want to lose her novice status over hurdles halfway through last season so decided to give her some experience in bumpers and she did extremely well.

"She ran a great race at Aintree and the track would definitely have been on the sharp side for her. There's much more to come from her over further and she does everything right at home.

"She has to prove she's good enough, but if she does Cheltenham will be on her agenda come March."

Frost is also excited by new recruit **Doc Penfro**, who cost £65,000 at the Tattersalls Cheltenham Ireland November Sale.

The five-year-old son of Dr Massini unshipped his rider at the last when in front in a point-to-point at Loughrea and will start off in novice hurdles this season.

Frost said: "We have high hopes for Doc

Penfro. He was going well when falling in a point-to-point and is a nice type."

Frost's yard favourite **Chieftain's Choice**, who finished a fine second in the conditional riders' handicap hurdle at the Grand National meeting in April, ran twice over fences during the summer and the Market Drayton trainer is set to vary the eight-year-old's campaign.

He said: "Chieftain's Choice goes on any ground, but I feel he's best suited by better ground these days and he likes a proper race where they go a good gallop.

"Brian Hughes rode him in two novice chases in the summer and said he's cut out for fences, but I'm not totally convinced. We'll probably mix it up with him as he's a versatile type."

Edgcote trainer *ALEX HALES* enjoyed a joint-best season last campaign and stable star **Duel At Dawn** can again fly the flag for the team as embarks on a novice chase campaign.

The seven-year-old finished third in the Grade 2 River Don Novices' Hurdle at Doncaster in January before proving that was no fluke by landing a competitive handicap hurdle at Bangor.

Drying ground ruled out a potential handicap hurdle raid at Punchestown in April, but it would be no surprise to see Duel At Dawn contesting some nice prizes at the spring festivals this time around, with the National Hunt Chase a potential long-term target.

Hales said: "Duel At Dawn did us proud last year and improved with each run over hurdles. He stays really well and is built for chasing, so we're really looking forward to getting him going."

New recruit **Topper Thornton** has an inconsistent profile, but the eight-year-old is well handicapped on the pick of his form and should be competitive in good staying handicap.

Huntsman Son, returning from injury after finishing third on his debut for owner Bill Booth at Worcester 15 months ago, should pay his way in novice hurdles, while Big Jim, who ran just once last season, remains open to improvement in 2m handicap chases.

Midlands magic

Duel At Dawn

North Hill Harvey

Our Kaempfer

DUEL AT DAWN (in front): embarks on a novice chase campaign

The South by Southerner

THERE is no question that *GARY MOORE* has taken his operation to another level in terms of quality in recent years, but there is still some frustration that even more big races haven't come his way.

Moore has suffered more than his fair share of bad luck with injuries to star horses, not least with **Ar Mad**, who has missed each of the last two Cheltenham Festivals and remains a horse of enormous untapped potential.

The seven-year-old won four in a row as a novice chaser two seasons ago but then suffered a condylar fracture as he was being prepared for the Racing Post Arkle.

Nothing went so badly wrong last season, but a series of minor setbacks and annoyances meant he made it to the racecourse only once when shaping with huge promise in the Tingle Creek.

Ar Mad threw in his worst ever round of jumping that day, clattering a series of fences, and it says a lot about his ability that he was still beaten only three and a half lengths, finishing strongly up the hill to suggest his future might well lie over further.

Moore even considered supplementing him for the King George after that, but he decided to wait for the Clarence House Chase only to swerve that race when it was switched to Cheltenham – he believes Ar Mad to be better going right-handed – and again wait for the Ascot Chase, before which he had a niggle that ruled him out of the spring.

Fingers crossed things will go more smoothly this term when Ar Mad could be a real force over a variety of trips.

Moore's desire to keep him to right-handed tracks – admittedly based on the limited evidence of a poor run at Plumpton as a novice, since when he has won again at that course and was a little better – will limit his options, but there is still the Tingle Creek and the Clarence House as well as the Ascot Chase and the King George over further.

Moore had a similar run of things with **Traffic Fluide**, who ran once in nearly two years after a promising novice campaign, confirming his potential by finishing third in the 2016 Clarence House behind Un De Sceaux.

Traffic Fluide at least got back on track at the start of last year and, keen to make up for lost time, Moore crammed five runs into him, which perhaps left its mark as he fell a little short of expectations.

Nonetheless, he was still a fair second to Menorah when stepped up in trip for the Oaksey Chase at Sandown on the last day of the season and could have more to offer.

The one horse who has really delivered at the top level for Moore is **Sire De Grugy**, most famously when winning the 2014 Champion Chase, and while those days are gone the evergreen 11-year-old may yet win more races.

He has already defied most pundits once when emerging from the doldrums last season to win a valuable handicap at Ascot and finish a length second in the Tingle Creek. Soft ground seems to be even more important to him as he gets older.

While those three are Moore's Grade 1 stars, he will be hoping **Baron Alco** can progress to a similar level via top handicaps.

The six-year-old wasn't out of the first two in five runs as a novice chaser last season and completed a really consistent campaign by finishing second in the Brown Advisory & Merriebelle Stable Plate at the Cheltenham Festival.

That looked a hot race and Baron Alco's performance would have been good

CAMPING GROUND: will go back over fences after winning the National Spirit

enough to win most handicaps, so a 2lb rise puts him right in the mix for something like the BetVictor Gold Cup in November.

Similar races might also be on the agenda for **Camping Ground** with Moore's mid-season recruit set to go back over fences after winning the National Spirit Hurdle at Fontwell on his only run for the yard.

A high-class but inconsistent performer for Robert Walford, Moore will be hoping to get a tune out of Camping Ground on a more regular basis and, while a mark of 152 won't make life easy, that is still 6lb lower than his hurdles rating.

Moore also has **All Yours** coming back from injury.

A Grade 1 winner for Paul Nicholls in his youth, the six-year-old switched to Moore in the summer of 2016 but soon suffered a season-ending setback.

In retrospect, Moore will be hugely relieved he was beaten at 1-5 in a novice chase at Worcester on his final run for Nicholls as it means he is still a novice over fences. If things don't work out in that sphere, there may still be scope in his handicap mark of 145 over hurdles.

Among the youngsters, Moore really likes **Kaveman**, a full brother to Champion Bumper winner Ballyandy who let himself down slightly in that sphere.

The Kayf Tara gelding has been beaten in three bumpers, twice at short prices, but he had a tendency to overrace and should prove much better than that as he gains experience.

EMMA LAVELLE enjoyed her best season for a few years last term, reaping the benefits of a fresh start after her move to the Bonita Racing Stables formerly owned by Peter Makin.

While that took Lavelle all the way to Marlborough, her yard remains a staple of the Southerner contact list and she has reported the exciting **Javert** to be on his way back from injury.

The eight-year-old has won all three of his completed starts over fences, although that's a slightly flattering record because he was well beaten when unseating his rider for the second time in the novice handicap chase at the 2016 Cheltenham Festival.

Still, Javert put that behind him by winning at Haydock that May before missing the rest of last season through injury.

He was raised 8lb for his Haydock win, but the handicapper might be more lenient in light of his subsequent layoff and he could prove a useful sort this season. Though untested beyond 2m5f110yds, Lavelle expects him to get 3m.

Junction Fourteen was at least seen a bit more last term, but it was still a stop-start campaign for him as he was being trained for the bet365 Gold Cup at Sandown only to pick up a knock when blundering badly and being pulled up at the Cheltenham Festival.

The Sandown race could still be a good spot for him this season, though, as he won a good novice handicap on the card two seasons ago and he promises to stay long distances, while decent ground is ideal.

Shotgun Paddy is another Lavelle horse cut out for marathon chases, although he is best through the winter when the mud is flying.

It's more than three years since the ten-year-old last won, landing the Classic Chase at Warwick as a novice, but he has run several fine races in defeat and the handicapper is starting to relent, so he could be one to watch in races like the Welsh National or the Eider.

SUZY SMITH enjoyed the biggest win of her career last season when **Clondaw Cian** struck at Cheltenham's November meeting and there could be more big days to come with the seven-year-old.

A much higher mark proved beyond

CLONDAW CIAN: novice chaser

Clondaw Cian after that Cheltenham success, but he is a strong stayer who may well make his mark in decent novice chases.

NICK GIFFORD also has a lovely long-term chasing prospect in **The Mighty Don**, who won a novice hurdle at Fakenham by ten lengths despite failing to impress with his jumping. There is clearly a big engine in this bumper winner and fences could be the making of him.

Gifford will also be hoping to get started with **Glen Rocco**, who was bought after winning a point-to-point last year and could be a Grand National horse one day according to the trainer.

Southern stars

Camping Ground
Clondaw Cian
Junction Fourteen

Newmarket by Aborigine

LUCY WADHAM has an abundance of promising young horses in her Newmarket string and the upwardly mobile **Potters Legend** could turn out to be one of the season's stars over fences.

The six-year-old started last year off a flourish, making a quick start to his chasing career with wins at Kempton and Bangor in November, and he justified his trainer's decision to send him to the Cheltenham Festival in the spring by finishing a close fourth in the Kim Muir.

There was also a lot to like about his final run of the campaign at Aintree as he kept on for fourth behind Sizing Codelco on Grand National day.

Wadham tells me the Midnight Legend gelding has thrived during the summer and it is indicative of her belief in him that the plan is to find a race to act as a springboard to what was the Hennessy.

Over a shorter trip, **Movie Legend** is also going to pay his way.

At first sight his form figures might not look all that encouraging as it took until his eighth and final outing to get off the mark at Market Rasen, where he eased home two and a quarter lengths ahead of the useful Crafty Roberto.

However, with his confidence boosted, there are more 2m handicaps to be won with him as he climbs the ladder.

Shanroe Santos made several friends last year, managing to win twice, and this bold jumper strikes me as the sort to climb the ladder towards a possible tilt at the Grand National.

Among the younger Wadham horses, her dual hurdles winner **Gregarious** will start off in that sphere but has already schooled well over fences, while Wadham also picked out **Shantung** and **Banjo Girl** for favourable mentions.

POTTERS LEGEND: Kim Muir fourth will be hoping for more success

JAMES EUSTACE holds out high hopes for promising young hurdler **Apache Song**.

This Mount Nelson filly had a couple of runs earlier this year and performed well, notably when second to a Nicky Henderson hotpot at Doncaster in February.

"She was too keen for her own good next time," reports Eustace, "but she still led until making a bad mistake at the last and would have been second again without that."

Eustace reckons she has tightened up in the jumping department and should pick up novice hurdles on the way up the ladder.

The ex-German Flat winner **Aviator** will also be running for Eustace over timber during the winter.

The nine-year-old was sidelined for a while because of injury, but Eustace is pleased with the way he has come out of a prep run on the Flat at Kempton and I reckon there is a decent staying hurdle in him before his attentions are turned to novice chases.

Eustace is obviously saddened to lose **Sir Note**, but that horse has gone back to his former trainer *NICK LITTMODEN*, who is back on the Newmarket jumping scene having come out of his 2015 retirement.

EXCELLENT RESULT: one to note

Littmoden won a couple of races with Sir Note at the start of his career, but while the seven-year-old went on to win a further six times for Eustace, his trainer moved to Norfolk, where he broke and prepared horses for other people.

Littmoden still came down to ride Sir Note on various work mornings and, back under his tutelage, Littmoden believes there is plenty more life in him yet, telling me: "He's had a good long summer break and I'll be planning a campaign for him in Grade 3 handicaps hoping he'll continue on the upgrade."

Adding strength to Littmoden's bow are a couple of horses he bought from France.

As he explained: "Both **Figeac** and **By Rail** have smart Flat form and I'll be finding suitable races for them. It's exciting being back in action and I hope we find our way back into the winner's enclosure before long."

RICHARD SPENCER has made a great start to his trainer career looking after the horses owned by Rebel Racing, whose interest in the game stemmed from their magic 2,000 Guineas triumph with Cockney Rebel.

Spencer quickly made his mark on the jumping scene, winning twice with **Excellent Result**. After a winning debut at Huntingdon in October, he acquitted himself well in good company and then won again in May when he beat Apasionado by a length and a quarter at Kempton.

His attempt to go into summer quarters on a winning note foundered when he was second to Hollywood Road at Huntingdon, but it was a sound effort considering he was attempting to defy a double penalty.

Spencer told me: "We'll stick to hurdling for a while but he'll go novice chasing when he's ready."

Stablemate **Movie Set** will be an exciting addition to the novice hurdling ranks as the Dubawi gelding looks the part, while keep an eye open for a newcomer to the yard called Aptly Put.

MARK TOMPKINS will also be in action over the winter. The St Leger-winning trainer – Bob's Return in 1993 – is keen on the prospects of **Bracken Brae**, who is a multiple winner on the Flat.

The five-year-old Champs Elysees mare is a lovely big individual who has shown ability over hurdles and we will be hearing more about her in due course.

HENRY SPILLER, whose father Charles was a bloodstock advisor to Sheikh Mohammed before setting up on his own, is one of the most recent additions to the HQ training ranks.

Already among the winners on the Flat, Spiller believes that in **Staff College** he has a jumper who can pay his way.

"He's got ability but remember that he needs plenty of give underfoot," he said.

Hot off the Heath

Excellent Result

Potters Legend

Sir Note

Hunter chasers by Nick Watts

COULD this be the year that **Wonderful Charm** sweeps all before him after some near misses last season?

It wouldn't take much for him to win one of the spring hunter chases and indeed he almost snared the biggest prize of the lot at Cheltenham in March, going down by a neck to Pacha Du Polder in the Foxhunter.

He was gaining on the winner all the way to the line and still has time on his side given he's just a nine-year-old.

Expect him to follow a similar path to last season, when he took in races at Musselburgh and Haydock – both in February – before arriving at the festival.

It's true to say he was beaten subsequently in two starts after Cheltenham, but both of those can be explained away.

The first of them came in the Grand National itself – and any horse can be excused a below-par display in that race.

Then he went to Stratford in June, finishing third behind Young Hurricane, when it's highly probable he was over the top by then.

What can be said about the new season is that the era of **On The Fringe** looks to be over.

Strangely, he ran the best race of his season first time back at Leopardstown, where he looked as good as ever in second behind Foxrock.

However, it was downhill from there. He never looked like winning at Cheltenham, he was worse at Aintree and couldn't even raise his game at his beloved Punchestown this time.

Enda Bolger keeps him in training, but he will be 13 next year and has surely seen better days.

A relative youngster who could be set for a decent season is **Vasco Du Mee**.

WONDERFUL CHARM (second left): just fails to catch Pacha Du Polder

FOXROCK: pulled up in the Irish National but unstoppable before that

He is an eight-year-old who claimed the notable scalp of Dineur when last seen on the racecourse at Chepstow in March.

That victory was achieved by 14 lengths, which may have flattered him a touch as Dineur had bigger fish to fry at Aintree's Grand National meeting subsequent to this run.

However, he is a useful horse at his best, as he proved the previous season when winning the four-miler at Cheltenham's hunter chase meeting in April.

What he does this season is open to question as he probably wouldn't be fast enough for Aintree, but Stratford in June for what used to be the Horse and Hound Gold Cup could be a possibility.

He was fifth in the race in 2016, but the race came quite quickly after his Cheltenham heroics and it may have been too much for him.

A darker one who may be able to make an impression in this sphere is the Sally Randell-trained **Wild Bill**.

He looked useful on more than one occasion for Evan Williams when trained under rules, but he can't have been the easiest to train as he isn't seen that often on the racecourse.

However, he won two point-to-points last season and was far from disgraced in the Champion Hunters' Chase at Stratford on his final start when fifth behind Young Hurricane, beaten around 20 lengths.

That was a bold piece of placing as his odds of 33-1 suggest, but he was bang there on the final circuit only to weaken late on.

The experience won't have been lost on him and, if he can stay injury-free, then he could yet make a mark in the hunter chase sphere – he is only eight so young enough to do so.

The obvious one to follow from Ireland is **Foxrock**, who was pulled up when last seen in the Irish National but prior to that had carried all before him in hunter chases, winning four races in succession culminating in the Raymond Smith in January.

He is a deceptive type as he can often race quite lazily, but he certainly knows how to get the job done having won eight times over fences already.

He is also extremely classy, once finishing second in what is now the Irish Gold Cup, so he will almost certainly be adding to his tally in 2018 as the hunter chase season gets into full swing.

Est. 1909
RACING & FOOTBALL OUTLOOK

Tipping Point
Ed Quigley

Raincoats and black pudding – it must be the jumps!

HERE we go again! It's that time of year when sunglasses get swapped for umbrellas, cereal and toast give way for black pudding and bacon and that favourite coat gets dusted off in anticipation for roaring on your selection from the rails among the pouring rain.

Well, maybe that's just me, but whatever your raceday ritual, it is the great annual buzz among racegoers which really sets the tone for the jumps season.

Last season was a brilliant one for Nicky Henderson, who will hoping the likes of Altior, Buveur D'Air and Might Bite can brush aside all before them once more.

Such is the strength at Seven Barrows that Paul Nicholls has already given up on the championship, but I still expect Nicholls to have another strong campaign as well. I've picked out a couple of his horses among my six to follow, but to that list you can also add the potentially top-class Clan Des Obeaux, exciting novice chaser Movewiththetimes and many more.

Throw in the new might of Colin Tizzard, who should have a returning Thistlecrack ready to throw big punches as well as the grand old Cue Card coming back for one more round, and the list of reasons to get excited goes on.

In Ireland, the rivalry between Gordon Elliott and Willie Mullins is arguably even more compelling.

While Mullins claimed the title, Elliott got the better of him in many of the big exchanges during the last campaign and continues to grow in strength and depth.

Nonetheless, Mullins' chief ally, Rich Ricci, has stepped up his operation, claiming to have "perhaps the biggest ever squad of young horses". Faugheen is due to return, while Douvan and Min should also be back at full fitness, so It will intriguing to see how that battle plays out.

A resurgent Jessica Harrington also ensured Mullins and Elliott didn't have things all their own way in Ireland as Sizing John landed a hat-trick of Gold Cup wins at Leopardstown, Cheltenham and Punchestown, while new kid on the block Our Duke is expected to go right to the top of the chasing tree after a facile success as a novice in the Irish Grand National.

Whatever your routine, one thing is for

sure, the jumps season should dish up plenty of exciting courses over the next six months or so and, as you can probably tell, I cannot wait.

Here is a selection of horses I think could pay their way to make the ride even more enjoyable.

Anibale Fly **7yo gelding**
112P142- (Tony Martin)

Anibale Fly should have a big prize in him over staying trips when the mud is flying.

The seven-year-old has a rather inconsistent profile, but when he is in full swing he is very effective.

Connections reported that the ground was too quick for him when he was pulled up in the Kauto Star Novices' Chase at Kempton over Christmas, but his final run of the campaign, when a staying-on second behind Disko in another Grade 1 at Punchestown, was smart form.

He should have more to offer from a mark of 149 should connections choose the handicap route.

Diego Du Charmil **5yo gelding**
19010- (Paul Nicholls)

Diego Du Charmil is another who can blow hot and cold, but the winner of the 2016 Fred Winter at Cheltenham has a lot of ability.

Always considered by connections as a long-term prospect over fences, he spent last season over hurdles gaining more vital experience but still managed an ultra-impressive display when winning the Scottish County Hurdle at Musselburgh in February.

Having reportedly been excellent in his schooling sessions over fences, he looked a natural when winning on his chasing debut at Newton Abbot in September and could develop into an Arkle candidate.

Fountains Windfall **7yo gelding**
173111- (Anthony Honeyball)

Anthony Honeyball has a progressive stayer on his hands in Fountains Windfall, who won his last three starts and improved 16lb to a mark of 146 over the course of last season.

He was remorseless in the manner in which he galloped his rivals ragged in a Grade 3 handicap at Aintree on his final start of the campaign.

He will now be stepped up in class, with a crack at the Long Distance Hurdle at Newbury earmarked as an early-season target.

ANIBALE FLY: Look out for him in a good handicap when the mud is flying

LE PREZIEN: already a winner at Cheltenham, could he be one for the BetVictor?

If he isn't up to Grade 1 level over hurdles, he should make a smashing novice chaser over staying trips. He looks one to keep in your notebooks.

L'Ami Serge 7yo gelding
2233251-21 (Nicky Henderson)

L'Ami Serge hasn't always been the punters' best friend, looking far from straightforward in the face of several near misses, but he may have turned a corner and could be worth backing for the Stayers' Hurdle at Cheltenham.

Staying trips appear to have given him a new lease of life and he could got the job done over 3m1½f at Auteuil this summer, staying on well to win the French Champion Hurdle to quash any doubts regarding his stamina.

Nicky Henderson has made some changes to the type of bit and mouthpiece he uses and connections think that has made a huge difference, allowing him to settle. The Stayers' Hurdle looks the natural long-term target.

Le Prezien 6yo gelding
21138P- (Paul Nicholls)

Le Prezien clearly has his jumping issues, but when he gets his act together he is more than useful.

The key to him appears to be the ground as, since joining Paul Nicholls, his form figures on soft or heavy read 11212113.

The ground was too quick for him at the Cheltenham Festival, but he was in the process of running a decent race at Punchestown until a jolting blunder four out put paid to his chance.

If he puts it all together, he is definitely better than a mark of 144, with races like the BetVictor Gold Cup within his compass granted proper winter ground.

Rock The Kasbah 7yo gelding
1324126- (Philip Hobbs)

In only seven runs over fences, Rock The Kasbah shapes like a horse who will relish a punch-up when the mud is flying.

Stepped up to 3m5f for the first time on his final run of last season, he did well to finish a staying-on sixth in the bet365 Gold Cup on ground that was too lively for him.

A mark of 142 probably underestimates him given his prerequisite conditions and, considering his love for a stamina test and form figures of 2211 at Chepstow, he looks to have cast-iron credentials for the Welsh National.

Est. 1909
RACING & FOOTBALL OUTLOOK

Richard Birch

Read Birchy every week in the RFO

Ten of the best to keep you warm during winter

MANY people may be surprised to read that **Un Noble**, who disappointed throughout last season, is top of my list of ten horses to follow for the 2017-18 jumps season.

Sometimes horses temporarily lose their form and 'miss out' a season, which is what I think happened to Un Noble last term.

Nothing went right for the Nicky Richards-trained chaser in five starts, starting with him unseating Craig Nichol when strongly fancied off a mark of 128 for a Kelso handicap chase.

As a result, Un Noble, who is still only seven, will begin the campaign 8lb lower and is well worth following in 2m4f handicap chases when the mud is flying.

Ayr provides plenty of races which Un Noble could go for and I expect him to get his career firmly on track and develop into the 130+ performer he once promised to become.

Yanmare did me a series of major favours last season when winning staying handicap chases at Uttoxeter, Warwick and Towcester.

The fact that he was able to rattle off a hat-trick at around 3m augurs well for this winter because Yanmare is an old-fashioned, out-and-out stayer who won't be seen to best effect until tackling marathon trips regularly.

Nigel Twiston-Davies's seven-year-old was probably on the verge of going over the top after a tough campaign when third to West Of The Edge at Warwick in March and will start the new season fresh and ready to continue his climb up the ratings.

There is a marathon handicap chase at Exeter in December which would suit Yanmare ideally and it would be no surprise if he progressed into a leading candidate for the Eider Chase after that.

Expect further improvement from **Mr Medic**, a six-year-old who created a most favourable impression when landing novice handicap chases at Lingfield and Plumpton early last winter.

Blessed with a high cruising speed and an excellent jumper of fences, the Robert Walford-trained gelding is rated only 112 and I doubt it will be long before he is plying his trade at a much higher level.

Arguably unfortunate not to have won his last three races – he slithered on landing and unseated James Best when still holding every chance three out at Taunton in March – Mr Medic rates an exciting prospect for 2m and 2m4f handicap chases in the south.

There is arguably no better jumper of a fence in training than **Sir Note**, who continued his progress into a really useful horse when winning three of his four races last winter.

The step up to 2m4f brought about further improvement in the dashing grey, whose slick, precision jumping is a joy to watch.

Now rated 137, he will prove harder to place this season, but he still has age on his side – he is a seven-year-old who hasn't been over-raced – and there will be obvious opportunities for him at places like Sandown, Kempton and Aintree.

Good ground is the key to Sir Note and, if allowed an uncontested lead on his favoured surface, he is lethal.

Ben Pauling did tremendously well with **Two Swallows** last season after the mare joined his fast-growing operation from Paul Webber.

A winner of three of her five races in 2016-17, culminating in a brave half-length defeat of Rolling Maul at Cheltenham in April, Two Swallows saw her rating rise from 104 to 127, but there is no reason why she cannot add to her tally, particularly if connections decide to go novice chasing with her.

A classy mare who boasts a decent turn of foot for a stayer, she is highly effective at 3m and seems to act on any going.

Connections of **Baywing** will be praying for a wet winter as the eight-year-old simply bulldozes his way through the mud.

SIR NOTE (left): there should be opportunities for this great jumper this season

TWO SWALLOWS (near side): a classy mare who acts on any ground

After winning four consecutive handicap hurdles in 2015-16, Baywing was sent novice chasing last term and responded by landing the Grade 2 Towton Chase at Wetherby by 22 lengths from a fair yardstick in Calett Mad.

He looks the perfect type for something like the Welsh Grand National – which is nearly always staged on bottomless ground at Chepstow – and remains totally unexposed over marathon trips as the furthest he has been sent so far is 3m2f.

Movie Legend was unfortunate not to win more races last season than the Market Rasen novices' handicap chase in April he took in smooth style by two and a quarter lengths from Crafty Roberto.

Placed on six of his seven other starts, Movie Legend jumps beautifully and possesses a cruising speed which makes me believe he will be able to hold his own at a higher level in due course.

Brave Encounter wasn't seen after landing a 3m2f Newton Abbot handicap chase in October by four lengths from Tikkapick off a mark of 87.

That was his second straight win since joining Jamie Snowden and he looked the type who could progress into a 110+ performer with his blend of stamina and accurate jumping potent weapons in low-grade staying events.

Hopefully he will be back to resume his career this winter as he looks a money-making machine off his current two-figure rating.

Bogoss Du Perret, a winner for Jimmy Frost at Newton Abbot in September, is just the type to thrive in similar events around the West Country tracks.

Punters must also look out for Ali Stronge's **Camakasi** in handicap hurdles.

An impressive winner of a Bath 1m2f handicap on the Flat in mid-August, Camakasi, who strolled home off a mark of 70 that day, could be absolutely thrown in over jumps off 87.

I have watched a couple of his hurdle races and he jumps well. There is no evidence he won't prove equally as good over hurdles, so be sure to keep this six-year-old firmly on side.

Time Test

Nothing between top staying chasers as rivals size up John

IT'S hard to recall a more open-looking jumps season, especially over fences as just four points separated the top ten chasers last season on Time Test figures.

As in the previous two campaigns, the Gold Cup was the race of the season and produced a fine effort from **Sizing John** (83), with those who chased him home also clocking big numbers.

Nonetheless, Jessica Harrington's seven-year-old wasn't as outstanding in victory as Don Cossack and Coneygree had been and the subsequent fates of that pair underline how much the Gold Cup can take out of a horse.

With connections outlining an ambitious plan to chase the British Triple Crown of the Betfair Chase, the King George and the Gold Cup, he also seems sure to endure a tough campaign.

Still, it's not long ago that he first stepped out of Douvan's shadow to tackle longer trips, since when he is unbeaten, and at the age of just seven he could still be improving.

The acid test will come in the King George, especially if Willie Mullins takes the plunge with **Un De Sceaux** (83), who shared top spot on last season's figures on the strength of his magnificent display in the Ryanair Chase.

His free-running and bold-jumping defeat of **Sub Lieutenant** (82) was perhaps the performance of the season given how hard he went early on and, as has always been the case with this horse, he will be a danger to all if he settles.

It was remarkable for **Thistlecrack** (76) to win last season's King George on only his fourth run over fences, but the clock showed it hadn't taken much winning and he actually produced a better effort in defeat when second to the ill-fated Many Clouds at Cheltenham next time. Hopes that he could rank higher are tempered by his injury layoff, although it shouldn't be forgotten that he achieved a mark as high as 83 over hurdles.

The other horse bound to be in the King George picture is **Might Bite** (64), who is clearly better than his bare figures having fallen at the last when set to win in a good time at Kempton and then nearly thrown away the RSA Chase with his antics in the straight. It's hard to get a handle on him but he clearly could be anything.

Similarly, **Yorkhill** (63) cost himself the chance to rank any higher with his wayward tendencies last season. That said, even his win in the JLT when on best behaviour was nothing special on the clock – nor was his Neptune victory at the meeting 12 months earlier – so he probably has more to prove.

So, too, does Sizing John's stablemate **Our Duke** (60), who is yet to produce a time to match his reputation, even when running away with an Irish Grand National in which the opposition was rather tame.

The 2m picture is less open but no less fascinating. Indeed, when Altior finally faces Douvan, it could rival Mayweather v McGregor for hype and would certainly produce much more of a contest.

Altior (79) has the edge according to the bookmakers and was by far the leading novice chaser of last season, but **Douvan** (80) is just ahead on the figures and, being the same age with similar racecourse experience, he could be just as open to improvement.

He achieved a figure that would have won the Champion Chase when scoring at Leopardstown in December only to go wrong on the big day itself. His comeback is eagerly anticipated.

The hurdling division, by comparison, looks light on quality and competition is scarce for the Champion Hurdle winner **Buveur D'Air** (85), who was some way ahead of his contemporaries last season.

Indeed, the next best performances over hurdles last season came from the placed horses in the Champion Hurdle and it's hard to see the veteran **My Tent Or Yours** (80) stepping up again this term.

Third-placed **Petit Mouchoir** (77) is set to go over fences and could be one for the Racing Post Arkle, while **Camping Ground** (75) and **Brain Power** (73) are also set to fences and Triumph Hurdle winner **Defi Du Seuil** (61) has a lot to find.

SIZING JOHN: last season's outstanding chaser – but not by much

Willie Mullins is hopeful of getting the 2015 Champion Hurdle winner **Faugheen** back this term, but even his peak figure of 77 lags a little way behind the current title-holder.

The biggest threat to Buveur D'Air could come from an adjoining box. It's unusual for the Supreme Novices' Hurdle to be run in a significantly slower time than the Champion and the slow pace didn't suit several of the inexperienced hurdlers, with **River Wylde** among those to race keenly.

He still finished a good third, just as Buveur D'Air had 12 months ago, and the benefits of Nicky Henderson's steady approach can be widely seen.

There's a big hole for an outstanding staying hurdler to fill despite the efforts of **Nichols Canyon** (70) and **Unowhatimeanharry** (66) last season. Neither ever clocked a truly top-notch figure last season despite dominating the Grade 1 races and the best figure in a staying hurdle came from the Pertemps Final winner **Presenting Percy** (71), who is a fine prospect, albeit perhaps over fences.

Top chasers of 2016-17

	Horse	*Speed rating*	*Distance in furlongs*	*Going*	*Track*	*Date achieved*
1	**Sizing John**	**83**	**26**	**GD**	**Cheltenham**	**Mar 17**
1	**Un De Sceaux**	**83**	**21**	**GD**	**Cheltenham**	**Mar 16**
3	Sub Lieutenant	82	21	GD	Cheltenham	Mar 16
4	Cue Card	81	24	GD	Haydock	Nov 19
5	Douvan	80	17	GS	Leopardstown	Dec 27
5	Minella Rocco	80	26	GD	Cheltenham	Mar 17
7	Altior	79	16	GD	Sandown	Apr 29
7	Native River	79	26	GD	Cheltenham	Mar 17
7	Sire De Grugy	79	17	SFT	Ascot	Nov 19
7	Special Tiara	79	16	GS	Cheltenham	Mar 15
7	The Last Samuri	79	26	GS	Aintree	Dec 3

Top hurdlers of 2016-17

	Horse	*Speed rating*	*Distance in furlongs*	*Going*	*Track*	*Date achieved*
1	**Buveur D'Air**	**85**	**16**	**GS**	**Cheltenham**	**Mar 14**
2	My Tent Or Yours	80	16	GS	Cheltenham	Mar 14
3	Petit Mouchoir	77	16	GS	Cheltenham	Mar 14
4	Camping Ground	75	19	GS	Fontwell	Feb 26
5	Brain Power	73	16	GS	Ascot	Dec 17
5	Footpad	73	16	GS	Cheltenham	Mar 14
5	The New One	73	16	GS	Cheltenham	Mar 14
8	Arctic Fire	72	16	GD	Cheltenham	Mar 17
8	Wicklow Brave	72	16	GY	Punchestown	Apr 28
10	Presenting Percy	71	24	GD	Cheltenham	Mar 16

Big-race review by Dylan Hill

1 188Bet Monet's Garden Old Roan Chase (Limited Handicap) (Grade 2) (2m3f200yds)

Aintree October 23 (Good)
1 **Third Intention** 9-10-7 Aidan Coleman
2 **God's Own** 8-11-9 A P Heskin
3 **Vibrato Valtat** 7-11-3 Nick Scholfield
5/1, 4/1, 9/1. 1¾l, 2½l. 7 ran. 4m 50.40s
(Colin Tizzard).

Third Intention had dropped 10lb in the previous 12 months and took full advantage as he saw off the unfortunate **God's Own**, who ran a stormer off a mark of 166 given he continues to look marginally better going right-handed. **Vibrato Valtat** was third ahead of **Smad Place**, who ran an excellent race over an inadequate trip, while **Royal Regatta** was also running well until a terrible blunder three out.

2 bet365 Charlie Hall Chase (Grade 2) (3m45yds)

Wetherby October 29 (Good)
1 **Irish Cavalier** 7-11-6 Jonathan Moore
2 **Menorah** 11-11-10 Richard Johnson
3 **Cue Card** 10-11-10 Paddy Brennan
[?]6/1, 12/1, 8/11F. ¾l, 2½l. 7 ran. 5m 59.70s
(Rebecca Curtis).

A below-par performance from **Cue Card** first time out left this race wide-open and **Irish Cavalier** was good enough to take advantage on a rare going day. Still inconsistent but a winner in similar conditions at Cheltenham and Punchestown in his time, Irish Cavalier just saw off the veteran **Menorah** as Cue Card's absence took its toll under an overly aggressive ride.

3 188Bet Haldon Gold Cup (Limited Handicap) (Grade 2) (2m1f109yds)

Exeter November 1 (Good)
1 **Sir Valentino** 7-10-8 A P Heskin
2 **Garde La Victoire** 7-10-12 R Johnson
3 **Dodging Bullets** 8-11-10 Nick Scholfield
10/1, EvensF, 5/1. shd, 11l. 8 ran. 3m 57.50s
(Tom George).

There was little depth to this race but two good horses came clear, with **Sir Valentino**, who proved a revelation over the season, just beating **Garde La Victoire**. Third in the Champion Chase in March and perhaps even better on a flatter track given he had run the winner, Special Tiara, to a neck on good ground in the Desert Orchid Chase when conceding 7lb, Sir Valentino kicked off that rapid progress by getting up to deny Garde La Victoire, who jumped much better than he has sometimes done. The pair pulled 11l clear of the regressive **Dodging Bullets**.

4 JNwine.com Champion Chase (Grade 1) (3m)

Down Royal (IRE) November 5 (Good)
1 **Valseur Lido** 7-11-10 R Walsh
2 **Silviniaco Conti** 10-11-10 Noel Fehily
3 **Lord Scoundrel** 7-11-10 Keith Donoghue
2/1F, 11/4, 25/1. 11l, 4½l. 7 ran. 6m 0.30s
(Henry De Bromhead).

Something of a false dawn for **Valseur Lido**, who looked highly impressive on his first run for Henry de Bromhead but failed to build on this in the Lexus as old stamina doubts resurfaced and then suffered a season-ending injury. Valseur Lido wasn't seriously tested by the veteran **Silviniaco Conti**, who had helped to set a modest gallop and held on for second from **Lord Scoundrel** as **Don Poli** disappointed.

5 BetVictor Gold Cup (Handicap Chase) (Grade 3) (2m4f78yds)

Cheltenham November 12 (Good To Soft)
1 **Taquin Du Seuil** 9-11-11 Aidan Coleman
2 **Village Vic** 9-11-10 Richard Johnson
3 **Buywise** 9-11-5 Paul Moloney
8/1, 20/1, 12/1. nk, 2l. 17 ran. 5m 16.60s (Jonjo O'Neill).

One for the old guard as **Taquin Du Seuil** held off **Village Vic** in a thriller ahead of **Buywise** – those three all packed with course-and-distance form – though unusually they probably didn't have to run much beyond their marks. Taquin Du Seuil bounced back to form with a tenacious effort, requiring virtually every yard to wear down the front-running Village Vic, but none of the first three would win another race all season. The youngsters were disappointing, particularly **More Of That**, with **Aso** overcoming several mistakes to do best of them in fourth ahead of **Bouvreuil**, who would have preferred quicker ground. **Frodon** was still going well until a terrible blunder four out.

6 Shloer Chase (registered as the Cheltenham Chase) (Grade 2) (1m7f199yds)

Cheltenham November 13 (Soft)
1 **Fox Norton** 6-11-4 Aidan Coleman
2 **Simply Ned** 9-11-4 Brian Harding
3 **Special Tiara** 9-11-0 Noel Fehily
5/2, 16/1, 2/1F. 9l, 9l. 8 ran. 4m 1.10s (Colin Tizzard).

Fox Norton was one of the most improved horses of the season and showed his early-season progress with this hugely impressive victory. Bought for big money after running away with a handicap at the course off 146, Fox Norton led three out and drew clear of **Simply Ned**, while subsequent Champion Chase winner **Special Tiara** ran a fair race in third on ground softer than ideal. **Top Gamble** was a below-par fifth.

7 StanJames.com Greatwood Handicap Hurdle (Grade 3) (2m87yds)

Cheltenham November 13 (Soft)
1 **North Hill Harvey** 5-11-0 Harry Skelton
2 **Modus** 6-10-10 Harry Cobden
3 **Song Light** 6-9-12 Kevin Jones
6/1, 5/1, 16/1. ½l, 1¼l. 16 ran. 3m 56.10s (Dan Skelton).

North Hill Harvey failed to build on this on much quicker ground in the spring, but there's no question this was strong form as he won one of the best handicaps of the season. Always prominent and in front between the last two, North Hill Harvey just held off **Modus**, who went on to win the Lanzarote off a 5lb higher mark, while only three of the other 14 runners finished within 18l.

8 Betfair Chase (Grade 1) (registered as the Lancashire Chase) (3m24yds)

Haydock November 19 (Heavy)
1 **Cue Card** 10-11-7 Paddy Brennan
2 **Coneygree** 9-11-7 Richard Johnson
3 **Vezelay** 7-11-7 Felix De Giles
15/8F, 2/1, 50/1. 15l, 13l. 6 ran. 6m 22.00s (Colin Tizzard).

This was billed as an epic clash between **Cue Card** and **Coneygree**, but the 2015 Gold Cup hero was well below his best following his injury problems and it ended up as little more than a training exercise for Cue Card. The hugely popular veteran was always travelling strongly and eased clear of Coneygree from the fourth-last, while French outsider **Vezelay** plugged on for third ahead of the bitterly disappointing **Silviniaco Conti**. The ground was much too soft for **Irish Cavalier** who was pulled up.

9 Stella Artois 1965 Chase (Grade 2) (2m5f8yds)

Ascot November 19 (Good To Soft)
1 **Royal Regatta** 8-11-7 Tom O'Brien
2 **Kylemore Lough** 7-11-7 Jamie Moore
3 **God's Own** 8-11-11 A P Heskin
10/1, 13/2, 7/2. hd, 1¾l. 7 ran. 5m 14.90s (Philip Hobbs).

A tremendously gutsy win from **Royal Regatta**, who made all the running and narrowly clung on as **Kylemore Lough** ate into his advantage after the last. The pace set by Royal Regatta seemed to get to the bottom of the stamina in **God's Own**, who was the class act and travelled strongly only to finish tamely in third.

10 StanJames.com Morgiana Hurdle (Grade 1) (2m)

Punchestown (IRE) November 20 (Soft)
1 **Nichols Canyon** 6-11-10 R Walsh
2 **Jer's Girl** 4-11-0 Barry Geraghty
3 **Ivanovich Gorbatov** 4-11-7 Davy Russell
8/13F, 3/1, 12/1. 12l, 5l. 5 ran. 3m 52.40s (W P Mullins).

Nichols Canyon would require a big step up in trip by the spring having slipped down the pecking order of Irish 2m hurdlers, but he was at least able to exploit his star stablemates' injuries on this occasion against a noderate field. Ridden to make the most of is stamina, Nichols Canyon was always in command and drew clear of **Jer's Girl** and **vanovich Gorbatov**, who both struggled to uild on their fine juvenile campaigns.

11 Hennessy Gold Cup (Handicap Chase) (Grade 3) (3m1f214yds)

Newbury November 26 (Good To Soft)

Native River 6-11-1 Richard Johnson
Carole's Destrier 8-10-8 Noel Fehily
Double Ross 10-10-6 Jamie Bargary
/2F, 25/1, 50/1. ½l, 5l. 19 ran. 6m 25.00s Colin Tizzard).

A battling win from the sharply progressive **Native River**, who was too good for some retty exposed rivals behind. Always prominent, Native River regained the lead two out and asserted his superiority from then on, winning with plenty in hand as he idled on the un-in to allow the strong-finishing **Carole's Destrier** to close in on him, with **Double Ross** and **Hadrian's Approach** next. **Blakion** travelled strongly but faded into fifth and was subsequently given a breathing operation, whereas **Vyta Du Roc** was outpaced but kept on well in sixth to point to his improvement over further. **Un Temps Pour Tout** was disappointing in tenth and **Saphir Du Rheu** fell early.

12 StanJames.com Fighting Fifth Hurdle (Grade 1) (2m98yds)

Newcastle November 26 (Soft)

1 **Irving** 8-11-7 Harry Cobden
2 **Apple's Jade** 4-11-0 Jack Kennedy
3 **Hidden Cyclone** 11-11-7 Danny Mullins
6/1, 15/8F, 12/1. nse, 2½l. 6 ran. 3m 56.30s (Paul Nicholls).

A second win in the race for **Irving**, who kept up his bizarre record of always producing by far his best form during the month of November. Irving just saw off **Apple's Jade**, who would prove better over further, and both would probably have lost out to **Petit Mouchoir** in light of his subsequent form had he not fallen three out. **Sceau Royal**, twice an impressive winner of weaker races earlier in

RVING: Fighting Fifth winner always produces his best form in November

UN DE SCEAUX: gutsy in the Tingle Creek despite proving better over further

the season, seemed to find this coming too quickly and was below his best in fourth, though he had his limitations exposed in the spring anyway.

13 Betfair Tingle Creek Chase (Grade 1) (1m7f119yds)

Sandown December 3 (Good To Soft)

1 **Un De Sceaux** 8-11-7 R Walsh
2 **Sire De Grugy** 10-11-7 Jamie Moore
3 **God's Own** 8-11-7 A P Heskin
5/4F, 5/1, 7/2. 1l, nk. 6 ran. 3m 51.35s (W P Mullins).

Two miles on decent ground certainly wasn't ideal for **Un De Sceaux**, as would become clear for the second successive spring at Punchestown, but he got the job done in gutsy fashion, helped by a shocking round of jumping from **Ar Mad**. Un De Sceaux, left in front six out, was headed after scratchy jumps at the last two fences, but he rallied strongly to hold off **Sire De Grugy** and **God's Own**. Ar Mad had set a blistering pace before losing all chance with a string of mistakes, yet he still stayed on strongly to finish within 3½l, suggesting he was the best horse in the race, with **Sir Valentino** also just 2l behind in fifth.

14 Bar One Racing Hatton's Grace Hurdle (Grade 1) (2m4f)

Fairyhouse (IRE) December 4 (Good To Yielding)

1 **Apple's Jade** 4-10-13 B J Cooper
2 **Vroum Vroum Mag** 7-11-3 R Walsh
3 **Shaneshill** 7-11-10 Paul Townend
4/1, 4/7F, 5/1. shd, 7l. 7 ran. 4m 57.80s (Gordon Elliott).

Vroum Vroum Mag came into this race unbeaten in ten races for Willie Mullins but met her match in **Apple's Jade**, who ground out a gutsy victory. Plenty of excuses were made for the winning machine, who had been off the track for more than six months in contrast to her race-fit rival and just ran out of steam after travelling strongly and even hitting the front at the last, but Apple's Jade would again prove she was the stronger stayer at Cheltenham. **Shaneshill** found the trip too short but would still have finished closer without a mistake at the last, while **Ivanovich Gorbatov** again disappointed in fourth.

15 Betfred Peterborough Chase (Grade 2) (2m3f189yds)

Huntingdon December 4 (Good To Soft)

1 **Josses Hill** 8-11-6 Noel Fehily
2 **Tea For Two** 7-11-5 Lizzie Kelly
3 **More Of That** 8-11-3 Aidan Coleman
7/4F, 6/1, 3/1. 6l, 3¾l. 5 ran. 4m 50.00s
(Nicky Henderson).

Josses Hill blotted his copybook later in the season, but it's still hard to find fault with this impressive all-the-way victory as he put a couple of talented opponents to the sword. With this trip on a right-handed track tailor-made for him, Josses Hill made all the running, jumping better as the race went on, and getting an easy lead was clearly vital given his disappointing effort when harried for the lead at Sandown on the final day of the season and well beaten by the retiring Menorah, with defeats over further and on left-handed tracks more forgiveable. **Tea For Two** and **More Of That** were unable to land a blow, though both would prove better over further.

16 Caspian Caviar Gold Cup (Handicap Chase) (Grade 3) (2m4f166yds)

Cheltenham December 10 (Soft)

1 **Frodon** 4-10-10 Sam Twiston-Davies
2 **Aso** 6-10-7 Charlie Deutsch
3 **Village Vic** 9-11-12 Richard Johnson
14/1, 13/2, 6/1J. 1½l, hd. 16 ran. 5m 18.00s
(Paul Nicholls).

A remarkable achievement for **Frodon** to win this race as a four-year-old, but he may just have dropped lucky in a modest renewal. Frodon was always to the fore and stayed on well up the hill after **Aso** and **Kylemore Lough**, who faded into fifth having been ridden into the lead, had made crucial late blunders. **Village Vic** managed to finish within 2l in third despite what was by now looking an almost impossible mark and less than 3l covered the first five, with **Bouvreuil** again finding the ground too soft in sixth.

17 StanJames.com International Hurdle (Grade 2) (2m179yds)

Cheltenham December 10 (Soft)

1 **The New One** 8-11-8 Richard Johnson
2 **My Tent Or Yours** 9-11-0 Barry Geraghty
3 **Old Guard** 5-11-8 Sam Twiston-Davies
13/8F, 7/4, 12/1. 3½l, 12l. 6 ran. 4m 6.90s
(Nigel Twiston-Davies).

While he again came up short against the very best, **The New One** remained prolific last season with this third International win to go with his third Champion Hurdle Trial at

JOSSES HILL: tailormade for the race conditions of the Peterborough

Haydock the following month. This was his best performance as he again proved ideally suited to the stiff 2m1f on Cheltenham's New Course, making all to give 8lb to old rival **My Tent Or Yours**, who would again show himself to be better when up against stronger opposition but finds it much harder to win. The pair were 12l clear of the 2015 winner **Old Guard**, who was crying out for further.

18 John Durkan Memorial Punchestown Chase (Grade 1) (2m4f)

Punchestown (IRE) December 11 (Yielding To Soft)

1 **Djakadam** 7-11-10 R Walsh
2 **Outlander** 8-11-10 Davy Russell
3 **Sub Lieutenant** 7-11-10 B J Cooper
4/5F, 9/1, 4/1. 1¼l, 1¼l. 5 ran. 5m 16.10s
(W P Mullins).

Djakadam underlined his class, showing the ability to become a dual winner of this 2m4f Grade 1 even with the stamina to have finished second in two Gold Cups. Facing quality rivals with the benefit of previous runs, Djakadam was always handy and shook off the subsequent Lexus winner **Outlander**. The trip should perhaps have favoured **Sub Lieutenant**, but he just came up short against two better horses.

19 JLT Long Walk Hurdle (Grade 1) (3m97yds)

Ascot December 17 (Good To Soft)

1 **Unowhatimeanharry** 8-11-7 B Geraghty
2 **Lil Rockerfeller** 5-11-7 Noel Fehily
3 **Un Temps Pour Tout** 7-11-7T Scudamore
6/5F, 8/1, 16/1. 4½l, 14l. 11 ran. 5m 54.30s
(Harry Fry).

Unowhatimeanharry confirmed his emergence as a major star of the staying hurdle division in the middle leg of a winter hat-trick of big-race victories that also saw him win the Long Distance Hurdle at Newbury and Cleeve Hurdle at Cheltenham. **Ballyoptic** made this a real stamina test from the front, but Unowhatimeanharry was already staying on far too strongly when that rival took a tired fall at the last. Unowhatimeanharry was left to come home in front of subsequent Stayers' Hurdle runner-up **Lil Rockerfeller**, who was a terrific second and pulled 14l clear of **Un Temps Pour Tout** and **Ptit Zig**.

20 Wessex Youth Trust Handicap Hurdle (Grade 3) (1m7f152yds)

Ascot December 17 (Good To Soft)

1 **Brain Power** 5-11-11 David Mullins
2 **Consul De Thaix** 4-10-11 J McGrath
3 **Fergall** 9-10-7 Kevin Jones
12/1, 6/1, 25/1, 4/1F. 5l, nk, 6l. 19 ran. 3m 39.90s
(Nicky Henderson).

Having already won a valuable contest at Sandown earlier in the month, **Brain Power** completed a big handicap double that propelled him out of handicaps into the Grade 1 arena. At his best off a strong gallop, Brain Power had the race run to suit and quickened clear from the last as only **Consul De Thaix** and **Fergall**, who would have been a fine second in the Swinton in May but for falling at the last, finished within 11l of him.

21 32Red King George VI Chase (Grade 1) (3m)

Kempton December 26 (Good)

1 **Thistlecrack** 8-11-10 Tom Scudamore
2 **Cue Card** 10-11-10 Paddy Brennan
3 **Silviniaco Conti** 10-11-10 Noel Fehily

YANWORTH: probably flattered by this Christmas Hurdle victory

1/10F, 5/4, 20/1. 3¼l, shd. 5 ran. 5m 53.50s
;olin Tizzard).

sensational achievement from the novice **histlecrack** to win on only his fourth run ver fences. Producing a spectacular round jumping, Thistlecrack led from halfway and owered into a decisive lead after the fourth-st, allowing his rider to ease him down on e run-in having never had to ask a serious uestion. **Cue Card** wasn't at his best in sec-nd as the rest of the field finished in a heap, ough that was partly because he paid the rice for trying to match strides with Thistle-ack and was a spent force in the straight. **lviniaco Conti** ran by far the best race of s final season in third, finishing just ahead subsequent Grade 1 winner **Tea For Two**, hile **Josses Hill** also ran well to finish within but didn't look a strong stayer.

22 32Red.com Christmas Hurdle (Grade 1) (2m)

empton December 26 (Good)

Yanworth 6-11-7 Barry Geraghty
The New One 8-11-7 Sam Twiston-Davies
Ch'Tibello 5-11-7 Harry Skelton
'4F, 13/8, 14/1. 3¼l, 2¼l. 5 ran. 3m 45.20s
lan King).

performance that ultimately made **Yan-orth** favourite for the Champion Hurdle but rely wasn't as good as it appeared at the ne. Rerouted down the 2m route after win-ng the Ascot Hurdle over 2m4f because of e success of his owner's Unowhatimean-arry, Yanworth looked to have the class to ucceed over any trip as he stormed home om the second-last. However, the sharp ack didn't suit **The New One** either and **y Tent Or Yours**, seemingly sacrificed as pacemaker, didn't enjoy new front-running ctics. **Ch'Tibello** ran on to split that pair in ird.

23 Coral Welsh Grand National (Handicap Chase) (Grade 3) m5f110yds)

hepstow December 27 (Soft)

Native River 6-11-12 Richard Johnson
Raz De Maree 11-10-7 Ger Fox
Houblon Des Obeaux 9-11-7 C Deutsch
/4F, 33/1, 33/1. 1¾l, 15l. 20 ran. 7m 49.80s
;olin Tizzard).

ative River pulled off a handicap double ot achieved since Playschool in 1987 in rilling fashion. Native River was helped by e race conditions – he escaped a penalty r his Hennessy win because it would have ken him above the maximum weight – but even so he stepped up again on his Newbury form, the extra distance and softer ground bringing his stamina to the fore as he led before halfway and kicked clear four out to run his rivals into the ground. **Raz De Maree** also ran a huge race in second as the pair pulled 15l clear of **Houblon Des Obeaux**.

24 Paddy Power Cashcard Chase (Grade 1) (2m1f)

Leopardstown (IRE) December 27 (Yielding)

1 **Douvan** 6-11-12 R Walsh
2 **Sizing John** 6-11-12 Robbie Power
3 **Simply Ned** 9-11-12 Brian Harding
1/8F, 10/1, 12/1. 8l, 7l. 5 ran. 4m 2.10s
(W P Mullins).

Douvan made an effortless step up to the top level as he stormed to his first Grade 1 win in open company, albeit without facing anything of Champion Chase quality. Douvan was always prominent and took over from **Alisier D'Irlande** at the second-last before quickening away from nearest rival **Simply Ned**, with **Sizing John** staying on late to finish second behind Douvan for the fifth time and prompt his step in trip.

25 Lexus Chase (Grade 1) (3m) Leopardstown (IRE) December 28 (Yielding)

1 **Outlander** 8-11-10 Jack Kennedy
2 **Don Poli** 7-11-10 David Mullins
3 **Djakadam** 7-11-10 R Walsh
11/1, 12/1, 5/4F. 2¼l, hd. 13 ran. 6m 2.40s
(Gordon Elliott).

A minor upset as **Outlander** broke through at the top level with **Djakadam** and **Valseur Lido**, both Grade 1 winners earlier in the season, behind. Outlander was probably flattered to reverse the John Durkan form with Djakadam, who should perhaps have been ridden more prominently and lacked the gears to come from behind, but he still beat another fair yardstick into second as **Don Poli** bounced back to form. Valseur Lido didn't appear to get home as he faded into fourth having held every chance, while **Taquin Du Seuil** had his limitations exposed in fifth, just holding off **More Of That** who was again below his best, and **Zabana** ran well for a long way on ground softer than ideal.

26 Squared Financial Christmas Hurdle (Grade 1) (3m)

Leopardstown (IRE) December 28 (Yielding)

1 **Vroum Vroum Mag** 7-11-3 R Walsh
2 **Clondaw Warrior** 9-11-10 Ms K Walsh

3 **Snow Falcon** 6-11-10 Sean Flanagan
8/15F, 8/1, 5/1. 1¼l, 2½l. 8 ran. 6m 6.90s
(W P Mullins).

Vroum Vroum Mag underlined her tremendous versatility as she became a Grade 1 winner over 2m and 3m, though she was all out to hold on over this longer trip and subsequently switched back to shorter. Vroum Vroum Mag had just taken over from **Shaneshill** at the last when that one fell and the way **Clondaw Warrior** closed her down suggested she may have struggled to hold on, though Shaneshill's rider felt he was tired having done plenty in front.

AGRAPART: relished soft ground at Cheltenham but has his limitations

27 Ryanair Hurdle (Grade 1) (2m) Leopardstown (IRE) Decembe 29 (Yielding)

1 **Petit Mouchoir** 5-11-10 B J Coope
2 **Nichols Canyon** 6-11-10 R Wals
3 **Ivanovich Gorbatov** 4-11-7 Davy Russe
6/1, 2/5F, 14/1. 7l, 2¼l. 5 ran. 3m 55.00s
(Henry De Bromhead).

Petit Mouchoir proved a revelation as h scored the first of his two Grade 1 victorie suggesting he would already have broken hi duck had he stayed upright in the Fightin Fifth. Petit Mouchoir made virtually all the run ning and was well in command once neares rival **Nichols Canyon** lost momentum with mistake at the second-last, causing him t struggle to hold off **Ivanovich Gorbatov** fo second. **Footpad** never got into the race bu plugged on for fourth ahead of **Jer's Girl**.

28 Dornan Engineering Relkeel Hurdle (Grade 2) (2m4f56yds) Cheltenham January 1 (Soft)

1 **Agrapart** 6-11-4 Lizzie Kell
2 **L'Ami Serge** 7-11-0 Daryl Jaco
3 **Cole Harden** 8-11-0 Richard Johnso
16/1, 2/1F, 7/1. hd, 7l. 6 ran. 5m 10.70s
(Nick Williams).

A tremendously gutsy win from **Agrapar** although subsequent events suggested th was more about the enigmatic French Cham pion Hurdle winner **L'Ami Serge** snatchin defeat as he finished tamely having ease into the lead after the last. Agrapart re ished the conditions and battled on far mo strongly, but a subsequent clearcut defe behind a rival past his best in **Zarkanda** albeit conceding 8lb, in the Rendlesha Hurdle confirmed his limitations. **Col Harden** found this trip too sharp in third o ground softer than ideal but was still thir ahead of the disappointing **Lil Rockerfell** and **Camping Ground**.

29 Peter Marsh Chase (Limited Handicap) (Grade 2) (3m24yds) Haydock January 21 (Soft)

1 **Bristol De Mai** 6-11-2 Daryl Jaco
2 **Otago Trail** 9-10-10 Charlie Deutsc
3 **Bishops Road** 9-10-11 Jamie Moor
4/1J, 11/1, 8/1. 22l, 3½l. 14 ran. 6m 21.80s
(Nigel Twiston-Davies).

An outstanding victory from **Bristol De Ma** comparable to the best staying performan es of the season, with soft ground seeming the key to him. Despite his big weight off mark of 154, Bristol De Mai jumped superbl much better than he has twice done on goo

ΛANY CLOUDS: magnificent at Cheltenham as he went out on his sword

ıround at Cheltenham, and was easing ef-
ɔrtlessly clear of **Otago Trail**, who went on
ɔ win a big 3m handicap at Sandown two
veeks later, when that one made a hash of
ıe second-last. Otago Trail still held on for
econd such was the pair's superiority, with
ishops Road next and just six of the 14 run-
ers getting round in a real test.

30 Spectra Cyber Security Solutions Clarence House Chase (Grade 1) 2m62yds)

;heltenham January 28 (Soft)

Un De Sceaux 9-11-7 R Walsh
Uxizandre 9-11-7 Barry Geraghty
Top Gamble 9-11-7 Davy Russell
/2F, 12/1, 5/1. 5l, 2¾l. 7 ran. 4m 11.70s
ΛV P Mullins).

his race was switched to Cheltenham after
ıscot's abandonment the previous week and
ıat made **Un De Sceaux**'s task a lot easier,
ıling out chief rival Ar Mad, though whether
ıe younger horse could have beaten him on
oft ground is another matter. With conditions
oming right for him, Un De Sceaux looked in
is element as he led five out and stayed on
trongly to beat **Uxizandre**, who produced
is best run of the season first time out after
a long absence, and **Top Gamble**, with that
trio 16l clear of **Dodging Bullets**. The ground
was too soft for **Special Tiara**, who was fifth,
while **Royal Regatta** was pulled up.

31 BetBright Trial Cotswold Chase (Grade 2) (3m1f56yds)

Cheltenham January 28 (Soft)

1 **Many Clouds** 10-11-10 Leighton Aspell
2 **Thistlecrack** 9-11-10 Tom Scudamore
3 **Smad Place** 10-11-10 Wayne Hutchinson
8/1, 4/9F, 7/1. hd, 17l. 7 ran. 6m 41.20s
(Oliver Sherwood).

An incredible race with a tragic postscript as **Many Clouds** collapsed and died after producing a career-best performance to inflict **Thistlecrack**'s first defeat over fences. Thistlecrack was less assured with his jumping than in the King George and paid the price as he was outstayed by Many Clouds from the last, casting some doubt over his Gold Cup credentials which will have to wait to 2018 to be answered after his subsequent season-ending injury. The pair pulled 17l clear of **Smad Place** and **Vezelay** would have been next but for falling at the last, with **Silviniaco Conti** and **Kylemore Lough**, who failed to stay, both tailed off.

BALLYANDY (right): much better off an end-to-end gallop in the Betfair Hurdle

32 galliardhomes.com Cleeve Hurdle (Grade 2) (2m7f213yds)
Cheltenham January 28 (Soft)
1 **Unowhatimeanharry** 9-11-8 B Geraghty
2 **Cole Harden** 8-11-0 Gavin Sheehan
3 **West Approach** 7-11-2 R Walsh
10/11F, 20/1, 14/1. 1¾l, 1½l. 15 ran. 5m 59.90s
(Harry Fry).

Another outstanding performance from **Unowhatimeanharry**, who easily gave weight to a hugely competitive field. Unowhatimeanharry was always travelling strongly and cosily shook off **Cole Harden**, who couldn't take advantage of the 8lb he received on ground softer than ideal although he ran well enough to suggest his preference for quicker had been exaggerated. The novice **West Approach** ran a cracker in third, pulling 6l clear of **Ballyoptic**, while **Un Temps Pour Tout**, **Old Guard** and **Ptit Zig** were among those behind.

33 BHP Insurance Irish Champion Hurdle (Grade 1) (2m)
Leopardstown (IRE) January 29 (Good)
1 **Petit Mouchoir** 6-11-10 David Mullins
2 **Footpad** 5-11-8 Daryl Jacob
3 **Ivanovich Gorbatov** 5-11-8 B Geraght
9/10F, 12/1, 13/2. 1l, 37l. 4 ran. 3m 41.30s
(Henry De Bromhead).

Another comfortable all-the-way win for **Pet Mouchoir**, who won with more in hand tha the winning margin as **Footpad** stayed o late for a never-nearer second. Petit Mou choir had been softened up slightly in fror by **Nichols Canyon** but again had that rival' measure when he took a crashing fall at th last. **Ivanovich Gorbatov** was tailed off i third.

34 Betfair Hurdle (Handicap) (Grad 3) (2m69yds)
Newbury February 11 (Soft)
1 **Ballyandy** 6-11-1 Sam Twiston-Davie
2 **Movewiththetimes** 6-11-2 Barry Geraght
3 **Clyne** 7-11-9 Adam Wedg
3/1F, 6/1, 6/1. ¾l, 6l. 16 ran. 3m 57.00s
(Nigel Twiston-Davies).

This was a red-hot contest dominated b two extremely well-handicapped novices i **Ballyandy** and **Movewiththetimes**. Muc better off an end-to-end gallop than he wa able to show in slowly run novice event Ballyandy travelled smoothly before quicl ening up well and just holding Movewiththetimes, the pair pulling clear of **Clyne**, who was officially 5lb well in after finishing second to The New One in Haydock's Champion Hurdle Trial. **Song Light** was the only other horse to finish within 13l.

35 Betfair Exchange Chase (Grade 2) (registered as the Game Spirit Chase) (2m92yds)

Newbury February 11 (Soft)

1 **Altior** 7-11-5 Nico de Boinville
2 **Fox Norton** 7-11-10 Aidan Coleman
3 **Dodging Bullets** 9-11-0 S Twiston-Davies
30/100F, 5/1, 20/1. 13l, 5l. 4 ran. 4m 5.80s (Nicky Henderson).

Outstanding novice **Altior** was campaigned with admirable aggression over the season and was hugely impressive as he stepped out of novice company for the first time, albeit against a below-par rival in **Fox Norton**. Altior jumped well and made most of the running, drawing clear from four out as Fox Norton was left trailing, but the runner-up was having his first three run for three months after an injury and would do much better at Cheltenham.

36 Stan James Irish Gold Cup (Grade 1) (3m60yds)

Leopardstown (IRE) February 12 (Soft)

1 **Sizing John** 7-11-10 Robbie Power
2 **Empire Of Dirt** 10-11-10 Jack Kennedy
3 **Don Poli** 8-11-10 David Mullins
100/30, 9/2, 9/4F. ¾l, ¾l. 7 ran. 6m 23.30s (Mrs John Harrington).

A tremendous race in which Gold Cup hero **Sizing John** pointed the way to Cheltenham by winning on his first run over 3m yet might not have done so had **Empire Of Dirt** jumped the last better. Sizing John was always travelling strongly and saw out the trip well, but Empire Of Dirt finished more strongly despite losing momentum at the final fence and, given how Sizing John franked the form, connections were surely left to rue their decision not to go for gold. **Don Poli** ran another solid race in third, helped by being able to dictate a steady gallop, while **More Of That** was running much better until unseating his rider when coming to challenge at the last. **Minella Rocco** had unseated his rider early.

37 Betfair Ascot Chase (Grade 1) (2m5f8yds)

Ascot February 18 (Soft)

1 **Cue Card** 11-11-7 Paddy Brennan
2 **Shantou Flyer** 7-11-7 Adam Wedge
3 **Royal Regatta** 9-11-7 Richard Johnson
4/9F, 22/1, 11/1. 15l, 3¾l. 6 ran. 5m 26.00s (Colin Tizzard).

A demolition job from **Cue Card**, who bounced back from his King George defeat with a terrific performance. The only horse able to lay up with the strong pace set by **Royal Regatta**, he led three out and drew clear as his stamina came to the fore. Royal Regatta made a bold bid to repeat his all-the-way win in the 1965 Chase, but for the second time in this race he was pressed into doing just too much at this higher level and was out on his feet as **Shantou Flyer** stayed on into second. **Taquin Du Seuil** and **Irish Cavalier** could never get on terms.

38 Betfred Grand National Trial (Handicap Chase) (Grade 3) (3m4f97yds)

Haydock February 18 (Good To Soft)

1 **Vieux Lion Rouge** 8-11-6 T Scudamore
2 **Blaklion** 8-11-12 William Twiston-Davies
3 **Vintage Clouds** 7-10-10 Brian Hughes
8/1, 7/2F, 5/1. 3¼l, 18l. 13 ran. 7m 25.10s (David Pipe).

Class came to the fore as **Vieux Lion Rouge** and **Blaklion** dominated the race. Vieux Lion Rouge, a winner of the Becher Chase over the Grand National fences but twice a non-stayer in the big race itself, confirmed he's a high-class chaser over slightly shorter trips as he raced prominently throughout and was always in command in the straight. RSA winner Blaklion, given a breathing operation after his Hennessy disappointment, relished a stiff test of stamina and enhanced his reputation in defeat as he pulled 18l clear of **Vintage Clouds** in third.

39 BetBright Handicap Chase (Grade 3) (3m)

Kempton February 25 (Good)

1 **Pilgrims Bay** 7-10-2 James Best
2 **Double Shuffle** 7-11-7 A P Heskin
3 **Theatre Guide** 10-11-11 Paddy Brennan
25/1, 11/2, 11/1. ½l, 2½l. 13 ran. 5m 56.20s (Neil Mulholland).

A competitive handicap in which little over 6l covered the first six, led by the novice **Pilgrims Bay**. Ridden with exaggerated waiting tactics, Pilgrims Bay came with a smooth run and took advantage of his featherweight as he just held off the progressive **Double Shuffle**. **Theatre Guide** ran a fine race in third ahead of **Aso**, who again missed a good opportunity to land a big handicap as he was given too much to do on his first attempt at 3m, with **Ballykan** and **Three Musketeers**

BUVEUR D'AIR: a good winner of what looked a weak Champion Hurdle

also not beaten far.

40 totepool National Spirit Hurdle (Grade 2) (2m3f33yds)

Fontwell February 26 (Good To Soft)

1 **Camping Ground** 7-11-11 Joshua Moore
2 **Le Rocher** 7-11-3 Tom Scudamore
3 **L'Ami Serge** 7-11-3 Daryl Jacob
9/1, 9/2, 2/1J. 29l, 22l. 7 ran. 4m 48.50s (Gary Moore).

Camping Ground had been one of the great unfulfilled talents having been out of sorts since a runaway win in the 2016 Relkeel Hurdle and gave another reminder of his potential on his first run for Gary Moore. The opposition admittedly amounted to little with joint-favourites **L'Ami Serge**, who lost a shoe, and **Different Gravey** tailed off, but Camping Ground had strung out the field by setting a strong pace and galloped on relentlessly for a remarkably easy triumph.

41 Ultima Handicap Chase (Grade 3) (3m1f)

Cheltenham March 14 (Good To Soft)

1 **Un Temps Pour Tout** 8-11-12 T Scudamore
2 **Singlefarmpayment** 7-10-13 A P Heskin
3 **Noble Endeavor** 8-11-11 Davy Russell
9/1, 5/1F, 15/2. shd, 3½l. 23 ran. 6m 20.00s (David Pipe).

Un Temps Pour Tout had won this race as a novice in 2016 when it was one of the strongest handicaps for many years and was able to win again off a 7lb higher mark in what may well prove to have been a weaker renewal. Seemingly a much better horse in the spring

Un Temps Pour Tout just held off the well-backed novice **Singlefarmpayment** with another horse at the top of the weights, **Noble Endeavor**, taking third ahead of the veteran **Buywise**.

42 Stan James Champion Hurdle Challenge Trophy (Grade 1) (2m87yds)

Cheltenham March 14 (Good To Soft)

1 **Buveur D'Air** 6-11-10 Noel Fehily
2 **My Tent Or Yours** 10-11-10 A Coleman
3 **Petit Mouchoir** 6-11-10 B J Cooper
5/1, 16/1, 6/1. 4½l, 3l. 11 ran. 3m 50.90s (Nicky Henderson).

A desperately weak Champion Hurdle, but **Buveur D'Air** won it with great authority. Switched back from fences little over a month earlier, Buveur D'Air made good headway to lead at the last and drew clear of **My Tent Or Yours**, who stuck on well to finish second in the race for the third time. Still, the ease with which the runner-up reversed form from earlier in the season with the likes of **The New One** and **Yanworth**, both horribly outpaced in fifth and seventh respectively, exposed the holes in that form and, allied to the absence of Annie Power and Faugheen, it suggests this didn't take much winning. **Petit Mouchoir** at least ran a solid race in third ahead of **Footpad** despite perhaps finding a stiffer track against him. **Sceau Royal** wasn't up to his level in sixth, but **Wicklow Brave** was a shade unlucky in eighth having lost ground at the start and **Brain Power** pulled far too hard.

43 OLBG Mares' Hurdle (Grade 1) (registered as the David Nicholson Mares' Hurdle) (2m3f200yds)

Cheltenham March 14 (Good To Soft)

1 **Apple's Jade** 5-11-5 B J Cooper
2 **Vroum Vroum Mag** 8-11-5 Paul Townend
3 **Limini** 6-11-5 R Walsh
7/2, 11/4, 6/4F. 1½l, nse. 17 ran. 4m 50.20s (Gordon Elliott).

By far the deepest ever running of this race, with three top-class mares involved in a thriller and **Apple's Jade** proving the best of them. Seemingly vulnerable having just edged out a less race-fit **Vroum Vroum Mag** in the Hatton's Grace and subsequently lost to **Limini** at Punchestown, Apple's Jade left that form behind given a stiffer test of stamina as she made most of the running and stayed on best from the last. Vroum Vroum Mag would surely have won over 2m, travelling strongly and just leading over the last, but she was found wanting in the final 50 yards and only just held off Limini for second.

SUPASUNDAE: showed his class by winning the Coral Cup

Indian Stream was just the best of the British mares in fourth ahead of **Briery Queen** as **Lifeboat Mona** disappointed.

44 Coral Cup (Handicap Hurdle) (Grade 3) (2m5f26yds)

Cheltenham March 15 (Good To Soft)

1 **Supasundae** 7-11-4 Robbie Power
2 **Taquin Du Seuil** 10-11-4 Aidan Coleman
3 **Who Dares Wins** 5-11-2 W Hutchinson
16/1, 12/1, 33/1. 2l, 2½l. 25 ran. 5m 4.60s (Mrs John Harrington).

The red-hot 2016 Supreme Novices' Hurdle

won by Altior had already produced Buveur D'Air and threw up another Cheltenham winner as **Supasundae**, not beaten far in seventh that day, won well in a strong handicap, with the first two mixing it at Grade 1 level at Aintree. Punters had latched on to Supreme fourth **Tombstone** for the same reason off a mark of 149, making him the shortest-priced handicap favourite of the week, but he trailed home in rear behind Supasundae, who was 1lb lower having finished just 1½l behind him 12 months earlier and running over this trip on decent ground for the first time since a win at Fairyhouse on New Year's Eve that also worked out well, with runner-up **Monksland** taking fourth here. **Taquin Du Seuil**, off a 12lb lower hurdles mark, and **Who Dares Wins** split that pair this time, with **Modus** and **Old Guard** running well just out of the places.

45 Betway Queen Mother Champion Chase (Grade 1) (1m7f199yds)

Cheltenham March 15 (Good To Soft)
1 **Special Tiara** 10-11-10 Noel Fehily
2 **Fox Norton** 7-11-10 Aidan Coleman
3 **Sir Valentino** 8-11-10 Paddy Brennan
11/1, 7/1, 33/1. hd, 6l. 10 ran. 3m 55.40s (Henry De Bromhead).

A massive shock as the mighty **Douvan**, who seemed head and shoulders above his rivals, finished lame in seventh behind the veteran **Special Tiara**. Third in the race in each of the previous two years, Special Tiara probably didn't have to step up on the best of those efforts to make the most of his golden opportunity, making virtually all the running and just holding on as **Fox Norton**, who finished strongest, ran a cracker in second. The pair pulled 6l clear of **Sir Valentino**, who was third ahead of the staying-on **Top Gamble**, with **God's Own** fading into fifth after a bad mistake two out just as he looked set to challenge. **Traffic Fluide** showed his first worthwhile piece of form of the season on his third run after a year absence when finishing sixth, beaten less than 8l, but **Garde La Victoire**'s jumping fell apart as he was tailed off along with **Simply Ned**.

46 Pertemps Network Final (Handicap Hurdle) (Listed Race) (2m7f213yds)

Cheltenham March 16 (Good)
1 **Presenting Percy** 6-11-11 Davy Russell
2 **Barney Dwan** 7-11-8 Paddy Brennan
3 **Jury Duty** 6-11-10 Jack Kennedy
11/1, 16/1, 9/1. 3¾l, 2l. 24 ran. 5m 49.40s (Patrick G Kelly).

A clearcut win for Irish novice **Presenting Percy**, who defied a big weight in terrific style, although the race may not have been as competitive as usual with several other fancied runners hit hard by the handicapper and the winner would come up well short at Grade 1 level next time. Presenting Percy had also taken a big hike, with his mark of 146 being 16lb higher than that he had won off in Ireland on his previous start, but he still quickened up well to beat **Barney Dwan** and **Jury Duty**.

47 Ryanair Chase (Grade 1) (2m4f166yds)

Cheltenham March 16 (Good)
1 **Un De Sceaux** 9-11-10 R Walsh
2 **Sub Lieutenant** 8-11-10 David Mullins
3 **Aso** 7-11-10 Charlie Deutsch
7/4F, 8/1, 40/1. 1½l, 6l. 8 ran. 5m 9.60s (W P Mullins).

Nothing special in terms of the bare form but an astonishing effort from **Un De Sceaux** to win despite pulling so hard early that Ruby Walsh was forced to dispense with plans to hold him up and send him storming into the lead after the fifth. Never headed from that point, Un De Sceaux was clear by halfway and, while he paid for his wasted energy by tiring up the hill, he had enough in hand to hold off the progressive **Sub Lieutenant** who was the only horse to emerge from the pack. **Aso** ran a cracker in third ahead of **Empire Of Dirt**, who was outpaced before staying on and looked badly in need of a return to 3m, though he still finished 9l clear of **Josses Hill** in fifth. **Uxizandre** failed to build on his promising return in seventh.

48 Sun Bets Stayers' Hurdle (Grade 1) (2m7f213yds)

Cheltenham March 16 (Good)
1 **Nichols Canyon** 7-11-10 R Walsh
2 **Lil Rockerfeller** 6-11-10 Trevor Whelan
3 **Unowhatimeanharry** 9-11-10 Noel Fehily
10/1, 33/1, 5/6F. ¾l, 3½l. 12 ran. 5m 49.60s (W P Mullins).

Stepping up to 3m proved the making of **Nichols Canyon**, who had the stamina to win even in a strongly run race that saw many others found wanting with only the next three finishing within 19l of him. Settled well off the pace and still with plenty to do coming down the hill, Nichols Canyon showed his class with a stunning turn of foot from the home turn that saw him cut down **Lil Rockerfeller** who proved a revelation on only his third run over 3m with the slightly quicker ground helping him to reverse Long Walk placings with **Unowhatimeanharry** in third. That said

ROAD TO RESPECT: won what looked the strongest of the festival handicaps

the favourite was certainly below the form he had shown earlier in the season and his subsequent win over Nichols Canyon at Punchestown suggests it wasn't just the ground to blame. **Cole Harden**, better suited by the conditions, was an honourable fourth, pulling 12l clear of **Snow Falcon** with **Clondaw Warrior**, **Zarkandar** and the non-staying **Jezki** behind. **Shaneshill** and **Ballyoptic** were pulled up.

49 Brown Advisory & Merriebelle Stable Plate Handicap Chase (Grade 3) (2m4f166yds)

Cheltenham March 16 (Good)

1 **Road To Respect** 6-10-13 B J Cooper
2 **Baron Alco** 6-11-0 Jamie Moore
3 **Bouvreuil** 6-10-13 Sam Twiston-Davies
14/1, 10/1, 10/1. 6l, 1¾l. 24 ran. 5m 8.90s (Noel Meade).

This was probably the strongest handicap of Cheltenham and dominated by two well-handicapped novices, with **Road To Respect** beating **Baron Alco**. Much improved on good ground, Road To Respect was always going well and took command two out as he drew clear of Baron Alco, with a subsequent Grade 1 win at Fairyhouse, albeit in bizarre circumstances, underlining how much he had in hand. **Bouvreuil**, placed at a third successive Cheltenham Festival, finally got his ground and ran a cracker in third ahead of **Thomas Crapper**, who was 11lb well in after a runaway win at Newbury earlier in the month, while the well-fancied **Starchitect** and close BetBright Chase fifth **Ballykan** were next, with those six 6l clear of the rest.

50 Randox Health County Handicap Hurdle (Grade 3) (2m179yds)

Cheltenham March 17 (Good)

1 **Arctic Fire** 8-11-12 Paul Townend

2 **L'Ami Serge** 7-11-6 Daryl Jacob
3 **Ozzie The Oscar** 6-10-3 Tom O'Brien
20/1, 25/1, 50/1. nk, nk. 25 ran. 4m 0.00s (W P Mullins).

A remarkable result for several reasons as **Arctic Fire** defied a layoff of more than a year to beat **L'Ami Serge**, the pair overcoming the biggest weights in a race those at the foot of the handicap tend to dominate. Given a little leeway by the handicapper even off a mark of 158 given he was rated 169 after his second in the 2015 Champion Hurdle, Arctic Fire looked close to his best as he stormed through from the rear to pip L'Ami Serge, who relished a strongly run race at this trip. The pair benefited from a lack of the usual well-handicapped youngsters, with 50-1 shot **Ozzie The Oscar** taking third ahead of **Air Horse One**, who was unable to defy an 8lb rise for winning at Ascot, and **Winter Escape**, who couldn't quite overcome a long layoff through sickness. **Ivanovich Gorbatov** was well backed but proved slightly disappointing again in sixth.

ROCK THE WORLD: atoned for managing only third in 2016

51 Timico Cheltenham Gold Cup (Grade 1) (3m2f70yds)

Cheltenham March 17 (Good)
1 **Sizing John** 7-11-10 Robbie Power
2 **Minella Rocco** 7-11-10 Noel Fehily
3 **Native River** 7-11-10 Richard Johnson
7/1, 18/1, 7/2. 2¾l, shd. 13 ran. 6m 36.10s (Mrs John Harrington).

A wide-open Gold Cup in which three progressive youngsters came to the fore, with the classy **Sizing John** seeing out this longer trip well enough at the expense of proven stayers **Minella Rocco** and **Native River**. Always going well, Sizing John showed the speed that had made him competitive in top 2m chases by quickening into a decisive lead between the last two and stayed on well enough up the hill as Minella Rocco got going too late, still just snatching second from Native River as he proved one-paced in a game third. Dual runner-up **Djakadam** had his best ever chance and looked likely to finally win until a mistake two out, which knocked the stuffing out of him disappointingly easily. **Saphir Du Rheu** was next ahead of **More Of That**, the two formerly exciting youngsters confirming recent returns to form with good efforts, though the first six were covered by less than 10l to back up the impression this was no more than an ordinary Gold Cup and **Bristol De Mai** would also have been in the mix but for a final-fence blunder having also made previous jumping errors. **Smad Place** was well beaten in seventh, with **Outlander** the big disappointment behind, while **Cue Card** was struggling to make an impression when falling three out and **Tea For Two** unseated his rider at the second.

52 Johnny Henderson Grand Annual Challenge Cup (Handicap Chase) (Grade 3) (2m62yds)

Cheltenham March 17 (Good)
1 **Rock The World** 9-11-5 Robbie Power
2 **Gardefort** 8-11-0 Daryl Jacob
3 **Theinval** 7-10-13 Jeremiah McGrath
10/1, 20/1, 9/1. 1¾l, nk. 24 ran. 4m 1.40s (Mrs John Harrington).

Third when heavily backed for the race 12 months earlier, **Rock The World** recouped those losses with a far more comfortable victory than the margins suggest, quickening up smartly from the rear after eight had jumped the second-last virtually in a line. Rock The World reversed 2016 form with **Dandridge**, who had been second that day and ran another cracker in fourth, the pair split by **Gardefort** and **Theinval**, who franked the

TEA FOR TWO: exploited the absence of the first six from the Gold Cup

form by finishing a length second off 3lb higher in the Red Rum at Aintree. The novice **Le Prezien** was a warm favourite but was outpaced in eighth.

53 Betway Bowl Chase (Grade 1) (3m210yds)

Aintree April 6 (Good)

1 **Tea For Two** 8-11-7 Lizzie Kelly
2 **Cue Card** 11-11-7 Paddy Brennan
3 **Smad Place** 10-11-7 Wayne Hutchinson
10/1, 2/1F, 10/1. nk, 15l. 7 ran. 6m 24.00s (Nick Williams).

A soft renewal with none of the first six from the Gold Cup involved and leading contender **Empire Of Dirt** going lame, but **Tea For Two** and **Cue Card** still served up a cracker. Cue Card again confirmed that, even at his age, he has good races in him with a gallant run in defeat and might well have won but for getting involved in a duel with **Silviniaco Conti** early on the final circuit, but the more patiently ridden Tea For Two had just too much toe between the last two and held on gamely. The pair pulled 15l clear of **Smad Place**, who reversed Gold Cup form with the below-par **Bristol De Mai**, with **Aso** splitting that pair and Silviniaco Conti retired after managing only sixth.

54 Betway Aintree Hurdle (Grade 1) (2m4f)

Aintree April 6 (Good)

1 **Buveur D'Air** 6-11-7 Barry Geraghty
2 **My Tent Or Yours** 10-11-7 A Coleman
3 **The New One** 9-11-7 S Twiston-Davies
4/9F, 8/1, 11/2. 5l, 1½l. 6 ran. 4m 55.80s (Nicky Henderson).

Another fine performance from **Buveur D'Air**, who proved equally effective over this longer trip to easily follow up his Champion Hurdle victory. **The New One**, much better over this trip, made a valiant attempt to stretch the favourite's stamina, but he had no answer to Buveur D'Air from the second-last and ended up compromising his own prospects of finishing second as **My Tent Or Yours**, never put in the race having failed to stay on his previous attempts at the trip, ran on into second. The New One was 11l clear of **Old Guard**.

55 JLT Melling Chase (Grade 1) (2m3f200yds)

Aintree April 7 (Good)

1 **Fox Norton** 7-11-7 Robbie Power
2 **Sub Lieutenant** 8-11-7 B J Cooper
3 **Traffic Fluide** 7-11-7 Joshua Moore
4/1, 100/30F, 14/1. 6l, 11l. 9 ran. 4m 58.00s (Colin Tizzard).

VICENTE (left): a second win in the Scottish National off the same mark

So close in the Champion Chase, **Fox Norton** produced a career-best performance on his first run over 2m4f as he ran out an easy winner over Ryanair second **Sub Lieutenant** with the rest of a decent field well strung out. Fox Norton came from off the pace to lead two out and was driven clear of Sub Lieutenant before being eased down. The first two were 11l clear of **Traffic Fluide** and **Kylemore Lough**, who perhaps found the ground quicker than ideal, while **God's Own** and **Josses Hill** were disappointing behind, **Uxizandre**'s jumping fell apart and a switch to waiting tactics failed to pay off with **Royal Regatta**, who was pulled up.

56 Ryanair Stayers Liverpool Hurdle (Grade 1) (3m149yds)

Aintree April 8 (Good)

1 **Yanworth** 7-11-7 Barry Geraghty
2 **Supasundae** 7-11-7 Robbie Power
3 **Snow Falcon** 7-11-7 Sean Flanagan

9/4F, 5/1, 9/1. 1l, ¾l. 11 ran. 6m 3.40s (Alan King).

A fascinating race which saw **Yanworth** and **Supasundae**, two exciting horses stepping up to 3m for the first time, finish first and second, albeit helped by the absence of any of the first three from the Stayers' Hurdle at Cheltenham and the below-par effort of **Cole Harden**. Yanworth, all out having taken the lead two out, was just too good for Supasundae, who confirmed Coral Cup form with **Taquin Du Seuil** on identical terms, that pair split by **Snow Falcon**. **Ballyoptic** finished closer than he had to Unowhatimeanharry in receipt of 4lb in the Cleeve despite jumping errors as the first five were separated by just 7l, though there was a big gap back to the disappointing **Ptit Zig**. **Cole Harden**, who didn't seem to enjoy a first-time visor, and **Different Gravey** were pulled up.

57 Randox Health Grand National (Handicap Chase) (Grade 3) (4m2f74yds)

Aintree April 8 (Good To Soft)

1 **One For Arthur** 8-10-11 Derek Fox
2 **Cause Of Causes** 9-10-13 Mr J J Codd
3 **Saint Are** 11-10-10 Davy Russell

14/1, 16/1, 25/1. 4½l, 3¾l. 40 ran. 9m 3.50s (Lucinda Russell).

The first National in which fancied horses came to the fore since significant changes were made to the course, with **One For Arthur** producing a sensational finish to come out on top. An impressive winner of the Classic Chase at Warwick in January, the fast-improving youngster did remarkably well to make up huge ground from the third-last even though the time of the leaders from that point was extremely quick and stormed home on the run-in. **Cause Of Causes**, who had become a three-time Cheltenham Festival winner when winning the Cross Country Chase, put to bed the notion that he couldn't put two good runs together by running a huge race in second from National specialist **Saint Are**. **Blaklion** travelled notably well and briefly looked to have swept into a decisive lead before running out of steam in fourth, with **Gas Line Boy** next ahead of another non-stayer in **Vieux Lion Rouge**. **Lord Windermere** was on a very lenient mark but lacked the legs to take advantage in seventh, while the most notable hard-luck stories were **Definitly Red**, who was pulled up after his saddle slipped at Becher's and may have been missed his chance given he was 10lb well in, and **Ucello Conti**, who was going notably well when departing at the second Becher's.

58 BoyleSports Irish Grand National (Handicap Chase) (3m5f)

Fairyhouse (IRE) April 17 (Good To Yielding)

1 **Our Duke** 7-11-4 Robbie Power
2 **Bless The Wings** 12-10-2 Jack Kennedy
3 **Abolitionist** 9-10-7 Rachael Blackmore
9/2F, 12/1, 14/1. 14l, ¾l. 28 ran. 7m 47.20s (Mrs John Harrington).

A sensational performance from the novice **Our Duke**, who became the first horse to win with more than 11st since 2000 – and off a higher mark than any winner in 20 years – and did so the hard way as he maintained a searching gallop throughout. Indeed, the pace was so strong that every other horse ridden prominently dropped out so quickly on the final circuit that they were all pulled up, but Our Duke galloped on relentlessly to an astonishing triumph worthy of a genuine Gold Cup horse. **Bless The Wings**, a short-head second in 2016, filled the same spot, albeit a long way further back, ahead of **Abolitionist** and 2015 winner **Thunder And Roses**, while **Noble Endeavor** was sixth.

59 Coral Scottish Grand National (Handicap Chase) (Grade 3) (3m7f176yds)

Ayr April 22 (Good)

1 **Vicente** 8-11-10 Sam Twiston-Davies
2 **Cogry** 8-10-6 Jamie Bargary
3 **Benbens** 12-10-8 Mr Z Baker
9/1J, 18/1, 50/1. nk, 2l. 30 ran. 8m 5.50s (Paul Nicholls).

Back down to the mark off which he had won a decent renewal in 2016, **Vicente** managed to repeat the trick in a thriller. Disappointing over shorter trips earlier in the season, often on softer ground, Vicente needed every yard to get up this time and deny the unfortunate **Cogry**, who had made virtually all the running and looked to have the race won at one point. **Benbens** was third ahead of 2016 runner-up **Alvarado** and **Lessons In Milan**.

60 QTS Scottish Champion Hurdle (Limited Handicap) (Grade 2) (2m)

Ayr April 22 (Good To Soft)

1 **Chesterfield** 7-10-5 Daniel Sansom
2 **Zubayr** 5-10-7 Sam Twiston-Davies
3 **Mohaayed** 5-10-4 Harry Skelton
12/1, 12/1, 5/1J. shd, 2¼l. 16 ran. 3m 43.20s (Seamus Mullins).

A big handicap double for **Chesterfield**, who had been raised 11lb for winning at Aintree but showed he was improving even faster than that by just edging out **Zubayr**, who made a vital mistake at the last just as he looked to have put the race to bed. Just 7l covered the first 11 with **L'Ami Serge** among those unsuited by the slow pace, though **Sceau Royal** again didn't look up to his mark of 155.

61 BoyleSports Champion Chase (Grade 1) (2m)

Punchestown (IRE) April 25 (Good To Yielding)

1 **Fox Norton** 7-11-12 Robbie Power
2 **Un De Sceaux** 9-11-12 R Walsh
3 **God's Own** 9-11-12 A P Heskin
5/2, 10/11F, 7/1. 1¾l, ½l. 8 ran. 4m 5.60s (Colin Tizzard).

With Special Tiara heading for Sandown and Douvan out of the season, this was all about two horses better over further and **Fox Norton** proved more adaptable than **Un De Sceaux**. Despite not travelling as smoothly, Fox Norton was driven along to join Un De Sceaux at the last and kept on strongly on the run-in. The 2016 winner **God's Own** got his ground and had everything in his favour

WICKLOW BRAVE: achieved a rare double when winning at Punchestown

again, but he could manage only third in a stronger renewal, still pulling 6½l clear of Grand Annual winner **Rock The World**. **Sir Valentino** was well below his best in sixth.

62 Coral Punchestown Gold Cup (Grade 1) (3m120yds)

Punchestown (IRE) April 26 (Good To Yielding)

1 **Sizing John** 7-11-10 Robbie Power
2 **Djakadam** 8-11-10 R Walsh
3 **Coneygree** 10-11-10 Nico de Boinville
9/10F, 5/2, 6/1. shd, 1½l. 6 ran. 6m 22.60s (Mrs John Harrington).

Sizing John backed up his Cheltenham triumph with another tremendous victory, just edging out **Djakadam**. Things went much less smoothly this time for Sizing John, who lost a front shoe and made a mistake at the second-last just as Djakadam was ridden into the lead, but he showed real guts and stamina to get up close home. Djakadam lost nothing in defeat, not helped by his own mistake at the last and perhaps doing better for the slightly shorter trip than at Cheltenham as he finished 1½l clear of **Coneygree**, who ran a stormer on his latest return from injury. The first three were a distance clear of the rest, with **Outlander** pulled up.

63 Ladbrokes Champion Stayers Hurdle (Grade 1) (3m)

Punchestown (IRE) April 27 (Good To Yielding)

1 **Unowhatimeanharry** 9-11-10 Noel Fehily
2 **Nichols Canyon** 7-11-10 R Walsh
3 **Footpad** 5-11-9 Daryl Jacob
4/1, 7/4F, 9/1. hd, 18l. 12 ran. 6m 1.40s (Harry Fry).

Unowhatimeanharry set the record straight as he beat his Cheltenham conqueror **Nichols Canyon** in another Punchestown race to produce a wonderful finish. In front after the second-last, Unowhatimeanharry was soon pressed by the strong-travelling Nichols Canyon but just held on as the pair both enhanced their reputations by pulling 18l clear of the chasing pack. Most of their main rivals were below their best, though, notably **Lil Rockerfeller** with **Snow Falcon** little better and **Shaneshill** last, while rising star **Sutton Place** went lame as he stepped up in class. Instead **Footpad**, ridden to get the longer trip, ran on into third ahead of **De Plotting Shed**, **One Track Mind** and Pertemps third **Jury Duty**, who was unable to bridge the gap from handicap company.

64 Betdaq Punchestown Champion Hurdle (Grade 1) (2m)

Punchestown (IRE) April 28 (Good To Yielding)

1 **Wicklow Brave** 8-11-12 Mr P W Mullins
2 **My Tent Or Yours** 10-11-12 A Coleman
3 **Arctic Fire** 8-11-12 Paul Townend
12/1, 8/1, 9/2. 1½l, nk. 10 ran. 3m 49.90s (W P Mullins).

Wicklow Brave achieved the rare feat of becoming a top-flight winner on the Flat and over hurdles as he translated his improvement at the summer game to timber, albeit in strange circumstances. Keen in the early stages, Wicklow Brave was allowed to stride clear and had a 10l advantage by the third-last, but the time of the race suggests the other jockeys certainly weren't giving him a soft lead and he did really well to hold off

THRILLER: the front-running Henllan Harri (left) held off allcomers at Sandown

the closing pack. **My Tent Or Yours** was the bridesmaid yet again ahead of **Arctic Fire** and the Supreme winner **Labaik**, while **Brain Power** put his Champion Hurdle flop behind him with a much better effort in fifth as little over 3l covered the leading quintet. It was 12l back to **Ivan Grozny** and **Vroum Vroum Mag**, who was found to be lame.

65 bet365 Gold Cup (Handicap Chase) (Grade 3) (3m4f166yds)

Sandown April 29 (Good)

1 **Henllan Harri** 9-10-0 Sean Bowen
2 **Vyta Du Roc** 8-10-11 Daryl Jacob
3 **Theatre Guide** 10-11-12 Paddy Brennan
40/1, 6/1, 20/1. hd, nk. 13 ran. 7m 22.60s
(Peter Bowen).

An incredibly tight finish to a marathon chase with the first four covered by ¾l and the first eight by less than 3l, with the easy lead enjoyed by **Henllan Harri** crucial in enabling him to hold off the pursuers. From 4lb out of the handicap, the seemingly exposed handicapper made all the running and just pipped the fast-finishing **Vyta Du Roc**. **Theatre Guide** and **Benbens** brought solid handicap form to the table and were next ahead of **Doing Fine**, who was given far too much to do in fifth.

66 bet365 Celebration Chase (Grade 1) (1m7f119yds)

Sandown April 29 (Good)

1 **Altior** 7-11-7 Nico de Boinville
2 **Special Tiara** 10-11-7 Noel Fehily
3 **San Benedeto** 6-11-7 S Twiston-Davies
30/100F, 4/1, 20/1. 8l, 4½l. 4 ran. 3m 48.00s
(Nicky Henderson).

A clash between Cheltenham winners Altior and **Special Tiara** remarkably had the novice priced at just 3-10 and that proved a fair guide to his superiority on the track as he proved himself an absolute superstar. Altior sat close to the front-running Special Tiara throughout and took over two out before bounding clear from the last. The other two runners, **San Benedeto** and **Vaniteux**, were ridden to pick up the pieces, with San Benedeto doing best though flattered to get so close to the principals.

67 bet365 Select Hurdle (Grade 2) (2m5f110yds)

Sandown April 29 (Good)

1 **L'Ami Serge** 7-11-0 Daryl Jacob
2 **Ptit Zig** 8-11-8 Noel Fehily
3 **Volnay De Thaix** 8-11-0 Nico de Boinville
7/2, 8/1, 16/1. 1½l, 6l. 8 ran. 5m 20.50s
(Nicky Henderson).

APPLE'S JADE: different class to the next generation

A long-overdue win for **L'Ami Serge**, who would go on to score again in the French Champion Hurdle in the summer. There's still an element of surprise that he was able to see out this race so well after pulling his way to the front two out given he also blotted his copybook with another weak finish in the Prix la Barka in between, but he was strongly favoured by the race conditions – **Ptit Zig** and **The New One** were giving him 8lb – and managed to make the most of it. Ptit Zig ran a cracker in second, pulling 6l clear of **Volnay De Thaix**, while The New One perhaps found this one race too many in fourth. **Modus** and **Old Guard** were among those behind.

68 Irish Stallion Farms European Breeders Fund Mares' Champion Hurdle (Grade 1) (2m4f)

Punchestown (IRE) April 29 (Good To Yielding)

1 **Apple's Jade** 5-11-7 B J Cooper
2 **Airlie Beach** 7-11-7 Danny Mullins
3 **Karalee** 6-11-7 R Walsh
EvensF, 16/1, 11/4. 14l, 1¾l. 7 ran. 4m 53.20s (Gordon Elliott).

An easy win for **Apple's Jade**, who proved herself vastly superior to the next generation as novice hurdlers provided the main opposition in the absence of Vroum Vroum Mag and Limini. **Airlie Beach** proved best of the novices, making a valiant attempt to make all the running, but she proved a sitting duck for Apple's Jade, who stormed to a clearcut victory. **Karalee** was a fair third on only her fourth run over hurdles, pulling well clear of the rest, who included the disappointing **Augusta Kate** and **Barra**.

Big-race index

All horses placed or commented on in our big-race review section, with race numbers

THE NEW ONE: again won his fair share of good hurdles races last season

Novice review by Dylan Hill

1 Neptune Investment Management Hyde Novices' Hurdle (Grade 2) (2m5f26yds)

Cheltenham November 11 (Good)

1 **Peregrine Run** 6-11-7 Roger Loughran
2 **Wholestone** 5-11-7 Daryl Jacob
3 **West Approach** 6-11-7 Aidan Coleman
13/2, 5/2F, 3/1. 1l, 3½l. 9 ran. 5m 5.90s (Peter Fahey).

A really strong contest in which Irish raider **Peregrine Run** came out on top. At his best on good ground, Peregrine Run relished the conditions and proved too strong for **Wholestone** and **West Approach**, both of whom went on to frank the form with Wholestone winning a couple of softer Grade 2 races at the track before finishing third in the Albert Bartlett and West Approach doing well in open Graded contests, notably when third in the Cleeve. The trio pulled 8l clear of the rest.

2 Sky Bet Supreme Trial Sharp Novices' Hurdle (Grade 2) (2m87yds)

Cheltenham November 13 (Soft)

1 **Moon Racer** 7-11-4 Tom Scudamore
2 **Mirsaale** 6-11-4 Brian Harding
3 **Ballyandy** 5-11-0 Ryan Hatch
9/4, 14/1, 5/4F. 2¼l, ½l. 6 ran. 4m 6.60s (David Pipe).

This was a second clash between the 2015 and 2016 Champion Bumper winners, **Moon Racer** and **Ballyandy**, as well as several other smart novices, but there was no pace and the form would prove highly questionable. Moon Racer had beaten Ballyandy on his hurdling debut at Perth and again did it nicely, but he was unable to build on this in the spring and the proximity of runner-up **Mirsaale** suggests he achieved little here. Ballyandy was badly outpaced, as was **Movewiththetimes** in fifth, though the pair would flourish given an end-to-end gallop when first and second in the Betfair Hurdle.

3 Racing Post Henry VIII Novices' Chase (Grade 1) (1m7f119yds)

Sandown December 3 (Good To Soft)

1 **Altior** 6-11-2 Noel Fehily
2 **Charbel** 5-11-2 David Bass
3 **Max Ward** 7-11-2 A P Heskin
2/7F, 11/2, 20/1. 6l, 14l. 4 ran. 3m 54.10s (Nicky Henderson).

Such a brilliant winner of the Supreme earlier in the year, **Altior** underlined his star potential over fences with this easy victory. Hinting at how their subsequent Arkle clash might have worked out had **Charbel** stood up, Charbel again managed to stay in front for a long way, leading until he jumped right at the last, but Altior then sprinted clear up the hill in hugely impressive fashion. It was another 14l back to subsequent Aintree Grade 1 fourth **Max Ward**.

4 32Red Kauto Star Novices' Chase (Grade 1) (3m)

Kempton December 26 (Good)

1 **Royal Vacation** 6-11-7 Paddy Brennan
2 **Virgilio** 7-11-7 Harry Skelton
3 **Amore Alato** 7-11-7 Richard Johnson
33/1, 10/1, 8/1. 12l, 8l. 10 ran. 5m 54.20s (Colin Tizzard).

Gut-wrenching for **Might Bite**, who had produced a stunning performance until a crashing fall at the final fence handed a hollow victory to **Royal Vacation**. Might Bite had proved much the best of a competitive field and was around 20l clear when kicked into the last and failing to respond, which seemed

DEFI DU SEUIL (left): carried all before him last season

an inexplicable move by Daryl Jacob, although the equally astonishing finish to the RSA suggests he may well have felt the horse idling. Royal Vacation picked up the pieces and franked the form when winning a novice handicap at Cheltenham next time off 143, while **Frodon**, who had been left second when falling at the last, had also won a big Cheltenham handicap, though he looked a non-stayer over this longer trip.

5 Racing Post Novice Chase (Grade 1) (2m1f)

Leopardstown (IRE) December 26 (Yielding)

1 **Min** 5-11-12 R Walsh
2 **Ordinary World** 6-11-12 Davy Russell
3 **Road To Respect** 5-11-12 Sean Flanagan
4/5F, 25/1, 20/1. 9l, ½l. 7 ran. 4m 6.70s (W P Mullins).

Unfortunately the last we would see of **Min** as a novice and this hugely impressive win suggests he would at least have made things interesting against Altior but for injury. Jumping well, Min made all the running and wasn't extended to beat **Ordinary World**, who was beaten only a shade further when placed in two more Grade 1 contests in the spring, including the Arkle. Subsequent Ryanair Gold Cup winner **Road To Respect** was third and while he wasn't suited by this softer ground and shorter trip, **Baily Cloud** wasn't beaten far in that race either having been ¾l further back in fourth here.

6 coral.co.uk Future Champions Finale Juvenile Hurdle (Grade 1) (2m11yds)

Chepstow December 27 (Soft)

1 **Defi Du Seuil** 3-11-0 Richard Johnson
2 **Evening Hush** 3-10-7 Paul Moloney
3 **Dolos** 3-11-0 Sam Twiston-Davies
4/5F, 5/2, 5/1. 13l, 5l. 5 ran. 4m 0.70s (Philip Hobbs).

An outstanding show of quality from **Defi Du Seuil**, who made a total hash of the final three flights yet still managed to destroy a strong opponent in **Evening Hush**. Defi Du Seuil was on the way to a stunning unbeaten juvenile season and this showed his effectiveness on soft ground as, even with his late nistakes, he beat Evening Hush by further han a very good Adonis winner in Master lueyes would at Kempton.

7 Neville Hotels Novice Chase (Grade 1) (3m)
eopardstown (IRE) December 29 (Yielding)

Our Duke 6-11-10 Robbie Power
Coney Island 5-11-10 Barry Geraghty
Disko 5-11-10 Jonathan Moore
/1, 5/2F, 20/1. ½l, ½l. 10 ran. 6m 7.20s
Mrs John Harrington).

he emergence of a new superstar as **Our Duke** stayed on strongly to see off a pair f fellow Grade 1 winners in **Coney Island** nd **Disko**. Stamina looked to be Our Duke's orte, as he would confirm with his brilliant ictory in the Irish Grand National, so it was o surprise that he failed to match this form hen beaten by Disko down in trip for the logas at Leopardstown on his next start. rinmore winner Coney Island split the pair nd may well have gone close in the RSA but r missing out with a badly bruised foot.

8 Betfred Challow Novices' Hurdle (Grade 1) (2m4f118yds)
ewbury December 31 (Good To Soft)

Messire Des Obeaux 4-11-7 Daryl Jacob
Baltazar D'Allier 5-11-7 Barry Geraghty
Ami Desbois 6-11-7 Kielan Woods
00/30, 9/2, 14/1. 2l, 4½l. 8 ran. 4m 57.70s
Alan King).

robably not the strongest Grade 1 but a pically solid performance from **Messire es Obeaux**, who ran out a comfortable inner. Messire Des Obeaux led two out and tayed on strongly, always holding Irish raider **altazar D'Allier**, who pulled 4½l clear of a ghtly bunched pack with the first two clearly uperior. **Ami Desbois**, second to Wholetone in a Grade 2 at Cheltenham but probbly better over that 3m trip, was third, while avourite **Robin Roe** was still going well in ear when he fell three out.

9 BetBright Dipper Novices' Chase (Grade 2) (2m4f166yds)
heltenham January 1 (Soft)

Whisper 9-11-7 Davy Russell
Clan Des Obeaux 5-11-2 S Twiston-Davies
Briery Belle 8-11-0 Tom O'Brien
1/4, 10/11F, 3/1. ½l, 20l. 4 ran. 5m 30.30s
Nicky Henderson).

second course win in successive months r **Whisper**, who had beaten subsequent cilly Isles runner-up Baron Alco in Decemer and claimed another notable scalp in **Clan Des Obeaux**. The runner-up was let down by his jumping later in the season, but he had stormed home in a Grade 2 at Newbury prior to this and again looked better in this race, jumping well in front bar a slight error two out that allowed Whisper to just take his measure.

10 32Red Tolworth Novices' Hurdle (Grade 1) (1m7f216yds)
Sandown January 7 (Soft)

1 **Finian's Oscar** 5-11-7 Tom O'Brien
2 **Capitaine** 5-11-7 Sam Twiston-Davies
3 **Chalonnial** 5-11-7 Noel Fehily
11/10F, 2/1, 8/1. 5l, 3¾l. 6 ran. 4m 7.50s
(Colin Tizzard).

A comfortable win for **Finian's Oscar**, who stormed clear between the last two and had more than enough in hand to survive a mistake at the final flight. The bare form was moderate, with main rival **Capitaine**, a Grade 2 winner at Ascot, found out subsequently in stronger races in that grade and the rest of the field 0-8 between them over the rest of the season, largely in moderate company, but Finian's Oscar at least backed up the good visual impression when stepped up in trip on better ground at Aintree.

11 Lawlor's Hotel Novice Hurdle (Grade 1) (2m4f)
Naas (IRE) January 8 (Soft)

1 **Death Duty** 6-11-10 Jack Kennedy
2 **Turcagua** 7-11-10 Paul Townend
3 **Blood Crazed Tiger** 6-11-10 D Mullins
5/6F, 7/1, 11/1. 9l, ½l. 6 ran. 5m 8.90s
(Gordon Elliott).

What would have been a good battle between **Death Duty** and **Augusta Kate** unfortunately failed to materialise when the latter fell at the last, leaving Death Duty clear. It was still enough to see Death Duty sent off a warm favourite at Cheltenham when failing to stay in the Albert Bartlett, but the way he and Let's Dance, a rival closely matched with Augusta Kate, were well beaten subsequently at Punchestown indicates this form had been overrated.

12 Neptune Investment Management Leamington Novices' Hurdle (Grade 2) (2m5f)
Warwick January 14 (Soft)

1 **Willoughby Court** 6-11-4 David Bass
2 **Gayebury** 7-11-0 Adam Wedge
3 **Peregrine Run** 7-11-7 Roger Loughran
11/4, 9/2, 11/2. 8l, 1¼l. 6 ran. 5m 14.40s
(Ben Pauling).

A precursor to the Neptune Hurdle as

WAITING PATIENTLY: made it three out of three when winning at Haydock

Willoughby Court again made all the running, proving his effectiveness on soft ground as he gave 4lb and a comprehensive beating to a useful rival in **Gayebury**, who won twice subsequently to end the season on a mark of 148. However, the ground was too soft for **Peregrine Run** in third.

13 Sky Bet Supreme Trial Rossington Main Novices' Hurdle (Grade 2) (1m7f144yds)

Haydock January 21 (Soft)

1 **Neon Wolf** 6-11-8 Noel Fehily
2 **Elgin** 5-11-11 Wayne Hutchinson
3 **Crievehill** 5-11-8 Sam Twiston-Davies
4/5F, 3/1, 12/1. 9l, 2l. 7 ran. 3m 55.80s
(Harry Fry).

The ill-fated **Neon Wolf** couldn't quite justify favouritism against Willoughby Court in the Neptune, but this was perhaps an even better performance than he produced a Cheltenham as he relished more cut in th ground and showed just what a loss he wi be to the sport. Neon Wolf was in front be fore the third-last and asserted betwee the last two, storming clear of a solid yarc stick in **Elgin**, who was seen off far mor easily than he was against Supreme thir River Wylde (also receiving 3lb) in the Dov cote at Kempton.

14 Star Sports Cheltenham Previe Evening Novices' Chase (Grad 2) (2m3f203yds)

Haydock January 21 (Soft)

1 **Waiting Patiently** 6-11-4 Brian Hughe
2 **Politologue** 6-11-7 Sam Twiston-Davie
3 **Its'afreebee** 7-11-4 Harry Skelto
11/4, 6/4F, 11/2. 1¼l, 20l. 6 ran. 5m 16.80s
(Malcolm Jefferson).

Three out of three for the unbeaten **Waitin Patiently**, who was always going well and ra out a smooth winner, though he was perhap flattered to beat a weaker stayer in **Polit logue**. Unlucky not to land a 2m Grade at Aintree, Politologue had also won over fu ther at this track as well as in a 2m5f Grade at Ascot, but he was just found wanting i better races at this sort of trip and lacked th legs to shake off the winner between the la two having jumped typically well in front.

15 Betfred TV Scilly Isles Novice Chase (Grade 1) (2m4f10yds)

Sandown February 4 (Soft)

1 **Top Notch** 6-11-3 Daryl Jaco
2 **Baron Alco** 6-11-3 Jamie Moor
3 **Le Prezien** 6-11-3 Barry Geraght
11/4, 7/1, 3/1. 5l, 1¼l. 5 ran. 5m 19.90s
(Nicky Henderson).

A very assured jumper for a small horse, **To Notch** made the most of that quality in an id al small field as he produced a far more con petent round than several of his key riva and comfortably saw off **Baron Alco**, wh franked the form when second in a red-h Cheltenham Festival handicap. **Le Prezie** did really well to finish a close third after se eral sketchy jumps, leading to a misplace gamble in the Grand Annual when he sug gested this longer trip was vital to him despi a 2m Grade 2 win at Cheltenham earlier in th season, while **Clan Des Obeaux** was taile off after his jumping fell apart.

16 Deloitte Novice Hurdle (Grade 1 (2m2f)

Leopardstown (IRE) February 12 (Soft)

1 **Bacardys** 6-11-10 Mr P W Mullin

Bunk Off Early 5-11-9 Paul Townend
Brelade 5-11-9 Barry Geraghty
2/1, 11/2, 8/1. ¾l, 2¼l. 10 ran. 4m 32.80s
V P Mullins).

nis is often the key trial for the Supreme, but went to more of a stayer in **Bacardys**, who as all out to get on top close home as **Bunk ff Early** paid the price for racing too keenly. **relade**, second to **Saturnas** in a Grade 1 Leopardstown over Christmas, was third, ough Saturnas, the 5-4 favourite to follow o, was tailed off in last.

17 Spring Juvenile Hurdle (Grade 1) (2m)

eopardstown (IRE) February 12 (Soft)
Mega Fortune 4-11-0 Davy Russell
Bapaume 4-11-0 R Walsh
Dinaria Des Obeaux 4-10-7 J Kennedy
'2, 7/4F, 100/30. 3½l, 7l. 8 ran. 4m 1.10s
Gordon Elliott).

he Irish juvenile form would prove really rong at Cheltenham, albeit no match for efi Du Seuil, and virtually all the best of them were involved in this race, which saw **Mega Fortune** gain an excellent win over Bapaume. Beaten by Bapaume three times over the season and only a short-head in front of him in the Triumph, Mega Fortune seemed to relish the soft ground more as he gained a decisive verdict this time. It was 7l back to **Dinaria Des Obeaux** and **Meri Devie**, whose trainer later said she needed the run, while **Ex Patriot** was a disappointing fifth.

18 Albert Bartlett Prestige Novices' Hurdle (Grade 2) (2m6f177yds)

Haydock February 18 (Good To Soft)
1 **The Worlds End** 6-11-7 A P Heskin
2 **No Hassle Hoff** 5-11-0 Bridget Andrews
3 **Ballyarthur** 7-11-4 William Twiston-Davies
11/4, 9/4F, 8/1. 9l, 16l. 7 ran. 5m 36.60s
(Tom George).

A tremendous performance from a major rising star in **The Worlds End**. Always prominent, The Worlds End led three out and drew clear of **No Hassle Hoff**, who was slightly impeded between the last two but still seen

'OP NOTCH (near side): jumping won the day in the Scilly Isles

off far more easily than he had been behind Constantine Bay and Wholestone in other Grade 2 races in receipt of the same 7lb.

19 BetBright Genius Adonis Juvenile Hurdle (Grade 2) (2m)

Kempton February 25 (Good)

1 **Master Blueyes** 4-11-2 Tom Bellamy
2 **Evening Hush** 4-10-12 Adam Wedge
3 **Fidux** 4-11-2 Tom Cannon
13/2, 6/1, 12/1. 11l, 4l. 10 ran. 3m 50.10s (Alan King).

A dramatic contest which saw hot favourite **Charli Parcs** fall when still very much in contention two out, though he would probably have struggled to beat the hugely impressive winner **Master Blueyes**. Travelling better than Charli Parcs at the time, Master Blueyes went on to storm clear of **Evening Hush** with subsequent Fred Winter winner **Flying Tiger** and Anniversary Hurdle third **Bedrock** among others left trailing in fourth and fifth, while he had also beaten Fred Winter second Divin Bere on his previous start.

20 Sky Bet Supreme Novices' Hurdle (Grade 1) (2m87yds)

Cheltenham March 14 (Good To Soft)

1 **Labaik** 6-11-7 Jack Kennedy
2 **Melon** 5-11-7 R Walsh
3 **River Wylde** 6-11-7 Nico de Boinville
25/1, 3/1J, 8/1. 2¼l, 8l. 14 ran. 3m 53.20s (Gordon Elliott).

This didn't look a vintage Supreme beforehand, with Moon Racer jumping ship to the Champion Hurdle and the likes of Neon Wolf and Bacardys stepping up in trip, and two horses coming from nowhere for very different reasons dominated as **Labaik** beat **Melon**. Labaik had all but refused to race three times, but he showed his ability when consenting to jump off as he travelled strongly in rear and produced a stunning turn of foot to deny Melon, who had run only once over hurdles but lived up to his lofty home reputation with a fine effort in second. The pair pulled 8l clear of the rest, though several behind had excuses with **River Wylde** racing too keenly and tiring up the hill whereas **Ballyandy** was outpaced before staying on strongly in fourth and could have done with a stiffer test of stamina. **Cilaos Emery** was another who pulled too hard in fifth, with **Beyond Conceit** and **Elgin** next, while **Pingshou** and **Bunk Off Early** were disappointing.

21 Racing Post Arkle Novices' Chase (Grade 1) (1m7f199yds)

Cheltenham March 14 (Good To Soft)

1 **Altior** 7-11-4 Nico de Boinvil
2 **Cloudy Dream** 7-11-4 Brian Hughe
3 **Ordinary World** 7-11-4 Davy Russe
1/4F, 12/1, 25/1. 6l, 9l. 9 ran. 3m 55.50s (Nicky Henderson).

Not quite the walk in the park many expecte for **Altior**, who was being put under seriou pressure when the unfortunate **Charbel** f two out, but the way he stormed up the h suggests he would ultimately have won w regardless. Altior held only a narrow lea over **Cloudy Dream** and **Ordinary Worl** when left in front by Charbel's departure, b by the line he had put 6l into the runner-u and 15l into the third, powering home in th manner of a strong stayer. Charbel, thoug certainly wasn't finished, confirming hims a very smart prospect having made all u to that point. Cloudy Dream was a fine se ond, pulling well clear of Ordinary World wi another 7l gap back to **Royal Caviar**, wh confirmed his superiority over **Some Pla** having gifted the Irish Arkle to that hor when departing at the last, while **Forest B han** split that pair despite jumping poorly.

22 JT McNamara National Hu Challenge Cup (Amateur Rider Novices' Chase) (Grade 2) (3m7f170yds)

Cheltenham March 14 (Good To Soft)

1 **Tiger Roll** 7-11-6 Ms L O'Ne
2 **Missed Approach** 7-11-6 Mr N McParla
3 **Haymount** 8-11-6 Mr P W Mullin
16/1, 50/1, 33/1. 3l, ¾l. 18 ran. 8m 22.50s (Gordon Elliott).

Class came to the fore in a race dominate by the two highest-rated horses, former T umph Hurdle winner **Tiger Roll** completin an unlikely double having been pushed clo est for most of the way by **Edwulf**, who brok a leg on the run-in but thankfully survive Rated 152 after winning the Munster Nationa Tiger Roll travelled supremely well throug out and had much more in hand over **Misse Approach**, **Haymount** and **Arpege D'Alen** than the official distances having tied up c the run-in to allow that trio to get to within 7l. was 17l back to favourite **A Genie In Abottl**

23 Close Brothers Novice Handicap Chase (Listed Rac (2m4f78yds)

Cheltenham March 14 (Good To Soft)

1 **Tully East** 7-11-8 Denis O'Rega
2 **Gold Present** 7-11-7 Jeremiah McGrat
3 **Two Taffs** 7-11-7 Davy Russe
8/1, 14/1, 7/1. 1¼l, nk. 20 ran. 5m 11.00s (Alan Fleming).

WILLOUGHBY COURT (right): won a really strong Neptune Hurdle

As has become the norm with this race, just 8lb covered the entire field and many well-fancied contenders (five of the first nine in the betting at declaration time) missed out, but it still looks a very strong race and the first three pulled clear, with **Tully East** proving best of them in impressive fashion. Tully East stayed on strongly having travelled notably well, with **Gold Present** and **Two Taffs**, who franked the form by winning a Listed handicap at Ayr next time, chasing him all the way. It was 6l back to **Powersbomb**, while those behind included **Double W's**, who didn't get home having led two out and went on to win back at 2m in the Red Rum at Aintree, in which the sixth, **Bun Doran**, also ran a big race.

24 Neptune Investment Management Novices' Hurdle (Grade 1) (2m5f26yds)

Cheltenham March 15 (Good To Soft)

1 **Willoughby Court** 6-11-7 David Bass
2 **Neon Wolf** 6-11-7 Noel Fehily
3 **Messire Des Obeaux** 5-11-7 Daryl Jacob
14/1, 2/1F, 8/1. hd, 3¾l. 15 ran. 5m 8.80s (Ben Pauling).

A high-class renewal with the form horses from either side of the Irish Sea opting for this race and the British novices held sway, with **Willoughby Court** just holding off **Neon Wolf**. Willoughby Court made all the running at a steady gallop and gamely found enough on the run-in, though Neon Wolf changed his legs a number of times, suggesting he was finding the ground plenty quick enough. Even so, the pair still pulled clear of Challow winner **Messire Des Obeaux**, with **Burbank** next ahead of leading Irish finisher **Kemboy**. Deloitte third **Brelade** was only sixth, suggesting **Bacardys** would have struggled to reach a place even without being hampered by a faller – the ill-fated **Consul De Thaix** – at the fifth, which led to him being pulled up.

25 RSA Novices' Chase (Grade 1) (3m80yds)

Cheltenham March 15 (Good To Soft)

1 **Might Bite** 8-11-4 Nico de Boinville
2 **Whisper** 9-11-4 Davy Russell
3 **Bellshill** 7-11-4 R Walsh
7/2F, 9/2, 5/1. nse, 10l. 12 ran. 6m 8.80s (Nicky Henderson).

Another superlative performance from **Might Bite** very nearly ended in heartbreak again as

FAYONAGH: took the Champion Bumper despite plenty going wrong

he came within a nose of throwing away what should have been a wide-margin win. Soon in front, Might Bite went clear after the fourth-last and had a 12l cushion when he blundered through the last and wandered right on the run-in before somehow getting back up when headed 100 yards out. **Whisper** was hugely flattered to finish so close but stayed on well and was 10l clear of **Bellshill** in third, although the race rather fell apart behind as the fourth, **Alpha Des Obeaux**, broke blood vessels for the second time and only two others finished, with **Royal Vacation** among those pulled up.

26 Fred Winter Juvenile Handicap Hurdle (Grade 3) (2m87yds)

Cheltenham March 15 (Good To Soft)

1 **Flying Tiger** 4-11-5 Richard Johnson
2 **Divin Bere** 4-11-10 Noel Fehily
3 **Nietzsche** 4-11-1 Danny Cook
33/1, 9/2F, 12/1. nk, nk. 22 ran. 3m 58.10s (Nick Williams).

A quality renewal with runner-up **Divin Bere** proving himself a very smart horse at Aintree and the fourth, **Project Bluebook**, going on to win a Grade 2 at Fairyhouse, but nothing could cope with **Flying Tiger**'s finishing burst. Flying Tiger pulled away his chance behind Divin Bere at Aintree, but an end-to-end gallop in this fiercely competitive handicap suited him perfectly and he was produced from off the pace to cut down Divin Bere and **Nietzsche** on the run-in. That trio pulled 5l clear of Project Bluebook, with **Diable De Sivola** next having been given far too much to do.

27 Weatherbys Champion Bumper (Grade 1) (2m87yds)

Cheltenham March 15 (Good To Soft)

1 **Fayonagh** 6-10-12 Mr J J Codd
2 **Debuchet** 4-10-11 Danny Mullins
3 **Claimantakinforgan** 5-11-5 N de Boinville
7/1, 10/1, 22/1. 1¼l, 1½l. 22 ran. 3m 51.10s (Gordon Elliott).

While the bare form looks nothing special, **Fayonagh** may well prove a good deal better than that having overcome plenty going wrong to win well. Intended to be ridden prominently, as she was when making all to win another Grade 1 at Punchestown next time, Fayonagh instead set off in last after a slow start and didn't get a clear run as she picked her way through, but she finished with a wet sail to mow down **Debuchet**, who ran a huge race for a four-year-old in second. The next three all finished within just over 3l of the winner, though, and the two British-trained runners involved – **Claimantakinforgan** and **Western Ryder** – were beaten similar distances at Aintree next time, while the fourth, **Next Destination**, was beaten at odds-on.

28 JLT Novices' Chase (Grade 1) (registered as the Golden Miller Novices' Chase) (2m3f198yds)

Cheltenham March 16 (Good)

1 **Yorkhill** 7-11-4 R Walsh
2 **Top Notch** 6-11-4 Daryl Jacob
3 **Disko** 6-11-4 B J Cooper
6/4F, 7/2, 4/1. 1l, 3l. 8 ran. 5m 0.20s (W P Mullins).

This race revolved around **Yorkhill**, who didn't impress many with his jumping over the season but stood out in terms of class, which carried him through despite continuing to jump to his left at times (electric at others) and showing signs of temperament on the run-in. Yorkhill at least settled well in rear and quickened up superbly in the straight before jinking and idling once he had put the race to bed. The placed horses, both Grade 1 winners, ran solid races to give the form a strong look, with **Top Notch**, who would have pushed Yorkhill harder but for a mistake two out, second ahead of **Disko**. It was 6l back to **Politologue**, while **Baily Cloud** was going well when falling six out, badly hampering **Flying Angel**, who was left with no chance, and **Balko Des Flos** was in front when falling four out.

29 Trull House Stud Mares' Novices' Hurdle (Grade 2) (registered as the Dawn Run Mares' Novices' Hurdle) (2m179yds)

Cheltenham March 16 (Good)

1 **Let's Dance** 5-11-7 R Walsh
2 **Barra** 6-11-2 B J Cooper
3 **Dusky Legend** 7-11-5 Wayne Hutchinson
11/8F, 12/1, 20/1. 2¾l, nk. 16 ran. 4m 2.00s (W P Mullins).

This was laid out on a plate for **Let's Dance**, who ran out a very easy winner. It had looked a much deeper edition of this race than the inaugural 2016 running, with **Airlie Beach** already a Grade 1 winner against geldings having thrashed Saturnas in the Royal Bond and not even favourite, but she took on leading British hope **La Bague Au Roi** up front and the pair cut each other's throats, allowing Let's Dance to cruise through from the rear before quickening clear. **Barra** ran on into second ahead of **Dusky Legend**, who had been second 12 months earlier and got a shade closer this time.

30 JCB Triumph Hurdle (Grade 1) (2m179yds)

Cheltenham March 17 (Good)

1 **Defi Du Seuil** 4-11-0 Richard Johnson
2 **Mega Fortune** 4-11-0 Davy Russell
3 **Bapaume** 4-11-0 R Walsh
5/2F, 7/1, 10/1. 5l, shd. 15 ran. 4m 0.20s (Philip Hobbs).

Defi Du Seuil had looked exceptional earlier in the season and proved arguably even better on good ground as he eased to another hugely impressive victory. Held up early, Defi Du Seuil easily made up ground to lead on the bridle between the last two and produced a stunning turn of foot to quicken clear. Irish horses filled the next four places, led by **Mega Fortune**, who ensured the race was a decent test of stamina and just got back up for second close home ahead of old rival **Bapaume**. **Ex Patriot** and **Landofhopeandglory** were next ahead of **Charli Parcs**, who paid the price for racing too freely, while **Master Blueyes** finished lame but was still in front of the disappointing **Dinaria Des Obeaux** and **Evening Hush**.

31 Albert Bartlett Novices' Hurdle (Grade 1) (registered as the Spa Novices' Hurdle) (2m7f213yds)

Cheltenham March 17 (Good)

1 **Penhill** 6-11-5 Paul Townend
2 **Monalee** 6-11-5 David Mullins
3 **Wholestone** 6-11-5 Daryl Jacob
16/1, 8/1, 13/2. 3½l, 4l. 15 ran. 5m 49.90s (W P Mullins).

The complexion of this race changed two out when **The Worlds End**, travelling like the winner, took a crashing fall and badly hampered **Constantine Bay**, though it's impossible to say whether either would have beaten the strong-staying **Penhill**. Constantine Bay recovered well enough to finish fourth, which further suggests The Worlds End would have gone very close given he comfortably held that horse on the form book after his Haydock win and beat him well at Aintree, but Penhill stormed up the hill after that having tanked through the race and the form looks decent, with **Monalee** second ahead of a rock-solid yardstick in **Wholestone**. **Ami Desbois** was fifth ahead of the below-par **Augusta Kate**, while **Death Duty** was struggling to stay in front of that pair when unseating his rider at the last and clearly failed to stay. **Turcagua** was among those pulled up.

32 Manifesto Novices' Chase (Grade 1) (2m3f200yds)

Aintree April 6 (Good)

1 **Flying Angel** 6-11-4 Noel Fehily
2 **Cloudy Dream** 7-11-4 Brian Hughes
3 **Top Notch** 6-11-4 Daryl Jacob
5/1, 4/1, 6/5F. 1l, 4½l. 6 ran. 5m 1.60s
(Nigel Twiston-Davies).

A high-class race on paper featuring two Cheltenham runners-up, but **Top Notch** was particularly disappointing and **Cloudy Dream** was beaten into second again by **Flying Angel**. A Grade 2 winner over 2m at Warwick earlier in the season but stepped up in trip at Cheltenham when unlucky in the JLT, Flying Angel just outstayed Cloudy Dream, who travelled particularly well, having been headed between the last two. Top Notch ran a flat race in third, while **Max Ward** was another 4l away in fourth before a big gap back to the below-par **Frodon**.

33 Doom Bar Anniversary 4YO Juvenile Hurdle (Grade 1) (2m209yds)

Aintree April 6 (Good)

1 **Defi Du Seuil** 4-11-0 Barry Geraghty
2 **Divin Bere** 4-11-0 Noel Fehily
3 **Bedrock** 4-11-0 Harry Skelton
4/11F, 7/2, 25/1. 1½l, 4½l. 8 ran. 4m 10.10s
(Philip Hobbs).

Seven out of seven for the mighty **Defi Du Seuil**, who probably wasn't at his best but was always unlikely to be pushed hard in the absence of any of the next seven from the Triumph Hurdle. Even so, **Divin Bere** proved a tough opponent in second and it was 4½l back to **Bedrock**, who also ran a cracker on only his second run over hurdles. The rest were well strung out, with Fred Winter winner **Flying Tiger**, who pulled far too hard, well beaten in fourth.

34 Crabbie's Top Novices' Hurdle (Grade 1) (2m103yds)

Aintree April 7 (Good)

1 **Pingshou** 7-11-4 Robbie Power
2 **Mount Mews** 6-11-4 Brian Hughes
3 **The Unit** 6-11-4 Wayne Hutchinson
16/1, 9/4J, 7/1. 4½l, 2½l. 9 ran. 4m 3.20s
(Colin Tizzard).

No fluke about this surprise victory for **Pingshou**, although he may have dropped lucky in a modest race for the grade. Pingshou was always handy and kicked into a decisive lead at the third-last, but he was going away again from the last in the manner of a strong stayer. **Mount Mews**, who boasted a wide-margin Grade 2 victrory at Kelso among his five wins out of six, was second ahead of another unexposed type in **The Unit**, but the highest rated horses failed to fire, with **River Wylde** and **Moon Racer** fifth and sixth.

35 Betway Mildmay Novices' Chase (Grade 1) (3m210yds)

Aintree April 7 (Good)

1 **Might Bite** 8-11-4 Nico de Boinville
2 **Whisper** 9-11-4 Davy Russell
3 **Virgilio** 8-11-4 Harry Skelton
8/13F, 9/4, 14/1. 2l, 18l. 5 ran. 6m 19.70s
(Nicky Henderson).

Another Grade 1 win for **Might Bite** that was rather ordinary compared to his previous victories, though he did the job well under a slightly more conservative ride from Nico de Boinville. Might Bite set a more sedate gallop than at Cheltenham and never had much of a gap on old rival **Whisper**, so much so the result briefly looked in doubt between the last two, but Might Bite produced a soaring jump at the last and stayed on for a cosy success. The pair pulled 18l clear of **Virgilio**, who franked the form by winning a handicap chase over course and distance off 142 the following month.

36 Doom Bar Sefton Novices' Hurdle (Grade 1) (3m149yds)

Aintree April 7 (Good)

1 **The Worlds End** 6-11-4 A P Heskin
2 **Beyond Conceit** 8-11-4 Barry Geraghty
3 **Debece** 6-11-4 Alan Johns
3/1, 9/1, 11/1. ½l, shd. 11 ran. 6m 5.80s
(Tom George).

Compensation for **The Worlds End** after his fall at Cheltenham, though his jumping almost cost him again as a final-flight blunder masked his superiority. Having travelled all over his rivals, The Worlds End quickened clear two out but fluffed the last and ended up all out to hold off **Beyond Conceit**, who benefited from stepping well up in trip after his Supreme sixth and just pipped **Debece** for second, with **Constantine Bay** only ¾l back in fourth. The rest were well strung out, with **West Approach** pulled up.

37 Betway Mersey Novices' Hurdle (Grade 1) (2m4f)

Aintree April 8 (Good)

1 **Finian's Oscar** 5-11-4 Robbie Power
2 **Captain Forez** 5-11-4 Harry Skelton
3 **Messire Des Obeaux** 5-11-4 Daryl Jacob
3/1F, 14/1, 7/2. 3l, 3¼l. 13 ran. 4m 51.40s
(Colin Tizzard).

Finian's Oscar had missed Cheltenham through injury but made a winning return, improving for the step up in trip as he stayed on strongly in the straight having come under pressure turning for home. **Messire Des Obeaux** was the highest-placed finisher from the Neptune but found a sharper test of speed against him, trying to stretch his field from the home turn and a sitting duck between the last two as he could only plug on at one pace, with **Captain Forez**, who travelled well, also staying on past him into second. The rest of the field was tightly bunched, with **Benatar** fourth ahead of **Brio Conti** and **La Bague Au Roi**.

38 Doom Bar Maghull Novices' Chase (Grade 1) (1m7f176yds)

Aintree April 8 (Good)

1 **San Benedeto** 6-11-4 Nick Scholfield
2 **Forest Bihan** 6-11-4 Brian Hughes
3 **Charbel** 6-11-4 David Bass
4/1, 6/1, 6/5F. hd, 13l. 5 ran. 3m 56.60s
(Paul Nicholls).

A modest race with **Charbel** well below his best, but **Politologue** still looked set to run out a good winner until a bizarre tumble handed a dramatic yet hollow victory to **San Benedeto**. Much happier back at 2m having failed to get home a couple of times over further, Politologue looked to have put the race to bed when he pinged the last, but he clipped his own heel a couple of strides later and came down. San Benedeto then finished strongly to pip **Forest Bihan**, who got back on track with a good run in second, perhaps preferring the flatter track given he had won a Grade 2 at Doncaster earlier in the season.

39 Irish Stallion Farms EBF Mares' Novice Hurdle Championship Final (Grade 1) (2m4f)

Fairyhouse (IRE) April 16 (Good To Yielding)

1 **Augusta Kate** 6-11-7 David Mullins
2 **Let's Dance** 5-11-7 R Walsh
3 **Barra** 6-11-7 Davy Russell
8/1, 8/13F, 14/1. ½l, 6½l. 7 ran. 4m 58.20s
(W P Mullins).

A terrific clash between two contrasting horses, with **Augusta Kate**'s stamina proving too much for the speedier **Let's Dance**, but the first four were all well beaten at Punchestown to suggest they may not have been the strongest bunch. Let's Dance travelled supremely well but found little as Augusta Kate wore her down, the pair pulling 6½l clear of **Barra** and **Good Thyne Tara**. **Airlie Beach**

DRAMA: they're on the run-in but disaster is about to strike leader Politologue

CILAOS EMERY: picked up the pieces from Melon and Pingshou

was well below her best, as she would show when reversing the form with the first and third behind Apple's Jade at Punchestown.

40 Ryanair Gold Cup (Novice Chase) (Grade 1) (2m4f)

Fairyhouse (IRE) April 16 (Good To Yielding)

1 **Road To Respect** 6-11-10 B J Cooper
2 **Yorkhill** 7-11-10 R Walsh
3 **Ball D'Arc** 6-11-10 Davy Russell
7/2, 4/7F, 5/1. nk, 5l. 6 ran. 5m 4.00s
(Noel Meade).

A dramatic contest which brought **Yorkhill**'s quirks into sharp focus but also emphasised the size of his engine as he conceded a huge amount of ground by jumping left throughout yet still came within a neck of victory. **Road To Respect** was the beneficiary, building on his Cheltenham Festival handicap win and beating some other useful rivals fair and square, with **Ball D'Arc** and **Baily Cloud** next, although Ball D'Arc's form tailed off slightly at the end of a long season having perhaps peaked with his close second to the prolific Ballycasey prior to this. However, Yorkhill was by far the best horse and still would have overcome all his errors but for one final jink left at the final fence.

41 Jordan Electrics Ltd Future Champion Novices' Chase (Grade 2) (2m4f110yds)

Ayr April 22 (Good)

1 **Cloudy Dream** 7-11-7 Brian Hughes
2 **Theinval** 7-11-4 Jeremiah McGrath
3 **Oldgrangewood** 6-11-7 Harry Skelton
11/4, 8/1, 14/1. 2l, 3¾l. 5 ran. 5m 2.00s
(Malcolm Jefferson).

A well-deserved win for **Cloudy Dream**, who took advantage of what was probably an easier opportunity than when outstayed at this trip by **Flying Angel** at Aintree, especially with that rival pulled up after a terrible blunder five out. Grand Annual third **Theinval** pushed Cloudy Dream closest ahead of another progressive handicapper, **Oldgrangewood**, while **Clan Des Obeaux** was again let down by his jumping but still beaten only 6l.

42 Herald Champion Novice Hurdle (Grade 1) (2m100yds)

Punchestown (IRE) April 25 (Good To Yielding)

1 **Cilaos Emery** 5-11-12 David Mullins
2 **Melon** 5-11-12 R Walsh
3 **Pingshou** 7-11-12 Davy Russell
8/1, 5/4F, 9/1. 1l, 3¼l. 7 ran. 3m 58.90s
(W P Mullins).

This looked a red-hot contest with Supreme one-two **Labaik** and **Melon** joined by Aintree hero **Pingshou**, but it slightly fell apart to hand victory to **Cilaos Emery**. Labaik reverted to type by refusing to race, while Melon and Pingshou took each other on up front at a brisk tempo, allowing Cilaos Emery to take a lead off them before swooping late. Melon and Pingshou did well to stay on so well in the circumstances as there were big gaps back to **Forge Meadow** and **Bunk Off Early** behind them.

43 Growise Champion Novice Chase (Grade 1) (3m120yds)

Punchestown (IRE) April 25 (Good To Yielding)

1 **Disko** 6-11-10 B J Cooper
2 **Anibale Fly** 7-11-10 Mark Walsh
3 **A Genie In Abottle** 6-11-10 S Flanagan

DISKO: set the standard in the Growise and duly delivered a second Grade 1

13/8F, 3/1, 8/1. 5l, ¾l. 7 ran. 6m 27.60s (Noel Meade).

A second Grade 1 win for **Disko**, who didn't need to improve on his previous form to justify favouritism. Always prominent and in command from the third-last, Disko stayed on well to beat Drinmore runner-up **Anibale Fly** and **A Genie In Abottle**, while **A Toi Phil** was 5½l further adrift with a bigger gap back to the disappointing **Acapella Bourgeois** and **Alpha Des Obeaux**.

44 Irish Daily Mirror Novice Hurdle (Grade 1) (3m)

Punchestown (IRE) April 26 (Good To Yielding)

1 **Champagne Classic** 6-11-10 B J Cooper
2 **Penhill** 6-11-10 R Walsh
3 **Tin Soldier** 6-11-10 Danny Mullins
14/1, 2/1F, 8/1. 2¼l, ½l. 8 ran. 5m 58.00s (Gordon Elliott).

This brought together three Cheltenham Festival winners and a steadily run race played into the hands of **Champagne Classic**, the only one whose victory had come over shorter. Much improved on good ground when thrown in for the Martin Pipe at Cheltenham, Champagne Classic stepped up again to see off **Penhill**, who would have appreciated a greater test of stamina, and **Tin Soldier**. It was 9l back to the below-par **Monalee**, while Pertemps Final winner **Presenting Percy** could manage only sixth.

45 Ryanair Novice Chase (Grade 1) (2m)

Punchestown (IRE) April 27 (Good To Yielding)

1 **Great Field** 6-11-10 Jody McGarvey
2 **Ordinary World** 7-11-10 Davy Russell
3 **Ball D'Arc** 6-11-10 B J Cooper
9/10F, 7/1, 11/2. 11l, 2¼l. 8 ran. 4m 6.50s (W P Mullins).

A terrific performance from yet another exciting 2m chaser in **Great Field**, who dismissed solid yardstick **Ordinary World** in a similar manner to Min and Altior earlier in the season. An easy winner of all three previous runs over fences, Great Field made all the running

BAPAUME: had too many gears for old rival Mega Fortune (partially hidden)

and stayed on strongly to see off Ordinary World and **Ball D'Arc**, who admittedly below his best. **Baily Cloud** also seemed to find this coming too soon after Fairyhouse and would have finished no better than fifth even without unseating his rider at the last.

46 Tattersalls Ireland Champion Novice Hurdle (Grade 1) (2m4f)

Punchestown (IRE) April 28 (Good To Yielding)

1 **Bacardys** 6-11-10 Mr P W Mullins
2 **Finian's Oscar** 5-11-10 Robbie Power
3 **Death Duty** 6-11-10 B J Cooper
10/1, 13/8F, 9/2. shd, 7l. 9 ran. 4m 53.90s (W P Mullins).

As at Aintree, this race lacked the Neptune one-two but **Finian's Oscar** couldn't quite take advantage this time as he just lost out to **Bacardys**. So unlucky at Cheltenham, Bacardys was able to show his true colours this time and got up close home under a patient ride after Finian's Oscar, driven clear after the second-last, had perhaps just idled in front given he rallied again as the winner got to him. **Death Duty**, back over a more suitable trip, was still found wanting in third, as was **Let's Dance** just a neck behind him, with excuses for the pair hard to swallow given they were always likely to finish close together on a line through **Augusta Kate**.

47 AES Champion Four-Year-Old Hurdle (Grade 1) (2m)

Punchestown (IRE) April 29 (Good To Yielding)

1 **Bapaume** 4-11-0 R Walsh
2 **Landofhopeandglory** 4-11-0 Mark Walsh
3 **Meri Devie** 4-10-7 David Mullins
2/1F, 4/1, 7/1. 1¼l, 1l. 7 ran. 3m 53.40s (W P Mullins).

Already placed twice at the top level, **Bapaume** turned the tables on **Mega Fortune** to run out a smooth winner. The surprising decision not to make the running with Mega Fortune seemed to backfire as Bapaume was able to deploy by far the greater turn of foot off a steady gallop, quickening clear before the home turn before holding off **Landofhopeandglory** and **Meri Devie**. Mega Fortune was next, the first four covered by just 2½l, before a 7l gap back to **Dinaria Des Obeaux**.

Novice index

All horses placed or commented on in our novice review section, with race numbers

A Genie In Abottle 22, 43
A Toi Phil 43
Acapella Bourgeois 43
Airlie Beach 29, 39
Alpha Des Obeaux 25, 43
Altior 3, 21
Ami Desbois 8, 31
Amore Alato 4
Anibale Fly 43
Arpege D'Alene 22
Augusta Kate 11, 31, 39, 46
Bacardys 16, 24, 46
Baily Cloud 5, 28, 40, 45
Balko Des Flos 28
Ball D'Arc 40, 45
Ballyandy 2, 20
Ballyarthur 18
Baltazar D'Allier 8
Bapaume 17, 30, 47
Baron Alco 15
Barra 29, 39
Bedrock 19, 33
Bellshill 25
Benatar 37
Beyond Conceit 20, 36
Blood Crazed Tiger 11
Brelade 16, 24
Briery Belle 9
Brio Conti 37
Bun Doran 23
Bunk Off Early 16, 20, 42
Burbank 24
Capitaine 10
Captain Forez 37
Chalonnial 10
Champagne Classic 44
Charbel 3, 21, 38
Charli Parcs 19, 30
Cilaos Emery 20, 42
Claimantakinforgan 27
Clan Des Obeaux 9, 15, 41
Cloudy Dream 21, 32, 41
Coney Island 7
Constantine Bay 31, 36
Consul De Thaix 24
Crievehill 13
Death Duty 11, 31, 46
Debece 36
Debuchet 27
Defi Du Seuil 6, 30, 33
Diable De Sivola 26
Dinaria Des Obeaux 17, 30, 47
Disko 7, 28, 43
Divin Bere 26, 33
Dolos 6
Double W's 23
Dusky Legend 29
Edwulf 22
Elgin 13, 20
Evening Hush 6, 19, 30
Ex Patriot 17
Fayonagh 27
Fidux 19
Finian's Oscar 10, 37, 46
Flying Angel 28, 32, 41
Flying Tiger 19, 26, 33
Forest Bihan 21, 38
Forge Meadow 42

DEATH DUTY: disappointing spring

WHISPER: ran consistently well in several top staying novice chases last term

Trainer Statistics

R.CURTIS 17/18
14/11/17 R W %
48 4 9

By race type

	Hurdles				Chases			
	W	R	%	£1 stake	W	R	%	£1 stake
Handicap	23	126	18	-14.13	28	184	15	-28.87
Novice	48	129	37	-11.89	40	127	31	-11.03
Maiden	15	42	36	-1.62	0	0	-	+0.00

By jockey

	Hurdles				Chases				Bumpers			
	W	R	%	£1 stake	W	R	%	£1 stake	W	R	%	£1 stake
S Twiston-Davies	38	129	29	-22.23	29	130	22	-43.89	3	9	33	+1.25
Harry Cobden	24	54	44	+16.92	5	26	19	+0.40	1	2	50	-0.56
Sean Bowen	6	31	19	-1.20	15	54	28	-2.30	0	1	-	-1.00
Nick Scholfield	10	56	18	-32.27	6	37	16	-7.17	1	3	33	+0.00
Jack Sherwood	4	11	36	+3.33	6	17	35	+14.75	0	1	-	-1.00
Stan Sheppard	6	26	23	-4.32	0	4	-	-4.00	2	7	29	+0.25
Barry Geraghty	3	10	30	+1.86	2	5	40	-1.36	0	0	-	+0.00
Mr W Biddick	0	0	-	+0.00	3	5	60	+2.17	0	0	-	+0.00
Miss B Frost	0	1	-	-1.00	2	6	33	+14.25	0	0	-	+0.00
Gary Derwin	1	1	100	+12.00	0	0	-	+0.00	0	0	-	+0.00

By month

	Hurdles				Chases				Bumpers			
	W	R	%	£1 stake	W	R	%	£1 stake	W	R	%	£1 stake
May 2016	5	19	26	-8.60	5	23	22	-13.11	1	3	33	+2.00
June	3	6	50	-1.89	2	11	18	-5.55	0	0	-	+0.00
July	2	7	29	-2.45	0	8	-	-8.00	1	1	100	+1.75
August	3	5	60	+2.79	0	6	-	-6.00	0	0	-	+0.00
September	1	4	25	-2.20	4	4	100	+3.74	0	0	-	+0.00
October	18	42	43	+9.84	8	25	32	+4.78	3	5	60	+5.25
November	13	47	28	+5.57	11	41	27	+9.38	0	5	-	-5.00
December	9	41	22	-9.76	11	45	24	+13.07	0	1	-	-1.00
January 2017	6	28	21	-4.21	2	30	7	-27.04	0	1	-	-1.00
February	7	43	16	-9.25	10	31	32	-12.81	0	1	-	-1.00
March	6	35	17	-11.70	9	37	24	+25.22	0	1	-	-1.00
April	19	53	36	-6.03	9	54	17	-20.32	2	6	33	-2.06

By horse

	Wins-Runs	%	£1 level stakes	Win prize	Total prize
San Benedeto	6-12	50	+8.52	£128,108.10	£152,430.30
Frodon	6-9	67	+15.78	£124,412.00	£127,062.00
Vicente	1-6	17	+4.00	£122,442.50	£125,524.50
Irving	1-4	25	+3.00	£67,843.20	£71,322.20
Politologue	3-6	50	+1.53	£46,981.00	£62,496.31
Present Man	4-8	50	+8.75	£52,422.50	£58,001.80
As De Mee	2-7	29	-0.09	£49,178.20	£57,484.20
Cliffs Of Dover	6-7	86	+10.49	£55,308.43	£56,739.43
Saphir Du Rheu	1-6	17	-4.86	£16,245.00	£55,177.00
Modus	1-6	17	+2.00	£22,780.00	£53,183.00
El Bandit	5-7	71	+16.37	£52,011.10	£52,011.10
Capitaine	3-7	43	+5.18	£28,620.80	£44,408.90
Silviniaco Conti	0-4	-	-4.00	£0.00	£43,272.77

Paul Nicholls

All runners

	Wins-Runs	%	Win prize	Total prize	£1 level stakes
Hurdle	92-330	28	£722,979.35	£1,047,262.37	-37.89
Chase	72-316	23	£989,001.45	£1,451,620.08	-35.45
Bumper	7-24	29	£21,612.80	£28,173.80	-2.06
TOTAL	171-670	26	£1,733,593.60	£2,527,056.25	-75.39

By course - last four seasons

	Hurdles				Chases				Bumpers			
	W	R	%	£1 stake	W	R	%	£1 stake	W	R	%	£1 stake
Aintree	4	48	8	-14.50	10	78	13	-24.13	0	5	-	-5.00
Ascot	10	61	16	-9.90	17	68	25	+3.93	1	4	25	-1.25
Ayr	6	19	32	+15.25	4	18	22	+16.75	1	2	50	+4.00
Bangor-On-Dee	1	1	100	+1.25	2	5	40	+0.25	0	0	-	+0.00
Carlisle	1	1	100	+2.50	3	5	60	+3.45	0	0	-	+0.00
Cartmel	0	1	-	-1.00	0	1	-	-1.00	0	0	-	+0.00
Catterick	0	2	-	-2.00	1	2	50	+0.50	0	1	-	-1.00
Cheltenham	18	164	11	-17.35	18	162	11	+19.73	2	7	29	+0.25
Chepstow	13	57	23	-17.96	6	49	12	-21.17	2	10	20	-4.50
Doncaster	6	28	21	-9.54	7	33	21	-5.96	1	2	50	-0.33
Exeter	21	62	34	-7.29	12	47	26	-20.97	2	6	33	+2.63
Fakenham	2	4	50	+0.32	4	9	44	+2.98	0	0	-	+0.00
Ffos Las	3	10	30	+4.10	2	7	29	-3.52	0	1	-	-1.00
Fontwell	8	28	29	-7.04	16	33	48	+14.30	0	1	-	-1.00
Haydock	4	35	11	-18.84	10	26	38	+5.73	0	2	-	-2.00
Hereford	1	4	25	-2.33	0	4	-	-4.00	0	0	-	+0.00
Hexham	0	0	-	+0.00	2	2	100	+2.40	0	0	-	+0.00
Huntingdon	2	8	25	-1.13	3	10	30	+6.50	1	1	100	+4.50
Kelso	2	4	50	+2.13	4	11	36	-2.57	0	0	-	+0.00
Kempton	12	63	19	+1.79	15	72	21	-9.45	0	4	-	-4.00
Kempton (AW)	0	0	-	+0.00	0	0	-	+0.00	1	17	6	-12.00
Leicester	1	3	33	-0.13	3	5	60	+0.24	0	0	-	+0.00
Lingfield	0	0	-	+0.00	1	1	100	+0.73	0	0	-	+0.00
Lingfield (AW)	0	0	-	+0.00	0	0	-	+0.00	1	3	33	+4.00
Ludlow	2	10	20	-6.04	2	14	14	-10.07	1	3	33	-0.38
Market Rasen	1	5	20	-3.33	2	14	14	-3.09	0	0	-	+0.00
Musselburgh	3	12	25	+4.17	3	6	50	-0.06	0	0	-	+0.00
Newbury	9	60	15	-16.33	15	79	19	+1.48	0	4	-	-4.00
Newcastle	2	3	67	+6.50	0	2	-	-2.00	0	0	-	+0.00
Newton Abbot	18	55	33	-18.17	13	58	22	-19.52	1	3	33	-0.25
Perth	1	2	50	-0.64	3	7	43	+5.80	0	0	-	+0.00
Plumpton	3	16	19	-5.17	2	7	29	-3.37	0	0	-	+0.00
Sandown	9	57	16	-3.22	15	97	15	-7.22	0	2	-	-2.00
Sedgefield	0	1	-	-1.00	1	1	100	+0.18	0	0	-	+0.00
Southwell	2	3	67	+2.30	0	1	-	-1.00	0	0	-	+0.00
Southwell (AW)	0	0	-	+0.00	0	0	-	+0.00	1	2	50	+2.00
Stratford	4	12	33	-4.56	0	13	-	-13.00	1	1	100	+4.00
Taunton	34	101	34	+8.91	12	37	32	+0.49	4	15	27	-1.75
Uttoxeter	0	1	-	-1.00	0	11	-	-11.00	0	0	-	+0.00
Warwick	3	15	20	-6.63	6	20	30	+2.01	1	4	25	-0.25
Wetherby	3	8	38	+6.00	2	9	22	-4.59	0	0	-	+0.00
Wincanton	50	123	41	+9.97	17	66	26	-21.73	7	22	32	+6.44
Worcester	7	19	37	+2.03	8	25	32	-1.72	0	0	-	+0.00

By race type

	Hurdles				Chases			
	W	R	%	£1 stake	W	R	%	£1 stake
Handicap	18	144	13	-43.13	8	89	9	-46.17
Novice	38	138	28	-38.01	33	95	35	+2.68
Maiden	19	48	40	+19.38	0	0	-	+0.00

By jockey

	Hurdles				Chases				Bumpers			
	W	R	%	£1 stake	W	R	%	£1 stake	W	R	%	£1 stake
Nico de Boinville	24	96	25	-22.49	15	48	31	-1.68	5	25	20	-7.09
Jerry McGrath	20	85	24	-6.76	6	45	13	-24.49	11	27	41	+16.93
Daryl Jacob	11	37	30	-4.11	5	17	29	-7.43	0	2	-	-2.00
Barry Geraghty	7	19	37	+1.15	2	9	22	-5.17	1	2	50	-0.47
Noel Fehily	3	16	19	-5.00	6	11	55	+0.44	0	0	-	+0.00
Ned Curtis	3	21	14	-15.14	0	0	-	+0.00	4	9	44	+2.33
Davy Russell	3	7	43	-2.30	2	4	50	+4.75	0	0	-	+0.00
David Bass	3	11	27	+2.75	2	9	22	-3.50	0	5	-	-5.00
Andrew Tinkler	4	17	24	-6.36	1	8	13	-1.00	0	2	-	-2.00
Freddie Mitchell	2	4	50	+0.07	0	0	-	+0.00	1	1	100	+3.33

By month

	Hurdles				Chases				Bumpers			
	W	R	%	£1 stake	W	R	%	£1 stake	W	R	%	£1 stake
May 2016	8	32	25	-2.28	4	12	33	-2.27	6	14	43	+4.73
June	5	14	36	+9.85	0	3	-	-3.00	1	3	33	+4.00
July	2	11	18	-4.00	0	3	-	-3.00	0	1	-	-1.00
August	1	6	17	-2.75	1	3	33	-0.90	0	0	-	+0.00
September	2	6	33	+1.88	0	1	-	-1.00	0	1	-	-1.00
October	4	17	24	-5.13	0	9	-	-9.00	0	3	-	-3.00
November	8	36	22	-12.10	9	24	38	+11.79	3	9	33	+1.75
December	12	61	20	-18.76	11	34	32	-8.97	2	9	22	-4.63
January 2017	13	34	38	+11.28	5	12	42	+2.33	2	6	33	-0.97
February	10	36	28	-11.83	5	18	28	-4.40	1	7	14	-4.13
March	7	44	16	-21.56	4	26	15	-14.11	4	15	27	+2.00
April	14	61	23	-4.65	5	32	16	-21.42	4	11	36	+5.15

By horse

	Wins-Runs	%	£1 level stakes	Win prize	Total prize
Buveur D'Air	5-5	100	+6.90	£371,069.50	£371,069.50
Altior	6-6	100	+1.40	£252,281.10	£252,281.10
My Tent Or Yours	0-5	-	-5.00	£0.00	£170,001.00
Might Bite	4-6	67	+2.76	£166,458.35	£167,984.75
Brain Power	2-4	50	+14.50	£119,187.00	£119,187.00
Top Notch	4-7	57	+1.08	£59,997.00	£105,432.61
Whisper	2-4	50	+4.75	£33,922.00	£92,429.50
L'Ami Serge	1-7	14	-2.50	£28,475.00	£81,029.2
Theinval	2-11	18	-7.27	£10,929.00	£71,982.77
Josses Hill	2-6	33	-1.63	£49,529.50	£70,064.70
Vaniteux	2-6	33	+0.25	£42,269.50	£60,944.00
Divin Bere	1-3	33	-0.25	£12,512.00	£50,769.42
Rather Be	3-6	50	+8.00	£46,536.80	£48,444.80

Nicky Henderson

All runners

	Wins-Runs	%	Win prize	Total prize	£1 level stakes
Hurdle	87-362	24	£1,025,762.02	£1,582,672.04	-62.48
Chase	44-177	25	£781,578.84	£1,162,977.58	-53.94
Bumper	23-79	29	£75,694.04	£100,837.71	+2.92
TOTAL	154-618	25	£1,883,034.90	£2,846,487.33	-113.50

By course - last four seasons

	Hurdles				Chases				Bumpers			
	W	R	%	£1 stake	W	R	%	£1 stake	W	R	%	£1 stake
Aintree	16	70	23	+21.82	6	43	14	-5.89	1	13	8	+2.00
Ascot	15	78	19	-21.66	6	27	22	-8.25	3	11	27	+0.64
Ayr	1	17	6	-15.09	1	11	9	-7.00	2	3	67	+2.23
Bangor-On-Dee	5	24	21	-9.25	2	6	33	-1.56	0	7	-	-7.00
Catterick	0	2	-	-2.00	1	2	50	+1.00	0	0	-	+0.00
Cheltenham	18	194	9	-73.23	10	100	10	-62.49	1	15	7	-8.00
Chepstow	5	23	22	-2.17	1	4	25	+3.00	1	5	20	+0.50
Doncaster	25	52	48	+54.73	8	24	33	-2.38	1	8	13	-3.50
Exeter	4	10	40	-1.21	1	5	20	+6.00	1	6	17	-4.09
Fakenham	6	16	38	-3.26	1	7	14	-5.60	3	4	75	+2.53
Ffos Las	8	18	44	-2.89	0	4	-	-4.00	1	4	25	-1.25
Fontwell	3	18	17	-6.64	2	8	25	-2.59	1	10	10	-8.20
Haydock	4	30	13	-15.85	1	6	17	-4.09	1	2	50	+1.75
Hereford	2	3	67	+3.00	0	1	-	-1.00	0	0	-	+0.00
Hexham	1	2	50	-0.17	0	0	-	+0.00	0	0	-	+0.00
Huntingdon	15	47	32	-2.22	7	14	50	+2.78	1	14	7	-12.27
Kelso	1	1	100	+0.36	2	2	100	+2.65	1	4	25	+2.50
Kempton	27	108	25	-12.10	18	56	32	+9.74	5	22	23	-2.68
Kempton (AW)	0	0	-	+0.00	0	0	-	+0.00	6	11	55	+11.45
Leicester	1	9	11	-7.20	1	6	17	-4.86	0	0	-	+0.00
Lingfield	2	3	67	-0.18	0	0	-	+0.00	0	0	-	+0.00
Lingfield (AW)	0	0	-	+0.00	0	0	-	+0.00	4	15	27	+0.67
Ludlow	15	48	31	-14.42	2	14	14	-5.63	8	19	42	+1.48
Market Rasen	10	36	28	-9.95	3	13	23	+9.10	6	15	40	+7.38
Musselburgh	6	20	30	-6.16	1	3	33	+0.00	0	1	-	-1.00
Newbury	27	90	30	-9.03	5	35	14	+0.05	5	20	25	-2.72
Newcastle	3	4	75	+1.25	0	0	-	+0.00	0	0	-	+0.00
Newton Abbot	4	15	27	-1.42	2	5	40	+1.41	1	2	50	+0.25
Perth	0	6	-	-6.00	0	3	-	-3.00	0	1	-	-1.00
Plumpton	4	11	36	+5.08	3	4	75	+0.58	0	1	-	-1.00
Sandown	23	80	29	+23.47	7	35	20	-5.90	1	4	25	-1.00
Southwell	3	27	11	-17.76	0	4	-	-4.00	7	14	50	+4.28
Stratford	5	29	17	-11.98	1	9	11	-7.43	0	7	-	-7.00
Taunton	6	22	27	-7.59	0	1	-	-1.00	2	5	40	-0.25
Towcester	8	16	50	+5.57	1	2	50	+1.25	3	14	21	-4.85
Uttoxeter	11	38	29	-4.53	2	13	15	-9.36	2	6	33	-0.22
Warwick	6	24	25	+1.40	3	7	43	-1.83	2	14	14	-8.09
Wetherby	4	12	33	-0.06	1	6	17	-4.83	1	2	50	+1.75
Wincanton	4	13	31	+0.83	2	6	33	-1.38	0	4	-	-4.00
Worcester	12	37	32	+1.40	3	8	38	+8.17	3	16	19	+0.83

By race type

	Hurdles W	Hurdles R	Hurdles %	Hurdles £1 stake	Chases W	Chases R	Chases %	Chases £1 stake
Handicap	27	212	13	-85.74	20	115	17	-28.25
Novice	31	168	18	-88.39	16	77	21	-28.43
Maiden	12	53	23	-19.03	0	0	-	+0.00

By jockey

	Hurdles W	Hurdles R	Hurdles %	Hurdles £1 stake	Chases W	Chases R	Chases %	Chases £1 stake	Bumpers W	Bumpers R	Bumpers %	Bumpers £1 stake
Harry Skelton	55	287	19	-102.54	26	127	20	-31.58	7	41	17	-17.36
Bridget Andrews	10	93	11	-60.93	1	14	7	-12.64	2	10	20	+1.50
Mr S Davies-Thomas	1	4	25	-2.60	4	10	40	+5.67	0	0	-	+0.00
Ian Popham	2	25	8	-9.00	2	10	20	-4.59	0	5	-	-5.00
Lewis Gordon	1	3	33	+0.50	0	0	-	+0.00	0	0	-	+0.00
Noel Fehily	1	5	20	-2.75	0	0	-	+0.00	0	1	-	-1.00
Davy Russell	0	2	-	-2.00	1	4	25	+0.00	0	1	-	-1.00
David England	0	17	-	-17.00	0	7	-	-7.00	0	2	-	-2.00
Mr J Andrews	0	1	-	-1.00	0	4	-	-4.00	0	0	-	+0.00
Tom Scudamore	0	2	-	-2.00	0	2	-	-2.00	0	0	-	+0.00

By month

	Hurdles W	Hurdles R	Hurdles %	Hurdles £1 stake	Chases W	Chases R	Chases %	Chases £1 stake	Bumpers W	Bumpers R	Bumpers %	Bumpers £1 stake
May 2016	3	26	12	-17.77	2	13	15	-5.63	0	4	-	-4.00
June	3	15	20	-2.30	0	8	-	-8.00	0	1	-	-1.00
July	3	17	18	-3.52	3	11	27	+4.25	0	0	-	+0.00
August	1	7	14	-4.90	3	8	38	-1.40	0	1	-	-1.00
September	1	13	8	-11.17	1	4	25	-1.25	0	2	-	-2.00
October	11	37	30	-7.72	3	18	17	-12.60	0	8	-	-8.00
November	8	56	14	-14.91	5	22	23	-6.17	1	6	17	-4.09
December	5	70	7	-44.27	5	27	19	-10.88	2	9	22	+2.50
January 2017	3	41	7	-34.21	2	19	11	-7.00	0	2	-	-2.00
February	8	50	16	-34.10	2	15	13	-3.50	2	8	25	+0.80
March	10	54	19	-32.45	5	15	33	+0.03	2	11	18	-3.67
April	13	60	22	-4.50	3	18	17	-4.00	2	9	22	-3.40

By horse

	Wins-Runs	%	£1 level stakes	Win prize	Total prize
Ch'Tibello	1-5	20	+1.00	£61,900.00	£93,450.00
Virgilio	2-6	33	-1.53	£25,169.20	£58,861.20
North Hill Harvey	1-3	33	+4.00	£56,950.00	£56,950.00
Two Taffs	2-7	29	-1.71	£31,724.00	£48,572.00
Stephanie Frances	4-6	67	+3.35	£36,232.44	£41,784.04
The Bay Oak	3-8	38	+0.78	£23,437.60	£30,020.20
Long House Hall	1-2	50	+5.00	£28,475.00	£29,667.50
Red Tornado	3-6	50	+6.30	£27,470.18	£29,235.68
Captain Forez	0-3	-	-3.00	£0.00	£28,939.90
Oldgrangewood	3-7	43	+4.75	£22,731.50	£28,872.87
Yorkist	1-5	20	-1.75	£14,620.50	£26,946.50
Superb Story	1-1	100	+1.38	£25,992.00	£25,992.00
No Hassle Hoff	1-6	17	-1.00	£2,729.16	£22,480.66

Dan Skelton

All runners

	Wins-Runs	%	Win prize	Total prize	£1 level stakes
Hurdle	70-449	16	£456,049.67	£785,988.77	-209.32
Chase	34-179	19	£290,493.86	£485,872.45	-57.14
Bumper	9-61	15	£18,380.06	£32,042.48	-25.86
TOTAL	113-689	16	£764,923.59	£1,303,903.70	-292.32

By course - last four seasons

	Hurdles				Chases				Bumpers			
	W	R	%	£1 stake	W	R	%	£1 stake	W	R	%	£1 stake
Aintree	5	32	16	-6.88	0	14	-	-14.00	0	3	-	-3.00
Ascot	2	25	8	-4.00	2	17	12	-3.50	0	3	-	-3.00
Ayr	6	22	27	+1.24	1	9	11	-5.00	1	2	50	+1.75
Bangor-On-Dee	5	28	18	-8.79	5	14	36	+4.20	1	7	14	-2.67
Carlisle	2	4	50	-1.38	0	2	-	-2.00	0	1	-	-1.00
Cartmel	0	5	-	-5.00	1	3	33	-0.13	0	0	-	+0.00
Catterick	3	10	30	-4.94	2	8	25	+2.25	1	1	100	+0.91
Cheltenham	8	71	11	-29.63	1	27	4	-17.00	0	5	-	-5.00
Chepstow	6	27	22	+3.75	0	8	-	-8.00	1	9	11	-1.00
Doncaster	1	35	3	-32.75	1	14	7	-12.00	0	4	-	-4.00
Exeter	3	12	25	-7.53	1	6	17	-4.43	0	0	-	+0.00
Fakenham	6	26	23	-7.84	6	17	35	+0.55	1	2	50	+5.00
Ffos Las	2	18	11	-8.50	2	7	29	+6.50	0	3	-	-3.00
Fontwell	3	23	13	-12.40	8	14	57	+10.66	1	12	8	-4.00
Haydock	5	32	16	-4.00	1	13	8	-10.13	0	1	-	-1.00
Hereford	2	8	25	-1.60	1	3	33	+3.50	0	0	-	+0.00
Hexham	1	5	20	-3.64	0	1	-	-1.00	0	0	-	+0.00
Huntingdon	10	55	18	-28.60	5	22	23	+0.13	1	15	7	-12.90
Kelso	0	3	-	-3.00	1	3	33	+2.00	0	0	-	+0.00
Kempton	6	54	11	-32.03	2	23	9	-18.43	0	7	-	-7.00
Kempton (AW)	0	0	-	+0.00	0	0	-	+0.00	0	1	-	-1.00
Leicester	1	12	8	-8.75	3	11	27	+7.75	0	0	-	+0.00
Lingfield	2	6	33	+4.25	3	4	75	+10.75	0	0	-	+0.00
Lingfield (AW)	0	0	-	+0.00	0	0	-	+0.00	0	1	-	-1.00
Ludlow	14	52	27	-6.73	2	14	14	-4.75	2	12	17	+1.80
Market Rasen	14	50	28	-4.89	6	27	22	+5.57	1	7	14	-2.67
Musselburgh	2	9	22	-4.25	0	2	-	-2.00	0	1	-	-1.00
Newbury	4	38	11	-18.13	2	11	18	+0.50	0	1	-	-1.00
Newcastle	1	5	20	-2.63	1	5	20	-3.71	1	1	100	+0.80
Newton Abbot	1	21	5	-19.09	2	10	20	-4.65	0	0	-	+0.00
Perth	1	2	50	+5.50	0	2	-	-2.00	0	0	-	+0.00
Plumpton	2	12	17	-5.88	0	6	-	-6.00	0	0	-	+0.00
Sandown	0	22	-	-22.00	1	9	11	-2.50	0	2	-	-2.00
Sedgefield	7	23	30	-7.03	2	11	18	-7.76	0	2	-	-2.00
Southwell	13	56	23	-9.15	5	19	26	-4.09	1	15	7	+0.00
Stratford	9	50	18	-10.37	4	24	17	-8.08	2	9	22	+2.00
Taunton	8	32	25	-9.15	1	7	14	+4.00	1	4	25	-0.50
Towcester	2	12	17	-7.00	2	5	40	-1.97	1	6	17	-2.00
Uttoxeter	6	33	18	+2.30	5	22	23	-9.04	0	7	-	-7.00
Warwick	9	62	15	-34.04	6	25	24	-4.47	5	20	25	+2.25
Wetherby	9	31	29	-0.13	6	18	33	+8.00	3	8	38	+1.04
Wincanton	5	22	23	+1.25	2	10	20	-1.00	1	3	33	+1.00
Worcester	7	41	17	-12.11	5	28	18	-14.40	1	10	10	-7.63

By race type

	Hurdles				Chases			
	W	R	%	£1 stake	W	R	%	£1 stake
Handicap	26	168	15	-4.25	22	168	13	-51.17
Novice	31	111	28	+17.26	6	55	11	-23.59
Maiden	14	64	22	-23.64	0	0	-	+0.00

By jockey

	Hurdles				Chases				Bumpers			
	W	R	%	£1 stake	W	R	%	£1 stake	W	R	%	£1 stake
Richard Johnson	44	182	24	+7.58	19	127	15	-29.67	3	24	13	-15.75
Tom O'Brien	8	50	16	+5.40	8	35	23	+10.24	0	7	-	-7.00
Barry Geraghty	8	16	50	-1.99	0	2	-	-2.00	0	0	-	+0.00
Ciaran Gethings	5	27	19	-11.34	0	9	-	-9.00	0	1	-	-1.00
Liam Heard	2	8	25	+2.00	2	3	67	+4.00	0	0	-	+0.00
Mr David Maxwell	0	0	-	+0.00	2	5	40	+0.00	0	0	-	+0.00
Mr Sean Houlihan	2	9	22	-2.75	0	1	-	-1.00	0	2	-	-2.00
Micheal Nolan	2	15	13	-1.67	0	12	-	-12.00	0	5	-	-5.00
Miss Natalie Parker	1	1	100	+5.00	0	0	-	+0.00	0	0	-	+0.00
Tom Scudamore	1	1	100	+4.00	0	0	-	+0.00	0	0	-	+0.00

By month

	Hurdles				Chases				Bumpers			
	W	R	%	£1 stake	W	R	%	£1 stake	W	R	%	£1 stake
May 2016	1	21	5	-16.50	8	21	38	+21.38	0	2	-	-2.00
June	1	7	14	-1.00	2	12	17	-4.25	0	1	-	-1.00
July	0	11	-	-11.00	2	12	17	+4.00	0	0	-	+0.00
August	5	10	50	+16.25	0	5	-	-5.00	0	0	-	+0.00
September	1	5	20	-3.47	0	3	-	-3.00	0	0	-	+0.00
October	10	45	22	-1.37	1	16	6	-9.00	0	5	-	-5.00
November	9	51	18	-17.47	4	25	16	-4.67	1	9	11	-6.63
December	7	49	14	-1.87	4	24	17	-0.50	0	6	-	-6.00
January 2017	9	37	24	+7.93	1	20	5	-17.50	0	3	-	-3.00
February	10	30	33	-2.26	3	22	14	-13.59	0	4	-	-4.00
March	10	43	23	-8.97	4	22	18	-1.67	1	7	14	-3.75
April	11	33	33	+26.88	2	21	10	-14.50	1	4	25	-1.38

By horse

	Wins-Runs	%	£1 level stakes	Win prize	Total prize
Defi Du Seuil	7-7	100	+6.03	£205,205.58	£205,205.58
Menorah	1-5	20	-1.75	£28,609.00	£62,077.00
Garde La Victoire	2-5	40	+1.25	£34,408.00	£58,464.25
Village Vic	0-5	-	-5.00	£0.00	£57,714.00
Royal Regatta	1-5	20	+6.00	£39,865.00	£57,644.00
Kruzhlinin	1-6	17	+4.00	£45,560.00	£51,831.80
Rock The Kasbah	2-7	29	+3.00	£25,992.00	£45,229.40
Sternrubin	1-3	33	+10.00	£34,170.00	£36,850.00
Verni	2-4	50	+1.50	£15,668.10	£31,496.10
Three Faces West	2-3	67	+5.50	£30,789.30	£30,789.30
Golden Doyen	2-7	29	+12.00	£26,275.20	£30,085.00
Ink Master	2-5	40	+1.13	£28,198.40	£29,575.20
No Comment	3-7	43	-0.50	£12,996.00	£29,362.40

Philip Hobbs

All runners

	Wins-Runs	%	Win prize	Total prize	£1 level stakes
Hurdle	75-344	22	£663,230.90	£880,757.15	-11.86
Chase	32-204	16	£331,812.08	£605,389.63	-46.18
Bumper	3-41	7	£5,458.32	£11,331.60	-32.75
TOTAL	110-589	19	£1,000,501.30	£1,497,478.38	-90.78

By course - last four seasons

	Hurdles				Chases				Bumpers			
	W	R	%	£1 stake	W	R	%	£1 stake	W	R	%	£1 stake
Aintree	5	45	11	-25.80	5	40	13	+13.50	0	5	-	-5.00
Ascot	7	34	21	+2.38	5	46	11	-14.77	2	5	40	+8.00
Ayr	1	4	25	+7.00	0	6	-	-6.00	0	0	-	+0.00
Bangor-On-Dee	3	14	21	-4.59	0	5	-	-5.00	0	2	-	-2.00
Carlisle	0	2	-	-2.00	1	2	50	-0.17	0	0	-	+0.00
Cartmel	0	0	-	+0.00	1	4	25	-0.50	0	0	-	+0.00
Catterick	1	2	50	-0.33	1	2	50	-0.75	0	1	-	-1.00
Cheltenham	13	92	14	+14.87	18	122	15	-17.00	2	13	15	-5.13
Chepstow	13	56	23	-10.24	11	51	22	+1.58	2	18	11	-10.25
Doncaster	2	14	14	-9.90	2	11	18	-2.25	0	0	-	+0.00
Exeter	22	96	23	-16.74	13	74	18	-10.09	4	13	31	-3.62
Fakenham	0	0	-	+0.00	1	2	50	-0.27	0	1	-	-1.00
Ffos Las	4	15	27	-6.92	2	10	20	+5.00	1	5	20	-2.50
Fontwell	8	33	24	-10.23	4	14	29	-2.43	0	4	-	-4.00
Haydock	5	30	17	+4.50	3	24	13	-10.75	0	4	-	-4.00
Hereford	2	12	17	-8.99	0	1	-	-1.00	0	0	-	+0.00
Hexham	1	1	100	+0.44	0	1	-	-1.00	0	0	-	+0.00
Huntingdon	4	24	17	-7.75	1	10	10	-2.50	3	7	43	+1.04
Kelso	1	2	50	-0.33	0	2	-	-2.00	0	0	-	+0.00
Kempton	5	46	11	-35.66	4	32	13	-9.63	0	7	-	-7.00
Leicester	3	10	30	+3.25	3	8	38	+0.25	0	0	-	+0.00
Lingfield	0	1	-	-1.00	0	1	-	-1.00	0	0	-	+0.00
Ludlow	13	45	29	-2.72	9	39	23	-4.67	1	8	13	+0.50
Market Rasen	5	19	26	+0.48	1	16	6	-13.25	2	6	33	-1.13
Musselburgh	0	2	-	-2.00	2	3	67	+1.53	0	0	-	+0.00
Newbury	9	51	18	+34.80	12	53	23	+25.67	0	7	-	-7.00
Newcastle	0	1	-	-1.00	0	2	-	-2.00	0	1	-	-1.00
Newton Abbot	19	81	23	+10.85	6	47	13	-0.45	2	7	29	-1.50
Perth	5	8	63	+7.01	2	9	22	-3.13	0	0	-	+0.00
Plumpton	4	13	31	-5.50	0	4	-	-4.00	0	0	-	+0.00
Sandown	7	25	28	+19.85	6	40	15	-12.25	1	5	20	-2.50
Sedgefield	0	2	-	-2.00	0	1	-	-1.00	0	0	-	+0.00
Southwell	3	11	27	-2.97	1	5	20	+0.50	1	5	20	-2.63
Stratford	4	20	20	+8.55	15	41	37	+36.43	0	4	-	-4.00
Taunton	12	69	17	-28.31	6	23	26	-1.88	3	14	21	-2.38
Towcester	3	7	43	+5.75	0	1	-	-1.00	0	1	-	-1.00
Uttoxeter	11	51	22	+4.44	3	35	9	-23.65	3	7	43	+17.38
Warwick	10	38	26	+5.35	6	28	21	-10.89	6	20	30	+0.15
Wetherby	5	13	38	-4.44	3	16	19	-1.42	0	0	-	+0.00
Wincanton	11	69	16	-4.00	7	47	15	-18.13	3	17	18	-5.75
Worcester	11	46	24	-11.59	8	31	26	+7.95	1	6	17	+0.00

By race type

	Hurdles				Chases			
	W	R	%	£1 stake	W	R	%	£1 stake
Handicap	41	193	21	+25.16	28	155	18	+13.00
Novice	17	106	16	-30.61	11	44	25	-12.14
Maiden	6	46	13	+1.88	0	0	-	+0.00

By jockey

	Hurdles				Chases				Bumpers			
	W	R	%	£1 stake	W	R	%	£1 stake	W	R	%	£1 stake
Noel Fehily	26	117	22	-22.51	16	63	25	+10.98	3	14	21	+3.00
Tom Scudamore	5	35	14	-14.14	4	14	29	-4.63	3	7	43	+5.83
Sean Corby	10	50	20	+39.40	0	2	-	-2.00	0	4	-	-4.00
Denis O'Regan	3	16	19	+8.50	2	12	17	-1.00	1	2	50	+13.00
Wayne Hutchinson	3	17	18	-2.13	2	9	22	+4.25	0	2	-	-2.00
Mr James King	3	25	12	-19.70	1	8	13	-2.50	1	4	25	+0.50
Richard Johnson	2	3	67	+6.00	2	4	50	+4.00	0	0	-	+0.00
David Noonan	1	9	11	-5.25	2	13	15	+7.00	0	0	-	+0.00
James Best	1	10	10	+24.00	2	16	13	+13.00	0	1	-	-1.00
Mark Quinlan	1	2	50	-0.27	1	1	100	+1.38	0	0	-	+0.00

By month

	Hurdles				Chases				Bumpers			
	W	R	%	£1 stake	W	R	%	£1 stake	W	R	%	£1 stake
May 2016	6	27	22	+13.88	4	12	33	+24.00	0	0	-	+0.00
June	2	14	14	-7.63	2	10	20	-4.75	0	1	-	-1.00
July	7	26	27	+1.95	0	13	-	-13.00	1	2	50	+13.00
August	5	15	33	+16.13	1	14	7	-12.82	0	1	-	-1.00
September	5	20	25	-3.22	2	10	20	-4.20	0	3	-	-3.00
October	5	30	17	-14.10	7	25	28	+1.17	0	2	-	-2.00
November	8	38	21	+19.68	4	20	20	+1.33	2	5	40	+2.75
December	6	31	19	-2.72	2	21	10	-7.50	0	9	-	-9.00
January 2017	6	32	19	+26.00	6	11	55	+17.13	0	2	-	-2.00
February	6	30	20	-5.15	2	12	17	+17.00	2	3	67	+6.83
March	5	43	12	-18.00	0	14	-	-14.00	1	3	33	+0.00
April	4	32	13	-25.41	4	13	31	-0.38	2	5	40	+8.75

By horse

	Wins-Runs	%	£1 level stakes	Win prize	Total prize
Pilgrims Bay	2-6	33	+30.00	£64,485.04	£69,064.24
Carole's Destrier	0-2	-	-2.00	£0.00	£42,740.00
Shantou Village	3-4	75	+2.85	£35,939.90	£35,939.90
Kalondra	4-11	36	+10.07	£29,025.88	£34,724.48
Indian Stream	2-6	33	+1.75	£23,458.85	£33,490.85
Fox Norton	1-1	100	+2.50	£31,280.00	£31,280.00
Bishops Court	4-9	44	+2.50	£23,169.24	£25,102.44
Doing Fine	1-5	20	-1.00	£7,507.20	£24,722.20
Peter The Mayo Man	3-5	60	+1.17	£16,050.06	£23,648.46
Hygrove Percy	3-7	43	+4.29	£15,752.10	£20,235.90
Impulsive Star	3-5	60	+2.79	£18,071.60	£19,670.60
Rossetti	3-7	43	+4.88	£16,569.90	£19,100.70
Pinkie Brown	2-6	33	-1.67	£14,698.00	£17,012.40

Neil Mulholland

All runners

	Wins-Runs	%	Win prize	Total prize	£1 level stakes
Hurdle	65-339	19	£287,832.76	£400,600.74	+0.41
Chase	34-175	19	£294,561.37	£422,133.06	+3.98
Bumper	8-36	22	£16,115.04	£20,664.51	+13.33
TOTAL	107-550	19	£598,509.17	£843,398.31	+17.73

By course - last four seasons

	Hurdles				Chases				Bumpers			
	W	R	%	£1 stake	W	R	%	£1 stake	W	R	%	£1 stake
Aintree	0	5	-	-5.00	1	10	10	+5.00	0	3	-	-3.00
Ascot	1	9	11	-1.00	2	7	29	-0.75	0	1	-	-1.00
Ayr	0	2	-	-2.00	0	1	-	-1.00	0	0	-	+0.00
Bangor-On-Dee	3	20	15	-9.10	0	6	-	-6.00	0	1	-	-1.00
Carlisle	1	4	25	-2.75	0	4	-	-4.00	0	3	-	-3.00
Cartmel	1	4	25	-1.38	1	5	20	+0.50	0	0	-	+0.00
Catterick	1	3	33	-1.33	0	2	-	-2.00	0	0	-	+0.00
Cheltenham	1	31	3	-25.50	7	32	22	+6.89	0	1	-	-1.00
Chepstow	5	39	13	-14.80	1	24	4	-15.00	1	4	25	+0.00
Doncaster	2	17	12	-6.75	1	7	14	-4.00	0	1	-	-1.00
Exeter	3	43	7	-33.25	2	9	22	-1.00	0	0	-	+0.00
Fakenham	12	29	41	+17.49	2	13	15	-9.23	0	1	-	-1.00
Ffos Las	4	31	13	+0.38	1	25	4	-12.00	2	6	33	+22.00
Fontwell	16	53	30	+37.88	10	39	26	-7.45	2	11	18	-7.47
Haydock	0	2	-	-2.00	0	3	-	-3.00	0	0	-	+0.00
Hereford	0	7	-	-7.00	0	2	-	-2.00	2	4	50	+5.83
Huntingdon	3	14	21	-1.51	4	14	29	-1.80	0	3	-	-3.00
Kelso	0	1	-	-1.00	0	1	-	-1.00	0	0	-	+0.00
Kempton	1	22	5	-7.00	2	9	22	+20.00	0	1	-	-1.00
Kempton (AW)	0	0	-	+0.00	0	0	-	+0.00	0	4	-	-4.00
Leicester	1	7	14	+6.00	0	5	-	-5.00	0	0	-	+0.00
Lingfield	2	12	17	+27.00	1	11	9	-1.00	0	0	-	+0.00
Lingfield (AW)	0	0	-	+0.00	0	0	-	+0.00	1	4	25	-0.75
Ludlow	3	16	19	-5.63	1	8	13	+0.00	0	1	-	-1.00
Market Rasen	3	13	23	-4.25	4	13	31	+1.75	1	2	50	-0.09
Musselburgh	1	4	25	+0.00	0	1	-	-1.00	0	0	-	+0.00
Newbury	4	17	24	+7.13	0	12	-	-12.00	0	1	-	-1.00
Newcastle	0	2	-	-2.00	1	2	50	+0.75	1	1	100	+3.50
Newton Abbot	6	49	12	-18.68	5	33	15	-4.00	0	5	-	-5.00
Perth	0	2	-	-2.00	0	2	-	-2.00	0	0	-	+0.00
Plumpton	4	34	12	-5.79	3	18	17	-4.25	0	3	-	-3.00
Sandown	1	6	17	-4.00	4	13	31	+16.00	0	0	-	+0.00
Sedgefield	7	15	47	+11.30	6	11	55	+4.89	1	2	50	+1.00
Southwell	4	34	12	-17.20	4	21	19	-8.75	1	6	17	+35.00
Stratford	7	33	21	+17.63	2	13	15	-8.95	1	4	25	+11.00
Taunton	5	50	10	-21.50	1	14	7	-10.00	0	8	-	-8.00
Towcester	4	10	40	+6.35	3	8	38	-0.67	1	3	33	-0.13
Uttoxeter	8	52	15	-19.09	2	21	10	-5.00	0	2	-	-2.00
Warwick	2	16	13	-6.56	4	16	25	-2.17	1	2	50	+2.50
Wetherby	4	16	25	+1.83	4	10	40	+1.49	1	3	33	-1.00
Wincanton	6	76	8	-16.40	4	35	11	-18.50	1	11	9	-8.25
Worcester	14	58	24	+11.15	9	40	23	+7.03	0	10	-	-10.00

By race type

	Hurdles				Chases			
	W	R	%	£1 stake	W	R	%	£1 stake
Handicap	23	131	18	-22.88	11	73	15	+15.88
Novice	28	101	28	-8.67	6	30	20	-7.30
Maiden	14	52	27	-14.80	0	0	-	+0.00

By jockey

	Hurdles				Chases				Bumpers			
	W	R	%	£1 stake	W	R	%	£1 stake	W	R	%	£1 stake
W Hutchinson	45	191	24	-51.97	10	55	18	+13.07	5	38	13	-16.18
Barry Geraghty	8	14	57	+8.37	1	4	25	-2.17	0	0	-	+0.00
Daryl Jacob	8	20	40	+5.25	0	0	-	+0.00	0	0	-	+0.00
Tom Cannon	7	46	15	-8.65	1	5	20	-2.63	0	8	-	-8.00
W Featherstone	4	14	29	+6.94	0	4	-	-4.00	1	1	100	+6.00
Tom Bellamy	2	16	13	-6.25	3	17	18	+6.75	0	2	-	-2.00
Kevin Dowling	3	14	21	+0.00	0	0	-	+0.00	0	0	-	+0.00
Denis O'Regan	2	4	50	+0.83	0	0	-	+0.00	0	0	-	+0.00
Davy Russell	1	1	100	+2.25	0	0	-	+0.00	0	0	-	+0.00
Richard Johnson	1	5	20	-3.80	0	1	-	-1.00	0	0	-	+0.00

By month

	Hurdles				Chases				Bumpers			
	W	R	%	£1 stake	W	R	%	£1 stake	W	R	%	£1 stake
May 2016	9	25	36	+3.45	3	11	27	+5.00	1	2	50	+0.75
June	2	5	40	+6.50	1	6	17	-3.63	0	1	-	-1.00
July	3	12	25	-3.25	1	5	20	-0.50	1	1	100	+2.00
August	2	5	40	-0.25	1	3	33	-1.39	0	2	-	-2.00
September	1	5	20	+1.00	0	1	-	-1.00	1	1	100	+6.00
October	7	28	25	-4.25	1	7	14	-3.00	0	4	-	-4.00
November	16	54	30	-13.77	1	13	8	-11.17	2	12	17	-2.93
December	15	52	29	+10.78	1	14	7	-9.00	1	8	13	-1.00
January 2017	10	31	32	+13.54	1	11	9	+0.00	1	4	25	+4.00
February	7	42	17	-16.95	3	9	33	+3.71	0	6	-	-6.00
March	5	46	11	-36.83	0	8	-	-8.00	0	6	-	-6.00
April	4	29	14	-16.00	2	9	22	+28.00	0	6	-	-6.00

By horse

	Wins-Runs	%	£1 level stakes	Win prize	Total prize
Yanworth	4-5	80	+3.70	£232,321.25	£232,321.25
Messire Des Obeaux	3-6	50	+4.08	£54,136.21	£84,509.71
Sceau Royal	2-6	33	+1.17	£57,749.20	£76,208.40
Ziga Boy	1-5	20	+6.00	£45,560.00	£48,470.60
Who Dares Wins	1-6	17	-1.00	£25,627.50	£40,767.50
Willoughby Hedge	2-5	40	+30.00	£40,334.00	£40,508.00
Dusky Legend	2-6	33	-2.42	£15,733.60	£38,072.70
Label Des Obeaux	3-7	43	+7.71	£30,399.90	£36,659.70
The Tourard Man	5-10	50	+7.99	£28,904.34	£35,014.34
Master Blueyes	2-6	33	+2.90	£22,283.40	£30,741.40
The Unit	3-7	43	+0.35	£17,858.40	£30,507.20
Smad Place	0-5	-	-5.00	£0.00	£30,408.00
Elgin	2-6	33	+3.75	£15,809.40	£29,585.40

Alan King

All runners

	Wins-Runs	%	Win prize	Total prize	£1 level stakes
Hurdle	81-335	24	£744,215.46	£1,062,341.25	-57.04
Chase	15-100	15	£169,147.84	£269,362.20	-3.97
Bumper	7-53	13	£20,763.02	£38,078.76	-16.18
TOTAL	103-488	21	£934,126.32	£1,369,782.21	-77.18

By course - last four seasons

	Hurdles				Chases				Bumpers			
	W	R	%	£1 stake	W	R	%	£1 stake	W	R	%	£1 stake
Aintree	3	35	9	-24.38	2	19	11	-10.75	1	11	9	+15.00
Ascot	6	46	13	-13.07	2	12	17	-2.67	1	6	17	-3.13
Ayr	1	13	8	-9.25	1	9	11	+2.00	1	1	100	+3.00
Bangor-On-Dee	8	26	31	-6.71	4	13	31	+22.15	3	9	33	+5.75
Catterick	3	4	75	+1.90	1	1	100	+0.83	0	0	-	+0.00
Cheltenham	9	90	10	-35.67	7	54	13	+4.63	1	12	8	-4.50
Chepstow	6	37	16	-17.23	2	9	22	+1.50	0	4	-	-4.00
Doncaster	15	50	30	+38.00	6	28	21	+10.38	1	7	14	-4.50
Exeter	7	45	16	-14.60	8	25	32	+5.74	1	8	13	-1.00
Fakenham	1	5	20	-3.00	0	1	-	-1.00	0	1	-	-1.00
Ffos Las	1	7	14	-4.50	1	4	25	-0.75	0	3	-	-3.00
Fontwell	9	33	27	-3.10	1	9	11	-6.38	1	7	14	-4.63
Haydock	1	23	4	-20.63	1	11	9	+15.00	2	4	50	+10.44
Hereford	1	2	50	+0.10	0	1	-	-1.00	0	1	-	-1.00
Huntingdon	11	56	20	-23.53	6	17	35	+9.06	4	19	21	-1.50
Kempton	16	84	19	-17.25	3	40	8	-32.25	3	15	20	+3.67
Kempton (AW)	0	0	-	+0.00	0	0	-	+0.00	0	3	-	-3.00
Leicester	2	11	18	+1.75	1	11	9	-7.25	0	0	-	+0.00
Lingfield	0	3	-	-3.00	1	3	33	+1.50	0	0	-	+0.00
Lingfield (AW)	0	0	-	+0.00	0	0	-	+0.00	1	11	9	-9.43
Ludlow	8	37	22	+2.88	2	9	22	-3.92	0	0	-	+0.00
Market Rasen	4	36	11	-12.15	1	20	5	-17.50	0	8	-	-8.00
Musselburgh	0	1	-	-1.00	0	0	-	+0.00	0	0	-	+0.00
Newbury	8	85	9	-39.73	5	31	16	-10.25	5	24	21	+1.85
Newcastle	1	3	33	+0.25	0	0	-	+0.00	0	0	-	+0.00
Newton Abbot	4	11	36	+6.80	2	8	25	+7.25	0	2	-	-2.00
Plumpton	9	26	35	-6.28	4	9	44	+2.58	0	2	-	-2.00
Sandown	8	32	25	-0.29	2	17	12	+5.00	0	4	-	-4.00
Sedgefield	1	2	50	+0.00	0	0	-	+0.00	0	0	-	+0.00
Southwell	5	27	19	-16.19	1	7	14	-5.39	0	7	-	-7.00
Stratford	9	30	30	+14.82	2	8	25	-1.38	1	5	20	+2.00
Taunton	2	32	6	-26.90	1	6	17	-1.00	1	6	17	-4.27
Towcester	5	19	26	+1.63	0	4	-	-4.00	4	8	50	+6.08
Uttoxeter	7	40	18	-17.68	3	16	19	-4.25	2	8	25	-2.00
Warwick	17	65	26	-17.98	5	20	25	-4.65	1	15	7	-13.20
Wetherby	4	25	16	-14.96	2	7	29	+1.25	0	3	-	-3.00
Wincanton	6	45	13	-29.11	3	15	20	+5.00	2	6	33	+10.00
Worcester	5	19	26	+4.75	1	10	10	-7.63	1	4	25	-1.50

Trainer interviews start on page 6

By race type

	Hurdles				Chases			
	W	R	%	£1 stake	W	R	%	£1 stake
Handicap	28	205	14	-30.44	33	191	17	-15.08
Novice	18	82	22	-32.21	10	59	17	-12.13
Maiden	6	33	18	-1.94	0	0	-	+0.00

By jockey

	Hurdles				Chases				Bumpers			
	W	R	%	£1 stake	W	R	%	£1 stake	W	R	%	£1 stake
S Twiston-Davies	20	87	23	+22.28	8	52	15	-13.93	1	17	6	-12.50
Jamie Bargary	12	95	13	-34.26	12	59	20	+9.34	1	9	11	-5.75
Ryan Hatch	10	50	20	+0.21	4	32	13	-17.38	0	5	-	-5.00
Daryl Jacob	5	10	50	+3.85	7	26	27	-0.84	0	0	-	+0.00
Tom Humphries	5	23	22	-9.80	0	3	-	-3.00	0	1	-	-1.00
Mr Z Baker	0	13	-	-13.00	3	14	21	+1.10	0	3	-	-3.00
W Twiston-Davies	1	21	5	-15.50	2	21	10	-7.00	0	4	-	-4.00
Dave Crosse	0	0	-	+0.00	1	3	33	+7.00	0	0	-	+0.00
Richard Johnson	1	4	25	-1.38	0	0	-	+0.00	0	0	-	+0.00
Noel Fehily	0	1	-	-1.00	1	5	20	+1.00	0	0	-	+0.00

By month

	Hurdles				Chases				Bumpers			
	W	R	%	£1 stake	W	R	%	£1 stake	W	R	%	£1 stake
May 2016	2	15	13	+2.50	0	7	-	-7.00	0	3	-	-3.00
June	3	11	27	+4.13	0	5	-	-5.00	0	3	-	-3.00
July	1	12	8	-8.00	1	3	33	-1.09	0	0	-	+0.00
August	4	9	44	+7.46	1	2	50	+2.50	0	0	-	+0.00
September	5	18	28	-4.99	3	10	30	+3.07	0	2	-	-2.00
October	10	33	30	+19.81	9	23	39	+6.18	1	6	17	-2.75
November	9	47	19	-21.82	6	29	21	-5.57	0	5	-	-5.00
December	8	47	17	-11.78	6	34	18	+5.21	0	3	-	-3.00
January 2017	9	35	26	+5.23	5	23	22	+12.50	0	3	-	-3.00
February	2	30	7	-17.00	2	28	7	-13.50	0	5	-	-5.00
March	1	29	3	+0.00	0	23	-	-23.00	1	7	14	-2.50
April	1	33	3	-30.13	4	32	13	-9.00	0	6	-	-6.00

By horse

	Wins-Runs	%	£1 level stakes	Win prize	Total prize
The New One	2-6	33	-0.88	£117,250.00	£173,105.00
Ballyandy	1-5	20	-1.00	£88,272.50	£105,510.00
Flying Angel	3-7	43	+5.07	£86,521.30	£88,621.88
Blaklion	0-5	-	-5.00	£0.00	£83,697.50
Cogry	1-10	10	-4.50	£12,512.00	£66,126.00
Wholestone	4-6	67	+5.10	£43,999.90	£63,785.90
Bristol De Mai	1-6	17	-1.00	£28,475.00	£60,942.75
Foxtail Hill	3-9	33	+15.00	£45,513.20	£56,961.40
Ballybolley	3-8	38	+0.80	£41,462.20	£52,106.20
Ballyoptic	1-7	14	-1.50	£28,475.00	£46,389.25
Double Ross	1-3	33	+1.00	£18,768.00	£40,861.00
Calett Mad	2-7	29	-0.75	£18,214.50	£37,564.50
Templehills	4-10	40	+12.98	£33,583.44	£34,155.84

Nigel Twiston-Davies

All runners

	Wins-Runs	%	Win prize	Total prize	£1 level stakes
Hurdle	55-320	17	£523,584.78	£781,842.13	-55.59
Chase	38-222	17	£422,995.94	£786,938.24	-30.70
Bumper	2-43	5	£3,898.80	£13,875.64	-35.25
TOTAL	95-585	16	£950,479.52	£1,582,656.01	-121.54

By course - last four seasons

	Hurdles				Chases				Bumpers			
	W	R	%	£1 stake	W	R	%	£1 stake	W	R	%	£1 stake
Aintree	5	37	14	-13.56	4	40	10	-13.00	1	6	17	+9.00
Ascot	1	20	5	-13.50	0	15	-	-15.00	0	1	-	-1.00
Ayr	0	2	-	-2.00	0	9	-	-9.00	0	0	-	+0.00
Bangor-On-Dee	4	21	19	+5.96	5	24	21	-6.19	0	7	-	-7.00
Carlisle	1	4	25	-1.20	1	8	13	-3.50	0	0	-	+0.00
Cartmel	1	10	10	-4.00	1	8	13	-5.25	0	0	-	+0.00
Cheltenham	9	79	11	-44.28	10	114	9	-52.79	2	11	18	+4.00
Chepstow	8	46	17	-6.54	7	40	18	+13.83	1	9	11	-2.50
Doncaster	1	20	5	-14.00	1	14	7	-10.25	0	2	-	-2.00
Exeter	1	21	5	-12.00	2	21	10	+1.00	0	0	-	+0.00
Fakenham	1	2	50	+6.00	1	8	13	+0.00	0	0	-	+0.00
Ffos Las	14	72	19	-5.28	13	56	23	+20.74	3	14	21	-2.75
Fontwell	0	3	-	-3.00	0	3	-	-3.00	0	1	-	-1.00
Haydock	7	30	23	+1.37	6	44	14	-9.42	1	2	50	+0.25
Hereford	1	6	17	-1.00	3	8	38	+2.25	0	2	-	-2.00
Huntingdon	4	34	12	-16.67	2	23	9	-17.95	0	7	-	-7.00
Kelso	1	3	33	-1.17	2	8	25	+0.25	0	0	-	+0.00
Kempton	5	24	21	-11.64	4	26	15	-4.50	0	4	-	-4.00
Leicester	6	25	24	+3.13	9	36	25	+18.33	0	0	-	+0.00
Lingfield	4	12	33	+7.58	2	9	22	+17.00	0	0	-	+0.00
Ludlow	8	66	12	-44.42	6	51	12	-15.33	1	5	20	-3.09
Market Rasen	5	21	24	+7.43	0	7	-	-7.00	0	1	-	-1.00
Newbury	6	35	17	+36.03	1	42	2	-35.00	1	8	13	-5.63
Newcastle	0	2	-	-2.00	1	8	13	-4.25	0	0	-	+0.00
Newton Abbot	5	18	28	-4.58	4	16	25	+2.75	0	2	-	-2.00
Perth	7	42	17	-18.24	6	28	21	-6.16	2	7	29	+9.00
Plumpton	0	6	-	-6.00	1	1	100	+5.50	0	1	-	-1.00
Sandown	4	23	17	+27.75	1	19	5	-17.09	0	0	-	+0.00
Sedgefield	1	1	100	+1.20	0	2	-	-2.00	0	0	-	+0.00
Southwell	3	30	10	-19.50	4	20	20	-3.91	3	9	33	+2.00
Stratford	7	40	18	-0.88	2	38	5	-27.63	0	6	-	-6.00
Taunton	2	23	9	-7.50	2	11	18	+1.00	0	1	-	-1.00
Towcester	3	35	9	-23.75	3	22	14	+0.38	3	11	27	+9.25
Uttoxeter	12	66	18	-11.54	10	50	20	+24.90	1	12	8	-9.90
Warwick	6	54	11	-36.98	10	51	20	-1.77	2	16	13	-7.00
Wetherby	4	16	25	-3.05	3	19	16	-8.75	0	1	-	-1.00
Wincanton	1	15	7	-8.50	4	15	27	+20.73	0	2	-	-2.00
Worcester	7	47	15	-7.88	7	31	23	+13.25	3	10	30	+10.91

By race type

	Hurdles				Chases			
	W	R	%	£1 stake	W	R	%	£1 stake
Handicap	32	226	14	-21.79	14	161	9	-84.50
Novice	30	127	24	+34.51	9	54	17	-16.50
Maiden	5	42	12	-18.17	0	0	-	+0.00

By jockey

	Hurdles				Chases				Bumpers			
	W	R	%	£1 stake	W	R	%	£1 stake	W	R	%	£1 stake
Will Kennedy	41	193	21	+31.17	12	123	10	-64.25	0	15	-	-15.00
James Cowley	12	68	18	+0.25	0	16	-	-16.00	0	3	-	-3.00
Harry Stock	4	21	19	+1.63	0	0	-	+0.00	0	1	-	-1.00
Mr T Gillard	2	13	15	+5.50	0	0	-	+0.00	0	1	-	-1.00
W Hutchinson	2	7	29	+5.00	0	7	-	-7.00	0	0	-	+0.00
Brian Hughes	2	12	17	-3.25	0	6	-	-6.00	0	0	-	+0.00
Daryl Jacob	0	0	-	+0.00	1	1	100	+3.50	0	0	-	+0.00
Miss G Andrews	0	0	-	+0.00	1	1	100	+9.00	0	0	-	+0.00
Henry Brooke	0	2	-	-2.00	1	4	25	+2.00	0	0	-	+0.00
Miss A McCain	1	12	8	-8.75	0	0	-	+0.00	0	0	-	+0.00

By month

	Hurdles				Chases				Bumpers			
	W	R	%	£1 stake	W	R	%	£1 stake	W	R	%	£1 stake
May 2016	6	30	20	-2.00	3	20	15	-6.25	0	2	-	-2.00
June	2	21	10	+1.00	1	7	14	-4.25	0	1	-	-1.00
July	4	17	24	+3.25	1	10	10	-6.75	0	1	-	-1.00
August	4	19	21	+12.88	2	8	25	+9.00	0	0	-	+0.00
September	3	19	16	-2.25	0	9	-	-9.00	0	1	-	-1.00
October	7	24	29	+22.00	0	14	-	-14.00	0	1	-	-1.00
November	5	36	14	-1.50	0	16	-	-16.00	0	5	-	-5.00
December	7	42	17	+0.88	0	17	-	-17.00	0	3	-	-3.00
January 2017	5	48	10	-20.67	3	21	14	+1.50	0	3	-	-3.00
February	7	37	19	-12.08	1	15	7	-12.25	0	5	-	-5.00
March	9	41	22	-4.95	1	12	8	-9.63	0	2	-	-2.00
April	5	40	13	-9.00	3	16	19	-1.13	0	3	-	-3.00

By horse

	Wins-Runs	%	£1 level stakes	Win prize	Total prize
Desert Cry	3-10	30	+7.08	£18,844.20	£25,749.60
Lastbutnotleast	3-3	100	+5.63	£25,408.50	£25,408.50
Venue	2-7	29	+7.00	£13,547.25	£19,173.25
Nefyn Bay	2-10	20	-2.25	£9,422.10	£19,027.50
Raise A Spark	3-9	33	+2.63	£11,046.60	£17,047.78
Clondaw Kaempfer	1-5	20	+2.50	£12,996.00	£16,656.18
Bourne	3-12	25	+3.38	£8,447.40	£15,613.19
Prince Khurram	1-13	8	-10.25	£4,548.60	£15,376.50
Thyne For Gold	3-12	25	+5.50	£10,752.12	£15,238.92
Witness In Court	1-11	9	-1.00	£6,498.00	£14,458.18
Ubaltique	1-7	14	-0.50	£9,747.00	£14,379.00
Move To The Groove	3-5	60	+7.38	£13,818.80	£13,818.80
Testify	2-5	40	+10.00	£11,046.60	£13,795.35

Donald McCain

All runners

	Wins-Runs	%	Win prize	Total prize	£1 level stakes
Hurdle	65-378	17	£273,686.15	£405,596.40	-10.45
Chase	15-165	9	£77,624.34	£169,172.42	-85.75
Bumper	0-27	-	£0.00	£2,972.73	-27.00
TOTAL	80-570	14	£351,310.49	£577,741.55	-123.20

By course - last four seasons

	Hurdles				Chases				Bumpers			
	W	R	%	£1 stake	W	R	%	£1 stake	W	R	%	£1 stake
Aintree	4	56	7	-35.79	1	47	2	-37.00	0	6	-	-6.00
Ascot	0	4	-	-4.00	0	4	-	-4.00	0	0	-	+0.00
Ayr	7	37	19	-14.16	3	31	10	-22.13	2	9	22	-1.10
Bangor-On-Dee	34	163	21	+34.41	10	65	15	-22.83	3	31	10	-21.50
Carlisle	18	98	18	-14.74	10	52	19	-11.50	4	13	31	-6.28
Cartmel	15	63	24	+1.11	4	30	13	-18.60	0	0	-	+0.00
Catterick	23	95	24	-6.68	10	39	26	+8.57	1	13	8	-8.50
Cheltenham	1	16	6	-1.00	1	19	5	-4.00	0	0	-	+0.00
Chepstow	1	8	13	-3.00	0	6	-	-6.00	0	1	-	-1.00
Doncaster	3	39	8	-25.60	1	19	5	-7.00	0	2	-	-2.00
Exeter	0	3	-	-3.00	1	4	25	+0.50	0	0	-	+0.00
Fakenham	1	5	20	+0.50	0	4	-	-4.00	0	0	-	+0.00
Ffos Las	0	0	-	+0.00	0	0	-	+0.00	0	1	-	-1.00
Fontwell	0	1	-	-1.00	1	3	33	+2.50	0	1	-	-1.00
Haydock	3	46	7	-35.25	5	25	20	+7.50	2	6	33	+0.06
Hereford	0	3	-	-3.00	0	3	-	-3.00	0	1	-	-1.00
Hexham	12	67	18	-28.54	0	20	-	-20.00	2	8	25	-2.00
Huntingdon	2	17	12	-4.50	0	5	-	-5.00	0	2	-	-2.00
Kelso	19	82	23	+5.55	9	47	19	-0.42	1	7	14	+0.00
Kempton	1	3	33	-1.43	0	5	-	-5.00	0	0	-	+0.00
Kempton (AW)	0	0	-	+0.00	0	0	-	+0.00	0	5	-	-5.00
Leicester	1	10	10	-3.50	1	8	13	-3.50	0	0	-	+0.00
Ludlow	1	37	3	-33.00	2	18	11	+5.00	0	4	-	-4.00
Market Rasen	4	54	7	-6.22	3	29	10	-7.00	0	7	-	-7.00
Musselburgh	15	71	21	+6.60	5	37	14	+7.75	4	6	67	+11.60
Newbury	0	7	-	-7.00	0	7	-	-7.00	0	1	-	-1.00
Newcastle	6	40	15	+0.48	4	25	16	-11.96	0	9	-	-9.00
Newton Abbot	0	7	-	-7.00	0	1	-	-1.00	0	0	-	+0.00
Perth	9	59	15	-24.47	6	28	21	+8.00	1	8	13	-5.63
Plumpton	0	1	-	-1.00	1	2	50	+0.00	0	0	-	+0.00
Sandown	1	9	11	+6.00	0	8	-	-8.00	0	0	-	+0.00
Sedgefield	28	142	20	-19.60	13	63	21	-9.38	6	21	29	-0.56
Southwell	0	19	-	-19.00	1	11	9	-7.50	0	0	-	+0.00
Southwell (AW)	0	0	-	+0.00	0	0	-	+0.00	1	2	50	+2.50
Stratford	2	23	9	-2.00	1	14	7	-4.00	1	3	33	+1.00
Taunton	1	5	20	-3.50	0	3	-	-3.00	0	0	-	+0.00
Towcester	1	16	6	-7.00	1	7	14	-0.50	0	2	-	-2.00
Uttoxeter	5	85	6	-39.50	2	31	6	-23.75	1	15	7	-2.00
Warwick	0	9	-	-9.00	2	9	22	-2.00	0	0	-	+0.00
Wetherby	9	74	12	-39.42	4	34	12	-3.00	0	5	-	-5.00
Wincanton	0	0	-	+0.00	2	2	100	+7.00	0	0	-	+0.00
Worcester	9	61	15	-11.83	5	31	16	-3.27	0	9	-	-9.00

By race type

	Hurdles				Chases			
	W	R	%	£1 stake	W	R	%	£1 stake
Handicap	20	169	12	-25.76	37	297	12	-97.80
Novice	7	107	7	-61.50	13	85	15	-25.55
Maiden	6	67	9	-37.75	0	0	-	+0.00

By jockey

	Hurdles				Chases				Bumpers			
	W	R	%	£1 stake	W	R	%	£1 stake	W	R	%	£1 stake
Aidan Coleman	22	148	15	-1.72	25	149	17	-37.80	2	17	12	+9.00
Jack Savage	3	11	27	+4.83	3	16	19	-1.75	0	0	-	+0.00
Killian Moore	2	37	5	-27.13	3	29	10	-14.75	0	2	-	-2.00
Noel Fehily	1	9	11	-5.50	3	10	30	+2.00	0	0	-	+0.00
Mr J J O'Neill	0	15	-	-15.00	1	12	8	-7.00	2	4	50	+1.75
Richard Johnson	1	30	3	-27.00	2	15	13	+3.00	0	1	-	-1.00
Barry Geraghty	0	10	-	-10.00	2	24	8	+13.50	0	0	-	+0.00
Richie McLernon	2	46	4	-13.50	0	44	-	-44.00	0	5	-	-5.00
Jordan Canavan	0	1	-	-1.00	1	1	100	+8.00	0	0	-	+0.00
Patrick Cowley	1	6	17	-2.50	0	1	-	-1.00	0	0	-	+0.00

By month

	Hurdles				Chases				Bumpers			
	W	R	%	£1 stake	W	R	%	£1 stake	W	R	%	£1 stake
May 2016	3	23	13	-3.50	1	19	5	-14.00	1	5	20	+8.00
June	2	18	11	-6.00	5	18	28	+1.85	0	1	-	-1.00
July	2	21	10	-15.63	3	26	12	-2.00	0	1	-	-1.00
August	0	7	-	-7.00	3	14	21	-2.40	0	0	-	+0.00
September	3	14	21	-1.75	3	14	21	+0.00	0	1	-	-1.00
October	2	33	6	-24.00	3	29	10	-15.50	0	8	-	-8.00
November	3	55	5	-22.50	2	43	5	-29.50	0	2	-	-2.00
December	4	52	8	-27.00	6	46	13	+9.75	1	2	50	+11.00
January 2017	1	29	3	-12.00	2	27	7	-19.50	0	0	-	+0.00
February	4	20	20	+17.38	2	22	9	-14.00	1	2	50	+1.50
March	4	22	18	-8.42	2	23	9	-14.00	1	3	33	-0.75
April	4	29	14	+1.91	8	39	21	+0.50	0	5	-	-5.00

By horse

	Wins-Runs	%	£1 level stakes	Win prize	Total prize
Minella Rocco	0-3	-	-3.00	£0.00	£128,227.50
Taquin Du Seuil	1-5	20	+4.00	£91,120.00	£128,047.75
Kelvingrove	2-6	33	+20.00	£36,798.20	£39,772.90
Upswing	2-8	25	+1.50	£22,259.00	£26,225.20
Dream Berry	1-5	20	+0.50	£7,797.60	£25,686.80
A Little Magic	3-9	33	+5.25	£22,743.00	£25,482.85
Go Conquer	0-6	-	-6.00	£0.00	£24,713.10
Festive Affair	1-6	17	-1.50	£12,558.40	£23,776.00
Foundation Man	3-9	33	+5.25	£15,978.45	£22,449.33
I'dliketheoption	1-9	11	-5.50	£11,371.50	£21,896.40
Forthefunofit	2-8	25	+16.50	£17,219.70	£19,081.70
Eastlake	1-6	17	+28.00	£18,768.00	£18,768.00
Doesyourdogbite	3-7	43	+32.50	£17,350.98	£17,886.98

Jonjo O'Neill

All runners

	Wins-Runs	%	Win prize	Total prize	£1 level stakes
Hurdle	32-329	10	£181,116.02	£314,806.47	-114.51
Chase	40-323	12	£338,081.65	£680,808.79	-101.80
Bumper	4-30	13	£8,642.34	£10,836.54	+1.75
TOTAL	76-682	11	£527,840.01	£1,006,451.80	-214.56

By course - last four seasons

	Hurdles				Chases				Bumpers			
	W	R	%	£1 stake	W	R	%	£1 stake	W	R	%	£1 stake
Aintree	4	44	9	-26.31	5	35	14	+1.55	1	6	17	-3.63
Ascot	2	22	9	+6.00	1	30	3	-24.50	0	0	-	+0.00
Ayr	1	3	33	+3.50	0	6	-	-6.00	0	0	-	+0.00
Bangor-On-Dee	3	52	6	-34.50	8	43	19	+1.38	3	5	60	+12.75
Carlisle	7	18	39	+2.08	1	15	7	-12.00	1	3	33	+0.50
Cartmel	3	8	38	+0.80	2	10	20	-2.50	0	0	-	+0.00
Catterick	4	16	25	+1.50	2	14	14	-8.34	1	2	50	+4.00
Cheltenham	6	74	8	-20.00	14	97	14	+21.21	0	6	-	-6.00
Chepstow	12	65	18	-4.21	1	36	3	-27.00	2	5	40	+4.50
Doncaster	3	42	7	-25.00	5	27	19	-7.84	0	2	-	-2.00
Exeter	5	41	12	-24.21	1	30	3	-23.50	0	3	-	-3.00
Fakenham	1	6	17	-4.56	1	7	14	-3.75	0	0	-	+0.00
Ffos Las	9	57	16	-22.92	7	36	19	-10.56	1	3	33	+10.00
Fontwell	4	22	18	-4.42	6	16	38	+9.38	0	0	-	+0.00
Haydock	4	33	12	-0.50	3	23	13	-6.77	0	1	-	-1.00
Hereford	1	6	17	+20.00	0	1	-	-1.00	0	0	-	+0.00
Hexham	0	1	-	-1.00	0	0	-	+0.00	0	0	-	+0.00
Huntingdon	14	56	25	+0.13	7	27	26	+9.00	3	7	43	+5.92
Kelso	0	1	-	-1.00	1	2	50	-0.75	0	0	-	+0.00
Kempton	7	48	15	-21.49	4	29	14	+0.10	0	3	-	-3.00
Kempton (AW)	0	0	-	+0.00	0	0	-	+0.00	0	8	-	-8.00
Leicester	1	21	5	-18.25	3	19	16	-10.25	0	0	-	+0.00
Lingfield	0	7	-	-7.00	0	4	-	-4.00	0	0	-	+0.00
Lingfield (AW)	0	0	-	+0.00	0	0	-	+0.00	1	4	25	+1.00
Ludlow	2	30	7	-25.88	5	41	12	-22.25	1	1	100	+8.00
Market Rasen	18	96	19	+0.83	12	76	16	-29.79	1	10	10	-7.50
Newbury	3	44	7	-30.35	4	34	12	-5.50	0	3	-	-3.00
Newcastle	0	2	-	-2.00	0	1	-	-1.00	0	0	-	+0.00
Newton Abbot	13	49	27	-0.13	1	33	3	-30.50	1	1	100	+2.75
Plumpton	1	12	8	-9.25	0	1	-	-1.00	0	0	-	+0.00
Sandown	1	27	4	-23.00	1	16	6	-12.50	0	2	-	-2.00
Sedgefield	4	7	57	+13.63	1	4	25	-1.00	0	1	-	-1.00
Southwell	15	96	16	-23.93	9	37	24	+4.47	1	11	9	-7.25
Stratford	9	49	18	+16.70	4	39	10	-19.58	2	6	33	+1.07
Taunton	2	16	13	-9.67	0	11	-	-11.00	0	1	-	-1.00
Towcester	4	39	10	-22.25	3	11	27	-0.25	0	2	-	-2.00
Uttoxeter	13	128	10	-71.42	10	80	13	-8.65	2	15	13	-9.25
Warwick	10	74	14	+7.49	4	27	15	+0.50	1	10	10	-7.75
Wetherby	10	45	22	-5.75	4	28	14	-10.50	0	2	-	-2.00
Wincanton	0	20	-	-20.00	1	6	17	+2.00	0	0	-	+0.00
Worcester	19	127	15	-51.27	25	97	26	+18.66	2	10	20	-5.22

By race type

	Hurdles				Chases			
	W	R	%	£1 stake	W	R	%	£1 stake
Handicap	10	51	20	-0.75	36	171	21	+28.23
Novice	9	47	19	-10.15	16	51	31	+24.06
Maiden	4	31	13	-17.88	0	0	-	+0.00

By jockey

	Hurdles				Chases				Bumpers			
	W	R	%	£1 stake	W	R	%	£1 stake	W	R	%	£1 stake
A P Heskin	15	77	19	-16.60	27	126	21	+16.48	7	15	47	+51.06
Paddy Brennan	7	29	24	+7.82	8	32	25	+13.25	1	8	13	-3.00
Mr N George	0	2	-	-2.00	2	11	18	+0.33	2	3	67	+4.50
Daryl Jacob	0	0	-	+0.00	1	1	100	+7.00	0	0	-	+0.00
Mark Quinlan	0	2	-	-2.00	1	5	20	+4.00	0	2	-	-2.00
B M Brooks	0	3	-	-3.00	0	0	-	+0.00	0	0	-	+0.00
Ciaran Gethings	0	3	-	-3.00	0	0	-	+0.00	0	0	-	+0.00
Richard Johnson	0	0	-	+0.00	0	3	-	-3.00	0	0	-	+0.00
Barry Geraghty	0	1	-	-1.00	0	3	-	-3.00	0	0	-	+0.00
James Best	0	1	-	-1.00	0	1	-	-1.00	0	0	-	+0.00

By month

	Hurdles				Chases				Bumpers			
	W	R	%	£1 stake	W	R	%	£1 stake	W	R	%	£1 stake
May 2016	2	10	20	+8.22	3	11	27	+8.75	0	4	-	-4.00
June	2	9	22	-3.90	1	6	17	-1.50	0	1	-	-1.00
July	0	4	-	-4.00	0	4	-	-4.00	0	0	-	+0.00
August	0	1	-	-1.00	1	2	50	+1.00	0	0	-	+0.00
September	0	0	-	+0.00	1	2	50	+4.00	0	0	-	+0.00
October	1	9	11	-4.00	3	21	14	+0.10	1	4	25	+30.00
November	5	19	26	-6.35	6	27	22	+14.75	3	7	43	+3.23
December	3	15	20	+1.50	7	27	26	+17.13	0	1	-	-1.00
January 2017	2	17	12	-8.75	2	19	11	-10.50	0	2	-	-2.00
February	1	13	8	-9.25	6	18	33	+6.00	2	3	67	+14.33
March	1	13	8	-8.00	5	22	23	+4.75	1	2	50	+2.50
April	4	11	36	+7.25	3	29	10	-19.42	2	4	50	+3.50

By horse

	Wins-Runs	%	£1 level stakes	Win prize	Total prize
Saint Are	0-5	-	-5.00	£0.00	£114,509.00
Sir Valentino	2-7	29	+14.00	£51,233.75	£113,847.80
The Worlds End	4-6	67	+9.00	£82,859.62	£83,336.62
Double Shuffle	1-6	17	+3.00	£25,024.00	£55,029.00
God's Own	0-5	-	-5.00	£0.00	£52,337.37
Max Ward	2-6	33	+2.25	£31,522.00	£43,515.00
Stamp Your Feet	3-7	43	+14.00	£38,839.52	£42,340.82
Singlefarmpayment	1-5	20	+0.50	£15,640.00	£41,286.10
Moss On The Mill	3-10	30	+8.50	£28,280.70	£33,092.50
O Maonlai	1-5	20	+8.00	£25,024.00	£28,157.00
Parsnip Pete	1-9	11	-4.50	£6,881.60	£23,813.90
Noche De Reyes	0-6	-	-6.00	£0.00	£23,313.60
Rocklander	2-8	25	-2.25	£11,528.40	£22,344.72

Tom George

All runners

	Wins-Runs	%	Win prize	Total prize	£1 level stakes
Hurdle	22-123	18	£193,316.22	£239,412.43	-25.78
Chase	39-189	21	£383,975.30	£830,197.17	+27.06
Bumper	10-29	34	£23,002.92	£26,127.63	+49.56
TOTAL	71-341	21	£600,294.44	£1,095,737.23	+50.84

By course - last four seasons

	Hurdles				Chases				Bumpers			
	W	R	%	£1 stake	W	R	%	£1 stake	W	R	%	£1 stake
Aintree	1	10	10	-6.00	7	39	18	+15.74	2	4	50	+32.00
Ascot	0	0	-	+0.00	2	18	11	-6.00	0	1	-	-1.00
Ayr	0	3	-	-3.00	0	7	-	-7.00	0	0	-	+0.00
Bangor-On-Dee	1	8	13	-6.78	0	9	-	-9.00	1	3	33	+2.00
Carlisle	0	0	-	+0.00	0	1	-	-1.00	0	0	-	+0.00
Cartmel	0	1	-	-1.00	0	1	-	-1.00	0	0	-	+0.00
Catterick	0	3	-	-3.00	1	5	20	-1.75	0	1	-	-1.00
Cheltenham	0	24	-	-24.00	5	56	9	-21.00	0	4	-	-4.00
Chepstow	5	24	21	-9.25	3	24	13	-15.50	5	7	71	+11.56
Doncaster	2	21	10	+33.00	3	25	12	+2.50	1	2	50	+2.33
Exeter	1	16	6	-8.00	5	20	25	+14.75	1	3	33	+10.00
Fakenham	0	2	-	-2.00	0	3	-	-3.00	0	0	-	+0.00
Ffos Las	0	7	-	-7.00	3	10	30	+3.45	0	2	-	-2.00
Fontwell	0	0	-	+0.00	0	4	-	-4.00	2	2	100	+12.00
Haydock	5	13	38	+10.75	1	19	5	-12.50	0	3	-	-3.00
Hereford	1	6	17	+0.00	1	2	50	+1.75	0	1	-	-1.00
Huntingdon	2	8	25	-2.25	3	14	21	+1.75	0	4	-	-4.00
Kelso	0	1	-	-1.00	1	1	100	+1.75	0	1	-	-1.00
Kempton	1	8	13	-4.25	8	43	19	+7.75	0	2	-	-2.00
Leicester	2	6	33	+1.75	12	35	34	+19.13	0	0	-	+0.00
Lingfield	0	0	-	+0.00	0	4	-	-4.00	0	0	-	+0.00
Ludlow	2	22	9	-16.50	13	45	29	+16.00	0	3	-	-3.00
Market Rasen	1	4	25	+0.00	2	9	22	+4.00	0	1	-	-1.00
Musselburgh	2	7	29	-1.63	0	4	-	-4.00	1	2	50	+1.25
Newbury	1	22	5	-17.50	4	37	11	-9.13	0	2	-	-2.00
Newcastle	2	3	67	+3.41	2	4	50	+0.63	0	1	-	-1.00
Newton Abbot	2	11	18	-6.45	1	8	13	-5.38	0	2	-	-2.00
Perth	2	14	14	-9.63	7	33	21	+1.50	1	2	50	+3.50
Plumpton	0	0	-	+0.00	0	3	-	-3.00	0	0	-	+0.00
Sandown	0	6	-	-6.00	2	24	8	-12.50	0	0	-	+0.00
Sedgefield	0	2	-	-2.00	0	3	-	-3.00	0	1	-	-1.00
Southwell	13	31	42	+10.83	4	11	36	+4.42	2	11	18	-0.75
Stratford	3	15	20	+7.75	8	22	36	+39.03	1	3	33	+1.50
Taunton	0	5	-	-5.00	1	13	8	-6.00	0	2	-	-2.00
Towcester	0	4	-	-4.00	2	8	25	+1.63	1	4	25	+2.50
Uttoxeter	3	21	14	-10.75	1	20	5	-17.90	0	4	-	-4.00
Warwick	0	10	-	-10.00	1	13	8	-9.25	1	5	20	+12.00
Wetherby	0	3	-	-3.00	0	8	-	-8.00	0	1	-	-1.00
Wincanton	1	10	10	-3.00	9	37	24	-2.79	0	4	-	-4.00
Worcester	1	16	6	-13.00	0	16	-	-16.00	0	3	-	-3.00

Top trainers by winners

All runs				First time out			Horses		
Won	Ran	%	Trainer	Won	Ran	%	Won	Ran	%
171	670	26	**Paul Nicholls**	43	161	27	87	161	54
154	618	25	**Nicky Henderson**	50	173	29	89	173	51
114	690	17	**Dan Skelton**	36	200	18	79	200	40
110	590	19	**Philip Hobbs**	27	158	17	70	158	44
107	551	19	**Neil Mulholland**	22	129	17	57	129	44
103	488	21	**Alan King**	30	128	23	59	128	46
95	585	16	**Nigel Twiston-Davies**	17	109	16	55	109	50
80	570	14	**Donald McCain**	10	114	9	48	114	42
76	683	11	**Jonjo O'Neill**	10	156	6	55	156	35
71	341	21	**Tom George**	20	76	26	46	76	61
70	535	13	**Tim Vaughan**	17	132	13	43	132	33
66	282	23	**Harry Fry**	24	87	28	39	87	45
60	327	18	**Fergal O'Brien**	14	81	17	36	81	44
59	486	12	**David Pipe**	19	116	16	41	116	35
57	405	14	**Colin Tizzard**	15	86	17	38	86	44
57	317	18	**Warren Greatrex**	17	91	19	36	91	40
51	460	11	**Evan Williams**	19	110	17	34	110	31
48	407	12	**Charlie Longsdon**	14	102	14	36	102	35
46	312	15	**Venetia Williams**	9	94	10	31	94	33
45	225	20	**Brian Ellison**	14	63	22	25	63	40
44	249	18	**Ian Williams**	8	61	13	25	61	41
44	237	19	**Nicky Richards**	10	65	15	30	65	46
43	407	11	**Lucinda Russell**	5	88	6	28	88	32
42	324	13	**Kim Bailey**	12	86	14	32	86	37
41	279	15	**Sue Smith**	5	59	8	25	59	42
40	339	12	**Gary Moore**	12	96	13	35	96	36
40	200	20	**Malcolm Jefferson**	11	51	22	23	51	45
40	300	13	**Peter Bowen**	5	55	9	26	55	47
35	185	19	**Emma Lavelle**	10	55	18	26	55	47
35	167	21	**Dr Richard Newland**	11	37	30	19	37	51
32	201	16	**Ben Pauling**	10	54	19	23	54	43
32	142	23	**Anthony Honeyball**	10	38	26	19	38	50
31	211	15	**Rebecca Curtis**	12	57	21	21	57	37
30	170	18	**Gordon Elliott**	16	94	17	22	94	23
28	227	12	**Nigel Hawke**	3	46	7	15	46	33
28	176	16	**Graeme McPherson**	6	40	15	18	40	45
26	130	20	**Michael Scudamore**	4	35	11	16	35	46
25	167	15	**Johnny Farrelly**	3	45	7	16	45	36
24	174	14	**Chris Gordon**	3	39	8	20	39	51
24	192	13	**Jeremy Scott**	6	37	16	17	37	46
24	204	12	**Jamie Snowden**	6	57	11	17	57	30
24	350	7	**Micky Hammond**	5	80	6	19	80	24
23	175	13	**Jennie Candlish**	2	39	5	12	39	31
23	120	19	**Charlie Mann**	6	31	19	14	31	45
22	160	14	**Kerry Lee**	2	40	5	14	40	35
22	195	11	**Oliver Sherwood**	8	60	13	17	60	28
21	148	14	**Henry Daly**	8	42	19	15	42	36

Top trainers by prize-money

Total prize-money	Trainer	Win prize-money	Wins	Class 1-3 Won	Class 1-3 Ran	Class 1-3 %	Class 4-6 Won	Class 4-6 Ran	Class 4-6 %
£2,846,487	**Nicky Henderson**	£1,883,035	154	66	345	19	88	273	32
£2,527,056	**Paul Nicholls**	£1,733,594	171	89	460	19	82	210	39
£2,040,578	**Colin Tizzard**	£1,449,147	57	39	252	15	18	153	12
£1,582,656	**Nigel Twiston-Davies**	£950,480	95	40	287	14	55	298	18
£1,497,478	**Philip Hobbs**	£1,000,501	110	50	302	17	60	288	21
£1,369,782	**Alan King**	£934,126	103	40	248	16	63	240	26
£1,305,853	**Dan Skelton**	£766,873	114	29	292	10	85	398	21
£1,095,737	**Tom George**	£600,294	71	33	190	17	38	151	25
£1,007,024	**Jonjo O'Neill**	£527,840	76	24	283	8	52	400	13
£941,892	**W P Mullins**	£754,757	9	9	52	17	0	0	—
£924,983	**Lucinda Russell**	£800,213	43	8	97	8	35	310	11
£901,405	**Gordon Elliott**	£454,054	30	11	68	16	19	102	19
£882,436	**Harry Fry**	£646,282	66	30	141	21	36	141	26
£843,398	**Neil Mulholland**	£598,509	107	25	162	15	82	389	21
£778,983	**David Pipe**	£538,975	59	30	248	12	29	238	12
£764,603	**Venetia Williams**	£449,363	46	25	173	14	21	139	15
£711,033	**Charlie Longsdon**	£482,531	48	24	176	14	24	231	10
£611,366	**Fergal O'Brien**	£433,222	60	23	132	17	37	195	19
£598,389	**Evan Williams**	£279,448	51	13	171	8	38	289	13
£577,742	**Donald McCain**	£351,310	80	13	134	10	67	436	15
£577,504	**Gary Moore**	£334,052	40	12	113	11	28	226	12
£523,388	**Henry De Bromhead**	£267,967	3	3	34	9	0	0	—
£515,061	**Warren Greatrex**	£294,871	57	11	105	10	46	212	22
£504,073	**Malcolm Jefferson**	£313,171	40	19	84	23	21	116	18
£477,948	**Mrs John Harrington**	£441,363	3	3	14	21	0	0	—
£476,683	**Peter Bowen**	£319,607	40	13	121	11	27	179	15
£473,465	**Tim Vaughan**	£314,550	70	11	105	10	59	430	14
£444,731	**Ian Williams**	£315,265	44	18	86	21	26	163	16
£432,231	**Rebecca Curtis**	£305,080	31	11	104	11	20	107	19
£430,524	**Brian Ellison**	£274,837	45	14	95	15	31	130	24
£408,370	**Kim Bailey**	£204,208	42	13	93	14	29	231	13
£373,745	**Emma Lavelle**	£211,474	35	13	84	15	22	101	22
£372,935	**Sue Smith**	£222,258	41	13	114	11	28	165	17
£369,928	**Nick Williams**	£241,073	19	7	69	10	12	78	15
£343,005	**Nicky Richards**	£223,254	44	12	87	14	32	150	21
£307,344	**Kerry Lee**	£124,390	22	6	78	8	16	82	20
£294,864	**Ben Pauling**	£224,682	32	8	87	9	24	114	21
£293,949	**Oliver Sherwood**	£195,477	22	10	81	12	12	114	11
£290,917	**Dr Richard Newland**	£181,180	35	7	87	8	28	80	35
£289,483	**Anthony Honeyball**	£213,711	32	4	41	10	28	101	28
£284,063	**Seamus Mullins**	£165,506	17	5	51	10	12	185	6
£276,737	**Neil King**	£78,961	17	3	69	4	14	112	13
£252,497	**Nigel Hawke**	£201,705	28	11	43	26	17	184	9
£249,055	**Michael Scudamore**	£188,745	26	8	36	22	18	94	19
£233,757	**David Dennis**	£133,327	20	6	60	10	14	208	7
£206,139	**Chris Gordon**	£133,244	24	5	61	8	19	113	17
£196,632	**Jeremy Scott**	£114,144	24	4	44	9	20	148	14

Top jockeys

Won	Ran	%	Jockey	Best Trainer	Won	Ran
187	1025	18	**Richard Johnson**	Philip Hobbs	66	333
144	859	17	**Brian Hughes**	Malcolm Jefferson	36	164
135	668	20	**Sam Twiston-Davies**	Paul Nicholls	70	268
121	756	16	**Aidan Coleman**	Jonjo O'Neill	49	314
117	541	22	**Noel Fehily**	Neil Mulholland	45	194
99	745	13	**Tom Scudamore**	David Pipe	40	292
98	525	19	**Harry Skelton**	Dan Skelton	88	455
95	453	21	**Paddy Brennan**	Fergal O'Brien	46	191
88	406	22	**Daryl Jacob**	Emma Lavelle	19	104
81	577	14	**Tom O'Brien**	Philip Hobbs	16	92
79	432	18	**Sean Bowen**	Peter Bowen	36	215
73	383	19	**Wayne Hutchinson**	Alan King	60	284
63	325	19	**Harry Cobden**	Paul Nicholls	30	82
63	461	14	**Will Kennedy**	Donald McCain	53	331
59	297	20	**Nico de Boinville**	Nicky Henderson	44	169
55	368	15	**Gavin Sheehan**	Warren Greatrex	32	174
54	296	18	**A P Heskin**	Tom George	49	218
51	274	19	**Danny Cook**	Sue Smith	32	161
48	386	12	**Henry Brooke**	Kenneth Slack	6	27
47	428	11	**Jamie Moore**	Gary Moore	20	162
45	324	14	**David Bass**	Kim Bailey	27	186
44	393	11	**Nick Scholfield**	Paul Nicholls	17	96
44	299	15	**Alan Johns**	Tim Vaughan	44	276
43	267	16	**Jeremiah McGrath**	Nicky Henderson	37	157
42	153	27	**Barry Geraghty**	Nicky Henderson	10	30
40	376	11	**Leighton Aspell**	Oliver Sherwood	15	127
38	343	11	**Sean Quinlan**	Jennie Candlish	20	145
36	344	10	**Tom Cannon**	Chris Gordon	15	98
35	375	9	**David Noonan**	David Pipe	10	103
34	319	11	**Paul Moloney**	Evan Williams	19	136
34	252	13	**Brian Harding**	Nicky Richards	12	65
31	160	19	**Harry Bannister**	Charlie Mann	12	32
29	273	11	**Jamie Bargary**	Nigel Twiston-Davies	25	163
29	326	9	**Trevor Whelan**	Neil King	14	134
29	315	9	**Brendan Powell**	Johnny Farrelly	13	78
28	422	7	**Richie McLernon**	Ben Haslam	6	55
28	181	15	**Stan Sheppard**	Matt Sheppard	12	91
27	303	9	**Adam Wedge**	Evan Williams	18	158
27	247	11	**Kielan Woods**	Graeme McPherson	17	115
27	305	9	**Craig Nichol**	Nicky Richards	14	89
26	154	17	**Jonathan Moore**	Rebecca Curtis	22	119
26	239	11	**Jake Greenall**	Mark Walford	11	65
25	154	16	**Charlie Deutsch**	Venetia Williams	19	110
25	238	11	**Robert Dunne**	Dai Burchell	8	59
25	212	12	**Tom Bellamy**	Kim Bailey	8	63
23	362	6	**James Best**	Robert Walford	9	51
23	216	11	**Jack Quinlan**	Robin Dickin	8	34
23	208	11	**Adam Nicol**	Philip Kirby	13	87

Big Race Dates, Fixtures and Track Facts

Perth
Musselburgh
Kelso
Ayr
Hexham
Newcastle
Carlisle
Cartmel
Sedgefield
Catterick
Wetherby
Aintree
Doncaster
Haydock
Bangor
Market Rasen
Southwell
Uttoxeter
Fakenham
Leicester
Ludlow
Huntingdon
Worcester
Warwick
Ffos Las
Stratford
Hereford
Towcester
Cheltenham
Chepstow
Newbury
Ascot
Kempton
Sandown
Lingfield
Taunton
Folkestone
Wincanton
Fontwell
Plumpton
Exeter
Newton Abbot

Fixtures

Key - Flat, **Jumps**

October

1 Sunday........Epsom, Musselburgh
2 Monday........Bath, **Newton Abbot**, **Stratford**
3 Tuesday........Ayr, **Sedgefield**, **Southwell**, Kempton
4 Wednesday........**Bangor**, Nottingham, Salisbury, Kempton
5 Thursday........**Huntingdon**, Lingfield, **Warwick**, Chelmsford City
6 Friday........Ascot, **Fontwell**, **Hexham**, Chelmsford City
7 Saturday........Ascot, **Fontwell**, Newmarket, Redcar, Wolverhampton
8 Sunday........**Kelso**, **Uttoxeter**
9 Monday........Pontefract, Salisbury, Windsor
10 Tuesday........Brighton, Catterick, Leicester, Newcastle
11 Wednesday........**Ludlow**, Nottingham, **Towcester**, Kempton
12 Thursday........Ayr, **Exeter**, **Worcester**, Chelmsford City
13 Friday........Newmarket, **Newton Abbot**, York, Kempton
14 Saturday........**Chepstow**, **Hexham**, Newmarket, York, Kempton
15 Sunday........**Chepstow**, Goodwood
16 Monday........Musselburgh, Windsor, Yarmouth
17 Tuesday........**Hereford**, **Huntingdon**, Leicester, Kempton
18 Wednesday........Bath, Nottingham, **Wetherby**, Kempton
19 Thursday........Brighton, **Carlisle**, **Uttoxeter**, Newcastle
20 Friday........**Fakenham**, Haydock, Redcar, **Wincanton**, Newcastle
21 Saturday........Ascot, Catterick, **Ffos Las**, **Market Rasen**, **Stratford**, ...Wolverhampton
22 Sunday........**Kempton**, Southwell
23 Monday........**Plumpton**, Pontefract, Windsor
24 Tuesday........**Exeter**, Newcastle, Yarmouth, Kempton
25 Wednesday........Newmarket, **Sedgefield**, **Worcester**, Kempton
26 Thursday........**Carlisle**, **Ludlow**, **Southwell**, Chelmsford City
27 Friday........**Cheltenham**, Doncaster, Newbury, Wolverhampton
28 Saturday........**Cheltenham**, Doncaster, **Kelso**, Newbury, Wolverhampton
29 Sunday........**Aintree**, **Wincanton**
30 Monday........**Ayr**, Leicester, Redcar
31 Tuesday........**Bangor**, Catterick, **Chepstow**, Wolverhampton

November

1 Wednesday........**Fakenham**, Nottingham, **Taunton**, Kempton
2 Thursday........Lingfield, **Sedgefield**, **Stratford**, Chelmsford City
3 Friday........Newmarket, **Uttoxeter**, **Wetherby**, Newcastle
4 Saturday........**Ascot**, **Ayr**, Newmarket, **Wetherby**, Newcastle
5 Sunday........**Carlisle**, **Huntingdon**
6 Monday........Kempton, **Plumpton**, **Southwell**
7 Tuesday........**Exeter**, Redcar, Wolverhampton, Kempton
8 Wednesday........**Chepstow**, **Musselburgh**, Nottingham, Kempton
9 Thursday........**Ludlow**, **Market Rasen**, **Newbury**, Chelmsford City

10 Friday .... **Fontwell**, **Hexham**, **Warwick**, Newcastle
11 Saturday .... **Aintree**, Doncaster, **Kelso**, **Wincanton**, Wolverhampton
12 Sunday .... **Ffos Las**, **Sandown**
13 Monday .... **Carlisle**, **Kempton**, Southwell
14 Tuesday .... **Hereford**, **Huntingdon**, **Lingfield**
15 Wednesday .... **Ayr**, **Bangor**, **Exeter**, Newcastle
16 Thursday .... **Ludlow**, Southwell, **Taunton**, Chelmsford City
17 Friday .... **Cheltenham**, Lingfield, **Newcastle**, Chelmsford City
18 Saturday ... **Cheltenham**, Lingfield, **Uttoxeter**, **Wetherby**, Wolverhampton
19 Sunday .... **Cheltenham**, **Fontwell**
20 Monday .... **Leicester**, **Plumpton**, Wolverhampton
21 Tuesday .... **Fakenham**, Lingfield, **Southwell**
22 Wednesday .... **Chepstow**, **Hexham**, **Warwick**, Kempton
23 Thursday .... **Market Rasen**, Newcastle, **Wincanton**, Chelmsford City
24 Friday .... **Ascot**, **Catterick**, **Ffos Las**, Newcastle
25 Saturday .... **Ascot**, **Haydock**, **Huntingdon**, Lingfield, Wolverhampton
26 Sunday .... **Exeter**, **Uttoxeter**
27 Monday .... **Ayr**, **Kempton**, **Ludlow**
28 Tuesday .... **Lingfield**, **Sedgefield**, Southwell
29 Wednesday .... **Hereford**, **Wetherby**, Wolverhampton, Kempton
30 Thursday .... **Musselburgh**, **Taunton**, **Towcester**, Newcastle

December

1 Friday .... **Doncaster**, **Newbury**, Southwell, Chelmsford City
2 Saturday .... **Bangor**, **Doncaster**, **Newbury**, **Newcastle**,
.... Wolverhampton
3 Sunday .... **Carlisle**, **Leicester**
4 Monday .... **Fakenham**, **Plumpton**, Southwell
5 Tuesday .... **Lingfield**, **Southwell**, Wolverhampton
6 Wednesday .... **Haydock**, Lingfield, **Ludlow**, Newcastle
7 Thursday .... **Leicester**, **Market Rasen**, **Wincanton**, Chelmsford City
8 Friday .... **Exeter**, **Sandown**, **Sedgefield**, Chelmsford City
9 Saturday .... **Aintree**, **Chepstow**, **Sandown**, **Wetherby**, Wolverhampton
10 Sunday .... **Huntingdon**, **Kelso**
11 Monday .... **Fontwell**, **Musselburgh**, Southwell
12 Tuesday .... **Ayr**, Lingfield, **Uttoxeter**
13 Wednesday .... **Hexham**, **Leicester**, Lingfield, Kempton
14 Thursday .... **Newcastle**, **Taunton**, **Warwick**, Chelmsford City
15 Friday .... **Bangor**, **Cheltenham**, **Doncaster**, Chelmsford City
16 Saturday .... **Cheltenham**, **Doncaster**, **Hereford**, Newcastle,
.... Wolverhampton
17 Sunday .... **Carlisle**, **Southwell**
18 Monday .... **Ffos Las**, **Plumpton**, Wolverhampton
19 Tuesday .... **Catterick**, **Fakenham**, Southwell
20 Wednesday .... Lingfield, **Ludlow**, **Newbury**, Kempton
21 Thursday .... **Exeter**, Southwell, **Towcester**, Chelmsford City
22 Friday .... **Ascot**, Southwell, **Uttoxeter**, Wolverhampton
23 Saturday .... **Ascot**, **Haydock**, Lingfield, **Newcastle**
26 Tuesday.... **Fontwell**, **Huntingdon**, **Kempton**, **Market Rasen**, **Sedgefield**,
.... **Wetherby**, **Wincanton**, Wolverhampton
27 Wednesday .... **Chepstow**, **Kempton**, **Wetherby**, Wolverhampton

28 Thursday .... **Catterick**, **Leicester**, Lingfield
29 Friday .... **Doncaster**, **Kelso**, Southwell
30 Saturday .... **Haydock**, Lingfield, **Newbury**, **Taunton**
31 Sunday .... Lingfield, **Uttoxeter**, **Warwick**

January

1 Mon .... **Catterick**, **Cheltenham**, **Exeter**, **Musselburgh**, **Fakenham**, ... Southwell
2 Tue .... **Ayr**, **Ffos Las**, Newcastle
3 Wed .... **Musselburgh**, **Ludlow**, Southwell, Wolverhampton
4 Thu .... Newcastle, **Bangor**, Chelmsford City, Wolverhampton
5 Fri .... **Wetherby**, Southwell, Kempton, **Lingfield**
6 Sat .... **Newcastle**, Kempton, Lingfield, **Sandown**, **Wincanton**
7 Sun .... **Chepstow**, **Plumpton**
8 Mon .... **Hereford**, **Fontwell**, Wolverhampton
9 Tue .... **Doncaster**, Southwell, **Taunton**
10 Wed .... **Ayr**, **Ludlow**, Kempton, Lingfield
11 Thu .... **Catterick**, **Leicester**, Chelmsford City, Newcastle
12 Fri .... Newcastle, **Huntingdon**, Lingfield, **Sedgefield**
13 Sat .... **Wetherby**, **Warwick**, **Kempton**, Wolverhampton, Lingfield
14 Sun .... **Kelso**, Southwell
15 Mon .... **Ayr**, Wolverhampton, **Plumpton**
16 Tue .... **Ayr**, **Hereford**, Kempton
17 Wed .... Newcastle, **Market Rasen**, Lingfield, **Newbury**
18 Thu .... **Ludlow**, Chelmsford City, Southwell, **Wincanton**
19 Fri .... **Musselburgh**, **Chepstow**, Newcastle, Lingfield
20 Sat .... **Haydock**, **Ascot**, Chelmsford City, Lingfield, **Taunton**
21 Sun .... **Newcastle**, **Fontwell**
22 Mon .... **Fakenham**, **Lingfield**, Wolverhampton
23 Tue .... **Wetherby**, **Leicester**, Southwell
24 Wed .... **Catterick**, **Exeter**, Kempton, Lingfield
25 Thu .... **Kelso**, Southwell, Chelmsford City, **Warwick**
26 Fri .... **Doncaster**, **Huntingdon**, Kempton, Lingfield
27 Sat .... **Doncaster**, **Cheltenham**, Kempton, **Uttoxeter**, Lingfield
28 Sun .... **Sedgefield**, **Fontwell**
29 Mon .... **Hereford**, **Plumpton**, Wolverhampton
30 Tue .... **Newcastle**, Southwell, **Lingfield**
31 Wed .... **Ayr**, **Leicester**, Chelmsford City, Newcastle

February

1 Thu .... Southwell, Kempton, **Towcester**, **Wincanton**
2 Fri .... **Catterick**, Wolverhampton, **Chepstow**, Lingfield
3 Sat .... **Musselburgh**, Kempton, **Wetherby**, Lingfield, **Sandown**
4 Sun .... **Musselburgh**, **Taunton**
5 Mon .... **Newcastle**, **Southwell**, Wolverhampton
6 Tue .... **Sedgefield**, **Market Rasen**, Southwell
7 Wed .... **Carlisle**, **Fakenham**, **Ludlow**, Wolverhampton
8 Thu .... **Doncaster**, **Huntingdon**, Chelmsford City, Newcastle
9 Fri .... Newcastle, **Bangor**, Chelmsford City, **Kempton**
10 Sat .... **Uttoxeter**, Lingfield, **Warwick**, **Newbury**, Wolverhampton
11 Sun .... **Ayr**, **Exeter**

12 Mon.......**Catterick**, Wolverhampton, **Plumpton**
13 Tue.......**Ayr**, Southwell, **Lingfield**
14 Wed.......**Musselburgh**, **Towcester**, Lingfield, Wolverhampton
15 Thu.......**Kelso**, **Leicester**, Chelmsford City, **Fontwell**
16 Fri.......Newcastle, **Fakenham**, Lingfield, **Sandown**
17 Sat.......**Haydock**, **Ascot**, Kempton, Lingfield, **Wincanton**
18 Sun.......**Market Rasen**, **Ffos Las**
19 Mon.......**Carlisle**, Kempton, **Lingfield**
20 Tue.......**Wetherby**, Wolverhampton, **Taunton**
21 Wed.......**Doncaster**, **Ludlow**, Kempton, Newcastle
22 Thu.......**Sedgefield**, **Huntingdon**, Chelmsford City, Southwell
23 Fri.......**Warwick**, **Exeter**, Wolverhampton, Lingfield
24 Sat.......**Newcastle**, Wolverhampton, **Chepstow**, **Kempton**, Lingfield
25 Sun.......**Southwell**, **Fontwell**
26 Mon.......**Ayr**, Wolverhampton, **Plumpton**
27 Tue.......**Catterick**, **Leicester**, Lingfield
28 Wed.......**Musselburgh**, **Market Rasen**, **Wincanton**, Newcastle

March

1 Thu.......Newcastle, **Ludlow**, Kempton, **Taunton**
2 Fri.......**Doncaster**, Chelmsford City, Lingfield, **Newbury**
3 Sat.......**Doncaster**, Chelmsford City, **Kelso**, Lingfield, **Newbury**
4 Sun.......**Sedgefield**, **Huntingdon**
5 Mon.......**Southwell**, **Lingfield**, Wolverhampton
6 Tue.......**Newcastle**, Southwell, **Exeter**
7 Wed.......**Catterick**, **Fontwell**, Kempton, Lingfield
8 Thu.......**Carlisle**, Southwell, **Wincanton**, Newcastle
9 Fri.......**Ayr**, **Leicester**, **Sandown**, Newcastle
10 Sat.......**Ayr**, **Hereford**, Chelmsford City, Wolverhampton, **Sandown**
11 Sun.......**Market Rasen**, **Warwick**
12 Mon.......**Stratford**, Chelmsford City, **Plumpton**, **Taunton**
13 Tue.......**Cheltenham**, Newcastle, **Sedgefield**, Southwell
14 Wed.......**Cheltenham**, **Huntingdon**, Southwell, Wolverhampton
15 Thu.......**Cheltenham**, **Hexham**, Chelmsford City, **Towcester**
16 Fri.......**Cheltenham**, Lingfield, **Fakenham**, Wolverhampton
17 Sat.......**Newcastle**, **Uttoxeter**, **Fontwell**, Wolverhampton, **Kempton**
18 Sun.......**Carlisle**, **Ffos Las**
19 Mon.......**Kelso**, **Southwell**, Lingfield
20 Tue.......Newcastle, **Exeter**, **Wetherby**
21 Wed.......**Haydock**, Southwell, **Chepstow**, Kempton
22 Thu.......**Ludlow**, Chelmsford City, Wolverhampton, **Chepstow**
23 Fri.......**Sedgefield**, Kempton, Lingfield, **Newbury**
24 Sat.......Doncaster, **Bangor**, Lingfield, Wolverhampton, **Newbury**
25 Sun.......Doncaster, **Ascot**
26 Mon.......**Huntingdon**, **Taunton**, **Market Rasen**
27 Tue.......Newcastle, **Hereford**, Southwell
28 Wed.......Newcastle, **Warwick**, **Wincanton**, Wolverhampton
29 Thu.......**Wetherby**, **Towcester**, Chelmsford City, Wolverhampton
30 Fri.......Newcastle, Bath, Lingfield
31 Sat.......**Carlisle**, Chelmsford City, **Haydock**, Kempton, Musselburgh, ...**Newton Abbot**

April

1 Sun........ Southwell, **Ffos Las**, **Plumpton**
2 Mon........ Redcar, **Fakenham**, **Chepstow**, **Huntingdon**, **Plumpton**, ... **Market Rasen**, Wolverhampton
3 Tue........ Pontefract, Lingfield, **Wincanton**
4 Wed........ Catterick, Southwell, Kempton, Lingfield
5 Thu........ Musselburgh, **Warwick**, Chelmsford City, Wolverhampton
6 Fri........ **Wetherby**, Chelmsford City, **Fontwell**, Lingfield
7 Sat........ **Kelso**, **Stratford**, Kempton, **Uttoxeter**, Wolverhampton
8 Sun........ **Carlisle**, **Exeter**
9 Mon........ **Ludlow**, **Kempton**, Wolverhampton
10 Tue........ **Hexham**, **Southwell**, Wolverhampton
11 Wed........ **Market Rasen**, Kempton, Nottingham, Lingfield
12 Thu........ **Aintree**, Southwell, Chelmsford City, **Taunton**
13 Fri........ **Aintree**, Leicester, Kempton, **Sedgefield**
14 Sat........ **Aintree**, Wolverhampton, **Chepstow**, **Newcastle**, Lingfield
15 Sun........ **Ffos Las**, **Plumpton**
16 Mon........ **Kelso**, Windsor, Redcar
17 Tue........ **Carlisle**, Newmarket, **Exeter**
18 Wed........ Beverley, **Cheltenham**, Kempton, Newmarket
19 Thu........ Newcastle, **Cheltenham**, Ripon, Newmarket
20 Fri........ **Ayr**, **Southwell**, Bath, **Fontwell**, Newbury
21 Sat........ **Ayr**, **Bangor**, Newbury, Thirsk, Nottingham, Wolverhampton
22 Sun........ **Stratford**, **Wincanton**
23 Mon........ **Hexham**, **Newton Abbot**, Pontefract, Windsor, **Sedgefield**
24 Tue........ **Huntingdon**, Brighton, **Ludlow**, **Exeter**, Yarmouth
25 Wed........ Catterick, Epsom, **Perth**, Lingfield, **Taunton**
26 Thu........ Beverley, **Warwick**, Chelmsford City, **Perth**, **Kempton**
27 Fri........ Doncaster, **Towcester**, **Chepstow**, **Perth**, Sandown
28 Sat........ Doncaster, Leicester, **Sandown**, Haydock, Wolverhampton, Ripon
29 Sun........ Wetherby, Salisbury
30 Mon........ Ayr, Southwell, Salisbury, Thirsk, Windsor

May

1 Tue........ Ayr, Nottingham, Brighton, Yarmouth, Kempton
2 Wed........ Pontefract, Wolverhampton, Ascot, Bath, Brighton
3 Thu........ Musselburgh, Southwell, Chelmsford City, Redcar, Lingfield
4 Fri........ Musselburgh, **Cheltenham**, Chepstow, Newcastle, Lingfield
5 Sat........ Doncaster, Newmarket, Goodwood, **Hexham**, **Uttoxeter**, Thirsk
6 Sun........ Hamilton, Newmarket
7 Mon........ Beverley, **Warwick**, Bath, **Kempton**, Windsor
8 Tue........ Wetherby, **Fakenham**, Brighton, **Ludlow**, **Exeter**
9 Wed........ **Kelso**, Chester, **Fontwell**, Wolverhampton, **Newton Abbot**
10 Thu........ Chester, Chelmsford City, **Huntingdon**, **Wincanton**, **Worcester**
11 Fri........ Ripon, Chester, Ascot, **Market Rasen**, Lingfield, Nottingham
12 Sat........ **Haydock**, Nottingham, Ascot, **Hexham**, **Warwick**, Lingfield, Thirsk
13 Sun........ Ludlow, Plumpton
14 Mon........ Catterick, **Towcester**, **Kempton**, Wolverhampton, Windsor
15 Tue........ Beverley, **Southwell**, Chepstow, **Sedgefield**, **Wincanton**

16 Wed..**Perth**, Yarmouth, Bath, York, **Newton Abbot**
17 Thu..**Perth**, Newmarket, **Fontwell**, York, Salisbury
18 Fri..**Aintree**, Newmarket, Newbury, Hamilton, York
19 Sat................Doncaster, **Bangor**, Newbury, Thirsk, Newmarket, **Uttoxeter**
20 Sun..Ripon, **Market Rasen**, **Stratford**
21 Mon..Carlisle, Leicester, Windsor, Redcar, **Towcester**
22 Tue..Ayr, **Huntingdon**, Chepstow, **Hexham**, Nottingham
23 Wed..Ayr, **Southwell**, Kempton, **Warwick**, Yarmouth
24 Thu................Catterick, Chelmsford City, Goodwood, Lingfield, Sandown
25 Fri..Haydock, **Worcester**, Bath, Pontefract, Goodwood
26 Sat......**Cartmel**, Chester, **Ffos Las**, Haydock, Goodwood, York, Salisbury
27 Sun..**Kelso**, **Uttoxeter**, **Fontwell**
28 Mon...**Cartmel**, **Huntingdon**, Chelmsford City, Redcar, Leicester, Windsor
29 Tue........................Redcar, Leicester, Brighton, Wolverhampton, Lingfield
30 Wed..Beverley, Nottingham, **Cartmel**, **Warwick**, Ripon
31 Thu..........Hamilton, Wolverhampton, Chelmsford City, **Ffos Las**, Lingfield

June

1 Fri............Catterick, **Market Rasen**, Bath, Doncaster, Epsom, Goodwood
2 Sat..... Doncaster, **Worcester**, Chepstow, **Hexham**, Epsom, Musselburgh,
....Lingfield
3 Sun..**Perth**, **Fakenham**
4 Mon..Ayr, Leicester, **Newton Abbot**, Windsor
5 Tue..Newcastle, **Bangor**, **Fontwell**, **Southwell**
6 Wed..................Hamilton, **Uttoxeter**, Kempton, Wetherby, Wolverhampton
7 Thu..Carlisle, Yarmouth, Sandown, Haydock, Ripon
8 Fri.....Carlisle, **Stratford**, Brighton, Haydock, Wolverhampton, Goodwood
9 Sat........... Beverley, Newmarket, Lingfield, Catterick, **Stratford**, Haydock,
....Musselburgh
10 Sun..Nottingham, Goodwood
11 Mon..Pontefract, **Worcester**, Brighton, Windsor
12 Tue..Thirsk, **Southwell**, Lingfield, Salisbury
13 Wed.................. Hamilton, Yarmouth, Chelmsford City, Haydock, Kempton
14 Thu........................ Haydock, Nottingham, Newbury, **Uttoxeter**, Yarmouth
15 Fri...........**Aintree**, Chepstow, York, Goodwood, **Newton Abbot**, Sandown
16 Sat................ **Hexham**, Chester, Bath, York, Leicester, **Fontwell**, Sandown
17 Sun..Doncaster, Salisbury
18 Mon..Ayr, Nottingham, Windsor, Carlisle
19 Tue................................ Royal Ascot, Beverley, **Stratford**, Thirsk, Brighton
20 Wed.................. Royal Ascot, Hamilton, **Uttoxeter**, Ripon, Chelmsford City
21 Thu..................... Royal Ascot, Ripon, Chelmsford City, **Ffos Las**, Lingfield
22 Fri...........Royal Ascot, Ayr, **Market Rasen**, Redcar, Newmarket, Wetherby
23 Sat......... Royal Ascot, Ayr, Newmarket, Haydock, Lingfield, **Perth**, Redcar
24 Sun..**Hexham**, **Worcester**, Pontefract
25 Mon................................**Southwell**, Chepstow, Wolverhampton, Windsor
26 Tue..Beverley, Brighton, Newbury, **Newton Abbot**
27 Wed..Carlisle, **Worcester**, Bath, Kempton, Salisbury
28 Thu..................... Hamilton, Leicester, Newcastle, Newmarket, Nottingham
29 Fri........... **Cartmel**, Chester, Doncaster, Newmarket, Newcastle, Yarmouth
30 Sat... Doncaster, Chester, Lingfield, Newcastle, Newmarket, Windsor, York

July

1 Sun......**Cartmel**, **Uttoxeter**, Windsor
2 Mon......Hamilton, Wolverhampton, Windsor, Pontefract
3 Tue ...... Hamilton, **Stratford**, Brighton, Chepstow
4 Wed......Musselburgh, **Worcester**, Bath, Thirsk, Kempton
5 Thu...... Haydock, Yarmouth, Epsom, **Perth**, Newbury
6 Fri...... Beverley, Chelmsford City, Doncaster, **Newton Abbot**, Haydock, ... Sandown
7 Sat...... Beverley, Leicester, Chelmsford City, Carlisle, Nottingham, ...Sandown, Haydock
8 Sun......Ayr, **Market Rasen**
9 Mon...... Ayr, **Worcester**, Windsor, Ripon
10 Tue ......Pontefract, **Uttoxeter**, Brighton, Wolverhampton
11 Wed......Catterick, Yarmouth, Bath, Kempton, Lingfield
12 Thu......Carlisle, Newmarket, Epsom, Doncaster, Newbury
13 Fri...... York, Chester, Ascot, Newmarket, Chepstow, **Ffos Las**
14 Sat...... Hamilton, Chester, Ascot, York, Newmarket, **Newton Abbot**, ...Salisbury
15 Sun...... **Perth**, **Southwell**, **Stratford**
16 Mon...... Ayr, Wolverhampton, Windsor, Ripon
17 Tue ......Beverley, **Worcester**, Bath, Thirsk
18 Wed...... Catterick, **Uttoxeter**, Lingfield, Wolverhampton, Yarmouth
19 Thu...... Doncaster, Leicester, Chepstow, Hamilton, Epsom
20 Fri......Hamilton, Newmarket, Newbury, Haydock, Nottingham, Pontefract
21 Sat....**Cartmel**, **Market Rasen**, Lingfield, Haydock, Newmarket, Newbury, ... Ripon
22 Sun......Redcar, **Stratford**, **Newton Abbot**
23 Mon...... Ayr, Windsor, Beverley, **Cartmel**
24 Tue ......Musselburgh, Nottingham, Chelmsford City, Ffos Las
25 Wed...... Catterick, Leicester, Bath, Lingfield, Sandown
26 Thu...... Doncaster, **Worcester**, Newbury, Yarmouth, Sandown
27 Fri......Thirsk, Newmarket, Ascot, York, **Uttoxeter**, Chepstow
28 Sat......Newcastle, Chester, Ascot, York, Newmarket, Lingfield, Salisbury
29 Sun...... Pontefract, **Uttoxeter**
30 Mon......Ayr, Wolverhampton, **Newton Abbot**, Windsor
31 Tue ...... Beverley, **Worcester**, Goodwood, **Perth**, Yarmouth

August

1 Wed......**Perth**, Leicester, Goodwood, Redcar, Sandown
2 Thu ......Nottingham, Epsom, **Stratford**, Ffos Las, Goodwood
3 Fri......Musselburgh, **Bangor**, Bath, Thirsk, Newmarket, Goodwood
4 Sat......Doncaster, Newmarket, Chelmsford City, Hamilton, Goodwood, ...Thirsk, Lingfield
5 Sun...... Chester, **Market Rasen**
6 Mon......Carlisle, **Newton Abbot**, Ripon, Windsor
7 Tue ......Ayr, Nottingham, Newbury, Catterick
8 Wed...... Pontefract, Yarmouth, Bath, Brighton, Kempton
9 Thu...... Haydock, Yarmouth, Brighton, Newcastle, Sandown
10 Fri......Haydock, Newmarket, Brighton, Musselburgh, Wolverhampton, ... Chelmsford City
11 Sat... Ayr, Newmarket, Ascot, Haydock, Chelmsford City, Redcar, Lingfield

12 Sun..Leicester, Windsor
13 Mon.. Ayr, Wolverhampton, Windsor, Ripon
14 Tue .... Thirsk, Nottingham, Chelmsford City, Ffos Las
15 Wed..................Beverley, **Worcester**, Kempton, **Newton Abbot**, Salisbury
16 Thu.................. Beverley, Wolverhampton, Chepstow, Yarmouth, Salisbury
17 Fri .... Catterick, Newmarket, Chelmsford City, Nottingham, Newbury,
....Wolverhampton
18 Sat.. Doncaster, **Market Rasen**, Bath, **Perth**, Newmarket, Newbury, Ripon
19 Sun...Pontefract, **Southwell**
20 Mon...Thirsk, **Bangor**, Windsor, Leicester
21 Tue .... Hamilton, Yarmouth, Brighton, Kempton, **Newton Abbot**
22 Wed...Carlisle, **Worcester**, Bath, York, Kempton
23 Thu..........................York, **Stratford**, Chepstow, Wolverhampton, **Fontwell**
24 Fri ...... York, Newmarket, Chelmsford City, Ffos Las, Goodwood, Salisbury
25 Sat........**Cartmel**, Newmarket, Chelmsford City, Redcar, Goodwood, York,
.... Windsor
26 Sun..Beverley, Yarmouth, Goodwood
27 Mon..................................**Cartmel**, Southwell, Chepstow, Ripon, Epsom
28 Tue ....Ripon, **Stratford**, Bath, Epsom
29 Wed......................Catterick, **Worcester**, Kempton, Musselburgh, Lingfield
30 Thu........... Carlisle, Chelmsford City, Musselburgh, **Fontwell**, **Sedgefield**
31 Fri ....Hamilton, **Bangor**, Sandown, Newcastle, Wolverhampton, Thirsk

September

1 Sat............. Beverley, Chester, Chelmsford City, Wolverhampton, Lingfield,
....**Newton Abbot**, Sandown
2 Sun..**Worcester**, Brighton
3 Mon.. Newcastle, Brighton, Chepstow, Windsor
4 Tue ....Leicester, Goodwood, **Stratford**, Kempton
5 Wed.........................**Southwell**, Bath, Wolverhampton, Ffos Las, Lingfield
6 Thu...................Carlisle, Chelmsford City, Haydock, Salisbury, **Sedgefield**
7 Fri ....Haydock, Ascot, Musselburgh, Kempton, Newcastle
8 Sat............. Haydock, **Stratford**, Ascot, Thirsk, Wolverhampton, Kempton
9 Sun..York, **Fontwell**
10 Mon..............................**Perth**, Brighton, Chelmsford City, **Newton Abbot**
11 Tue .... Catterick, Leicester, Salisbury, **Worcester**
12 Wed.. Carlisle, **Uttoxeter**, Kempton, Doncaster
13 Thu...Doncaster, Chepstow, Hamilton, Epsom
14 Fri ....Doncaster, Chester, Salisbury, Sandown
15 Sat...... Doncaster, Chester, Bath, Musselburgh, Chelmsford City, Lingfield
16 Sun.. Bath, Ffos Las
17 Mon... **Hexham**, **Worcester**, Brighton, Kempton
18 Tue ....Redcar, Yarmouth, Chepstow, Kempton
19 Wed.. Beverley, Yarmouth, Sandown, **Kelso**
20 Thu..Ayr, Yarmouth, Chelmsford City, Pontefract
21 Fri ....Ayr, Newbury, Newcastle, **Newton Abbot**
22 Sat.............. Ayr, Newmarket, Chelmsford City, Catterick, Wolverhampton,
.... Newbury
23 Sun...Hamilton, **Uttoxeter**, **Plumpton**
24 Mon..Hamilton, Leicester, Kempton, Newcastle
25 Tue ....Beverley, **Warwick**, Chelmsford City, Lingfield
26 Wed....................................**Perth**, Wolverhampton, Goodwood, Redcar

7 Thu .... **Perth**, Newmarket, Kempton, Pontefract
8 Fri .... Haydock, Newmarket, Newcastle, **Worcester**
9 Sat .... Haydock, Chester, Chelmsford City, Ripon, **Market Rasen**, ... Newmarket
0 Sun .... Musselburgh, Epsom

October

1 Mon .... Catterick, Bath, Kempton, **Newton Abbot**
2 Tue .... Ayr, **Southwell**, Kempton, **Sedgefield**
3 Wed .... Newcastle, **Bangor**, Salisbury, Nottingham
4 Thu .... **Huntingdon**, Chelmsford City, **Warwick**, Lingfield
5 Fri .... **Hexham**, Wolverhampton, Ascot, **Fontwell**
6 Sat .... Redcar, Newmarket, Ascot, Wolverhampton, **Fontwell**
7 Sun .... **Kelso**, **Uttoxeter**
8 Mon .... Pontefract, **Stratford**, Kempton, Windsor
9 Tue .... Catterick, Leicester, Brighton, Newcastle
0 Wed .... **Ludlow**, Kempton, Nottingham, **Towcester**
1 Thu .... Ayr, **Worcester**, Chelmsford City, **Exeter**
2 Fri .... York, Newmarket, **Newton Abbot**, Wolverhampton
3 Sat .... **Hexham**, Newmarket, Chelmsford City, York, **Chepstow**
4 Sun .... **Chepstow**, Goodwood
5 Mon .... Musselburgh, Yarmouth, Kempton, Windsor
6 Tue .... **Hereford**, Kempton, **Huntingdon**, Leicester
7 Wed .... Newcastle, Nottingham, Bath, **Wetherby**
8 Thu .... **Carlisle**, **Uttoxeter**, Brighton, Chelmsford City
9 Fri .... Haydock, **Fakenham**, **Wincanton**, Newcastle, Redcar
0 Sat .... Catterick, **Market Rasen**, Ascot, **Stratford**, **Ffos Las**, ... Wolverhampton
1 Sun .... **Sedgefield**, **Kempton**
2 Mon .... Pontefract, Kempton, **Plumpton**, Windsor
3 Tue .... Newcastle, Yarmouth, **Exeter**, Kempton
4 Wed .... Newcastle, Newmarket, **Fontwell**, **Worcester**
5 Thu .... **Carlisle**, **Ludlow**, Chelmsford City, **Southwell**
6 Fri .... Doncaster, **Cheltenham**, Kempton, Newbury
7 Sat .... Doncaster, **Cheltenham**, Kempton, **Kelso**, Newbury
8 Sun .... **Aintree**, **Wincanton**
9 Mon .... **Ayr**, Leicester, Chelmsford City, Redcar
0 Tue .... Catterick, **Bangor**, **Chepstow**, Wolverhampton
1 Wed .... **Fakenham**, Kempton, Nottingham, **Taunton**

November

1 Thu .... **Sedgefield**, **Stratford**, Lingfield, Wolverhampton
2 Fri .... **Wetherby**, Newmarket, Kempton, **Uttoxeter**
3 Sat .... **Ayr**, Newmarket, **Ascot**, Newcastle, **Wetherby**
4 Sun .... **Carlisle**, **Huntingdon**
5 Mon .... **Hereford**, Kempton, **Plumpton**
6 Tue .... Redcar, Wolverhampton, **Exeter**, Kempton
7 Wed .... **Musselburgh**, Nottingham, **Chepstow**, Newcastle
8 Thu .... **Sedgefield**, **Market Rasen**, Chelmsford City, **Newbury**
9 Fri .... **Hexham**, **Warwick**, **Fontwell**, Newcastle
0 Sat .... **Aintree**, Chelmsford City, Doncaster, **Wincanton**, **Kelso**

11 Sun ... **Ffos Las**, **Sandow**

12 Mon ... **Carlisle**, Southwell, **Kempto**

13 Tue ... **Hereford**, Chelmsford City, **Huntingdon**, **Lingfiel**

14 Wed ... **Ayr**, **Bangor**, **Exeter**, Kempto

15 Thu ... **Ludlow**, Chelmsford City, Southwell, **Taunto**

16 Fri ... **Newcastle**, **Cheltenham**, Lingfield, Wolverhampto

17 Sat ... **Wetherby**, **Cheltenham**, Lingfield, **Uttoxeter**, Wolverhampto

18 Sun ... **Cheltenham**, **Fontwel**

19 Mon ... **Leicester**, Kempton, **Plumpto**

20 Tue ... **Fakenham**, Lingfield, **Southwel**

21 Wed ... **Hexham**, **Warwick**, **Chepstow**, Kempto

22 Thu ... Newcastle, **Market Rasen**, **Wincanton**, Wolverhampto

23 Fri ... **Catterick**, **Ascot**, **Ffos Las**, Kempto

24 Sat ... **Haydock**, **Huntingdon**, **Ascot**, Wolverhampton, Lingfiel

25 Sun ... **Uttoxeter**, **Exete**

26 Mon ... **Musselburgh**, **Ludlow**, **Kempto**

27 Tue ... **Sedgefield**, Southwell, **Lingfiel**

28 Wed ... Newcastle, **Hereford**, **Wetherby**, Wolverhampto

29 Thu ... **Ayr**, **Towcester**, Chelmsford City, **Taunto**

30 Fri ... **Doncaster**, Southwell, **Newbury**, Newcastl

December

1 Sat ... **Doncaster**, **Bangor**, **Newbury**, **Newcastle**, Wolverhampto

2 Sun ... **Carlisle**, **Leiceste**

3 Mon ... **Musselburgh**, Wolverhampton, **Plumpto**

4 Tue ... **Fakenham**, Lingfield, **Southwel**

5 Wed ... **Haydock**, **Ludlow**, Kempton, Lingfiel

6 Thu ... **Leicester**, Chelmsford City, **Market Rasen**, **Wincanto**

7 Fri ... **Sedgefield**, **Exeter**, Kempton, **Sandow**

8 Sat ... **Aintree**, Wolverhampton, **Chepstow**, **Wetherby**, **Sandow**

9 Sun ... **Kelso**, **Huntingdo**

10 Mon ... **Musselburgh**, Wolverhampton, **Lingfiel**

11 Tue ... Southwell, **Fontwell**, **Uttoxete**

12 Wed ... **Hexham**, **Leicester**, Kempton, Lingfiel

13 Thu ... **Newcastle**, **Warwick**, Chelmsford City, **Taunto**

14 Fri ... **Doncaster**, **Bangor**, Kempton, **Cheltenha**

15 Sat ... **Doncaster**, **Cheltenham**, Newcastle, **Hereford**, Wolverhampto

16 Sun ... **Carlisle**, **Southwel**

17 Mon ... Wolverhampton, **Ffos Las**, **Plumpto**

18 Tue ... **Catterick**, **Fakenham**, Southwe

19 Wed ... Newcastle, **Ludlow**, Lingfield, **Newbur**

20 Thu ... Southwell, Chelmsford City, **Towcester**, **Exete**

21 Fri ... Southwell, **Ascot**, **Uttoxeter**, Wolverhampto

22 Sat ... **Haydock**, **Ascot**, **Newcastle**, Lingfiel

26 Wed ... **Sedgefield**, **Huntingdon**, **Fontwell**, **Wetherby**, **Market Rasen**
... **Kempton**, Wolverhampton, **Wincanto**

27 Thu ... **Wetherby**, Wolverhampton, **Chepstow**, **Kempto**

28 Fri ... **Catterick**, **Leicester**, Lingfiel

29 Sat ... **Doncaster**, Southwell, **Newbury**, **Kels**

30 Sun ... **Haydock**, Lingfield, **Taunto**

31 Mon ... **Uttoxeter**, Lingfield, **Warwic**

Big-race dates

November

4 Wetherby .... Charlie Hall Chase
11 Wincanton .... Elite Hurdle
18 Cheltenham .... BetVictor Gold Cup
25 Haydock .... Betfair Chase
25 Haydock .... Ascot Hurdle

December

2 Newbury .... Ladbrokes Gold Cup
2 Newcastle .... Fighting Fifth Hurdle
9 Sandown .... Tingle Creek Trophy
9 Aintree .... Becher Chase
16 Cheltenham .... Caspian Caviar Gold Cup
23 Ascot .... Long Walk Hurdle
26 Kempton .... King George VI Chase
27 Chepstow .... Welsh Grand National
30 Newbury .... Challow Novices' Hurdle

January

6 Sandown .... Tolworth Hurdle
13 Warwick .... Classic Chase
20 Ascot .... Clarence House Chase
20 Haydock .... Peter Marsh Chase
27 Cheltenham .... Festival Trials Day

February

10 Newbury .... Betfair Hurdle
17 Ascot .... Ascot Chase
17 Haydock .... Grand National Trial
24 Kempton .... BetBright Chase

March

10 Sandown .... Imperial Cup
13 Cheltenham .... Champion Hurdle
14 Cheltenham .... Champion Chase
15 Cheltenham .... Stayers' Hurdle
16 Cheltenham .... Cheltenham Gold Cup

April

2 Fairyhouse .... Irish Grand National
12 Aintree .... Betfred Bowl
13 Aintree .... Melling Chase
14 Aintree .... Crabbie's Grand National
21 Ayr .... Scottish Grand National
28 Sandown .... bet365 Gold Cup

Big-race records

BetVictor Gold Cup (2m4½f) Cheltenham

Year	Winner	Age-wgt	Trainer	Jockey	SP	Ra
2007	**L'Antartique**	7-10-13	F Murphy	G Lee	13-2	2
2008	**Imperial Commander**	7-10-7	N Twiston-Davies	P Brennan	13-2	1
2009	**Tranquil Sea**	7-10-13	E O'Grady	A McNamara	11-2f	1
2010	**Little Josh**	8-10-8	N Twiston-Davies	S Twiston-Davies (3)	20-1	1
2011	**Great Endeavour**	7-10-3	D Pipe	T Murphy	8-1	2
2012	**Al Ferof**	7-11-8	P Nicholls	R Walsh	8-1	1
2013	**Johns Spirit**	6-10-2	J O'Neill	R McLernon	7-1	2
2014	**Caid Du Berlais**	5-10-13	P Nicholls	S Twiston-Davies	10-1	1
2015	**Annacotty**	7-11-0	A King	I Popham	12-1	2
2016	**Taquin Du Seuil**	9-11-11	J O'Neill	A Coleman	8-1	1

Course form is the key factor as 20 of the last 25 winners had previously been successf at Cheltenham and two of the exceptions had been placed at the Cheltenham Festiva That's even more remarkable considering winners tend to be so inexperienced, with 1 of the last 43 being second-season chasers aged five to eight. The last winner to hav had more than 15 chase runs was The Outback Way in 1999 and the last older winne was Clear Cut in 1975. There have been several great weight-carrying performance down the years, most recently Taquin Du Seuil and Al Ferof, but they are the only wir ners in the last decade to have carried more than 11st.

Betfair Chase (3m1f) Haydock

Year	Winner	Age-wgt	Trainer	Jockey	SP	Ra
2007	**Kauto Star**	7-11-7	P Nicholls	S Thomas	4-5f	
2008	**Snoopy Loopy**	10-11-7	P Bowen	S Durack	33-1	
2009	**Kauto Star**	9-11-7	P Nicholls	R Walsh	4-6f	
2010	**Imperial Commander**	9-11-7	N Twiston-Davies	P Brennan	10-11f	
2011	**Kauto Star**	11-11-7	P Nicholls	R Walsh	6-1	
2012	**Silviniaco Conti**	6-11-7	P Nicholls	R Walsh	7-4	
2013	**Cue Card**	7-11-7	C Tizzard	J Tizzard	9-1	
2014	**Silviniaco Conti**	8-11-7	P Nicholls	N Fehily	10-3	
2015	**Cue Card**	9-11-7	C Tizzard	P Brennan	7-4	
2016	**Cue Card**	10-11-7	C Tizzard	P Brennan	15-8f	

First run in 2005, this race has quickly become the first port of call for proven top-clas staying chasers. As such 11 of the 12 winners had already secured a top-two finish a Grade 1 level and the sole exception, Snoopy Loopy, is the only winner priced bigge han 9-1. Tactical speed is vital at Haydock and form over shorter trips has been more elling than proven stamina – every winner since Kingscliff in the inaugural running had reviously won over 2m or 2m1f whereas four hadn't won over the big-race trip itself.

Ladbrokes Gold Cup (3m2f) Newbury

007	**Denman**	7-11-12	P Nicholls	S Thomas	5-1	18
008	**Madison Du Berlais**	7-11-4	D Pipe	T Scudamore	25-1	15
009	**Denman**	9-11-12	P Nicholls	R Walsh	11-4f	19
010	**Diamond Harry**	7-10-0	N Williams	D Jacob	6-1	18
011	**Carruthers**	8-10-4	M Bradstock	M Batchelor	10-1	18
012	**Bobs Worth**	7-11-6	N Henderson	B Geraghty	4-1f	19
013	**Triolo D'Alene**	6-11-1	N Henderson	B Geraghty	20-1	21
014	**Many Clouds**	7-11-6	O Sherwood	L Aspell	8-1	19
015	**Smad Place**	8-11-4	A King	W Hutchison	7-1	15
016	**Native River**	6-11-1	C Tizzard	R Johnson	7-2f	19

ust about the most high-quality handicap of the season, won by some very special orses including twice by Denman as well as subsequent Gold Cup and Grand National vinners since then. The increasing quality has seen 11 of the last 14 winners carry 11st r more to victory after 16 out of 18 prior to Strong Flow in 2003 had been below that enchmark. Eleven out of 18 winners since 1999 were second-season chasers (includ-ng three winners of the RSA Chase) and one of the exceptions, Strong Flow, was a ovice, so lack of experience isn't a worry. Be My Royal was also a winning novice in 002 but was disqualified due to a banned substance, leaving Ireland without a winner ince 1980. In contrast, no horse older than nine has won since Diamond Edge in 1981, vith 83 beaten in the meantime. The Badger Ales Trophy is best of the traditional trials, although six of the last 11 winners were making their seasonal debuts.

Tingle Creek Trophy (2m) Sandown

007	**Twist Magic**	5-11-7	P Nicholls	S Thomas	5-1	8
008	**Master Minded**	5-11-7	P Nicholls	A McCoy	4-7f	7
009	**Twist Magic**	7-11-7	P Nicholls	R Walsh	9-4	5
010*	**Master Minded**	7-11-7	P Nicholls	N Fehily	10-11f	9
011	**Sizing Europe**	9-11-7	H de Bromhead	A Lynch	11-8f	7
012	**Sprinter Sacre**	6-11-7	N Henderson	B Geraghty	4-11f	7
013	**Sire De Grugy**	7-11-7	G Moore	J Moore	7-4jf	9
014	**Dodging Bullets**	6-11-7	P Nicholls	S Twiston-Davies	9-1	10
015	**Sire De Grugy**	9-11-7	G Moore	J Moore	10-3	7
016	**Un De Sceaux**	8-11-7	W Mullins	R Walsh	5-4f	6

run at Cheltenham

This changed from a handicap to a Grade 1 conditions event prior to the 1994 renewal and has grown to rank alongside the Champion Chase in terms of quality. Moscow Flyer's epic 2004 win over Well Chief and Azertyuiop was the most memorable running and since then the Irish legend has been matched by Master Minded, Sprinter Sacre, Sire De Grugy and Dodging Bullets in doubling up at Cheltenham, while Un De Sceaux went on to win the Ryanair. As well as going on to big things, winners also tend to have proved themselves already at the highest level as Dodging Bullets, Sire De Grugy (for his first win in 2013) and Kauto Star (for his first win in 2005) are the only ones since Direct Route in 1998 not to have previously landed a Grade 1 chase. As a result no winner has returned bigger than 9-1 since the race gained Grade 1 status.

Caspian Caviar Gold Cup (2m5f) Cheltenham

2007	**Tamarinbleu**	7-11-8	D Pipe	D O'Regan	22-1	[illegible]
2008	*Abandoned*					
2009	**Poquelin**	6-11-8	P Nicholls	R Walsh	7-2f	[illegible]
2010	**Poquelin**	7-11-12	P Nicholls	I Popham (5)	16-1	[illegible]
2011	**Quantitativeeasing**	6-10-7	N Henderson	B Geraghty	6-1	[illegible]
2012	**Unioniste**	4-10-0	P Nicholls	H Derham (5)	15-2	[illegible]
2013	**Double Ross**	8-10-8	N Twiston-Davies	S Twiston-Davies	14-1	[illegible]
2014	**Niceonefrankie**	8-11-5	V Williams	A Coleman	16-1	[illegible]
2015	**Village Vic**	8-10-0	P Hobbs	R Johnson	8-1	[illegible]
2016	**Frodon**	4-10-10	P Nicholls	S Twiston-Davies	14-1	[illegible]

Not surprisingly, the BetVictor Gold Cup, held at the same venue four weeks earlie is the most useful guide to this event as six of the last 12 winners ran in that race, wit Exotic Dancer doing the double (to emulate Pegwell Bay and Senor El Betrutti in th previous 20 years) and Quantitativeeasing, Poquelin (for his 2009 victory) and Monke hostin improving on their second-placed efforts. Even compared to the BetVictor, it's great race for young horses – four-year-olds Frodon and Unioniste are the best exampl and three winners since 2006 were only six, while Double Ross was another successfu novice in 2013 – whereas Fragrant Dawn was the last winner older than eight in 1993 The race has featured some notable weight-carrying performances and five of the las ten winners carried 11st 4lb or more.

Long Walk Hurdle (3m½f) Ascot

2007	**Lough Derg**	7-11-7	D Pipe	T Scudamore	14-1	[illegible]
2008	**Punchestowns**	5-11-7	N Henderson	B Geraghty	3-1f	[illegible]
2009*	**Big Buck's**	6-11-7	P Nicholls	R Walsh	1-2f	[illegible]
2010*	**Big Buck's**	7-11-7	P Nicholls	A McCoy	2-13f	[illegible]
2011	**Big Buck's**	8-11-7	P Nicholls	R Walsh	3-10f	[illegible]
2012	**Reve De Sivola**	7-11-7	N Williams	R Johnson	9-2	[illegible]
2013	**Reve De Sivola**	8-11-7	N Williams	R Johnson	9-4	[illegible]
2014	**Reve De Sivola**	9-11-7	N Williams	D Jacob	13-2	[illegible]
2015	**Thistlecrack**	7-11-7	C Tizzard	T Scudamore	2-1f	[illegible]
2016	**Unowhatimeanharry**	8-11-7	H Fry	B Geraghty	6-5f	[illegible]

**run at Newbury*

Defending champions deserve the utmost respect because ten of the 17 runnings sinc 2000 were won by just three horses – Baracouda leads the way with four victories fron 2000 to 2004 (he was also second at 4-11 to Deano's Beeno in between), Big Buck's reeled off a hat-trick from 2009 to 2011 and Reve De Sivola did likewise from 2012 t 2014 before finishing second the following year. Four-year-olds fare better than they d at Cheltenham aged five – Silver Wedge and Ocean Hawk were successful in the 1990s – but generally you want an older horse with the last seven winners aged at least seven

King George VI Chase (3m) Kempton

2007	**Kauto Star**	7-11-10	P Nicholls	R Walsh	4-6f	[illegible]
2008	**Kauto Star**	8-11-10	P Nicholls	R Walsh	10-11f	[illegible]
2009	**Kauto Star**	9-11-10	P Nicholls	R Walsh	8-13f	[illegible]
2010*	**Long Run**	6-11-10	N Henderson	Mr S W-Cohen	9-2	[illegible]
2011	**Kauto Star**	11-11-10	P Nicholls	R Walsh	3-1	[illegible]
2012	**Long Run**	7-11-10	N Henderson	Mr S W-Cohen	15-8f	[illegible]

FRODON: the second four-year-old in five seasons to win the Caspian Caviar Gold Cup, which has been a terrific race for youngsters over many years

2013	**Silviniaco Conti**	7-11-10	P Nicholls	N Fehily	7-2	9
2014	**Silviniaco Conti**	8-11-10	P Nicholls	N Fehily	15-8f	10
2015	**Cue Card**	9-11-10	C Tizzard	P Brennan	9-2	9
2016	**Thistlecrack**	8-11-10	C Tizzard	T Scudamore	11-10f	5

**run in January 2011*

A race the best horses often manage to win several times. It's not just the amazing Kauto Star, who landed a fifth win in 2011, as Silviniaco Conti, Long Run, Kicking King, See More Business and One Man are also multiple winners since the days of the legendary Desert Orchid. That also emphasises the importance of experience as 15 of the last 18 winners were in at least their third season of chasing – although, staggeringly, Thistlecrack somehow managed to prevail as a novice last year. The Kauto Star Novices' Chase, run over the same course and distance, is often seen as a good trial yet has seen only Long Run follow up. Kempton's relatively sharp three miles provides slightly less of a stamina test than other major tracks, particularly Cheltenham, and the importance of tactical speed is shown by the fact that the 13 winners prior to Thistlecrack had all landed a Graded chase from 2m4f to 2m6f. That means those who have just failed to see out the Gold Cup trip often make amends here, such as One Man and Florida Pearl, while Kauto Star was also more vulnerable in March, there were stamina doubts about Kicking King prior to his first win and Edredon Bleu was a 2m performer stepping into the unknown. Thistlecrack was also the first winner not to have previously landed a Grade 1 chase since Teeton Mill in 1998.

Christmas Hurdle (2m) Kempton

2007	**Straw Bear**	6-11-7	N Gifford	A McCoy	9-2	6
2008	**Harchibald**	9-11-7	N Meade	P Carberry	7-1	7
2009	**Go Native**	6-11-7	N Meade	D Condon	5-2	7
2010*	**Binocular**	7-11-7	N Henderson	A McCoy	13-8f	6
2011	**Binocular**	7-11-7	N Henderson	A McCoy	5-4f	5

NATIVE RIVER: it takes a special horse to win the Welsh National under a big weight as those at the foot of the handicap are generally favoured

2012	**Darlan**	5-11-7	N Henderson	A McCoy	3-1	7
2013	**My Tent Or Yours**	6-11-7	N Henderson	A McCoy	11-8	6
2014	**Faugheen**	6-11-7	W Mullins	R Walsh	4-11f	6
2015	**Faugheen**	7-11-7	W Mullins	R Walsh	1-4f	5
2016	**Yanworth**	6-11-7	A King	B Geraghty	5-4f	5

**run in January 2011*

Forget Harchibald's trend-busting win in 2008 as this sharp two miles is ideal for young, improving types. Apart from Harchibald and 1-4 certainty Faugheen in 2015, every winner since 2000 would have been aged five or six had Binocular not had his first win forced over into 2011 by bad weather and then pipped Rock On Ruby by a nose at the end of that year. Six of the last ten winners were getting off the mark for the season and two of the four exceptions had won the Fighting Fifth.

Welsh Grand National (3m5f) Chepstow

2007	**Miko De Beauchene**	7-10-5	R Alner	A Thornton	13-2	18
2008	**Notre Pere**	7-11-0	T Dreaper	A Lynch	16-1	20
2009	**Dream Alliance**	8-10-8	P Hobbs	T O'Brien	20-1	18
2010*	**Synchronised**	8-11-6	J O'Neill	A McCoy	5-1	18
2011	**Le Beau Bai**	8-10-1	R Lee	C Poste	10-1	20
2012	**Monbeg Dude**	8-10-1	M Scudamore	P Carberry	10-1	17
2013	**Mountainous**	8-10-0	R Lee	P Moloney	20-1	20
2014	**Emperor's Choice**	7-10-8	V Williams	A Coleman	9-1	19
2015**	**Mountainous**	11-10-6	K Lee	J Moore	9-1	20
2016	**Native River**	6-11-12	C Tizzard	R Johnson	11-4f	20

**run in January 2011* ***run in January 2016*

Chepstow lost a key trial for this race with the Rehearsal Chase moving to Newcastle, but it has basically been replaced by another handicap in early December – aptly named the Welsh Grand National Trial – and course form remains pivotal. Six of the last ten winners had previously triumphed at the track, making 13 of the last 19 in all, which tends to eliminate the vast majority of the field. As with most staying handicap chases that are often run in the mud, horses at the foot of the weights are massively favoured. Only nine winners since 1976 carried more than 11st and the last three show the quality needed as Synchronised went on to win the Gold Cup and Native River and Halcon Genelardais were third and fourth in that race. Generally punters should not even rule out any horse from out of the handicap, with Mountainous the latest to defy extra weight in 2013, and Kendal Cavalier was as much as 13lb wrong in 1997. Silver Birch was a rare winning favourite in 2004, while remarkably Native River was the first winner to have run in the Hennessy since Playschool in 1987.

Betfair Hurdle (2m½f) Newbury

2008	**Wingman**	6-10-0	G Moore	J Moore	14-1	24
2009	*Abandoned*					
2010	**Get Me Out Of Here**	6-10-6	J O'Neill	A McCoy	6-1	23
2011	**Recession Proof**	5-10-8	J Quinn	D Costello	12-1	15
2012	**Zarkandar**	5-11-1	P Nicholls	R Walsh	11-4f	20
2013	**My Tent Or Yours**	6-11-2	N Henderson	A McCoy	5-1f	19
2014	**Splash Of Ginge**	6-10-10	N Twiston-Davies	R Hatch (7)	33-1	20
2015	**Violet Dancer**	5-10-9	G Moore	Joshua Moore	20-1	23
2016	**Agrapart**	5-10-10	N Williams	L Kelly (5)	16-1	22
2017	**Ballyandy**	6-11-1	N Twiston-Davies	S Twiston-Davies	3-1f	16

A top-class handicap hurdle which has been rewarded for a big increase in prize-money in recent times. Young improvers with Grade 1 potential are preferred to experienced handicappers – the last ten winners were five or six, six of the last eight were novices and the same number were making their handicap debuts. Nine of the last 19 winners carried more than 11st, yet no horse has defied a burden in excess of 11st 7lb since Persian War in 1968. Eight of the last 24 winners were officially ahead of the handicapper having had their mark raised since the publication of the weights.

Grand National Trial (3m4½f) Haydock

2008	**Miko De Beauchene**	8-11-12	R Alner	A Thornton	17-2	16
2009	**Rambling Minster**	11-11-0	K Reveley	J Reveley (3)	18-1	16
2010	**Silver By Nature**	8-10-11	L Russell	P Buchanan	7-1	14
2011	**Silver By Nature**	9-11-12	L Russell	P Buchanan	10-1	14
2012	**Giles Cross**	10-10-5	V Dartnall	D O'Regan	4-1f	14
2013	**Well Refreshed**	9-10-0	G Moore	J Moore (3)	9-2f	14
2014	**Rigadin De Beauchene**	9-10-8	V Williams	R Dunne (3)	16-1	14
2015	**Lie Forrit**	11-11-6	L Russell	P Buchanan	8-1	12
2016	**Bishops Road**	8-11-7	K Lee	R Johnson	13-2	8
2017	**Vieux Lion Rouge**	8-11-6	D Pipe	T Scudamore	8-1	13

This race is usually run on soft ground and can be a real test of stamina, so it's extremely rare for winners not to have already triumphed over at least 3m1f. That fact seems to have finally got through to punters in recent years as dour stayers Well Refreshed and Giles Cross were the first winning favourites since Frantic Tan in 2001 and three of the subsequent four winners were priced in single figures. None of the last 14 winners had run more than 14 times over fences even though four were aged in double figures during that time. Neptune Collonges followed up his 2012 second by winning at Aintree, but the race has been overrated as a National trial with the winner no better than fifth since 2000 and several running poorly when well fancied.

BetBright Chase (3m) Kempton

2008	**Gungadu**	8-11-12	P Nicholls	R Walsh	4-1f	15
2009	**Nacarat**	8-10-13	T George	A McCoy	10-1	20
2010	**Razor Royale**	8-10-5	N Twiston-Davies	P Brennan	11-1	13
2011	**Quinz**	7-11-0	P Hobbs	R Johnson	8-1	16
2012	**Nacarat**	11-11-8	T George	P Brennan	9-2	10
2013	**Opening Batsman**	7-10-5	H Fry	N Fehily	12-1	13
2014	**Bally Legend**	9-10-12	C Keevil	I Popham	28-1	13
2015	**Rocky Creek**	9-11-11	P Nicholls	S Twiston-Davies	8-1	14
2016	**Theatre Guide**	9-10-6	C Tizzard	P Brennan	6-1	15
2017	**Pilgrims Bay**	7-10-2	N Mulholland	J Best	25-1	13

It's remarkable how many horses manage to defy big weights to win this top prize as 11 of the last 18 winners carried more than 11st including Gungadu, Farmer Jack, Marlborough and Gloria Victis from the top of the handicap. Course form is a handy asset with 11 of the last 18 winners having previously been successful at Kempton, while Pilgrims Bay and Bally Legend are the only winners priced bigger than 12-1 since 1997. Novices have a decent record, including three of the last seven winners in Pilgrims Bay, Opening Batsman and Quinz.

Imperial Cup (2m) Sandown

2008	**Ashkazar**	4-10-12	D Pipe	T Murphy	10-3f	22
2009	**Dave's Dream**	6-10-13	N Henderson	B Geraghty	12-1	19
2010	**Qaspal**	6-10-3	P Hobbs	A McCoy	11-4f	23
2011	**Alarazi**	7-10-3	L Wadham	D Elsworth	10-1	24
2012	**Paintball**	5-10-7	C Longsdon	N Fehily	20-1	24
2013	**First Avenue**	8-11-1	L Mongan	N Baker (10)	20-1	19
2014	**Baltimore Rock**	5-10-12	D Pipe	T Scudamore	7-1	14
2015	**Ebony Express**	6-11-7	Dr R Newland	W Kennedy	33-1	23
2016	**Flying Angel**	5-10-10	N Twiston-Davies	R Hatch (3)	9-1	14
2017	**London Prize**	6-11-2	I Williams	T O'Brien	10	13

This falls on the eve of the Cheltenham Festival and, with the sponsors putting up a bonus for horses doubling up, a strong and competitive field is always assured. Unexposed youngsters hold the key as 12 of the last 15 winners were novices – seven having raced no more than four times over hurdles – and nine of the last 20 were five-year-olds, with two of the exceptions aged just four. David Pipe has won three of the last 11 runnings to maintain a strong family tradition as his father Martin also won three of the last five in which he had runners. No winner has carried more than 11st 2lb since 2003.

Supreme Novices' Hurdle (2m½f) Cheltenham

2008	**Captain Cee Bee**	7-11-7	E Harty	R Thornton	17-2	22
2009	**Go Native**	6-11-7	N Meade	P Carberry	12-1	20
2010	**Menorah**	5-11-7	P Hobbs	R Johnson	12-1	18
2011	**Al Ferof**	6-11-7	P Nicholls	R Walsh	10-1	15
2012	**Cinders And Ashes**	5-11-7	D McCain	J Maguire	10-1	19
2013	**Champagne Fever**	6-11-7	W Mullins	R Walsh	5-1	12

2014	**Vautour**	5-11-7	W Mullins	R Walsh	7-2jf	18
2015	**Douvan**	5-11-7	W Mullins	R Walsh	2-1f	12
2016	**Altior**	6-11-7	N Henderson	N de Boinville	4-1	14
2017	**Labaik**	6-11-7	G Elliott	J Kennedy	25-1	14

This traditionally gets Ireland off to a flying start at the Cheltenham Festival as the raiders have taken 12 of the last 19 runnings, including three of the last five for Willie Mullins. The success of the Mullins team has started to reverse the dreadful record of favourites, though Douvan is still the only successful outright market leader since Brave Inca in 2004 and just three of the last 13 horses sent off at 2-1 or shorter came out on top. Many of the beaten favourites, such as Cue Card, Dunguib and Cousin Vinny, had won the previous year's Champion Bumper so don't be sucked in by winners of that race, with Champagne Fever the only one to follow up since Montelado in 1992. Labaik and Melon were first and second for the ex-Flat brigade last year, but they are only horses who started on the Flat to have finished in the first four since Binocular in 2008 and 43 others have fallen short in that time. The Tolworth Hurdle is a terrible guide despite being the only Grade 1 novice hurdle over the trip in Britain earlier in the season, even with Noland doing the double in 2006. Seventeen of the last 21 winners had run in the previous 45 days, showing recent match practice is vital, and 18 of those 21 had won last time out.

Racing Post Arkle Chase (2m) Cheltenham

2008	**Tidal Bay**	7-11-7	H Johnson	D O'Regan	6-1	14
2009	**Forpadydeplasterer**	7-11-7	T Cooper	B Geraghty	8-1	17
2010	**Sizing Europe**	8-11-7	H de Bromhead	A Lynch	6-1	12
2011	**Captain Chris**	7-11-7	P Hobbs	R Johnson	6-1	10
2012	**Sprinter Sacre**	6-11-7	N Henderson	B Geraghty	8-11f	6
2013	**Simonsig**	7-11-7	N Henderson	B Geraghty	8-15f	7
2014	**Western Warhorse**	6-11-4	D Pipe	T Scudamore	33-1	9
2015	**Un De Sceaux**	7-11-4	W Mullins	R Walsh	4-6f	11
2016	**Douvan**	6-11-4	W Mullins	R Walsh	1-4f	7
2017	**Altior**	7-11-4	N Henderson	N de Boinville	1-4f	9

A typical Arkle winner tends to be well fancied with proven class over hurdles and plenty of chasing experience. Eight of the last 11 winners had won a Graded race over hurdles (six at Grade 1 level) and all but one of the exceptions had been placed, while only Western Warhorse and Simonsig hadn't run at least three times over fences since Well Chief in 2004. Western Warhorse is also the only winner priced bigger than 11-1 since 1989 and it was perhaps inevitable that the moderate record of favourites would be put right with wins for odds-on shots Altior, Douvan, Un De Sceaux, Simonsig and Sprinter Sacre in recent times. Three of those were trained by Nicky Henderson, who has won the race six times. The abolition of an overly generous weight-for-age allowance in 2008 has ended the dominance of French-bred five-year-olds, with seven of the last 11 winners aged seven or eight, although that's as old as you want to go. No horse older than eight has won since Danish Flight in 1989 and since 2000 alone that includes several fancied horses such as Ned Kelly, Adamant Approach, Barton, Captain Cee Bee, Overturn, Rock On Ruby and Royal Caviar.

Ultima H'cap Chase (3m1f) Cheltenham

2008	**An Accordion**	7-10-12	D Pipe	T Scudamore	7-1	14
2009	**Wichita Lineman**	8-10-9	J O'Neill	A McCoy	5-1f	21
2010	**Chief Dan George**	10-10-10	J Moffatt	P Aspell	33-1	24

2011	**Bensalem**	8-11-2	A King	R Thornton	5-1	19
2012	**Alfie Sherrin**	9-10-0	J O'Neill	R McLernon	14-1	19
2013	**Golden Chieftain**	8-10-5	C Tizzard	B Powell (5)	28-1	24
2014	**Holywell**	7-11-6	J O'Neill	R McLernon	10-1	23
2015	**The Druids Nephew**	8-11-3	N Mulholland	B Geraghty	8-1	24
2016	**Un Temps Pour Tout**	7-11-7	D Pipe	T Scudamore	11-1	23
2017	**Un Temps Pour Tout**	8-11-12	D Pipe	T Scudamore	9-1	23

Youth has taken over this contest. Fourteen of the last 17 winners were novices (five) or second-season chasers (nine) and The Druids Nephew is the only one to have raced more than 11 times over fences since 2007 hero Joes Edge, whereas just two horses older than ten have even made the frame since 1997 out of many to have tried. A strong stayer is essential as only three of the last 21 winners lacked previous winning form at 3m or further and all three had been placed over that trip on soft ground. Long-standing trends in favour of those near the bottom of the weights have been turned around in recent years by the last four winners all carrying more than 11st to victory, although Un Temps Pour Tout was the first to defy a mark of more than 150 since 1983 when landing his second victory last year. That has also helped those near the front of the market, with all four no bigger than 11-1 after three of the previous seven had been 28-1 or bigger.

Stan James Champion Hurdle (2m½f) Cheltenham

2008	**Katchit**	5-11-10	A King	R Thornton	10-1	15
2009	**Punjabi**	6-11-10	N Henderson	B Geraghty	22-1	23
2010	**Binocular**	6-11-10	N Henderson	A McCoy	9-1	12
2011	**Hurricane Fly**	7-11-10	W Mullins	R Walsh	11-4f	11
2012	**Rock On Ruby**	7-11-10	P Nicholls	N Fehily	11-1	10
2013	**Hurricane Fly**	9-11-10	W Mullins	R Walsh	13-8f	9
2014	**Jezki**	6-11-10	J Harrington	B Geraghty	9-1	9
2015	**Faugheen**	7-11-10	W Mullins	R Walsh	4-5f	8
2016	**Annie Power**	8-11-3	W Mullins	R Walsh	5-2f	12
2017	**Buveur D'Air**	6-11-10	N Henderson	N Fehily	5-1	11

This race has been dominated in recent times by great Irish champions with Hurricane Fly, Hardy Eustace and Istabraq all multiple winners, though Hurricane Fly was the first to regain the crown since Comedy Of Errors in 1975. He was also unusual as a nine-year-old winner because younger horses have been faring much better in recent times. Katchit defied the biggest trend of all as a winning five-year-old in 2008 and six others have been placed in the last ten years, with seven of the nine subsequent winners aged six or seven. Three of the last five favourites have won, but this is traditionally the toughest of Cheltenham's four championship races to call with form in slowly run trials often proving misleading and instead previous festival form is the key. Plenty of horses step up having been placed the previous year, with wins for Hurricane Fly, Binocular, Punjabi and Brave Inca since 2006 after they were third 12 months earlier. Of the other winners in that time, Buveur D'Air, Jezki and Sublimity had top-four finishes in the Supreme, Faugheen and Rock On Ruby were first and second in the Neptune, Katchit won the Triumph and Annie Power would have won the Mares' Hurdle but for falling at the last.

Neptune Novices' Hurdle (2m5f) Cheltenham

2008	**Fiveforthree**	6-11-7	W Mullins	R Walsh	7-1	15
2009	**Mikael D'Haguenet**	5-11-7	W Mullins	R Walsh	5-2f	14
2010	**Peddlers Cross**	5-11-7	D McCain	J Maguire	7-1	17

2011	**First Lieutenant**	6-11-7	M Morris	D Russell	7-1	12
2012	**Simonsig**	6-11-7	N Henderson	B Geraghty	2-1f	17
2013	**The New One**	5-11-7	N Twiston-Davies	S Twiston-Davies	5-1	8
2014	**Faugheen**	6-11-7	W Mullins	R Walsh	6-4f	15
2015	**Windsor Park**	6-11-7	D Weld	D Russell	9-2	10
2016	**Yorkhill**	6-11-7	W Mullins	R Walsh	3-1	11
2017	**Willoughby Court**	6-11-7	B Pauling	D Bass	14-1	15

Much like the Supreme, this often throws up a supposed good thing who will be worth opposing. There have been just three winning favourites since 2000 and plenty of short-priced jollies have been turned over in that time, mainly from Ireland with Pont Alexandre, So Young and Rite Of Passage recent examples. Even so, the Irish have a good record overall with six winners in the last ten years. Fifteen of the last 18 winners hadn't run on the Flat, with seven recording a top-six finish in one of the big bumpers at Cheltenham, Aintree and Punchestown the previous spring. There has been only one winner older than six since 1974, with 52 beaten since 1998, while all 16 Challow Hurdle winners to run have been beaten.

RSA Chase (3m½f) Cheltenham

2008	**Albertas Run**	7-11-4	J O'Neill	A McCoy	4-1f	11
2009	**Cooldine**	7-11-4	W Mullins	R Walsh	9-4f	15
2010	**Weapon's Amnesty**	7-11-4	C Byrnes	D Russell	10-1	9
2011	**Bostons Angel**	7-11-4	Mrs J Harrington	R Power	16-1	12
2012	**Bobs Worth**	7-11-4	N Henderson	B Geraghty	9-2	9
2013	**Lord Windermere**	7-11-4	J Culloty	D Russell	8-1	11
2014	**O'Faolains Boy**	7-11-4	R Curtis	B Geraghty	12-1	15
2015	**Don Poli**	6-11-4	W Mullins	B Cooper	13-8f	8
2016	**Blaklion**	7-11-4	N Twiston-Davies	R Hatch	8-1	8
2017	**Might Bite**	8-11-4	N Henderson	N de Boinville	7-2f	12

UN TEMPS POUR TOUT (centre): the first horse to win Cheltenham's big 3m handicap chase off a mark higher than 150 since 1983

DON POLI: broke the mould of RSA winners, who tend to have had more recent match practice and greater experience, when scoring in 2015

Five winning favourites in 11 years have redressed the balance somewhat, but this still justifies its reputation as a race for upsets with plenty of bubbles getting burst. Eight beaten favourites this century had come into the race unbeaten over fences, with only Denman and Don Poli surviving with their records intact in that time. It's worth bearing in mind that many horses in the field will be getting better and better with experience having wasted little time over hurdles as 12 of the last 16 winners spent no more than one season in that sphere, three of the exceptions raced no more than once outside their novice campaign and the horse to break that streak, Might Bite, had tried chasing the previous season before reverting to hurdles when things went wrong. It's therefore vital to have had enough runs over fences, though, with Don Poli the only winner since Florida Pearl in 1998 not to have run in at least three chases and the only one in more than 50 years not to have run since the turn of the year. Don Poli is also one of five Irish-trained horses to have won in the last nine years and the only one not to have won or finished close in what is now the Flogas Novice Chase at Leopardstown on their previous start. Seven-year-olds have a remarkable record with nine of the last 11 winners, while four of the last seven winners ran in the previous season's Albert Bartlett.

Coral Cup (2m5f) Cheltenham

2008	**Naiad Du Misselot**	7-10-13	F Murphy	D Russell	7-1	24
2009	**Ninetieth Minute**	6-10-3	T Taaffe	P W Flood	14-1	27
2010	**Spirit River**	5-11-2	N Henderson	B Geraghty	14-1	28
2011	**Carlito Brigante**	5-11-0	G Elliott	D Russell	16-1	22
2012	**Son Of Flicka**	8-10-6	D McCain	J Maguire	16-1	28
2013	**Medinas**	6-11-10	A King	W Hutchinson	33-1	28
2014	**Whisper**	6-11-11	N Henderson	N de Boinville (5)	14-1	28
2015	**Aux Ptits Soins**	5-10-7	P Nicholls	S Twiston-Davies	9-1	25

2016	**Diamond King**	8-11-3	G Elliott	D Russell	12-1	26
2017	**Supasundae**	7-11-4	J Harrington	R Power	16-1	25

It seems incredible that Sky's The Limit in 2006 was the first winning five-year-old in this race 13 years after its inception as three more have followed up since and younger, progressive horses have increasingly taken over with nine of the last 12 winners being second-season hurdlers. A light but successful campaign is key as the last ten winners had run no more than four times earlier in the season, though not necessarily with an eye on a plot. After all, 14 of the last 15 had managed a victory, nine of them last time out, and this is such a quality race these days that connections being too clever with the handicapper are likely not to get a run at all. That has also given those near the top of the handicap a chance, shown by the victories of Medinas and Whisper under big weights. Aux Ptits Soins is the only winner since 2008 priced in single figures and there has been just one winning outright favourite in the race's history.

Queen Mother Champion Chase (2m) Cheltenham

2008	**Master Minded**	5-11-10	P Nicholls	R Walsh	3-1	8
2009	**Master Minded**	6-11-10	P Nicholls	R Walsh	4-11f	12
2010	**Big Zeb**	9-11-10	C Murphy	B Geraghty	10-1	9
2011	**Sizing Europe**	9-11-10	H de Bromhead	A Lynch	10-1	11
2012	**Finian's Rainbow**	9-11-10	N Henderson	B Geraghty	4-1	8
2013	**Sprinter Sacre**	7-11-10	N Henderson	B Geraghty	1-4f	7
2014	**Sire De Grugy**	8-11-10	G Moore	J Moore	11-4f	11
2015	**Dodging Bullets**	7-11-10	P Nicholls	S Twiston-Davies	9-2	9
2016	**Sprinter Sacre**	10-11-10	N Henderson	N de Boinville	5-1	10
2017	**Special Tiara**	10-11-10	H de Bromhead	N Fehily	11-1	10

The 2006 winner Newmill is the only one out of the last 25 to return bigger than 11-1 and, while it would be wrong to say that was easy to predict, it was nonetheless forecast in the pages of the RFO – Nick Watts tipped Newmill ante-post at 100-1! Newmill is also one of only three winners out of the last 18 to return bigger than 5-1. The previous year's Arkle is the best pointer as Sprinter Sacre (for his first win), Sizing Europe, Voy Por Ustedes, Azertyuiop and Moscow Flyer have all followed up since 2003 and Douvan (injured when a 2-9 shot last year) is the only winner among the last 14 to run the following year not to be at least placed, while Dodging Bullets and Finian's Rainbow were also the highest-placed representatives from the Arkle when victorious. Also look at the Tingle Creek as five of the last 13 winners had won the Sandown Grade 1 earlier in the season, including three of the last five. However, defending champions have a poor record with just one of the last 14 to take part hanging on to their crown.

Weatherbys Champion Bumper (2m½f) Cheltenham

2008	**Cousin Vinny**	5-11-5	W Mullins	Mr P Mullins	12-1	23
2009	**Dunguib**	6-11-5	P Fenton	Mr B O'Connell	9-2	24
2010	**Cue Card**	4-10-12	C Tizzard	J Tizzard	40-1	24
2011	**Cheltenian**	5-11-5	P Hobbs	R Johnson	14-1	24
2012	**Champagne Fever**	5-11-5	W Mullins	Mr P Mullins	16-1	20
2013	**Briar Hill**	5-11-5	W Mullins	R Walsh	25-1	23
2014	**Silver Concorde**	6-11-5	D Weld	Mr R McNamara	16-1	22
2015	**Moon Racer**	6-11-5	D Pipe	T Scudamore	9-2f	23
2016	**Ballyandy**	5-11-5	N Twiston-Davies	S Twiston-Davies	5-1	23
2017	**Fayonagh**	6-10-12	G Elliott	Mr J Codd	7-1	22

Bonanza time for Ireland, winners of 18 of the 25 runnings and within a nose of another in 2016. Willie Mullins has led the way in style, winning the race eight times, although not since 2013. British trainers have cottoned on to the strength of Irish bumper form and also now try to buying the best Irish prospects, so in total 15 of the 17 winners this century made their debut in Ireland, with Ballyandy and Cue Card the exceptions. Cue Card is also the only successful four-year-old since Dato Star in 1995 as older horses tend to prove too strong, with the early dominance of five-year-olds now challenged by more and more top-class six-year-olds being held back for the race. Favourites have a poor record with just three winners, while horses who have been off the track since the turn of the year have accounted for seven of the last 16 winners from very few runners.

Pertemps Final (3m) Cheltenham

2008	**Ballyfitz**	8-10-8	N Twiston-Davies	P Brennan	18-1	24
2009	**Kayf Aramis**	7-10-5	V Williams	A Coleman	16-1	22
2010	**Buena Vista**	9-10-4	D Pipe	H Frost (3)	16-1	24
2011	**Buena Vista**	10-10-8	D Pipe	C O'Farrell (5)	20-1	23
2012	**Cape Tribulation**	8-10-11	M Jefferson	D O'Regan	14-1	24
2013	**Holywell**	6-11-4	J O'Neill	R McLernon	25-1	24
2014	**Fingal Bay**	8-11-12	P Hobbs	R Johnson	9-2f	23
2015	**Call The Cops**	6-10-12	N Henderson	A Tinkler	9-1	23
2016	**Mall Dini**	6-10-11	P Kelly	D Russell	14-1	24
2017	**Presenting Percy**	6-11-11	P Kelly	D Russell	11-1	24

This race is desperately hard to call and the best policy for punters is to embrace its unpredictability and ignore those near the head of the market, with Fingal Bay the only winning favourite since 2003 and nine of the last 12 winners priced at least 14-1. Tellingly, Fingal Bay was an eight-year-old and older horses deserve plenty of respect because, even amid a run of success for six-year-olds, seven of the last 12 winners being older than seven is a remarkable record for a handicap hurdle. Successive victories for Irish trainer Pat Kelly's novices Mall Dini and Presenting Percy show you should never dismiss the youngsters, but Call The Cops is the only winner out of 34 horses aged seven or younger sent off in single figures since 2003 so it's not worth taking short prices about any of them. It's generally best to stick to lower weights with seven of the last ten winners carrying no more than 10st 12lb, although even that trend is weakening with Presenting Percy and Fingal Bay defying hefty burdens.

Ryanair Chase (2m5f) Cheltenham

2008	**Our Vic**	10-11-10	D Pipe	T Murphy	4-1	9
2009	**Imperial Commander**	8-11-10	N Twiston-Davies	P Brennan	6-1	10
2010	**Albertas Run**	9-11-10	J O'Neill	A McCoy	14-1	13
2011	**Albertas Run**	10-11-10	J O'Neill	A McCoy	6-1	11
2012	**Riverside Theatre**	8-11-10	N Henderson	B Geraghty	7-2f	12
2013	**Cue Card**	7-11-10	C Tizzard	J Tizzard	7-2	8
2014	**Dynaste**	8-11-10	D Pipe	T Scudamore	3-1f	11
2015	**Uxizandre**	7-11-10	A King	T McCoy	16-1	14
2016	**Vautour**	7-11-10	W Mullins	R Walsh	Evsf	15
2017	**Un De Sceaux**	9-11-10	W Mullins	R Walsh	7-4f	8

Upgraded to Grade 1 status in 2008, this race has become a firm feature of Cheltenham since first being run three years earlier. Course form is the key as Riverside Theatre is the only winner not to have been successful at Cheltenham before. In the early days of the race that made the BetVictor Gold Cup and the December Gold Cup the key guides, but as the race has got classier it's Grade 1 form that holds the key and five of the last eight winners were previous Cheltenham Festival heroes, with Uxizandre also beaten less than a length. At the same time, stamina has also become more important and six of the ten winners since the upgrade had posted their best Racing Post Rating at 3m or beyond (two at intermediate trips and two at around 2m), while six of those ten were also beaten in that season's King George. Four of the last five winners were second-season chasers.

Sun Bets Stayers' Hurdle (3m) Cheltenham

2008	**Inglis Drever**	9-11-10	H Johnson	D O'Regan	11-8f	17
2009	**Big Buck's**	6-11-10	P Nicholls	R Walsh	6-1	14
2010	**Big Buck's**	7-11-10	P Nicholls	R Walsh	5-6f	14
2011	**Big Buck's**	8-11-10	P Nicholls	R Walsh	10-11f	13
2012	**Big Buck's**	9-11-10	P Nicholls	R Walsh	5-6f	11
2013	**Solwhit**	9-11-10	C Byrnes	P Carberry	17-2	13
2014	**More Of That**	6-11-10	J O'Neill	B Geraghty	15-2	10
2015	**Cole Harden**	6-11-10	W Greatrex	G Sheehan	14-1	16
2016	**Thistlecrack**	8-11-10	C Tizzard	T Scudamore	Evsf	12
2017	**Nichols Canyon**	7-11-10	W Mullins	R Walsh	10-1	12

An amazing race for former champions, with three horses – Big Buck's, Inglis Drever and Baracouda – sharing nine of the last 16 renewals between them and only one subsequent winner returning to defend their crown 12 months on. That's largely because 3m form stands up so strongly. Horses beaten in the race previously rarely step up – the last horse to win having finished out of the first two 12 months earlier was Derring Rose in 1981 – and only three winners this century had been beaten in a 3m Graded hurdle earlier in the season. For that reason the market has been a strong guide in this time – 16 out of 17 winners came from the first four in the betting – with the danger to the defending champion or established form horse coming from those stepping up in trip. In fact a lack of proven stamina shouldn't be considered a negative at all as seven of the last 12 first-time winners were triumphing over 3m for the first time and class is more important as Cole Harden and Thistlecrack are the only winners since Princeful in 1998 not to have won a Graded race shorter than 2m5f. In contrast, the Albert Bartlett, a race far more about stamina than speed, has proved a woeful guide with the six winners to take their chance 12 months later finishing no better than third.

Triumph Hurdle (2m1f) Cheltenham

2008	**Celestial Halo**	4-11-0	P Nicholls	R Walsh	5-1	14
2009	**Zaynar**	4-11-0	N Henderson	B Geraghty	11-2	18
2010	**Soldatino**	4-11-0	N Henderson	B Geraghty	6-1	17
2011	**Zarkandar**	4-11-0	P Nicholls	D Jacob	13-2	23
2012	**Countrywide Flame**	4-11-0	J Quinn	D Costello	33-1	20
2013	**Our Conor**	4-11-0	D Hughes	B Cooper	4-1	17
2014	**Tiger Roll**	4-11-0	G Elliott	D Russell	10-1	15
2015	**Peace And Co**	4-11-0	N Henderson	B Geraghty	2-1f	16
2016	**Ivanovich Gorbatov**	4-11-0	A O'Brien	B Geraghty	9-2f	15
2017	**Defi Du Seuil**	4-11-0	P Hobbs	R Johnson	5-2f	15

The juvenile championship has benefited greatly from the advent of the Fred Winter in 2005, with the loss of many of the also-rans helping the cream to rise to the top. Of the 13 subsequent winners, only Tiger Roll and the vastly underrated Countrywide Flame weren't priced in single figures and among the first four in the betting. At the same time experience has become less of a factor, with Zarkandar even winning after just one outing over hurdles and three of the last four winners never having run on the Flat, which used to be almost guaranteed with 12 of the previous 13 having done so. If still considering one coming via the Flat, bear in mind that Our Conor is the only winner in recent times who ran on the Flat but wasn't tried over at least 1m4f. The last five Irish-trained winners had run in the Grade 1 Spring Hurdle at Leopardstown on their previous start, while six of the last ten British-trained winners had landed the Finesse Hurdle at Cheltenham or the Adonis Hurdle at Kempton. Nineteen of the last 24 winners passed the post first on their previous run (Scolardy had been disqualified before winning in 2002).

County Hurdle (2m1f) Cheltenham

2008	**Silver Jaro**	5-10-13	T Hogan	N Fehily	50-1	22
2009	**American Trilogy**	5-11-0	P Nicholls	R Walsh	20-1	27
2010	**Thousand Stars**	6-10-5	W Mullins	Ms K Walsh	20-1	28
2011	**Final Approach**	5-10-12	W Mullins	R Walsh	10-1	26
2012	**Alderwood**	8-11-1	T Mullins	A McCoy	20-1	26
2013	**Ted Veale**	6-10-6	T Martin	B Cooper	10-1	28
2014	**Lac Fontana**	5-10-11	P Nicholls	D Jacob	11-1	28
2015	**Wicklow Brave**	6-11-4	W Mullins	P Townend	25-1	24
2016	**Superb Story**	5-10-12	D Skelton	H Skelton	8-1	26
2017	**Arctic Fire**	8-11-12	W Mullins	P Townend	20-1	25

Much like in the Imperial Cup, another fiercely competitive 2m handicap hurdle, young horses have a big edge. Ten five-year-olds have won in the last 16 years and the 14 winners prior to Arctic Fire last year were all novices (six) or had been novices the previous season (eight), although the last winner without handicap experience was Thumbs Up in 1993 with more than 60 having failed since. Ireland have won eight of the last 11 runnings, which is remarkable given that Pedrobob was only the second in 25 years when he won in 2007, and five of the last nine Irish winners were at least placed in the BoyleSports or Betfair Hurdles. The last two exceptions, Arctic Fire and Wicklow Brave, were both trained by Willie Mullins and are also the only winners to carry more than 11st 1lb since Spirit Leader in 2003.

Albert Bartlett Novices' Hurdle (3m) Cheltenham

2008	**Nenuphar Collonges**	7-11-7	A King	R Thornton	9-1	18
2009	**Weapon's Amnesty**	6-11-7	C Byrnes	D Russell	8-1	17
2010	**Berties Dream**	7-11-7	P J Gilligan	A Lynch	33-1	19
2011	**Bobs Worth**	6-11-7	N Henderson	B Geraghty	15-8f	18
2012	**Brindisi Breeze**	6-11-7	L Russell	C Gillies	7-1	20
2013	**At Fishers Cross**	6-11-7	R Curtis	A McCoy	11-8f	13
2014	**Very Wood**	5-11-7	N Meade	P Carberry	33-1	18
2015	**Martello Tower**	7-11-4	M Mullins	A Heskin	14-1	19
2016	**Unowhatimeanharry**	8-11-5	H Fry	N Fehily	11-1	19
2017	**Penhill**	6-11-5	W Mullins	P Townend	16-1	15

Though not run as a Grade 1 until 2008, this has always been a level-weights affair since its inception three years earlier. Unowhatimeanharry won as an eight-year-old last year and there have been four winning seven-year-olds, which is very unusual for a top novice hurdle. The importance of stamina and experience is also shown by the fact that all 13 winners had run at least three times over hurdles (five of them at least six times) and ten

SUPERB STORY: one of ten five-year-olds in 16 years to win the County Hurdle

had also been tried over at least 3m. Seven of the eight non-Irish winners (French-trained Moulin Riche won the inaugural running) had run at least twice at Cheltenham and finished first or second, five of them winning.

Cheltenham Gold Cup (3m2½f) Cheltenham

2008	**Denman**	8-11-10	P Nicholls	S Thomas	9-4	12
2009	**Kauto Star**	9-11-10	P Nicholls	R Walsh	7-4f	16
2010	**Imperial Commander**	9-11-10	N Twiston-Davies	P Brennan	7-1	11
2011	**Long Run**	6-11-10	N Henderson	Mr S W-Cohen	7-2f	13
2012	**Synchronised**	9-11-10	J O'Neill	A McCoy	8-1	14
2013	**Bobs Worth**	8-11-10	N Henderson	B Geraghty	11-4f	9
2014	**Lord Windermere**	8-11-10	J Culloty	D Russell	20-1	13
2015	**Coneygree**	8-11-10	M Bradstock	N de Boinville	7-1	16
2016	**Don Cossack**	9-11-10	G Elliott	B Cooper	9-4f	9
2017	**Sizing John**	7-11-10	J Harrington	R Power	7-1	13

As the Gold Cup has increasingly become the be-all and end-all for top staying chasers, winners tend to be proven top-class performers who have been wrapped in cotton wool during the season. Don Cossack is the only winner since Kauto Star in 2007 to have run more than three times earlier in the campaign and even he had been off since early January, while the last 18 winners had already struck at the top level. That's certainly made the race more predictable as eight of the last 15 favourites have won, with just one winner since 1999 priced bigger than 8-1. Lord Windermere was the exception, but even he was a solid trends pick having won the previous year's RSA Chase, which has provided four of the last ten winners with Lord Windermere, Bobs Worth and Denman doing the double. That trio are among a raft of winners for inexperienced horses, with eight of the last 13 in their first or second season over fences, headed of course by the remarkable Coneygree, who was the first winning novice since Captain Christy in 1974. The key races during the season are the King George and the Lexus Chase as 15 of the last 18 winners ran in one of those contests. Horses older than nine struggle, with Cool Dawn the last to win in 1998 – there have since been 15 sent off at 8-1 or shorter including four favourites – while See More Business's win the following year was the last time a horse beaten on their first attempt in the race made the required improvement, with 66 beaten subsequently including last year's favourite Djakadam.

Christie's Foxhunter Chase (3m2½f) Cheltenham

2008	**Amicelli**	9-12-0	C Coward	Mr O Greenall	33-1	23
2009	**Cappa Bleu**	7-12-0	Mrs E Crow	Mr R Burton	11-2	24
2010	**Baby Run**	10-12-0	N Twiston-Davies	Mr S Twiston-Davies	9-2jf	24
2011	**Zemsky**	8-12-0	I Ferguson	Mr D O'Connor	33-1	24
2012	**Salsify**	7-12-0	R Sweeney	Mr C Sweeney	7-1	22
2013	**Salsify**	8-12-0	R Sweeney	Mr C Sweeney	2-1f	23
2014	**Tammys Hill**	9-12-0	L Lennon	Mr J Smyth	15-2	24
2015	**On The Fringe**	10-12-0	E Bolger	Ms N Carberry	6-1	24
2016	**On The Fringe**	11-12-0	E Bolger	Ms N Carberry	13-8f	24
2017	**Pacha Du Polder**	10-12-0	P Nicholls	Miss B Frost	16-1	23

This is regarded as a lottery by many punters and five of the last 12 winners were at least 16-1, but with the other seven no bigger than 15-2 it's clearly been kind to some. The key is generally to rule out any horse older than ten, thereby wiping out half the field at a stroke in most years, as On The Fringe in 2016 was the first such winner since Earthmover 12 years earlier. That pair were both previous winners and the only first-time winner older than ten since 1989 is the 2000 hero Cavalero. Cappa Bleu was very unusual in winning on his debut under rules in 2009, while six of the subsequent eight runnings have gone to Ireland.

Grand Annual H'cap Chase (2m½f) Cheltenham

2008	**Tiger Cry**	10-10-6	A Moore	D Russell	15-2	17
2009	**Oh Crick**	6-10-0	A King	W Hutchinson	7-1	18
2010	**Pigeon Island**	7-10-1	N Twiston-Davies	P Brennan	16-1	19

PACHA DU POLDER (right): broke Ireland's stranglehold on the Foxhunters

2011	**Oiseau De Nuit**	9-11-6	C Tizzard	S Clements (7)	40-1	23
2012	**Bellvano**	8-10-2	N Henderson	P Carberry	20-1	21
2013	**Alderwood**	9-10-11	T Mullins	A McCoy	3-1f	23
2014	**Savello**	8-11-5	T Martin	D Russell	16-1	23
2015	**Next Sensation**	8-11-2	M Scudamore	T Scudamore	16-1	20
2016	**Solar Impulse**	6-11-0	P Nicholls	S Twiston-Davies	28-1	24
2017	**Rock The World**	9-11-5	J Harrington	R Power	10-1	24

Cheltenham is one of the few places where you see 2m handicaps run at such a fast and furious pace and those who have excelled at the course before, especially in this race, tend to go well. Seven of the last ten British-trained winners had previously been successful at Cheltenham, with one of the exceptions, Next Sensation, placed in this race, and while Irish horses are an increasing factor with seven winners in the last 18 runnings, even then Rock The World and Tiger Cry had been placed in this race and Alderwood had won a County Hurdle. It takes a strong, mature horse to cope with the demands of the Grand Annual yet you also want one unexposed enough to still be ahead of the handicapper. Ten of the last 14 winners were eight or older even though most of those at head of the market are younger, including nine favourites in that time, but even so just one of the last 16 winners had run more than 12 times over fences. Long-standing trends in favour of lightly weighted runners have become largely obsolete due to the compressed nature of the handicap, although you still want to steer clear right at the top of the weights with Edredon Bleu the last winner to carry more than 11st 5lb in 1999.

Betfred Bowl (3m1f) Aintree

2008	**Our Vic**	10-11-10	D Pipe	T Murphy	9-1	5
2009	**Madison Du Berlais**	8-11-10	D Pipe	T Scudamore	12-1	10
2010	**What A Friend**	7-11-7	P Nicholls	R Walsh	5-2	5
2011	**Nacarat**	10-11-7	T George	P Brennan	7-2	6
2012	**Follow The Plan**	9-11-7	O McKiernan	T Doyle	50-1	11
2013	**First Lieutenant**	8-11-7	M Morris	T Cooper	7-2	8
2014	**Silviniaco Conti**	8-11-7	P Nicholls	N Fehily	9-4	6
2015	**Silviniaco Conti**	9-11-7	P Nicholls	N Fehily	7-4f	7
2016	**Cue Card**	10-11-7	C Tizzard	P Brennan	6-5f	9
2017	**Tea For Two**	8-11-7	N Williams	L Kelly	10-1	7

This race is Aintree's version of the Gold Cup, but it rarely attracts the winner of the big one and the record of the three who have tried to do the double – Imperial Commander, Desert Orchid and Dawn Run – won't tempt many more to try it as all of them failed to complete. That's part of a wider trend because, of the 21 winners to have come via the Gold Cup, 14 of them finished outside the top four at Cheltenham. Not only were they likely to have avoided a harder race, but Prestbury Park form can always be turned around at this sharp, flat course that, despite being left-handed, has more in common with Kempton. Indeed, form at the Sunbury track seems to be key as ten of the last 18 winners had been first or second in a King George, with Silviniaco Conti winning both races twice and Cue Card also doing the double. Of the exceptions, Tea For Two and Madison Du Berlais had produced their best runs at Kempton and Nacarat had twice won the Racing Post Chase.

Randox Health Grand National (4m2½f) Aintree

2008	**Comply Or Die**	9-10-9	D Pipe	T Murphy	7-1jf	40
2009	**Mon Mome**	9-11-0	V Williams	L Treadwell	100-1	40

2010	**Don't Push It**	10-11-5	J O'Neill	A McCoy	10-1jf	40
2011	**Ballabriggs**	10-11-0	D McCain	J Maguire	14-1	40
2012	**Neptune Collonges**	11-11-6	P Nicholls	D Jacob	33-1	40
2013	**Auroras Encore**	11-10-3	S Smith	R Mania	66-1	40
2014	**Pineau De Re**	11-10-6	Dr R Newland	L Aspell	25-1	40
2015	**Many Clouds**	8-11-9	O Sherwood	L Aspell	25-1	39
2016	**Rule The World**	9-10-7	M Morris	D Mullins	33-1	39
2017	**One For Arthur**	8-10-11	L Russell	D Fox	14-1	40

For such a unique challenge, it's remarkable that previous Grand Nationals are such a poor guide to this race. Twenty of the last 25 winners had never run in it before and four of the five exceptions failed to complete, with no horse winning it more than once since Red Rum and Amberleigh House the only winner in this period to have placed previously as others get weighted out of contention. The Becher and the Topham over the same fences have thrown up a fair number of winners, but the best guides are other major staying handicaps like the Hennessy Gold Cup, the Welsh National and the Irish National. A light weight used to be the key trend and remains a big help – 50 of the 55 top-11 finishers in the last five years were below 11st – but the condensing of the handicap in recent years has given class horses more of a chance, with Many Clouds, Neptune Collonges, Ballabriggs, Don't Push It and Mon Mome all defying 11st or more in the last seven years after Hedgehunter in 2005 had been the first since Corbiere 22 years earlier. Winners still tend to have hidden their ability from the handicapper that season – ten of the last 18 winners hadn't won at all over fences and 16 of them no more than once – but it's vital to have plenty of experience. Even Rule The World, the first winning novice in more than a century, had run 13 times over fences and finished second in an Irish National, with One For Arthur and Many Clouds the least experienced winners in recent times on their 11th chase starts and the only winning eight-year-olds since Party Politics in 1992, with no younger winner since 1940. Don't back at starting price but take the best available odds non-runner no-bet in the days before the race as prices tend to shorten dramatically close to start time.

Scottish Grand National (4m) Ayr

2008	**Iris De Balme**	8-10-0	S Curran	C Huxley (7)	66-1	24
2009	**Hello Bud**	11-10-9	N Twiston-Davies	P Brennan	12-1	17
2010	**Merigo**	9-10-0	A Parker	T Murphy	18-1	30
2011	**Beshabar**	9-10-4	T Vaughan	R Johnson	15-2	28
2012	**Merigo**	11-10-2	A Parker	T Murphy	15-2	24
2013	**Godsmejudge**	7-11-3	A King	W Hutchinson	12-1	24
2014	**Al Co**	9-10-0	P Bowen	J Moore	40-1	29
2015	**Wayward Prince**	11-10-1	H Parrott	R Dunne	25-1	29
2016	**Vicente**	7-11-3	P Nicholls	S Twiston-Davies	14-1	28
2017	**Vicente**	8-11-10	P Nicholls	S Twiston-Davies	9-1jf	30

This has been a lean race for punters, with 9-1 shot Vicente the first winning favourite since Paris Pike in 2000 and some real skinners in that time, topped by 66-1 shot Iris De Balme romping to victory in 2008. Vicente had fallen at the first in the Grand National, but in general running at Aintree is a big negative as he is the only winner to come via the National since Little Polveir in 1987. Similarly, ignore Cheltenham Festival winners as none have followed up in more than 30 years, though the ground tends to be fast which can also render soft-ground winter form redundant. Instead it's best to look back at previous Scottish Nationals, with Vicente and Merigo winning four of the last eight renewals between them and Godsmejudge also finishing second 12 months after his 2013 victory. There are no conclusive trends with regard to weight – 12 of the last 28 winners carried the minimum of 10st, ranging up to 26lb out of the handicap, but seven of the last 19 winners carried more than 11st and Vicente, Grey Abbey and Young Kenny defied welter burdens. The best bet is to side with a novice, with nine winners in 24 years from small representation.

Irish Grand National (3m5f) Fairyhouse

2008	**Hear The Echo**	7-10-0	M Morris	P Flood	33-1	23
2009	**Niche Market**	8-10-5	R Buckler	H Skelton (5)	33-1	28
2010	**Bluesea Cracker**	8-10-4	J Motherway	A J McNamara	25-1	26
2011	**Organisedconfusion**	6-9-13	A Moore	Miss N Carberry	12-1	25
2012	**Lion Na Bearnai**	10-10-5	T Gibney	A Thornton	33-1	29
2013	**Liberty Counsel**	10-9-10	D Love	B Dalton (5)	50-1	28
2014	**Shutthefrontdoor**	7-10-13	J O'Neill	B Geraghty	8-1f	26
2015	**Thunder And Roses**	7-10-6	S Hughes	K Walsh	20-1	28
2016	**Rogue Angel**	8-10-9	M Morris	G Fox (3)	16-1	27
2017	**Our Duke**	7-11-4	J Harrington	R Power	9-2f	28

A race whose history is littered with great winners, most notably Desert Orchid, and Our Duke was the latest with his stunning success last season, which was all the more remarkable given the previous 16 winners carried less than 11st. The main reason is that this tends to be a race for young horses just starting to realise their potential as they step up in trip, with Rogue Angel the only winner since Mudahim in 1998 to have run more than 13 times over fences and Our Duke was the ninth in that time carrying novice status. That can also make it a hard race to call, with nine of the last 12 winners sent off 20-1 or bigger. British raiders have traditionally had an awful record, but that's changed in recent times with Shuttthefrontdoor the fourth successful raider in 11 years when he won in 2014.

bet365 Gold Cup (3m5f) Sandown

2008	**Monkerhostin**	11-10-13	P Hobbs	R Johnson	25-1	19
2009	**Hennessy**	8-10-7	C Llewellyn	A McCoy	13-2	14
2010	**Church Island**	11-10-5	M Hourigan	A Heskin (7)	20-1	19
2011	**Poker De Sivola**	8-10-12	F Murphy	T Murphy	11-1	18
2012	**Tidal Bay**	11-11-12	P Nicholls	D Jacob	9-1	19
2013	**Quentin Collonges**	9-10-12	H Daly	A Tinkler	14-1	19
2014	**Hadrian's Approach**	7-11-0	N Henderson	B Geraghty	10-1	19
2015	**Just A Par**	8-10-3	P Nicholls	S Bowen (3)	14-1	20
2016	**The Young Master**	7-11-1	N Mulholland	Mr S Waley-Cohen (3)	8-1	20
2017	**Henllan Harri**	9-10-0	P Bowen	S Bowen	40-1	13

As in so many staying chases, light weights are favoured – 24 of the last 29 winners carried less than 11st (including The Young Master with Sam Waley-Cohen's 3lb claim) and the best winner of recent times, Tidal Bay, was a rare beast indeed when defying 11st 12lb. However, that still hasn't helped punters as the race is a graveyard for favourites, with Mr Frisk the last outright market leader to prevail when becoming the only horse to follow up a Grand National victory in 1990. He's one of ten winners to have come via Aintree since 1973, but seven of them had failed to get beyond Becher's on the second circuit. Most winners had run at the Cheltenham Festival – 27 of the last 43 in all – but none of them had won there.

Track Facts

YOU WANT course statistics? Look no further - this section contains all the numbers you'll need for every jumps track in the country.

Course by course, we've set out four-year trainer and jockey statistics, favourites' records, winning pointers and three-dimensional racecourse maps, plus details of how to get there and fixtures for the new season.

Following this, from page 220, we've got details of course records and standard times for each track. Note that we have been unable to produce standard times in a few cases as there have not been enough recent races over the trip at the track in question.

See also our statistical assessment of last season's records from Britain's top ten trainers (page 119).

Ormskirk Rd, Liverpool,
L9 5AS. Tel: 0151 523 2600

AINTREE

How to get there Road: M6, M62, M57, M58. Rail: Liverpool Lime Street and taxi.

Features The left-handed 2m2f giant triangular Grand National course is perfectly flat. Inside it, the sharp left-handed Mildmay course is 1m4f in circumference.

2017-18 Fixtures
October 29, November 11, December 9, April 12-14

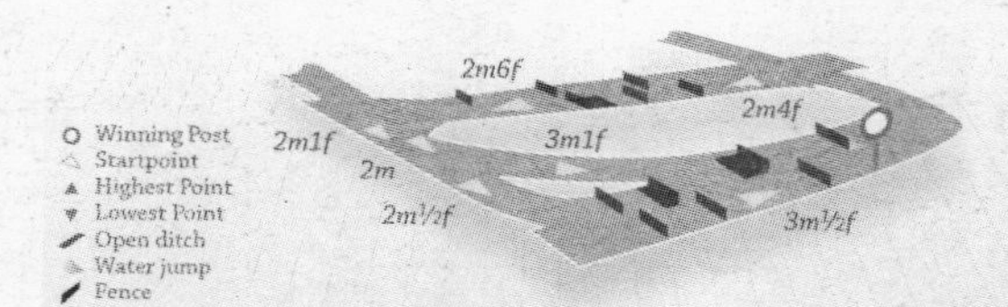

Trainers	Wins-Runs	%	Hurdles	Chases	£1 level stks
Nicky Henderson	23-126	18	16-70	6-43	+17.93
Paul Nicholls	14-131	11	4-48	10-78	-43.63
Philip Hobbs	10-90	11	5-45	5-40	-16.80
Jonjo O'Neill	10-85	12	4-44	5-35	-27.89
Nigel Twiston-Davies	10-83	12	5-37	4-40	-17.56
W P Mullins	10-57	18	6-27	3-25	-9.15
Tom George	10-53	19	1-10	7-39	+41.74
Colin Tizzard	10-35	29	4-12	6-23	+94.99
Alan King	6-65	9	3-35	2-19	-20.13
Peter Bowen	6-62	10	1-30	3-26	-32.50
Donald McCain	5-109	5	4-56	1-47	-78.79
Dan Skelton	5-49	10	5-32	0-14	-23.88
David Pipe	4-66	6	2-24	2-42	-19.38

Jockeys	Wins-Rides	%	£1 level stks	Best Trainer	W-R
A P McCoy	15-57	26	+3.38	Jonjo O'Neill	7-19
Richard Johnson	11-98	11	+1.14	Philip Hobbs	6-51
Barry Geraghty	11-57	19	+13.56	Nicky Henderson	6-22
Nico de Boinville	8-43	19	+12.12	Nicky Henderson	7-29
Brian Hughes	7-87	8	+14.33	Kevin Frost	2-6
Sam Twiston-Davies	7-81	9	-32.43	Paul Nicholls	4-42
Tom Scudamore	7-73	10	+10.91	David Pipe	4-43
Noel Fehily	7-61	11	-27.92	Paul Nicholls	2-10
Paddy Brennan	7-45	16	+3.94	Tom George	6-28
Paul Townend	6-33	18	+5.32	W P Mullins	4-14
Aidan Coleman	5-79	6	-53.00	Harry Whittington	1-1
Ryan Hatch	5-28	18	+8.50	Nigel Twiston-Davies	5-26
Nick Scholfield	4-48	8	-26.00	Paul Nicholls	3-31

Favourites

Hurdle 32.7% -9.74 Chase 26.3% -16.79 TOTAL 29.1% -33.66

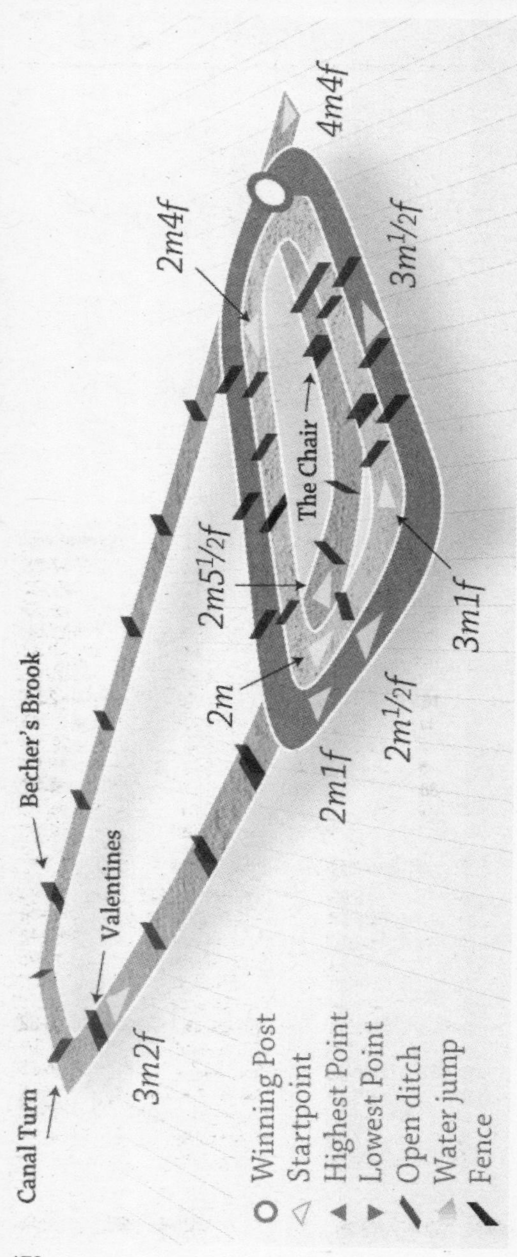

Aintree's Grand National course - used in the Becher Chase, the Grand Sefton Chase, the Topham Chase, the Foxhunters' Chase and the Grand National

ASCOT

Ascot, Berkshire SL5 7JX
0870 7227 227

How to get there Road: M4 junction 6 or M3 junction 3 on to A332. Rail: Frequent service from Reading or Waterloo

Features Right-handed

2017-18 Fixtures November 4, 24-25, December 22-23, January 20, February 17, March 25

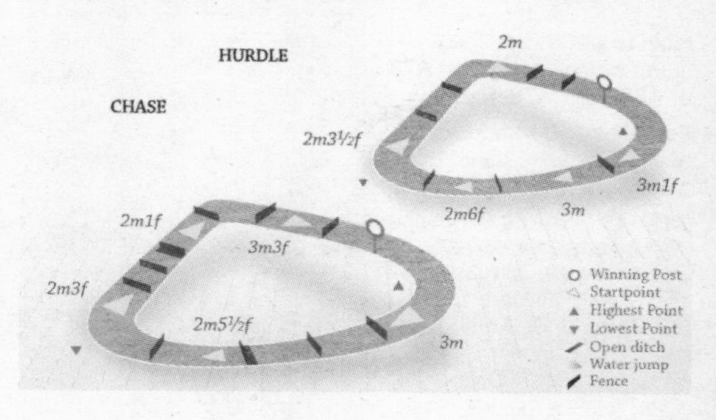

Trainers	*Wins-Runs*	*%*	*Hurdles*	*Chases*	*£1 level stks*
Paul Nicholls	28-133	21	10-61	17-68	-7.21
Nicky Henderson	24-116	21	15-78	6-27	-29.27
Philip Hobbs	14-85	16	7-34	5-46	-3.89
Venetia Williams	14-71	20	4-19	10-51	+53.50
Harry Fry	12-40	30	11-23	1-12	+9.54
Alan King	9-64	14	6-46	2-12	-18.86
David Pipe	9-58	16	6-34	1-20	-2.53
Colin Tizzard	8-48	17	3-14	5-28	+11.28
Charlie Longsdon	7-54	13	2-23	3-23	+22.50
Gary Moore	5-61	8	1-32	4-24	-19.50
W P Mullins	5-13	38	3-8	2-4	-5.57
Dan Skelton	4-45	9	2-25	2-17	-10.50
Rebecca Curtis	4-38	11	2-12	2-19	-2.50

Jockeys	*Wins-Rides*	*%*	*£1 level stks*	*Best Trainer*	*W-R*
Barry Geraghty	22-86	26	+15.61	Nicky Henderson	9-42
Aidan Coleman	17-87	20	+57.25	Venetia Williams	11-39
Sam Twiston-Davies	12-74	16	-24.14	Paul Nicholls	10-42
Richard Johnson	11-87	13	-34.70	Philip Hobbs	8-48
Noel Fehily	11-69	16	-0.39	Paul Nicholls	5-8
Nico de Boinville	9-34	26	+11.05	Nicky Henderson	8-18
Tom Scudamore	8-57	14	-12.03	David Pipe	6-32
R Walsh	8-15	53	+2.37	W P Mullins	5-9
Jamie Moore	7-42	17	+20.50	Gary Moore	5-26
Daryl Jacob	7-42	17	-16.17	Nicky Henderson	2-6
Wayne Hutchinson	7-39	18	+3.01	Alan King	7-32
Tom O'Brien	5-40	13	+2.50	Philip Hobbs	4-22
Jack Sherwood	5-13	38	+19.38	Paul Nicholls	4-6

Favourites

Hurdle 43.8% +12.06   Chase 33.3% -12.67   TOTAL 38% -3.59

AYR

Whitletts Road, Ayr, KA8 0JE
Tel: 01292 264 179

How to get there Road: south from Glasgow on A77 or A75, A70, A76. Rail: Ayr

Features Left-handed 1m4f oval, easy turns, slight uphill finish

2017-18 Fixtures October 30, November 4, 15, 27, December 12, January 2, 10, 15-16, 31, February 11, 13, 26, March 9-10, April 20-21

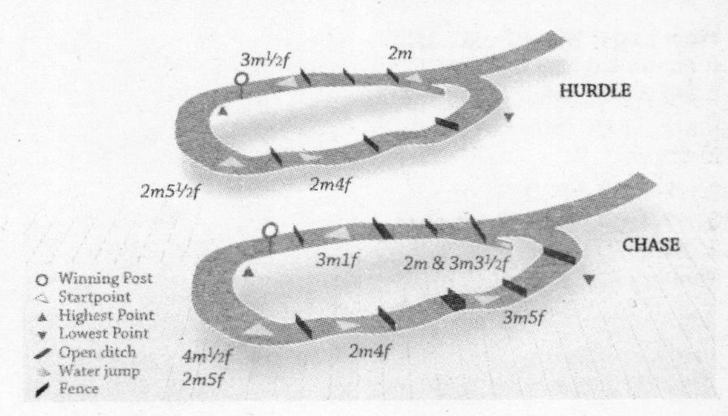

Trainers	*Wins-Runs*	*%*	*Hurdles*	*Chases*	*£1 level stks*
Nicky Richards	28-118	24	12-68	9-33	-21.25
Lucinda Russell	25-239	10	12-122	13-92	-127.26
N W Alexander	24-171	14	10-105	12-51	-14.73
S R B Crawford	15-112	13	10-68	3-25	-39.38
Jim Goldie	12-99	12	8-65	4-29	-36.08
Donald McCain	12-77	16	7-37	3-31	-37.39
Paul Nicholls	11-39	28	6-19	4-18	+36.00
James Ewart	9-81	11	6-39	2-22	-20.00
Martin Todhunter	9-54	17	3-24	6-29	+11.48
Stuart Coltherd	8-43	19	5-22	3-19	+20.50
Dan Skelton	8-33	24	6-22	1-9	-2.01
Ian Duncan	7-56	13	6-42	1-10	+16.75
Malcolm Jefferson	7-37	19	4-13	2-18	+0.80

Jockeys	*Wins-Rides*	*%*	*£1 level stks*	*Best Trainer*	*W-R*
Brian Hughes	37-180	21	+19.20	N W Alexander	5-7
Brian Harding	27-132	20	+22.48	Nicky Richards	17-64
Peter Buchanan	14-89	16	-13.59	Lucinda Russell	12-72
Craig Nichol	10-114	9	-33.25	Nicky Richards	4-19
Wilson Renwick	10-57	18	+24.60	Martin Todhunter	4-16
Derek Fox	9-94	10	-3.38	Lucinda Russell	4-56
Sam Twiston-Davies	9-32	28	+35.25	Paul Nicholls	9-27
Lucy Alexander	8-94	9	-31.00	N W Alexander	7-61
Stephen Mulqueen	8-65	12	-41.11	Nicky Richards	3-5
Henry Brooke	7-79	9	-26.25	Martin Todhunter	3-21
James Reveley	7-64	11	-40.33	Jim Goldie	3-25
Dale Irving	7-33	21	+19.25	James Ewart	5-22
Jason Maguire	7-30	23	-6.37	Donald McCain	6-23

Favourites

Hurdle 38.1% -7.62 Chase 36.4% +3.75 TOTAL 38.3% -4.05

BANGOR

Bangor-on-Dee, nr Wrexham
Clwyd. Tel: 01948 860 438

How to get there Road: A525. Rail: Wrexham

Features Left-handed, 1m4f round, quite sharp, final fence gets plenty of fallers

2017-18 Fixtures October 4, 31, November 15, December 2, 15, January 4, February 9, March 24, April 21

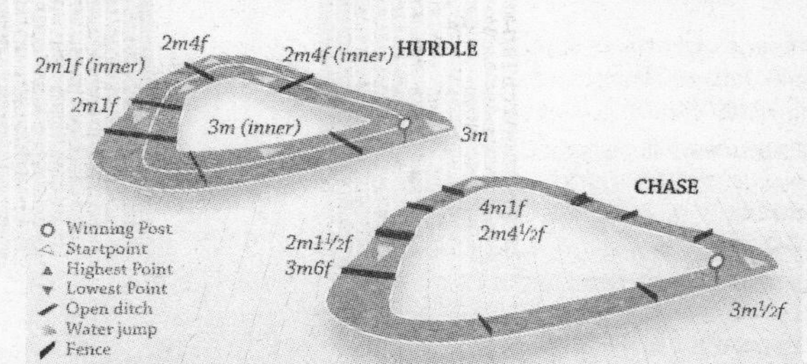

R-CURTIS - 16/17
R W
14 2

BUMPERS - 5 YR
R W
23 3

Trainers	Wins-Runs	%	Hurdles	Chases	£1 level stks
Donald McCain	47-259	18	34-163	10-65	-9.92
Rebecca Curtis	18-73	25	9-31	7-26	-4.28
Alan King	15-48	31	8-26	4-13	+21.19
Jonjo O'Neill	14-100	14	3-52	8-43	-20.38
Charlie Longsdon	12-56	21	6-34	4-17	-14.61
Warren Greatrex	12-36	33	6-22	2-7	+17.89
Venetia Williams	11-84	13	3-38	8-45	-24.01
Dan Skelton	11-49	22	5-28	5-14	-7.26
Nigel Twiston-Davies	9-52	17	4-21	5-24	-7.23
Peter Bowen	8-40	20	5-18	2-17	+9.20
Jennie Candlish	7-51	14	5-33	2-12	-25.15
Henry Daly	7-46	15	6-24	1-15	-1.50
Nicky Henderson	7-37	19	5-24	2-6	-17.81

Jockeys	Wins-Rides	%	£1 level stks	Best Trainer	W-R
Jason Maguire	18-70	26	+2.77	Donald McCain	15-60
Noel Fehily	15-61	25	+4.15	Charlie Longsdon	5-11
Will Kennedy	14-90	16	+2.17	Donald McCain	12-50
Richard Johnson	13-67	19	+3.45	Charlie Longsdon	3-5
Wayne Hutchinson	13-62	21	-2.81	Alan King	11-30
A P McCoy	13-49	27	-11.89	Jonjo O'Neill	5-24
Gavin Sheehan	11-43	26	+29.79	Warren Greatrex	8-23
Tom O'Brien	9-49	18	-9.09	Henry Daly	3-7
Tom Scudamore	9-46	20	-13.63	David Pipe	5-15
Brian Hughes	8-46	17	+12.75	Patrick Griffin	3-7
Sean Quinlan	8-36	22	+4.25	Jennie Candlish	5-26
Harry Skelton	8-36	22	-2.51	Dan Skelton	8-33
Sean Bowen	8-29	28	+23.00	Peter Bowen	6-17

Favourites

Hurdle 33.8% -44.18 | Chase 42.6% +16.57 | TOTAL 37.8% -29.40

CARLISLE

Blackwell, Carlisle, CA2 4TS
Tel: 01228 522 973

How to get there Road: M6 Jctn 42. Rail: 2m from Citadel Station, Carlisle

Features Pear-shaped, 1m5f circuit, right-handed, undulating, uphill home straight

2017-18 Fixtures October 19, 26, November 5, 13, December 3, 17, February 7, 19, March 8, 18, 31, April 8, 17

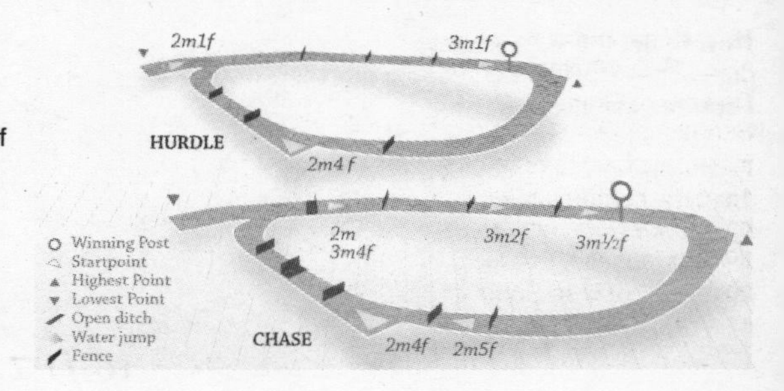

Trainers	*Wins-Runs*	*%*	*Hurdles*	*Chases*	*£1 level stks*
Donald McCain	32-163	20	18-98	10-52	-32.51
Nicky Richards	16-72	22	8-36	6-31	+16.27
Sue Smith	14-92	15	0-25	13-59	-14.04
Alan Swinbank	11-37	30	6-23	3-7	+10.98
Malcolm Jefferson	9-38	24	1-3	6-26	-1.47
Jonjo O'Neill	9-36	25	7-18	1-15	-9.42
Lucinda Russell	8-141	6	3-62	5-67	-88.55
Jennie Candlish	8-57	14	2-27	6-25	-19.25
Maurice Barnes	8-56	14	0-32	8-20	+8.75
Charlie Longsdon	8-29	28	3-9	4-17	-13.45
Nigel Hawke	8-20	40	5-10	1-6	+9.13
Venetia Williams	7-26	27	2-10	4-14	+12.41
Rose Dobbin	6-56	11	2-29	4-19	-27.50

Jockeys	*Wins-Rides*	*%*	*£1 level stks*	*Best Trainer*	*W-R*
Brian Hughes	30-170	18	-38.52	Malcolm Jefferson	9-38
Brian Harding	17-121	14	-24.39	Nicky Richards	14-43
Will Kennedy	14-50	28	+5.69	Donald McCain	11-39
A P McCoy	13-35	37	-2.10	Jonjo O'Neill	5-16
Danny Cook	12-61	20	-1.58	Sue Smith	7-28
Wilson Renwick	11-71	15	-11.00	Keith Dalgleish	3-3
Richard Johnson	11-33	33	-2.92	Charlie Longsdon	2-5
Jason Maguire	10-57	18	-21.96	Donald McCain	8-44
Paul Moloney	10-32	31	+10.93	Alan Swinbank	7-23
James Reveley	9-53	17	+6.08	Philip Kirby	2-5
Sam Twiston-Davies	9-24	38	+5.03	Paul Nicholls	4-6
Daragh Bourke	8-40	20	+21.75	Maurice Barnes	6-25
Tom Scudamore	8-29	28	-3.55	David Pipe	4-11

Favourites

Hurdle 41.6% -12.67 Chase 37.1% -6.74 TOTAL 40.5% -15.79

Grange-over-Sands, Penrith
CA10 2HG. Tel: 01593 536 340

CARTMEL

How to get there Road: M6 Jctn 36, A591. Rail: Cark-in-Cartmel or Grange-over-Sands

Features Tight, left-handed 1m circuit, undulating, half-mile run-in from last (longest in Britain)

2017-18 Fixtures Summer jumping only

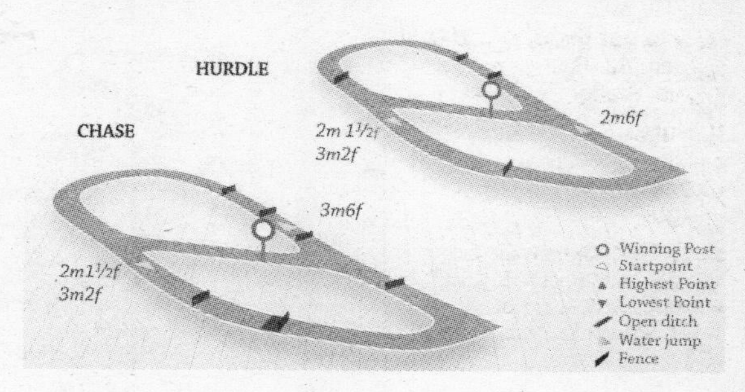

Trainers	Wins-Runs	%	Hurdles	Chases	£1 level stks
Donald McCain	19-93	20	15-63	4-30	-17.49
James Moffatt	14-108	13	8-77	6-31	-0.75
Gordon Elliott	10-38	26	8-25	2-13	-4.55
Dianne Sayer	9-86	10	2-49	7-37	-34.17
Peter Bowen	8-30	27	3-17	5-13	+5.13
Micky Hammond	5-41	12	1-21	4-20	-4.25
Jonjo O'Neill	5-18	28	3-8	2-10	-1.70
Martin Todhunter	4-36	11	3-22	1-14	-8.50
Brian Ellison	4-27	15	2-19	2-8	-8.00
Maurice Barnes	4-27	15	0-14	4-13	+5.00
Joanne Foster	4-26	15	0-5	4-21	+6.75
Kenneth Slack	4-13	31	4-11	0-2	+43.00
Julia Brooke	4-12	33	4-9	0-3	+10.33

Jockeys	Wins-Rides	%	£1 level stks	Best Trainer	W-R
Henry Brooke	17-94	18	+48.75	Kenneth Slack	3-8
Brian Hughes	16-125	13	-16.63	James Moffatt	5-38
Richard Johnson	14-67	21	-13.80	Gordon Elliott	6-29
Brian Harding	6-52	12	+24.23	Pauline Robson	2-4
Wilson Renwick	6-31	19	-1.00	Brendan Powell	1-1
A P McCoy	6-23	26	-8.34	Donald McCain	4-9
Sean Bowen	6-19	32	+7.88	Peter Bowen	5-16
Lucy Alexander	5-38	13	+14.71	Dianne Sayer	2-5
Paul Moloney	5-35	14	+0.50	Evan Williams	2-8
Sam Twiston-Davies	5-26	19	-4.61	Dr Richard Newland	2-5
Tom Scudamore	5-22	23	+5.38	David Pipe	2-6
Callum Bewley	4-39	10	-22.25	Harriet Graham	3-11
Derek Fox	4-31	13	-0.50	Mark Michael McNiff	2-8

Favourites

Hurdle 30% -18.62 Chase 26.8% -26.12 TOTAL 28.6% -44.74

CATTERICK

Catterick Bridge, Richmond, N Yorks
DL10 7PE. Tel: 01748 811 478

How to get there Road: A1. Rail: Darlington

Features Left-handed, 1m2f oval, undulating, sharp turns, favours small, handy horses

2017-18 Fixtures November 24, December 19, 28, January 1, 11, 24, February 2, 12, 27, March 7

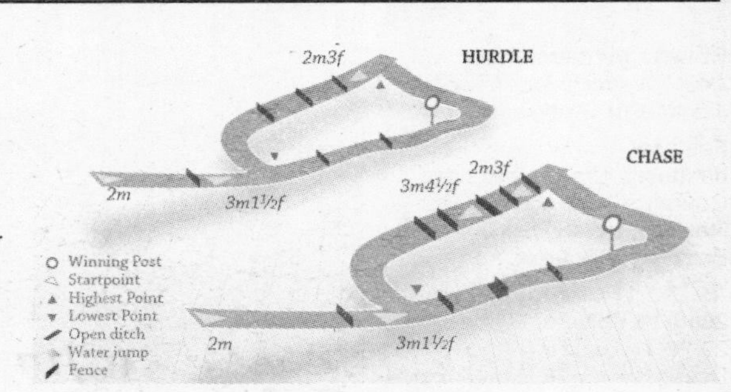

Trainers	Wins-Runs	%	Hurdles	Chases	£1 level stks
Donald McCain	34-147	23	23-95	10-39	-6.11
Sue Smith	24-78	31	8-37	16-32	+78.92
Brian Ellison	17-61	28	11-37	3-16	-14.32
Micky Hammond	9-125	7	3-81	6-38	-68.00
John Ferguson	9-15	60	7-9	0-3	+9.22
Jonjo O'Neill	7-32	22	4-16	2-14	-2.84
Kenneth Slack	7-26	27	4-16	3-10	+12.00
Dan Skelton	6-19	32	3-10	2-8	-1.78
Malcolm Jefferson	5-32	16	0-11	4-13	+1.50
Pam Sly	5-13	38	4-9	1-4	+11.56
Dianne Sayer	4-31	13	4-27	0-4	+60.00
Keith Reveley	4-27	15	4-16	0-4	-11.75
Rebecca Menzies	4-22	18	1-9	3-12	-2.13

Jockeys	Wins-Rides	%	£1 level stks	Best Trainer	W-R
Brian Hughes	19-115	17	-14.25	Malcolm Jefferson	3-25
Danny Cook	18-57	32	+17.08	Sue Smith	13-29
Jason Maguire	15-54	28	-7.57	Donald McCain	14-46
A P McCoy	13-29	45	+16.07	Jonjo O'Neill	4-12
Joe Colliver	8-69	12	-23.10	Micky Hammond	5-48
Henry Brooke	7-86	8	-42.88	Donald McCain	3-10
Will Kennedy	7-36	19	-10.97	Donald McCain	4-20
James Reveley	7-35	20	-7.75	Keith Reveley	4-14
Aidan Coleman	6-22	27	-4.18	John Ferguson	4-5
Richard Johnson	6-16	38	+11.92	David O'Meara	1-1
Jonathan England	5-36	14	-4.50	Sam England	2-7
Tony Kelly	4-43	9	-13.50	Rebecca Menzies	2-11
James Cowley	4-28	14	-4.50	Donald McCain	4-24

Favourites

Hurdle 45.3% -0.66 Chase 44.7% +19.72 TOTAL 45.3% +20.78

Prestbury Park, Cheltenham, GL50 4SH. Tel: 01242 513 014

CHELTENHAM

How to get there Road: A435, five miles north of M5 Jctns 9, 10, 11

Features There are two left-handed courses - the Old Course is 1m4f around, the New Course slightly longer. Both are undulating and end with a testing uphill finish

2017-18 Fixtures October 27-28, November 17-19, December 15-16, January 1, 27, March 13-16, April 18-19

VILLAGE VIC: course specialist has helped Philip Hobbs to the best strike-rate among Cheltenham's top ten trainers in the last four seasons

New Course

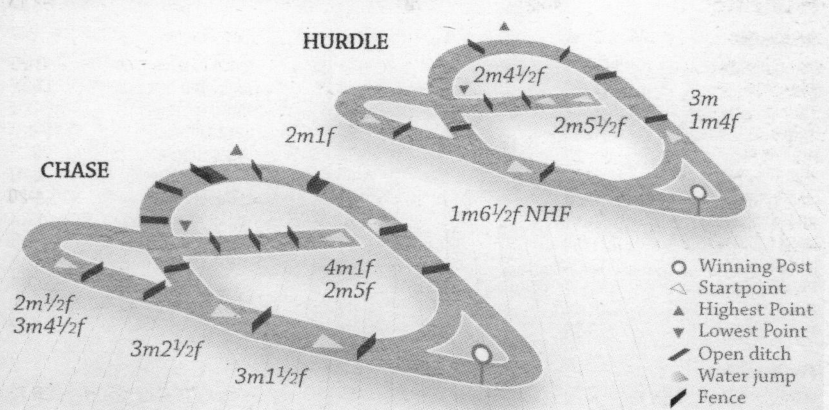

Old Course

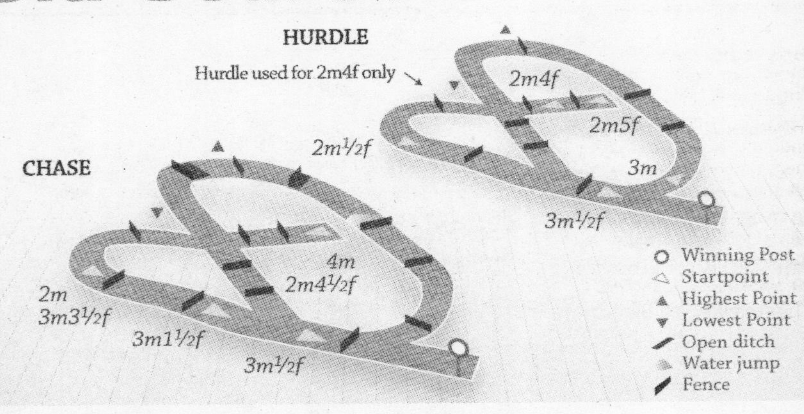

Trainers	*Wins-Runs*	*%*	*Hurdles*	*Chases*	*£1 level stks*
Paul Nicholls	38-333	11	18-164	18-162	+2.63
Philip Hobbs	33-227	15	13-92	18-122	-7.25
Nicky Henderson	29-309	9	18-194	10-100	-143.72
W P Mullins	27-220	12	18-130	9-68	-67.01
David Pipe	22-193	11	10-91	9-93	+2.53
Nigel Twiston-Davies	21-204	10	9-79	10-114	-93.07
Jonjo O'Neill	20-177	11	6-74	14-97	-4.79
Alan King	17-156	11	9-90	7-54	-35.04
Colin Tizzard	12-155	8	3-45	9-102	-68.06
Gordon Elliott	12-102	12	6-53	5-45	+16.13
Harry Fry	12-66	18	8-39	3-21	-1.74
Fergal O'Brien	11-89	12	2-24	6-45	+33.88
Dan Skelton	9-103	9	8-71	1-27	-51.63

Jockeys	*Wins-Rides*	*%*	*£1 level stks*	*Best Trainer*	*W-R*
Richard Johnson	32-232	14	-41.02	Philip Hobbs	24-138
Barry Geraghty	29-200	14	-42.73	Nicky Henderson	7-88
Tom Scudamore	24-171	14	+4.48	David Pipe	17-115
Sam Twiston-Davies	23-244	9	-59.65	Paul Nicholls	15-131
R Walsh	21-81	26	-19.76	W P Mullins	20-73
Aidan Coleman	17-197	9	-40.42	Jonjo O'Neill	4-18
Noel Fehily	17-179	9	-56.48	Harry Fry	6-46
Nico de Boinville	17-80	21	+23.28	Nicky Henderson	11-58
Daryl Jacob	14-134	10	-74.76	Paul Nicholls	8-48
Davy Russell	12-66	18	+59.03	Nicky Henderson	3-6
Paddy Brennan	11-112	10	-6.13	Fergal O'Brien	6-38
A P McCoy	11-89	12	-12.77	Jonjo O'Neill	6-31
Harry Skelton	8-82	10	-36.63	Dan Skelton	8-80

Favourites

Hurdle 29% -45.17 Chase 27.5% -52.36 TOTAL 28.1% -101.03

Chepstow, Gwent, NP6 5YH
Tel: 01291 622 260

CHEPSTOW

How to get there Road: three miles west of Severn Bridge (M4). Rail: Chepstow

Features Left-handed, undulating oval, nearly 2m round, suits long-striding front-runners

2017-18 Fixtures October 14-15, 31, November 8, 22, December 9, 27, January 7, 19, February 2, 24, March 21-22, April 2, 14, 27

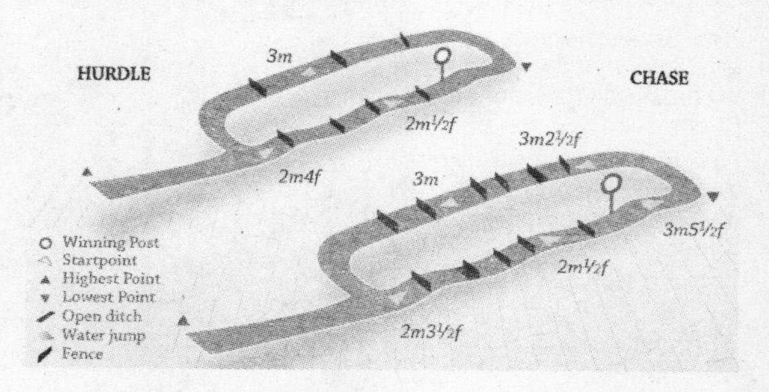

Trainers	*Wins-Runs*	*%*	*Hurdles*	*Chases*	*£1 level stks*
Philip Hobbs	26-125	21	13-56	11-51	-18.91
Evan Williams	23-149	15	13-82	9-61	+22.78
Paul Nicholls	21-116	18	13-57	6-49	-43.63
Peter Bowen	19-95	20	8-51	8-33	+34.23
Rebecca Curtis	16-117	14	9-46	5-49	-31.27
Nigel Twiston-Davies	16-95	17	8-46	7-40	+4.79
Jonjo O'Neill	15-106	14	12-65	1-36	-26.71
Venetia Williams	15-87	17	2-36	12-47	-6.48
David Pipe	13-92	14	7-54	4-29	-33.46
Tom George	13-55	24	5-24	3-24	-13.19
Colin Tizzard	10-118	8	4-48	6-55	-50.58
Matt Sheppard	10-53	19	6-34	4-17	+33.38
Tim Vaughan	9-107	8	7-77	2-22	-44.75

Jockeys	*Wins-Rides*	*%*	*£1 level stks*	*Best Trainer*	*W-R*
Richard Johnson	27-127	21	-0.33	Philip Hobbs	12-52
Sean Bowen	24-84	29	+81.98	Peter Bowen	15-47
Sam Twiston-Davies	21-110	19	-38.92	Paul Nicholls	10-45
Paul Moloney	18-116	16	+61.35	Evan Williams	10-55
Tom O'Brien	14-92	15	-5.26	Philip Hobbs	5-31
Tom Scudamore	13-97	13	-42.79	David Pipe	6-42
Aidan Coleman	11-82	13	-2.93	Venetia Williams	3-19
Adam Wedge	9-69	13	-22.05	Evan Williams	7-42
Paddy Brennan	9-64	14	-22.42	Tom George	5-25
James Best	8-93	9	-61.52	Philip Hobbs	4-14
Jamie Moore	8-57	14	+4.75	Gary Moore	2-10
Daryl Jacob	8-56	14	-21.60	Nigel Twiston-Davies	2-3
Stan Sheppard	8-27	30	+32.88	Matt Sheppard	7-23

Favourites

Hurdle 38.3% -8.90   Chase 32.9% -14.34   TOTAL 35.6% -31.65

DONCASTER

Grand Street, Leger Way, Doncaster
DN2 6BB. Tel: 01302 320 666/7

How to get there Road: M18 Jctn 3, A638, A18 towards Hull. Rail: Doncaster Central

Features Left-handed, flat, 2m round, run-in of just over a furlong, rarely heavy, favours speed horses

2017-18 Fixtures December 1-2, 15-16, 29, January 9, 26-27, February 8, 21, March 2-3

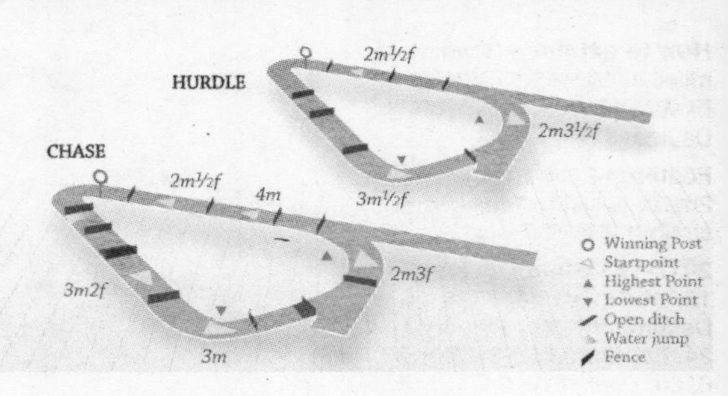

Trainers	*Wins-Runs*	*%*	*Hurdles*	*Chases*	*£1 level stks*
Nicky Henderson	34-84	40	25-52	8-24	+48.85
Alan King	22-85	26	15-50	6-28	+43.87
Paul Nicholls	14-63	22	6-28	7-33	-15.83
Keith Reveley	11-97	11	3-48	8-41	-31.20
Kim Bailey	9-53	17	6-35	3-14	+4.85
Emma Lavelle	9-30	30	3-10	3-13	+4.33
Jonjo O'Neill	8-71	11	3-42	5-27	-34.84
Ben Pauling	8-33	24	5-19	3-12	+10.40
Harry Fry	8-23	35	0-10	6-10	+3.92
Warren Greatrex	7-37	19	2-21	4-12	-11.97
Nicky Richards	7-32	22	4-20	2-9	+16.75
Brian Ellison	7-28	25	2-13	3-10	-2.34
Charlie Longsdon	6-61	10	2-29	3-28	-22.53

Jockeys	*Wins-Rides*	*%*	*£1 level stks*	*Best Trainer*	*W-R*
James Reveley	14-97	14	+48.13	Keith Reveley	10-78
Andrew Tinkler	13-48	27	+48.60	Nicky Henderson	10-21
Nico de Boinville	13-33	39	+22.87	Nicky Henderson	9-19
Brian Hughes	11-98	11	-47.64	Malcolm Jefferson	4-23
Noel Fehily	11-52	21	+17.59	Neil Mulholland	2-6
David Bass	11-51	22	-10.33	Kim Bailey	6-27
Nick Scholfield	11-39	28	+50.79	Paul Nicholls	5-19
A P McCoy	10-39	26	-9.65	Jonjo O'Neill	3-15
Richard Johnson	9-66	14	-31.08	Philip Hobbs	3-16
Wayne Hutchinson	9-31	29	+16.13	Alan King	5-15
Aidan Coleman	8-56	14	-16.92	Emma Lavelle	2-7
Leighton Aspell	8-46	17	-10.43	Emma Lavelle	4-7
Paddy Brennan	7-49	14	+43.75	Tom George	5-32

Favourites

Hurdle 41.3% -6.31 Chase 37.7% -8.86 TOTAL 39.1% -20.08

EXETER

Kennford, nr Exeter, Devon
EX6 7XS. Tel: 01392 832 599

How to get there Road: five miles south of M5, A38. Rail: Exeter Central or Exeter St Davids

Features Right-handed, 2m, hilly, stiff half-mile home straight with 300-yard run-in

2017-18 Fixtures October 12, 24, November 7, 15, 26, December 8, 21, January 1, 24, February 11, 23, March 6, 20, April 8, 17, 24

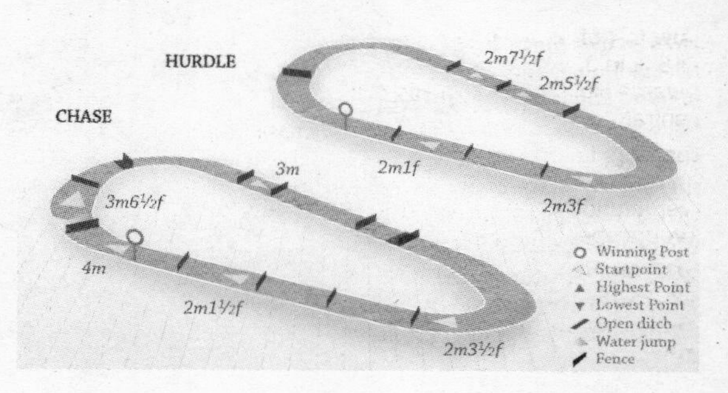

Trainers	Wins-Runs	%	Hurdles	Chases	£1 level stks
Philip Hobbs	39-183	21	22-96	13-74	-30.45
Paul Nicholls	35-115	30	21-62	12-47	-25.63
Harry Fry	24-58	41	17-42	5-11	+46.28
David Pipe	23-170	14	19-123	3-39	-47.37
Alan King	16-78	21	7-45	8-25	-9.86
Colin Tizzard	15-126	12	7-60	8-57	-59.90
Venetia Williams	13-71	18	6-32	7-38	+21.83
Sue Gardner	10-90	11	6-67	4-16	-30.04
Victor Dartnall	10-85	12	7-51	3-28	-44.25
Emma Lavelle	9-51	18	2-26	7-22	-7.75
Fergal O'Brien	9-44	20	3-23	5-18	+29.83
Chris Down	8-87	9	5-69	3-12	-29.75
Robert Walford	8-52	15	0-26	8-26	-6.25

Jockeys	Wins-Rides	%	£1 level stks	Best Trainer	W-R
Richard Johnson	39-152	26	-2.54	Philip Hobbs	29-97
Noel Fehily	21-94	22	-3.43	Harry Fry	18-38
Aidan Coleman	20-115	17	-8.42	Venetia Williams	8-41
Nick Scholfield	19-145	13	-53.68	Paul Nicholls	10-28
Sam Twiston-Davies	18-111	16	-50.06	Paul Nicholls	14-48
Tom Scudamore	16-108	15	-44.68	David Pipe	9-69
James Best	15-138	11	+20.00	Kevin Bishop	4-18
Tom O'Brien	12-115	10	-46.70	Philip Hobbs	4-42
Paddy Brennan	11-58	19	+46.50	Fergal O'Brien	5-21
Brendan Powell	10-78	13	-16.83	Colin Tizzard	5-35
Lucy Gardner	9-71	13	-17.04	Sue Gardner	9-71
Gavin Sheehan	9-54	17	-10.27	Warren Greatrex	5-23
Daryl Jacob	8-85	9	-48.61	Emma Lavelle	2-8

Favourites

Hurdle 41.7% -11.51 | Chase 32.7% -39.70 | TOTAL 37.4% -65.60

FAKENHAM

Fakenham, Norfolk, NR21 7NY
Tel: 01328 862 388

How to get there Road: A1065 from Swaffham, A148 King's Lynn, A1067 from Norwich. Rail: Kings Lynn, Norwich

Features Left-handed, 1m circuit, undulating, unsuitable for long-striding horses

2017-18 Fixtures October 20, November 1, 21, December 4, 19, January 1, 22, February 7, 16, March 16, April 2

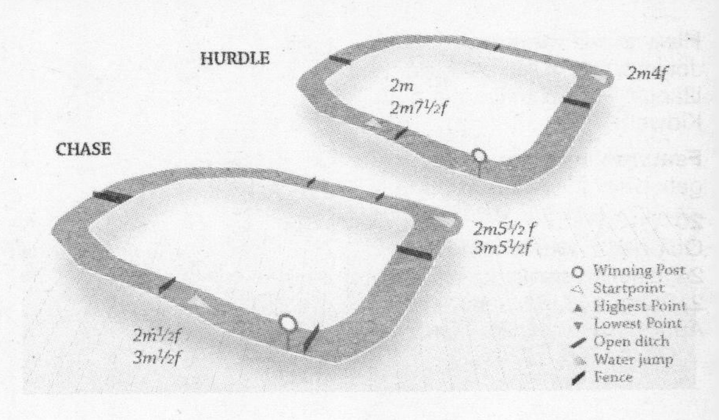

Trainers	Wins-Runs	%	Hurdles	Chases	£1 level stks
Lucy Wadham	15-56	27	7-35	5-16	+14.60
Neil Mulholland	14-43	33	12-29	2-13	+7.26
Dan Skelton	13-45	29	6-26	6-17	-2.29
Nicky Henderson	10-27	37	6-16	1-7	-6.32
Neil King	8-58	14	4-35	3-22	+4.97
David Pipe	8-16	50	6-11	2-5	+1.22
Tim Vaughan	7-49	14	5-35	2-14	-27.65
Alex Hales	6-38	16	3-27	3-10	-2.27
Paul Nicholls	6-13	46	2-4	4-9	+3.30
Dr Richard Newland	6-11	55	4-8	2-3	+8.99
David Thompson	5-26	19	4-22	1-4	+50.50
Ben Case	5-22	23	3-12	2-9	+2.38
Michael Gates	5-21	24	0-9	5-12	+7.50

Jockeys	Wins-Rides	%	£1 level stks	Best Trainer	W-R
Harry Skelton	14-39	36	+13.51	Dan Skelton	10-27
Leighton Aspell	11-43	26	+7.75	Lucy Wadham	8-25
Tom Scudamore	10-35	29	-5.33	David Pipe	7-13
Noel Fehily	10-27	37	+14.85	Neil Mulholland	8-15
James Banks	8-50	16	-10.75	Emma Baker	3-12
Richard Johnson	8-36	22	-11.40	Tim Vaughan	4-14
Tom O'Brien	7-38	18	-0.83	Henry Daly	1-1
Brian Hughes	7-18	39	+46.63	David Thompson	3-3
Jack Quinlan	6-71	8	-36.25	John Ferguson	1-3
A P McCoy	6-18	33	-2.10	Kim Bailey	1-1
Daryl Jacob	6-15	40	+1.63	Paul Nicholls	3-3
Adam Wedge	5-40	13	+5.00	Ali Stronge	4-8
Tom Messenger	5-23	22	+11.00	Chris Bealby	4-17

Favourites

Hurdle 40.8% -9.31 Chase 40.5% -13.69 TOTAL 40.8% -25.22

FFOS LAS

Trimsaran, Carmarthenshire
SA17 4DE. Tel: 01554 811 092

How to get there Road: M4 Jctn 48, follow A4138 to Llanelli. Rail: Llanelli, Kidwelly, Carmarthen

Features Left-handed, flat, galloping

2017-18 Fixtures October 21, November 12, 24, December 18, January 2, February 18, March 18, April 1, 15

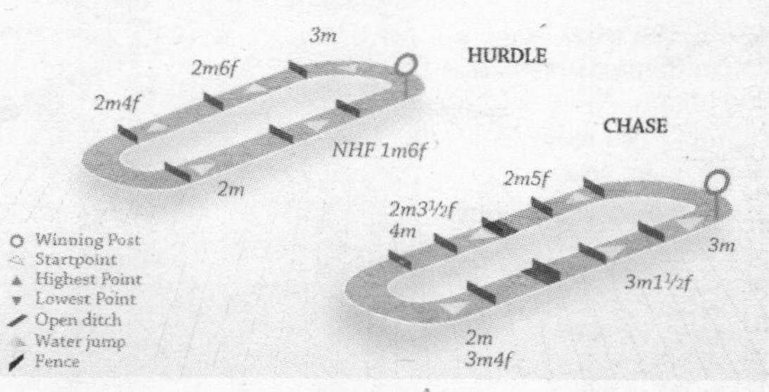

CURTIS 16/17 - 10%

Trainers	Wins-Runs	%	Hurdles	Chases	£1 level stks
Peter Bowen	44-237	19	21-134	17-73	-12.85
Rebecca Curtis	34-134	25	15-79	13-33	+17.87
Evan Williams	31-266	12	19-143	7-100	-84.45
Nigel Twiston-Davies	30-142	21	14-72	13-56	+12.72
Jonjo O'Neill	17-96	18	9-57	7-36	-23.47
Bernard Llewellyn	12-80	15	11-66	1-10	+15.14
David Pipe	11-82	13	5-51	3-15	-23.66
Debra Hamer	11-66	17	4-36	7-27	+13.13
Tim Vaughan	10-134	7	4-73	6-52	-84.02
Kim Bailey	9-30	30	8-24	1-5	+21.87
Nicky Henderson	9-26	35	8-18	0-4	-8.14
Warren Greatrex	8-39	21	4-19	1-10	-17.67
Sophie Leech	8-31	26	6-15	2-13	+7.38

Jockeys	Wins-Rides	%	£1 level stks	Best Trainer	W-R
Sam Twiston-Davies	27-133	20	+24.46	Nigel Twiston-Davies	20-98
Sean Bowen	21-98	21	-8.64	Peter Bowen	16-79
Tom Scudamore	20-102	20	+4.00	David Pipe	10-47
Paul Moloney	19-154	12	-10.73	Evan Williams	11-88
Richard Johnson	18-111	16	-36.70	Tim Vaughan	7-51
A P McCoy	15-53	28	-8.66	Jonjo O'Neill	8-29
Adam Wedge	14-127	11	-38.75	Evan Williams	14-100
Tom O'Brien	14-93	15	-24.50	Peter Bowen	4-23
Jamie Moore	12-77	16	-29.88	Peter Bowen	12-53
Donal Devereux	12-75	16	+7.48	Peter Bowen	11-65
David Bass	12-30	40	+46.28	Kim Bailey	6-13
Gavin Sheehan	9-58	16	-18.03	Warren Greatrex	7-29
Robert Williams	8-55	15	+6.14	Bernard Llewellyn	7-44

Favourites

Hurdle 42.8% +7.90 Chase 34.7% -8.84 TOTAL 39.8% -4.63

FONTWELL

Fontwell Park, nr Arundel, W Sussex
BN18 0SX. Tel: 01243 543 335

How to get there Road: A29 to Bognor Regis. Rail: Barnham

Features Left-handed, 1m4f circuit, quite sharp

2017-18 Fixtures October 6-7, November 10, 19, December 11, 26, January 8, 21, 28, February 15, 25, March 7, 17, April 6, 20

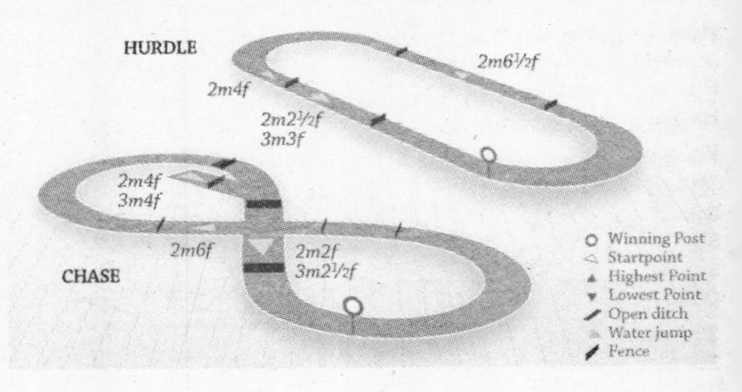

Trainers	*Wins-Runs*	*%*	*Hurdles*	*Chases*	*£1 level stks*
Gary Moore	41-255	16	25-166	11-68	-8.97
Chris Gordon	34-227	15	21-140	12-73	-16.54
Neil Mulholland	28-103	27	16-53	10-39	+22.95
Paul Nicholls	24-62	39	8-28	16-33	+6.26
Anthony Honeyball	21-69	30	8-35	8-21	+13.87
Charlie Longsdon	18-76	24	10-43	6-23	-5.51
Colin Tizzard	13-82	16	5-39	8-33	-30.34
Jamie Snowden	12-64	19	6-34	2-14	+8.55
Philip Hobbs	12-51	24	8-33	4-14	-16.66
Caroline Keevil	12-50	24	6-29	5-17	+59.28
Dan Skelton	12-49	24	3-23	8-14	-5.74
Neil King	11-58	19	5-34	5-18	+30.41
Alan King	11-49	22	9-33	1-9	-14.10

Jockeys	*Wins-Rides*	*%*	*£1 level stks*	*Best Trainer*	*W-R*
Tom Cannon	37-269	14	-61.04	Chris Gordon	26-152
Jamie Moore	27-195	14	-78.27	Gary Moore	22-131
Richard Johnson	24-114	21	-14.01	Philip Hobbs	8-24
Aidan Coleman	23-95	24	+12.52	Charlie Longsdon	5-15
Tom O'Brien	18-126	14	-5.46	Jamie Snowden	3-8
Noel Fehily	18-86	21	-31.59	Neil Mulholland	9-36
Gavin Sheehan	17-70	24	+14.35	Warren Greatrex	9-23
Joshua Moore	16-106	15	+7.00	Gary Moore	13-72
Leighton Aspell	15-164	9	-68.11	Oliver Sherwood	5-45
Sam Twiston-Davies	15-57	26	-4.33	Paul Nicholls	7-22
A P McCoy	15-52	29	+3.28	Jonjo O'Neill	5-14
Marc Goldstein	13-190	7	-41.75	Lydia Richards	5-45
Brendan Powell	12-101	12	-34.45	Jamie Snowden	5-24

Favourites

Hurdle 36.2% -34.94 Chase 37.7% -29.18 TOTAL 36% -82.49

HAYDOCK

Newton-Le-Willows, Lancashire
WA12 0HQ. Tel: 01942 725 963

How to get there Road: M6 Jctn 23 on A49 to Wigan. Rail: Wigan or Warrington Bank Quay (main line)

Features Flat, left-handed, 1m5f circuit, quarter-mile run-in, chase track much sharper (like hurdles track) since introduction of portable fences

2017-18 Fixtures November 25, December 6, 23, 30, January 20, February 17, March 21, 31

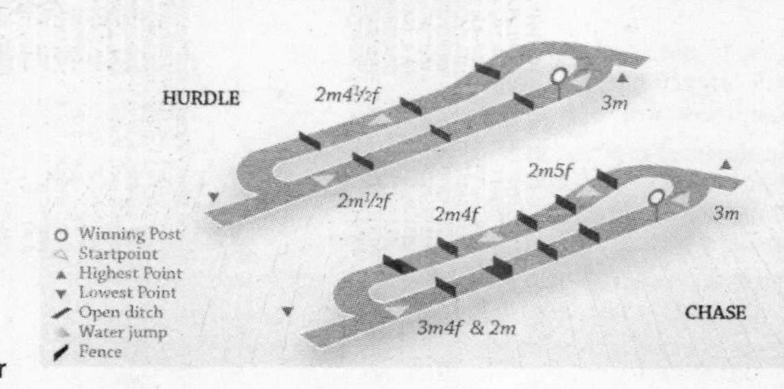

Trainers	Wins-Runs	%	Hurdles	Chases	£1 level stks
Nigel Twiston-Davies	14-76	18	7-30	6-44	-7.80
Paul Nicholls	14-63	22	4-35	10-26	-15.12
Venetia Williams	13-78	17	6-27	6-50	-4.25
David Pipe	12-66	18	7-38	5-28	+50.00
Sue Smith	10-93	11	3-34	7-58	+16.70
Donald McCain	10-77	13	3-46	5-25	-27.69
Lucinda Russell	9-65	14	5-30	4-33	+30.83
Philip Hobbs	8-58	14	5-30	3-24	-10.25
Jonjo O'Neill	7-57	12	4-33	3-23	-8.27
Evan Williams	7-54	13	6-27	1-26	+41.50
Dan Skelton	6-46	13	5-32	1-13	-15.13
Nicky Henderson	6-38	16	4-30	1-6	-18.19
Tom George	6-35	17	5-13	1-19	-4.75

Jockeys	Wins-Rides	%	£1 level stks	Best Trainer	W-R
Daryl Jacob	13-35	37	+25.11	Nigel Twiston-Davies	4-4
Brian Hughes	9-96	9	-62.00	Malcolm Jefferson	5-29
Sam Twiston-Davies	9-57	16	-28.95	Nigel Twiston-Davies	6-25
Richard Johnson	9-41	22	+15.75	Philip Hobbs	4-25
Aidan Coleman	8-59	14	-5.72	Venetia Williams	4-28
Paddy Brennan	8-36	22	-8.21	Tom George	4-16
Tom Scudamore	6-49	12	-8.50	David Pipe	6-33
Harry Skelton	6-39	15	-6.13	Dan Skelton	5-33
Peter Buchanan	6-32	19	+27.83	Lucinda Russell	6-29
Sean Bowen	6-20	30	+9.03	Paul Nicholls	3-6
Noel Fehily	5-41	12	-19.87	Charlie Longsdon	2-11
Jason Maguire	5-41	12	-13.17	Donald McCain	3-25
Liam Treadwell	5-29	17	-3.00	Venetia Williams	5-26

Favourites

Hurdle 32.8% -7.19 Chase 28% -26.75 TOTAL 31.7% -32.65

HEREFORD

Roman Road, Holmer, Hereford HR 4 9QU. Tel 01981 250 436

How to get there Road: A49 1m north of Hereford. Rail: Hereford

Features Right-handed, predominately galloping track with stiffer fences than at many minor courses

2017-18 Fixtures
October 17, November 14, 29, December 16, January 8, 16, 29, March 10, 27

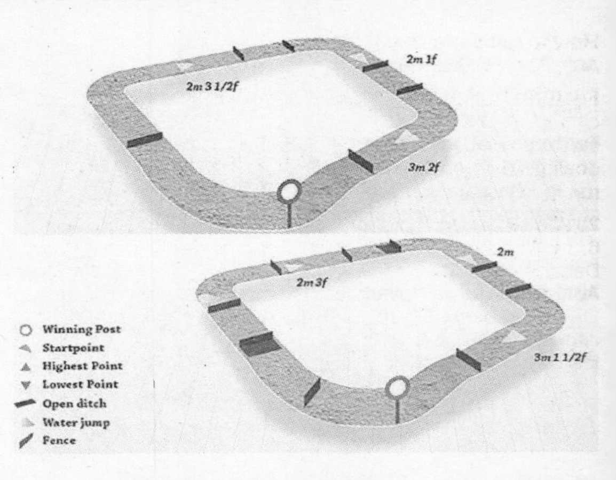

Trainers	Wins-Runs	%	Hurdles	Chases	£1 level stks
Nigel Twiston-Davies	4-16	25	1-6	3-8	-0.75
Venetia Williams	3-20	15	2-12	1-8	-11.03
Henry Oliver	3-12	25	2-8	1-3	+11.50
Dan Skelton	3-11	27	2-8	1-3	+1.90
Nikki Evans	3-7	43	3-6	0-1	+9.75
Harry Fry	3-6	50	1-3	2-3	+6.45
Kerry Lee	2-17	12	1-5	1-12	-5.00
Tim Vaughan	2-15	13	0-6	2-9	-4.50
Philip Hobbs	2-13	15	2-12	0-1	-9.99
Neil Mulholland	2-13	15	0-7	0-2	-3.17
Tom George	2-9	22	1-6	1-2	+0.75
Warren Greatrex	2-8	25	1-3	1-3	-1.88
Rebecca Curtis	2-8	25	0-2	1-4	-2.13

Jockeys	Wins-Rides	%	£1 level stks	Best Trainer	W-R
Noel Fehily	5-9	56	+7.06	Harry Fry	3-4
Aidan Coleman	3-14	21	-3.88	Anthony Honeyball	1-1
Sam Twiston-Davies	3-12	25	-2.83	Nigel Twiston-Davies	2-5
Gavin Sheehan	3-11	27	-1.13	David Dennis	1-1
Jake Greenall	3-7	43	+18.00	Oliver Greenall	2-4
Richard Johnson	2-27	7	-23.18	Rebecca Curtis	1-1
Tom O'Brien	2-14	14	-8.68	Colin Tizzard	1-2
Paddy Brennan	2-11	18	+3.50	Paul Henderson	1-1
James Davies	2-11	18	+8.00	Henry Oliver	2-6
Tom Scudamore	2-11	18	-1.17	Neil Mulholland	2-2
A P Heskin	2-8	25	+1.75	Tom George	2-7
Andrew Tinkler	2-7	29	-2.00	Alastair Ralph	1-1
Wayne Hutchinson	2-7	29	-1.65	Warren Greatrex	1-1

Favourites

Hurdle 28.2% -16.35 Chase 44% +7.71 TOTAL 35.8% -7.45

High Yarridge, Hexham, Northumberland
NE46 2JP. Tel: 01434 606 881

HEXHAM

How to get there Road: A69. Rail: Hexham

Features Left-handed, 1m4f circuit, very stiff, back straight runs nearly all downhill before steep uphill run from home turn

2017-18 Fixtures October 6, 14, November 10, 22, December 13, March 15, April 10, 23

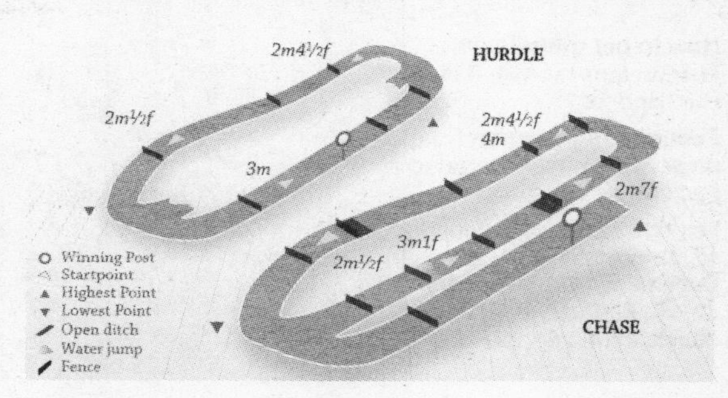

Trainers	*Wins-Runs*	*%*	*Hurdles*	*Chases*	*£1 level stks*
Lucinda Russell	36-199	18	14-101	21-90	+42.22
Sue Smith	14-101	14	6-51	7-46	-32.58
Donald McCain	14-95	15	12-67	0-20	-50.54
Stuart Coltherd	14-59	24	4-28	10-31	+42.50
Malcolm Jefferson	13-50	26	6-30	2-8	-8.00
Maurice Barnes	12-85	14	6-42	6-40	-11.00
Nicky Richards	12-37	32	7-26	5-10	+22.40
James Ewart	11-47	23	4-19	7-22	+11.13
Brian Ellison	11-47	23	8-34	2-11	+10.54
Micky Hammond	9-80	11	6-41	3-33	-51.18
Martin Todhunter	9-77	12	5-43	4-32	-18.63
George Bewley	9-56	16	3-36	6-17	+17.25
Jonathan Haynes	8-66	12	7-42	1-19	-1.72

Jockeys	*Wins-Rides*	*%*	*£1 level stks*	*Best Trainer*	*W-R*
Brian Hughes	34-175	19	-42.06	Malcolm Jefferson	13-41
Peter Buchanan	15-93	16	-5.54	Lucinda Russell	12-54
Wilson Renwick	14-74	19	-15.18	Donald McCain	4-13
Brian Harding	13-115	11	-51.63	Nicky Richards	10-22
Craig Nichol	11-96	11	-33.65	Lucinda Russell	6-20
Ryan Mania	11-57	19	+70.04	Sue Smith	5-25
James Reveley	11-50	22	+10.87	Stuart Coltherd	2-5
Daragh Bourke	11-41	27	+20.00	Maurice Barnes	5-19
Henry Brooke	10-136	7	-78.33	Alistair Whillans	2-4
Thomas Dowson	10-58	17	+4.50	Jonathan Haynes	4-14
Tony Kelly	9-91	10	-41.80	Rebecca Menzies	3-36
Derek Fox	9-86	10	-41.29	Lucinda Russell	4-33
Danny Cook	9-38	24	+11.50	Brian Ellison	4-13

Favourites

Hurdle 35.9% -32.54 Chase 30.7% -20.02 TOTAL 35.6% -43.96

HUNTINGDON

Brampton, Huntingdon, Cambs PE18 8NN. Tel: 01480 453 373

How to get there Road: Follow signs off A14. Rail: Huntingdon

Features Right-handed, flat track, short run-in of around 200 yards

2017-18 Fixtures October 5, 17, November 5, 14, 25, December 10, 26, January 12, 26, February 8, 22, March 4, 14, 26, April 2, 24

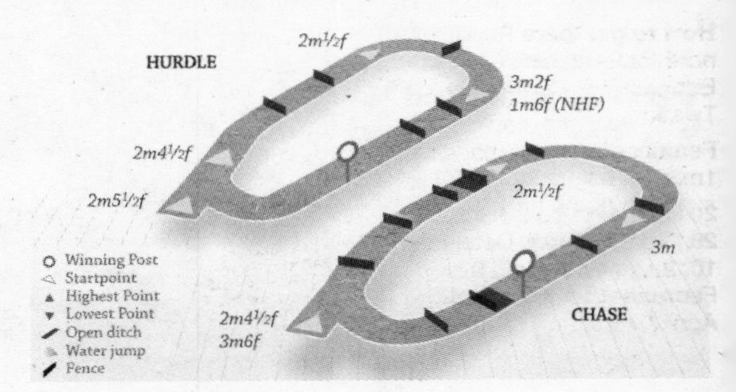

Trainers	Wins-Runs	%	Hurdles	Chases	£1 level stks
Jonjo O'Neill	24-90	27	14-56	7-27	+15.04
Nicky Henderson	23-75	31	15-47	7-14	-11.71
Alan King	21-92	23	11-56	6-17	-15.98
John Ferguson	19-49	39	14-39	1-3	+8.55
Dan Skelton	16-92	17	10-55	5-22	-41.38
Kim Bailey	16-72	22	8-38	6-24	+30.48
Gary Moore	14-80	18	10-55	4-21	+10.71
Charlie Longsdon	13-79	16	8-53	4-17	-12.15
Venetia Williams	9-48	19	4-25	5-22	-15.59
Neil King	8-67	12	6-42	2-15	+17.75
Ian Williams	8-51	16	3-33	5-14	-9.25
Tim Vaughan	8-48	17	6-32	1-12	-15.97
Philip Hobbs	8-41	20	4-24	1-10	-9.21

Jockeys	Wins-Rides	%	£1 level stks	Best Trainer	W-R
Richard Johnson	25-108	23	-1.68	Philip Hobbs	7-25
Aidan Coleman	21-102	21	-10.46	Venetia Williams	7-24
Noel Fehily	21-86	24	-6.64	Charlie Longsdon	5-21
A P McCoy	19-49	39	+5.63	Jonjo O'Neill	6-18
Wayne Hutchinson	16-71	23	-9.03	Alan King	14-52
Leighton Aspell	15-116	13	-35.99	Lucy Wadham	4-24
Harry Skelton	14-86	16	-30.38	Dan Skelton	11-62
Sam Twiston-Davies	14-74	19	-0.25	Paul Nicholls	3-10
Trevor Whelan	13-93	14	+46.83	Neil King	6-49
Jamie Moore	12-60	20	+68.75	Gary Moore	6-31
David Bass	11-59	19	+61.99	Kim Bailey	7-28
Andrew Tinkler	10-60	17	+27.92	Nicky Henderson	5-13
Will Kennedy	9-56	16	-6.88	Jonjo O'Neill	4-8

Favourites

Hurdle 37.5% -28.68 Chase 36.5% -12.70 TOTAL 37% -54.36

Kelso, Roxburghshire.
Tel: 01668 281 611

KELSO

How to get there Road: 1m north of Kelso on B6461 to Ednam. Rail: Berwick-on-Tweed

Features Tight, left-handed, 1m3f circuit

2017-18 Fixtures October 8, 28, November 11, December 10, 29, January 14, 25, February 15, March 3, 19, April 7, 16

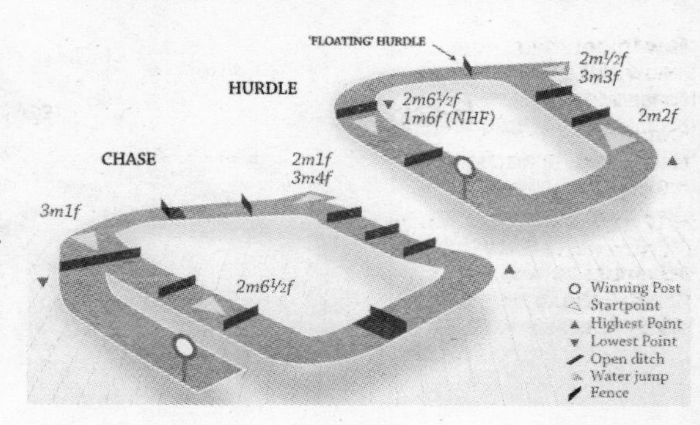

Trainers	*Wins-Runs*	*%*	*Hurdles*	*Chases*	*£1 level stks*
Lucinda Russell	31-233	13	11-121	19-103	-49.32
Donald McCain	29-136	21	19-82	9-47	+5.13
Nicky Richards	26-110	24	16-62	8-38	+6.19
N W Alexander	22-161	14	15-87	7-65	+15.58
Rose Dobbin	13-109	12	5-73	7-31	+16.25
James Ewart	13-85	15	9-46	4-34	-0.04
Malcolm Jefferson	13-57	23	6-21	3-25	-9.09
Sandy Thomson	10-75	13	4-38	6-35	+47.08
Stuart Coltherd	8-85	9	3-37	5-47	-36.63
Chris Grant	8-60	13	4-35	3-17	+89.13
George Bewley	8-59	14	5-31	3-23	+16.00
Dianne Sayer	7-85	8	3-56	4-28	-46.00
Michael Smith	6-38	16	4-20	1-13	-0.38

Jockeys	*Wins-Rides*	*%*	*£1 level stks*	*Best Trainer*	*W-R*
Brian Hughes	39-213	18	+12.41	Malcolm Jefferson	12-50
Brian Harding	27-171	16	-52.21	Nicky Richards	16-61
Peter Buchanan	17-113	15	-13.15	Lucinda Russell	13-81
Jason Maguire	16-52	31	+18.19	Donald McCain	16-45
Craig Nichol	14-127	11	-56.37	Rose Dobbin	6-41
Lucy Alexander	13-118	11	+0.13	N W Alexander	10-76
Derek Fox	12-91	13	-17.08	Lucinda Russell	7-53
Tony Kelly	9-79	11	-28.00	Chris Grant	2-6
Ryan Mania	9-70	13	-18.92	Dianne Sayer	2-13
Henry Brooke	8-78	10	+34.38	Kenneth Slack	3-5
James Reveley	8-62	13	-20.63	Keith Reveley	3-11
Danny Cook	8-55	15	-5.63	Michael Smith	4-15
Dale Irving	8-35	23	+9.83	James Ewart	7-25

Favourites

Hurdle 36.4% -21.63 | Chase 37.3% +11.96 | TOTAL 35.7% -20.84

KEMPTON

Staines Rd East, Sunbury-on-Thames
TW16 5AQ. Tel: 01932 782 292

How to get there Road: M3 Jctn 1, A308 towards Kingston-on-Thames. Rail: Kempton Park from Waterloo

Features A sharp right-handed track with the emphasis very much on speed

2017-18 Fixtures October 22, November 13, 27, December 26-27, January 13, February 9, 24, March 17, April 9, 26

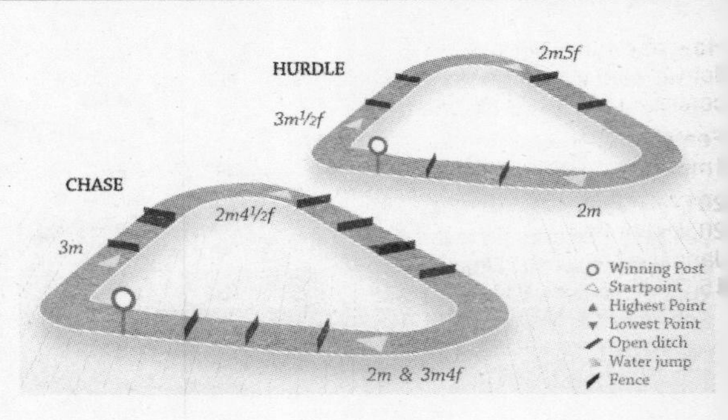

Trainers	*Wins-Runs*	*%*	*Hurdles*	*Chases*	*£1 level stks*
Nicky Henderson	50-186	27	27-108	18-56	-5.04
Paul Nicholls	27-139	19	12-63	15-72	-11.65
Alan King	22-139	16	16-84	3-40	-45.83
Jonjo O'Neill	11-80	14	7-48	4-29	-24.39
Colin Tizzard	10-59	17	3-19	6-35	+15.23
Philip Hobbs	9-85	11	5-46	4-32	-52.28
Emma Lavelle	9-64	14	4-30	4-27	-33.40
Nigel Twiston-Davies	9-54	17	5-24	4-26	-20.14
Tom George	9-53	17	1-8	8-43	+1.50
Harry Fry	9-49	18	8-29	1-13	-19.80
Dan Skelton	8-84	10	6-54	2-23	-57.46
Chris Gordon	8-43	19	2-18	6-24	+48.18
Charlie Longsdon	7-50	14	2-28	5-20	+1.70

Jockeys	*Wins-Rides*	*%*	*£1 level stks*	*Best Trainer*	*W-R*
Barry Geraghty	27-108	25	-1.80	Nicky Henderson	18-65
Noel Fehily	21-121	17	-40.06	Harry Fry	5-28
Nico de Boinville	20-71	28	+3.45	Nicky Henderson	14-43
Richard Johnson	19-111	17	-30.37	Philip Hobbs	9-41
Sam Twiston-Davies	17-111	15	-41.78	Nigel Twiston-Davies	8-24
Tom Cannon	15-79	19	+81.10	Chris Gordon	7-24
Aidan Coleman	13-110	12	-50.18	Emma Lavelle	3-26
Wayne Hutchinson	13-79	16	-12.00	Alan King	12-64
Nick Scholfield	13-73	18	+22.52	Paul Nicholls	7-23
A P McCoy	11-42	26	-2.21	Jonjo O'Neill	5-16
Daryl Jacob	10-76	13	-34.37	Paul Nicholls	4-19
Paddy Brennan	10-72	14	+21.50	Tom George	6-32
Harry Skelton	8-68	12	-19.96	Dan Skelton	6-61

Favourites

Hurdle 44% +3.31 Chase 38% -14.26 TOTAL 40.9% -16.87

eicester, LE2 4AL
el: 0116 271 6515

LEICESTER

low to get there Road: M1 ctn 21, 2m south of city entre on A6. Rail: Leicester

'eatures Right-handed, m6f circuit, stiff uphill run-in

017-18 Fixtures November 0, December 3, 7, 13, 28, anuary 11, 23, 31, February 5, 27, March 9

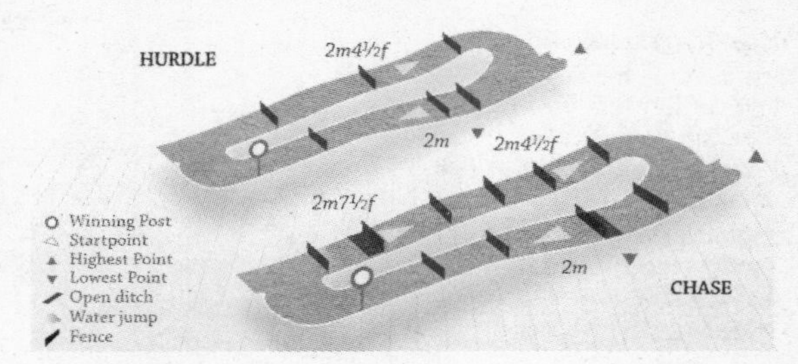

Trainers	*Wins-Runs*	*%*	*Hurdles*	*Chases*	*£1 level stks*
Nigel Twiston-Davies	15-61	25	6-25	9-36	+21.46
Tom George	14-41	34	2-6	12-35	+20.88
David Pipe	11-24	46	6-13	5-11	+15.06
Caroline Bailey	9-39	23	2-11	7-28	-1.21
Venetia Williams	8-38	21	2-17	6-21	-14.38
Fergal O'Brien	7-41	17	0-10	7-31	+23.13
Philip Hobbs	6-18	33	3-10	3-8	+3.50
Ian Williams	6-17	35	3-8	3-9	+0.57
Tony Carroll	4-56	7	2-35	2-21	-26.00
Jonjo O'Neill	4-40	10	1-21	3-19	-28.50
Henry Oliver	4-26	15	2-12	2-14	-11.50
Dan Skelton	4-23	17	1-12	3-11	-1.00
Charlie Longsdon	4-22	18	0-11	4-11	-10.40

Jockeys	*Wins-Rides*	*%*	*£1 level stks*	*Best Trainer*	*W-R*
Sam Twiston-Davies	18-60	30	+14.83	Nigel Twiston-Davies	11-38
Aidan Coleman	12-48	25	-9.10	Venetia Williams	5-22
Paddy Brennan	11-66	17	+3.13	Tom George	6-24
Richard Johnson	10-41	24	-5.95	Philip Hobbs	5-13
Tom Scudamore	8-34	24	-8.44	David Pipe	8-18
Conor Shoemark	6-30	20	+11.63	Fergal O'Brien	3-15
Will Kennedy	6-22	27	-2.81	Ian Williams	4-7
Noel Fehily	6-18	33	-3.42	Charlie Longsdon	3-4
Liam Treadwell	5-26	19	+12.13	Venetia Williams	3-7
Lee Edwards	4-50	8	-24.00	Tony Carroll	3-40
Trevor Whelan	4-37	11	-8.25	Neil King	2-13
Charlie Poste	4-26	15	-9.50	Matt Sheppard	2-5
Harry Skelton	4-26	15	-2.38	Dan Skelton	3-18

Favourites

Hurdle 46.8% +18.68 Chase 35.9% -19.36 TOTAL 40.2% -0.68

LINGFIELD

Lingfield, Surrey, RH7 6PC
Tel: 01342 834 80(

How to get there Road: M25 Jctn 6, south on A22. Rail: Lingfield from London Bridge and Victoria

Features Left-handed, 1m4f circuit, hilly

2017-18 Fixtures November 14, 28, December 5, January 5, 22, 30, February 13, 19, March 5

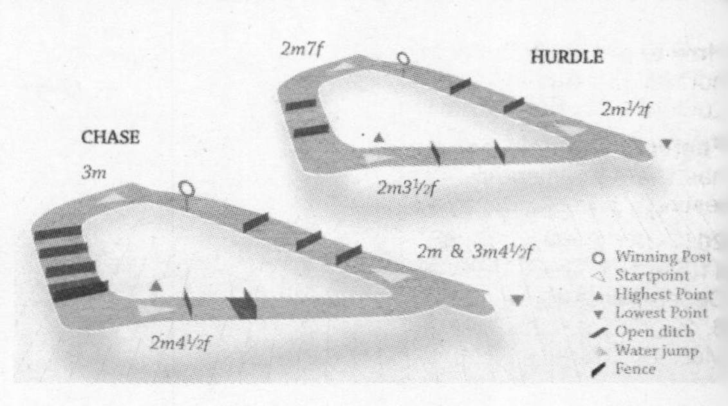

Trainers	*Wins-Runs*	*%*	*Hurdles*	*Chases*	*£1 level stks*
Gary Moore	9-69	13	2-40	7-29	-13.25
Warren Greatrex	9-17	53	7-12	2-5	+6.47
Chris Gordon	7-31	23	4-18	3-13	-3.25
Nigel Twiston-Davies	6-21	29	4-12	2-9	+24.58
Dan Skelton	5-10	50	2-6	3-4	+15.00
Seamus Mullins	4-32	13	1-17	3-15	-15.00
Venetia Williams	4-27	15	1-9	3-18	-11.63
Tim Vaughan	4-20	20	1-9	3-11	-7.40
Dr Richard Newland	4-6	67	2-3	2-3	+3.95
Neil Mulholland	3-23	13	2-12	1-11	+26.00
Anna Newton-Smith	3-18	17	2-9	1-9	+0.00
Evan Williams	3-13	23	0-8	3-5	+0.00
Oliver Sherwood	3-10	30	3-7	0-3	-3.14

Jockeys	*Wins-Rides*	*%*	*£1 level stks*	*Best Trainer*	*W-R*
Leighton Aspell	9-39	23	-4.51	Lucy Wadham	3-7
Tom Scudamore	8-29	28	+4.49	Anabel K Murphy	2-2
Gavin Sheehan	8-23	35	+5.23	Warren Greatrex	7-15
Tom Cannon	7-46	15	-11.25	Chris Gordon	6-20
Jamie Moore	5-47	11	-10.50	Gary Moore	5-30
Joshua Moore	5-32	16	-5.25	Gary Moore	3-27
Noel Fehily	5-22	23	+3.64	Harry Fry	2-2
Sam Twiston-Davies	5-12	42	+10.83	Nigel Twiston-Davies	4-9
Paddy Brennan	4-19	21	-1.25	Colin Tizzard	1-1
Daryl Jacob	4-10	40	+4.10	Dr Richard Newland	2-2
Andrew Thornton	3-26	12	-13.50	Seamus Mullins	3-13
Aidan Coleman	3-19	16	-6.63	Venetia Williams	3-11
Alan Johns	3-14	21	-7.40	Tim Vaughan	3-14

Favourites

Hurdle 43.7% -2.58   Chase 40.3% +0.25   TOTAL 42% -2.32

LUDLOW

romfield, Ludlow, Shrewsbury,
hropshire. Tel: 01981 250 052

low to get there Road: 2m orth of Ludlow on A49. Rail: udlow

eatures Flat, right-handed, as sharp turns and a esting run-in of 450 yards

017-18 Fixtures October 1, 26, November 9, 16, 27, ecember 6, 20, January , 10, 18, February 7, 21, larch 1, 22, April 9, 24

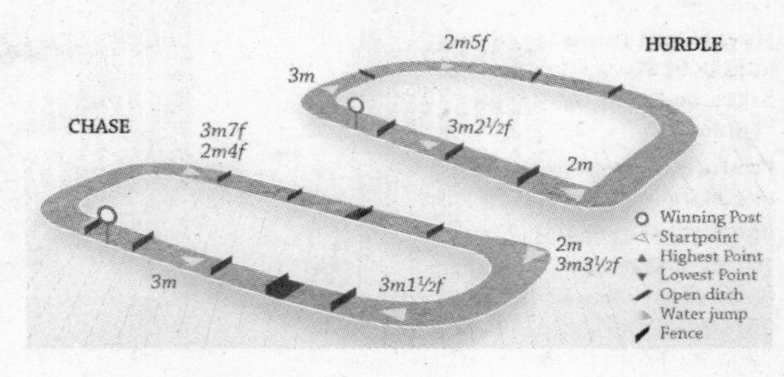

Trainers	Wins-Runs	%	Hurdles	Chases	£1 level stks
Evan Williams	35-210	17	13-88	18-107	-36.59
Nicky Henderson	25-81	31	15-48	2-14	-18.56
Philip Hobbs	23-92	25	13-45	9-39	-6.90
Dan Skelton	18-78	23	14-52	2-14	-9.68
Henry Daly	17-88	19	6-36	9-37	-17.02
Nigel Twiston-Davies	15-122	12	8-66	6-51	-62.85
Tom George	15-70	21	2-22	13-45	-3.50
Venetia Williams	12-116	10	2-54	9-61	-62.28
Ian Williams	11-54	20	8-36	3-18	+3.82
Kim Bailey	10-78	13	6-52	1-20	-9.57
Alan King	10-46	22	8-37	2-9	-1.03
Jonjo O'Neill	8-72	11	2-30	5-41	-40.13
Tim Vaughan	8-66	12	2-38	6-19	+9.12

Jockeys	Wins-Rides	%	£1 level stks	Best Trainer	W-R
Richard Johnson	30-142	21	-35.90	Philip Hobbs	13-56
Paddy Brennan	21-84	25	+18.75	Tom George	12-40
Paul Moloney	18-118	15	-51.83	Evan Williams	16-89
Harry Skelton	18-70	26	-1.68	Dan Skelton	18-64
Adam Wedge	14-92	15	-6.51	Evan Williams	14-75
Sam Twiston-Davies	11-132	8	-80.68	Nigel Twiston-Davies	7-64
Aidan Coleman	10-104	10	-34.79	Venetia Williams	6-47
Wayne Hutchinson	10-46	22	-1.53	Alan King	9-31
Tom Scudamore	10-45	22	+17.03	David Pipe	7-20
A P McCoy	10-45	22	-15.32	Neil Mulholland	2-3
Andrew Tinkler	8-53	15	+9.07	Nicky Henderson	3-21
David Bass	8-44	18	-15.29	Kim Bailey	5-30
Nico de Boinville	7-32	22	-10.27	Nicky Henderson	5-16

Favourites

Hurdle 43.2% -2.74 Chase 38.3% +7.53 TOTAL 41.4% +9.26

MARKET RASEN

Legsby Road, LN8 3E
Tel: 01673 843 43

How to get there Road: A46 to Market Rasen, course on A631. Rail: Market Rasen (1m walk)

Features Right-handed, easy fences, run-in of 250 yards

2017-18 Fixtures
October 21, November 9, 23, December 7, 26, January 17, February 6, 18, 28, March 11, 26, April 2, 11

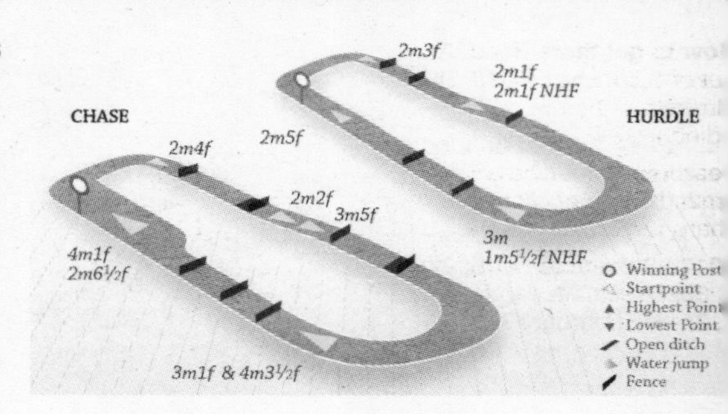

Trainers	Wins-Runs	%	Hurdles	Chases	£1 level stks
Jonjo O'Neill	31-182	17	18-96	12-76	-36.47
Charlie Longsdon	26-120	22	14-62	10-43	-28.18
Brian Ellison	23-126	18	18-86	3-34	-11.79
Dan Skelton	21-84	25	14-50	6-27	-1.98
Nicky Henderson	19-64	30	10-36	3-13	+6.53
Dr Richard Newland	17-64	27	10-40	7-24	+24.51
Malcolm Jefferson	15-78	19	7-36	4-17	+16.88
Peter Bowen	14-67	21	5-26	6-31	-15.53
Fergal O'Brien	14-61	23	6-29	7-28	+53.00
John Ferguson	14-48	29	13-39	0-5	+4.55
David Pipe	11-51	22	5-28	6-19	-13.60
Nigel Hawke	10-42	24	4-20	6-21	+22.96
Tim Vaughan	9-96	9	4-61	4-27	-59.13

Jockeys	Wins-Rides	%	£1 level stks	Best Trainer	W-R
A P McCoy	28-104	27	-25.94	Jonjo O'Neill	12-51
Noel Fehily	27-104	26	-10.37	Charlie Longsdon	14-42
Richard Johnson	26-159	16	-76.64	Philip Hobbs	7-27
Aidan Coleman	25-129	19	+17.19	Jonjo O'Neill	7-25
Tom Scudamore	23-107	21	+16.82	David Pipe	10-35
Brian Hughes	21-177	12	-68.37	Malcolm Jefferson	12-60
Harry Skelton	18-78	23	-6.73	Dan Skelton	18-68
Sam Twiston-Davies	17-71	24	-7.51	Dr Richard Newland	9-28
Danny Cook	13-72	18	-16.96	Sue Smith	6-20
Paddy Brennan	13-65	20	+18.13	Fergal O'Brien	7-31
Gavin Sheehan	12-70	17	-17.30	Warren Greatrex	7-27
Leighton Aspell	10-65	15	-29.96	Oliver Sherwood	4-16
Kielan Woods	9-69	13	-10.95	Pam Sly	4-14

Favourites

Hurdle 39.3% -17.24 Chase 34.1% -34.35 TOTAL 38.3% -43.88

ast Lothian
el: 01316 652 859

MUSSELBURGH

low to get there Road: A1 ut of Edinburgh. Rail: Musselburgh from Edinburgh

eatures Right-handed, m2f circuit, very flat with harp turns

017-18 Fixtures November , 30, December 11, January , 3, 19, February 3-4, 14, 28

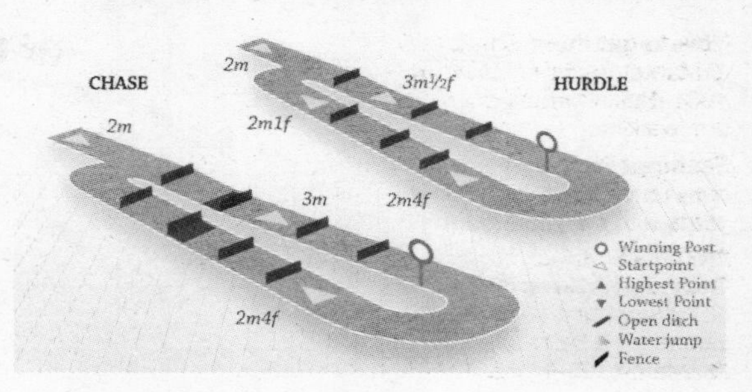

Trainers	Wins-Runs	%	Hurdles	Chases	£1 level stks
Lucinda Russell	27-208	13	12-113	13-83	-29.15
Donald McCain	24-114	21	15-71	5-37	+25.95
James Ewart	13-74	18	11-49	1-16	+15.05
Sandy Thomson	10-47	21	7-25	3-20	+40.30
Jim Goldie	8-83	10	8-78	0-4	-22.59
Dianne Sayer	8-61	13	5-40	3-19	+1.75
John Ferguson	8-26	31	7-21	0-3	-0.46
Chris Grant	7-61	11	1-26	4-24	-13.00
Rose Dobbin	7-57	12	1-29	5-25	+10.25
Nicky Henderson	7-24	29	6-20	1-3	-7.16
John Quinn	7-21	33	7-19	0-1	+7.85
Keith Dalgleish	6-30	20	4-21	2-4	-3.25
Paul Nicholls	6-18	33	3-12	3-6	+4.11

Jockeys	Wins-Rides	%	£1 level stks	Best Trainer	W-R
Brian Hughes	28-156	18	-30.74	James Moffatt	4-14
Jason Maguire	14-60	23	-8.55	Donald McCain	14-54
James Reveley	12-58	21	+9.49	Jim Goldie	3-13
Craig Nichol	11-87	13	-32.17	Lucinda Russell	5-28
Peter Buchanan	10-62	16	+36.38	Lucinda Russell	7-50
Denis O'Regan	10-31	32	+32.54	John Ferguson	5-10
Derek Fox	9-68	13	-18.63	Lucinda Russell	8-48
Wilson Renwick	9-45	20	+3.00	Peter Niven	2-5
Richard Johnson	8-42	19	-20.15	Gordon Elliott	3-6
Henry Brooke	7-73	10	+9.08	David Thompson	2-2
Danny Cook	7-59	12	-10.54	Brian Ellison	3-31
Ryan Mania	7-19	37	+41.75	Sandy Thomson	3-5
Brian Harding	6-82	7	-49.75	Jim Goldie	2-6

Favourites

Hurdle 40.9% -3.26 Chase 34.7% -1.43 TOTAL 39% -3.26

NEWBURY

Newbury, Berkshire, RG14 7
Tel: 01635 400 15 or 414

How to get there Road: Follow signs from M4 or A34. Rail: Newbury Racecourse

Features Flat, left-handed, 1m6f circuit, suits galloping sorts with stamina, tough fences

2017-18 Fixtures November 9, December 1-2, 20, 30, January 17, February 10, March 2-3, 23-24

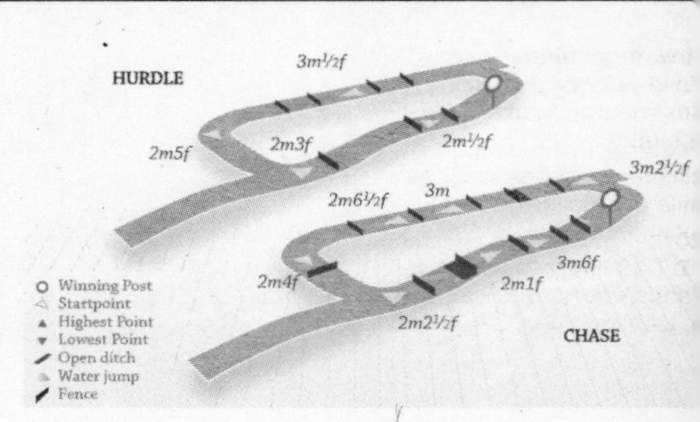

Trainers	Wins-Runs	%	Hurdles	Chases	£1 level stks
Nicky Henderson	37-145	26	27-90	5-35	-11.71
Paul Nicholls	24-143	17	9-60	15-79	-18.86
Philip Hobbs	21-111	19	9-51	12-53	+53.47
Alan King	18-140	13	8-85	5-31	-48.13
David Pipe	13-90	14	7-54	6-33	-11.97
Warren Greatrex	11-58	19	6-38	4-13	-4.00
Colin Tizzard	10-67	15	2-23	7-34	-15.53
Harry Fry	10-48	21	6-25	2-13	-8.33
Venetia Williams	9-82	11	1-26	8-55	-27.63
Nigel Twiston-Davies	8-85	9	6-35	1-42	-4.59
Jonjo O'Neill	7-81	9	3-44	4-34	-38.85
Ben Pauling	7-25	28	4-17	2-6	+3.74
Rebecca Curtis	6-58	10	1-27	5-25	-10.67

Jockeys	Wins-Rides	%	£1 level stks	Best Trainer	W-R
Richard Johnson	28-135	21	+74.19	Philip Hobbs	19-81
Barry Geraghty	27-100	27	+9.40	Nicky Henderson	21-54
Noel Fehily	16-109	15	-21.63	Harry Fry	6-33
Tom Scudamore	15-100	15	-3.85	David Pipe	9-56
A P McCoy	15-75	20	-3.63	Jonjo O'Neill	4-29
Gavin Sheehan	11-77	14	-5.38	Warren Greatrex	7-40
Sam Twiston-Davies	10-129	8	-72.88	Paul Nicholls	7-66
Aidan Coleman	9-126	7	-84.53	Venetia Williams	5-50
Wayne Hutchinson	9-87	10	-37.82	Alan King	8-76
Daryl Jacob	9-64	14	-23.77	Paul Nicholls	7-22
Tom O'Brien	8-66	12	-8.00	Hughie Morrison	3-9
Nico de Boinville	8-50	16	-15.58	Nicky Henderson	4-26
Paddy Brennan	7-78	9	-42.63	Tom George	4-38

Favourites

Hurdle 39.5% -8.00 Chase 27.7% -30.88 TOTAL 33.6% -46.75

High Gosforth Park, Newcastle
NE3 5HP. Tel: 01912 362 020

NEWCASTLE

How to get there Road: Follow signs from A1. Rail: 4m from Newcastle Central

Features Left-handed, 1m6f circuit, tough fences, half-mile straight is all uphill

2017-18 Fixtures November 17, December 2, 14, 23, January 6, 21, 30, February 5, 24, March 6, 17, April 14

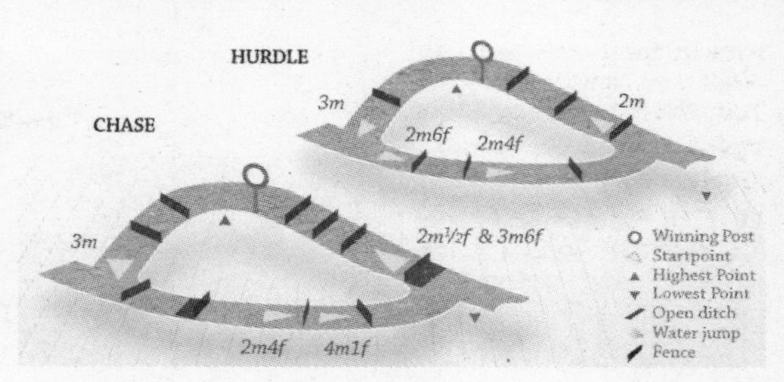

Trainers	Wins-Runs	%	Hurdles	Chases	£1 level stks
Sue Smith	15-100	15	3-38	11-55	-28.22
Lucinda Russell	14-115	12	4-50	8-56	-42.47
N W Alexander	13-92	14	8-50	5-35	-27.43
Nicky Richards	12-53	23	4-21	3-22	-6.24
Donald McCain	10-74	14	6-40	4-25	-20.48
Brian Ellison	10-51	20	4-21	6-25	-11.83
Malcolm Jefferson	10-37	27	4-15	3-13	-6.90
Keith Reveley	9-59	15	4-32	4-18	-21.88
Keith Dalgleish	9-18	50	4-11	4-5	+28.88
Micky Hammond	8-57	14	5-25	3-25	-0.13
Sandy Thomson	8-34	24	3-14	3-16	+7.53
Ann Hamilton	7-26	27	3-5	4-20	+3.82
Rose Dobbin	4-54	7	2-36	2-15	-34.81

Jockeys	Wins-Rides	%	£1 level stks	Best Trainer	W-R
Brian Hughes	29-149	19	-48.24	Malcolm Jefferson	10-33
Brian Harding	15-100	15	-22.86	Nicky Richards	9-34
James Reveley	14-79	18	-8.36	Keith Reveley	6-40
Wilson Renwick	11-57	19	-9.13	Keith Dalgleish	4-8
Craig Nichol	9-78	12	-38.99	Lucinda Russell	3-14
Danny Cook	9-51	18	-15.57	Sue Smith	7-32
Lucy Alexander	8-53	15	-3.13	N W Alexander	7-37
Henry Brooke	7-77	9	-9.50	Donald McCain	2-6
Joe Colliver	7-35	20	+8.88	Micky Hammond	6-23
Jason Maguire	7-34	21	+27.68	Donald McCain	5-23
Grant Cockburn	6-37	16	+5.50	Lucinda Russell	4-19
Tony Kelly	5-59	8	-18.00	Henry Hogarth	3-15
Ryan Mania	5-32	16	+1.25	Sue Smith	3-19

Favourites

Hurdle 40% -10.04 Chase 41.6% -1.41 TOTAL 40.7% -11.79

NEWTON ABBOT

Devon, TQ12 3A[illegible]
Tel: 01626 532 3[illegible]

How to get there Road: On A380 from Newton Abbot to Torquay. Rail: Newton Abbot

Features Tight, left-handed, 1m1f circuit

2017-18 Fixtures October 2, 13, March 31, April 23

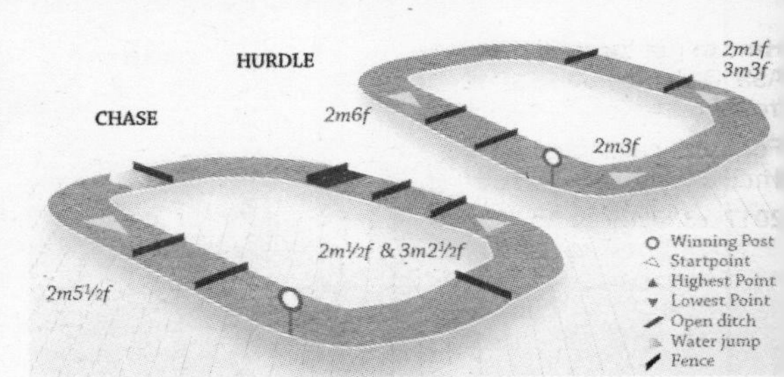

Trainers	*Wins-Runs*	*%*	*Hurdles*	*Chases*	*£1 level stks*
Paul Nicholls	32-116	28	18-55	13-58	-37.94
Philip Hobbs	27-135	20	19-81	6-47	+8.90
Martin Hill	16-104	15	11-75	4-24	+27.88
Evan Williams	15-92	16	6-47	9-44	-19.36
Jonjo O'Neill	15-83	18	13-49	1-33	-27.88
Tim Vaughan	14-85	16	11-62	2-17	-21.50
John Ferguson	14-37	38	10-29	2-5	+10.16
Jimmy Frost	13-134	10	10-95	3-38	-18.88
David Pipe	13-120	11	9-88	4-27	-66.16
Neil Mulholland	11-87	13	6-49	5-33	-27.68
Jeremy Scott	11-63	17	3-38	8-25	+19.25
Colin Tizzard	10-98	10	4-53	5-40	-36.88
David Bridgwater	9-38	24	3-16	6-21	-0.27

Jockeys	*Wins-Rides*	*%*	*£1 level stks*	*Best Trainer*	*W-R*
Richard Johnson	34-176	19	-16.42	Philip Hobbs	14-67
Sam Twiston-Davies	34-145	23	-48.77	Paul Nicholls	21-67
Tom Scudamore	26-149	17	-39.93	David Pipe	10-68
A P McCoy	24-83	29	-19.45	Jonjo O'Neill	7-32
Tom O'Brien	19-137	14	-35.40	Philip Hobbs	7-23
Nick Scholfield	19-130	15	-25.29	Jeremy Scott	6-25
Noel Fehily	17-74	23	+18.12	Harry Fry	5-15
Aidan Coleman	16-73	22	+24.31	John Ferguson	8-13
Hadden Frost	15-72	21	+46.75	Martin Hill	8-36
Paul Moloney	13-98	13	-38.05	Evan Williams	9-43
Gavin Sheehan	10-49	20	+7.42	Warren Greatrex	4-10
James Best	9-103	9	-24.25	Kevin Bishop	3-13
Daryl Jacob	8-57	14	-0.85	Emma Lavelle	2-6

Favourites

Hurdle 36.8% -11.86 Chase 34.8% -29.66 TOTAL 36.7% -35.96

PERTH

cone Palace Park, Perth
'H2 6BB. Tel: 01683 220 131

low to get there Road:
.93. Rail: Free bus service
rom Perth

eatures Flat, right-handed,
m2f circuit

017-18 Fixtures April 25-27

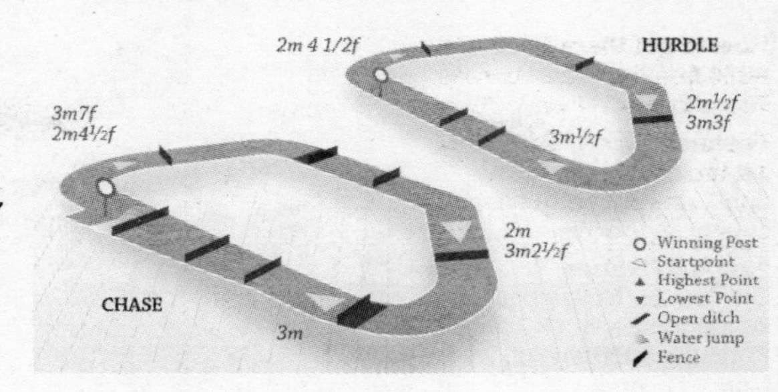

Trainers	Wins-Runs	%	Hurdles	Chases	£1 level stks
Gordon Elliott	60-211	28	42-126	14-68	+13.81
Lucinda Russell	25-316	8	18-198	7-104	-111.54
Lisa Harrison	19-125	15	10-76	9-39	+16.08
Nicky Richards	18-102	18	11-71	5-26	+7.00
Fergal O'Brien	17-61	28	8-28	8-27	+29.88
Donald McCain	16-95	17	9-59	6-28	-22.09
Nigel Twiston-Davies	15-77	19	7-42	6-28	-15.39
S R B Crawford	13-121	11	7-78	2-25	-52.07
David Pipe	13-24	54	6-13	7-11	+23.11
Tom George	10-49	20	2-14	7-33	-4.63
Dianne Sayer	9-87	10	7-62	2-25	-28.25
Peter Bowen	9-28	32	4-9	3-15	+2.90
N W Alexander	8-114	7	3-69	5-38	-30.50

Jockeys	Wins-Rides	%	£1 level stks	Best Trainer	W-R
Richard Johnson	51-182	28	-22.00	Gordon Elliott	32-123
Brian Hughes	20-179	11	-45.42	Robert Alan Hennessy	3-14
Craig Nichol	19-148	13	-41.60	Nicky Richards	5-21
Paddy Brennan	18-78	23	+9.00	Fergal O'Brien	11-32
Sam Twiston-Davies	17-74	23	-6.14	Nigel Twiston-Davies	10-52
Tom Scudamore	13-53	25	-6.02	David Pipe	12-22
Jason Maguire	12-47	26	-4.81	Gordon Elliott	8-18
Brian Harding	11-111	10	-41.86	Nicky Richards	7-46
Henry Brooke	10-112	9	-39.50	Alistair Whillans	2-5
Callum Bewley	10-75	13	+11.88	Lisa Harrison	4-35
Wilson Renwick	10-64	16	-19.36	Gordon Elliott	3-10
Ryan Day	10-51	20	+6.33	Lisa Harrison	8-31
Tony Kelly	9-62	15	+10.25	Jackie Stephen	6-35

Favourites

Hurdle 36.8% -30.72 Chase 25.9% -62.82 TOTAL 33.2% -95.73

PLUMPTON

Plumpton, Sussex
Tel: 01273 890 383

How to get there Road: A274 or A275 to B2116. Rail: Plumpton

Features Quirky, undulating, left-handed 1m1f circuit, uphill straight, has several course specialists

2017-18 Fixtures
October 23, November 6, 20, December 4, 18, January 7, 15, 29, February 12, 26, March 12, April 1-2, 15

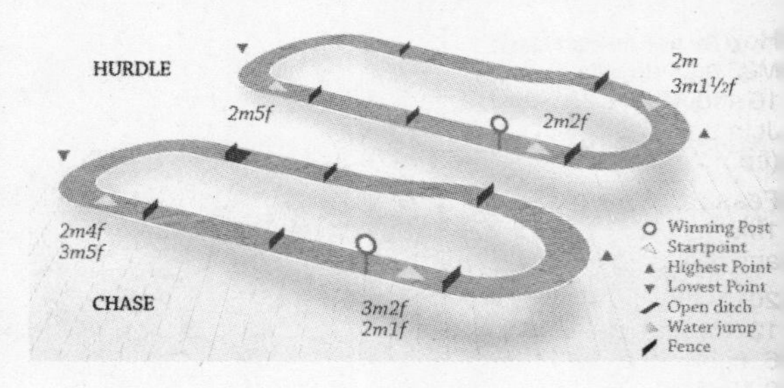

Trainers	*Wins-Runs*	*%*	*Hurdles*	*Chases*	*£1 level stks*
Gary Moore	43-218	20	27-150	16-63	-18.52
Chris Gordon	20-127	16	11-90	9-29	+21.66
Paul Henderson	13-62	21	4-25	9-37	+13.63
Suzy Smith	13-43	30	11-37	0-0	+66.88
Anthony Honeyball	13-40	33	7-27	4-9	-1.86
Alan King	13-37	35	9-26	4-9	-5.71
Seamus Mullins	12-110	11	5-51	7-55	-49.42
Sheena West	12-82	15	7-61	5-19	+1.67
David Bridgwater	11-58	19	1-26	9-30	-22.34
David Pipe	11-46	24	6-29	2-9	+12.98
Warren Greatrex	10-38	26	8-34	0-1	+7.65
Colin Tizzard	9-48	19	6-25	3-20	-14.67
Venetia Williams	9-36	25	7-21	2-15	-13.32

Jockeys	*Wins-Rides*	*%*	*£1 level stks*	*Best Trainer*	*W-R*
Joshua Moore	25-130	19	-23.60	Gary Moore	24-96
Tom Cannon	24-180	13	+0.41	Chris Gordon	14-77
Tom Scudamore	23-78	29	+31.02	David Bridgwater	8-27
Marc Goldstein	21-167	13	+28.67	Sheena West	10-70
Jamie Moore	20-143	14	-33.98	Gary Moore	14-85
Aidan Coleman	18-75	24	-19.92	Venetia Williams	7-24
Gavin Sheehan	17-64	27	+26.27	Warren Greatrex	9-27
Leighton Aspell	12-109	11	-57.87	Oliver Sherwood	7-21
Wayne Hutchinson	12-36	33	-5.13	Alan King	10-24
Paddy Brennan	11-43	26	+23.70	Paul Henderson	4-13
Tom O'Brien	10-70	14	+0.67	Paul Henderson	6-21
Nick Scholfield	8-59	14	-14.34	Lawney Hill	4-13
Noel Fehily	8-54	15	-30.53	Harry Fry	3-8

Favourites

Hurdle 43.4% +19.52   Chase 38.4% -10.27   TOTAL 40.6% +1.54

Esher, Surrey, KT10 9AJ
Tel: 01372 463 072 or 464 348

SANDOWN

How to get there Road: M25 anti-clockwise Jctn 10 and A3, M25 clockwise Jctn 9 and A224. Rail: Esher (from Waterloo)

Features Right-handed, 1m5f circuit, tough fences and stiff uphill finish

2017-18 Fixtures November 12, December 8-9, January 6, February 3, 16, March 9-10, April 28

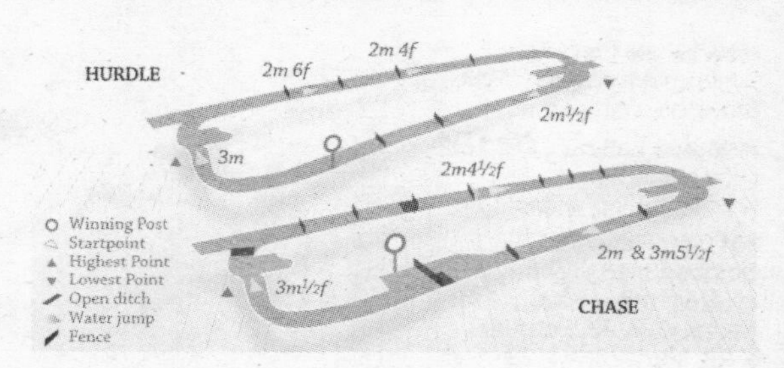

Trainers	*Wins-Runs*	*%*	*Hurdles*	*Chases*	*£1 level stks*
Nicky Henderson	31-119	26	23-80	7-35	+16.57
Paul Nicholls	24-156	15	9-57	15-97	-12.44
Gary Moore	21-91	23	9-55	11-35	+87.48
Philip Hobbs	14-70	20	7-25	6-40	+5.10
Alan King	10-53	19	8-32	2-17	+0.71
Venetia Williams	8-90	9	1-32	7-57	-52.00
Fergal O'Brien	7-17	41	3-6	3-7	+25.96
David Pipe	6-51	12	3-39	3-12	-24.79
Lucy Wadham	6-25	24	2-13	4-11	+12.83
W P Mullins	6-17	35	3-8	2-7	+19.19
Nigel Twiston-Davies	5-42	12	4-23	1-19	+10.66
Oliver Sherwood	5-35	14	2-20	3-13	+2.25
Neil Mulholland	5-19	26	1-6	4-13	+12.00

Jockeys	*Wins-Rides*	*%*	*£1 level stks*	*Best Trainer*	*W-R*
Richard Johnson	20-87	23	+42.18	Philip Hobbs	13-44
Jamie Moore	19-76	25	+26.89	Gary Moore	12-44
Daryl Jacob	19-60	32	+39.56	Nicky Henderson	5-9
Noel Fehily	14-67	21	+4.57	Neil Mulholland	4-8
Sam Twiston-Davies	12-85	14	+9.95	Paul Nicholls	9-58
Barry Geraghty	11-57	19	-1.81	Nicky Henderson	10-39
Joshua Moore	10-46	22	+75.88	Gary Moore	8-30
Aidan Coleman	9-93	10	-28.00	Venetia Williams	6-51
Leighton Aspell	7-59	12	-19.42	Lucy Wadham	3-13
A P McCoy	6-40	15	-8.50	Nicky Henderson	2-3
Wayne Hutchinson	6-33	18	-5.29	Alan King	6-28
Paddy Brennan	5-36	14	-2.00	Fergal O'Brien	3-6
David Bass	5-18	28	+18.25	Nicky Henderson	4-7

Favourites

Hurdle 28.7% -25.92 Chase 38.7% +3.69 TOTAL 33.2% -24.85

SEDGEFIELD

Sedgefield, Cleveland, TS21 2HW
Tel: 01740 621 925

How to get there Road: 2m from A1 on A689. Rail: Stockton, Darlington

Features Left-handed, 1m2f circuit, sharp and undulating, no water jump

2017-18 Fixtures
October 3, 25, November 2, 28, December 8, 26, January 12, 28, February 6, 22, March 4, 13, 23, April 13, 23

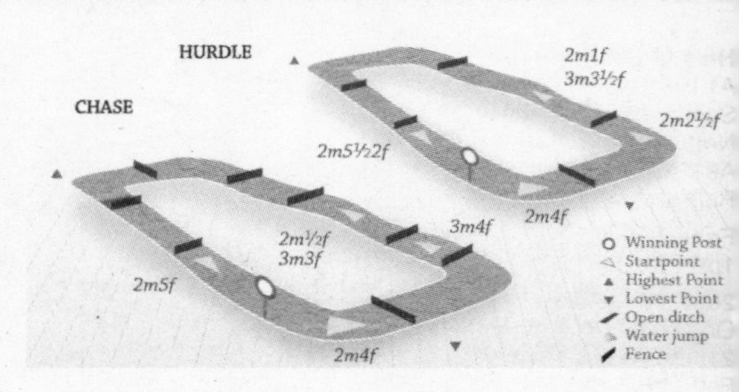

Trainers	Wins-Runs	%	Hurdles	Chases	£1 level stks
Donald McCain	47-226	21	28-142	13-63	-29.55
Brian Ellison	28-117	24	22-83	3-24	-6.41
Micky Hammond	25-168	15	13-101	10-57	-22.69
Malcolm Jefferson	25-92	27	9-47	10-26	+17.63
Sue Smith	20-166	12	9-77	11-78	-52.48
Kenneth Slack	19-55	35	11-40	8-15	+38.58
Dianne Sayer	14-71	20	10-49	4-20	+2.25
Neil Mulholland	14-28	50	7-15	6-11	+17.19
Chris Grant	12-114	11	5-64	5-33	-30.70
Keith Reveley	11-27	41	9-19	2-7	+23.67
Dan Skelton	9-36	25	7-23	2-11	-16.78
James Ewart	8-48	17	5-23	3-23	+3.00
Sam England	8-31	26	4-17	4-14	+17.90

Jockeys	Wins-Rides	%	£1 level stks	Best Trainer	W-R
Brian Hughes	61-285	21	+39.80	Malcolm Jefferson	23-76
Henry Brooke	30-156	19	+32.50	Kenneth Slack	12-31
Wilson Renwick	21-99	21	+12.57	Donald McCain	9-28
Jason Maguire	18-59	31	-2.41	Donald McCain	12-49
Brian Harding	17-117	15	-5.98	William Amos	4-18
James Reveley	17-62	27	+12.57	Keith Reveley	7-17
Jonathan England	13-77	17	-0.22	Sam England	7-26
Danny Cook	11-80	14	-29.10	Brian Ellison	8-31
Dougie Costello	10-83	12	-20.52	Joanne Foster	3-10
Adam Nicol	10-77	13	+2.50	Philip Kirby	3-31
Joe Colliver	9-66	14	-32.51	Micky Hammond	7-45
Craig Nichol	8-85	9	-32.30	Alistair Whillans	2-7
Sean Quinlan	8-85	9	-35.01	Sue Smith	5-30

Favourites

Hurdle 42.8% -12.15 Chase 35.4% -19.11 TOTAL 39% -48.08

SOUTHWELL

Rolleston, nr Newark, Notts
NG25 0TS. Tel: 01636 814 481

How to get there Road: A1 to Newark and A617 to Southwell or A52 to Nottingham (off M1) and A612 to Southwell. Rail: Rolleston

Features Flat, left-handed, 1m2f circuit

2017-18 Fixtures October 3, 26, November 6, 21, December 5, 17, February 5, 25, March 5, 19, April 10, 20

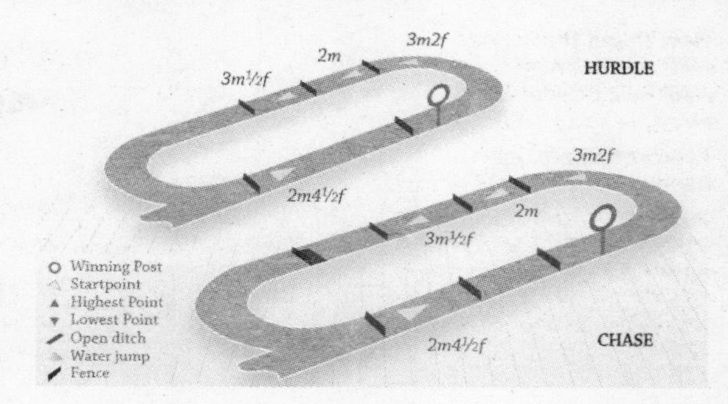

Trainers	*Wins-Runs*	*%*	*Hurdles*	*Chases*	*£1 level stks*
Jonjo O'Neill	25-144	17	15-96	9-37	-26.70
Dan Skelton	19-90	21	13-56	5-19	-13.24
Caroline Bailey	19-80	24	11-50	8-28	+50.85
Tom George	19-53	36	13-31	4-11	+14.50
Charlie Longsdon	17-74	23	10-47	5-16	+0.09
Tim Vaughan	12-79	15	8-50	3-20	+5.40
Nigel Twiston-Davies	10-59	17	3-30	4-20	-21.41
Kim Bailey	10-51	20	7-34	3-12	+11.73
Nicky Henderson	10-45	22	3-27	0-4	-17.48
Sue Smith	9-70	13	3-35	5-29	-25.50
Neil Mulholland	9-61	15	4-34	4-21	+9.05
Seamus Mullins	9-53	17	2-27	4-19	+22.13
David Bridgwater	9-34	26	1-13	8-19	-5.48

Jockeys	*Wins-Rides*	*%*	*£1 level stks*	*Best Trainer*	*W-R*
Richard Johnson	26-118	22	-16.08	Tim Vaughan	6-25
Harry Skelton	25-105	24	+15.63	Dan Skelton	16-67
A P McCoy	23-69	33	-3.08	Jonjo O'Neill	7-32
Paddy Brennan	22-94	23	+26.28	Tom George	13-38
Noel Fehily	17-62	27	+12.10	Charlie Longsdon	8-29
Tom Scudamore	14-75	19	-23.07	David Bridgwater	5-15
Leighton Aspell	14-65	22	+17.57	Lucy Wadham	6-19
Aidan Coleman	13-108	12	-60.87	Jonjo O'Neill	5-21
Sam Twiston-Davies	13-80	16	-27.14	Nigel Twiston-Davies	5-33
Andrew Thornton	12-88	14	+7.48	Caroline Bailey	7-38
Trevor Whelan	11-78	14	+50.38	Neil King	3-17
Richie McLernon	11-65	17	+1.43	Jonjo O'Neill	6-28
Kielan Woods	11-64	17	-8.96	Phil Middleton	3-3

Favourites

Hurdle 44.5% +31.17 Chase 34% -34.18 TOTAL 38.6% -27.47

STRATFORD

Luddington Road, Stratford CV37 9SE. Tel: 01789 267 94[illegible]

How to get there Road: M40 Jctn 15, A3400, B439, A46. Rail: Stratford-Upon-Avon

Features Sharp, left-handed, 1m2f circuit

2017-18 Fixtures October 2, 21, November 2, March 12, April 7, 22

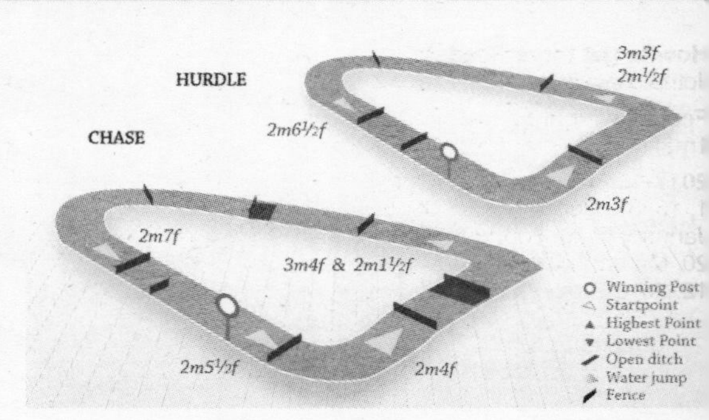

Trainers	*Wins-Runs*	*%*	*Hurdles*	*Chases*	*£1 level stks*
Warren Greatrex	21-54	39	12-34	6-13	+42.88
Philip Hobbs	19-65	29	4-20	15-41	+40.98
John Ferguson	18-42	43	14-33	1-3	+7.88
Jonjo O'Neill	15-94	16	9-49	4-39	-1.81
Dan Skelton	15-83	18	9-50	4-24	-16.45
Tim Vaughan	13-92	14	8-66	4-21	-26.55
Alan King	12-43	28	9-30	2-8	+15.45
Tom George	12-40	30	3-15	8-22	+48.28
Neil Mulholland	10-50	20	7-33	2-13	+19.68
Nigel Twiston-Davies	9-84	11	7-40	2-38	-34.50
David Bridgwater	9-82	11	4-44	4-34	+14.00
Charlie Longsdon	9-47	19	8-29	1-15	-2.92
David Pipe	8-57	14	5-35	2-19	-15.21

Jockeys	*Wins-Rides*	*%*	*£1 level stks*	*Best Trainer*	*W-R*
Richard Johnson	34-153	22	-1.07	Philip Hobbs	10-33
Aidan Coleman	25-111	23	+21.23	John Ferguson	9-14
Tom Scudamore	17-97	18	+28.63	David Pipe	8-34
Noel Fehily	17-75	23	-2.76	Warren Greatrex	4-4
Sam Twiston-Davies	16-115	14	-22.67	Paul Nicholls	4-14
Tom O'Brien	16-93	17	+9.58	Philip Hobbs	7-19
A P McCoy	15-60	25	-6.08	Jonjo O'Neill	7-25
Harry Skelton	14-67	21	-10.45	Dan Skelton	13-59
Paddy Brennan	12-70	17	+15.92	Tom George	6-25
Gavin Sheehan	11-71	15	-11.75	Warren Greatrex	6-30
Wayne Hutchinson	10-46	22	+3.00	Alan King	8-27
Daryl Jacob	10-42	24	+6.75	Emma Lavelle	4-11
Harry Bannister	10-23	43	+34.20	Charlie Mann	5-6

Favourites

Hurdle 37.8% -12.97 Chase 28.8% -43.21 TOTAL 33.7% -69.66

Orchard Portman, Taunton, Somerset
TA3 7BL. Tel: 01823 337 172

TAUNTON

How to get there Road: M5 Jctn 25. Rail: Taunton

Features Right-handed, 1m2f circuit

2017-18 Fixtures November 1, 16, 30, December 14, 30, January 9, 20, February 4, 20, March 1, 12, 26, April 12, 25

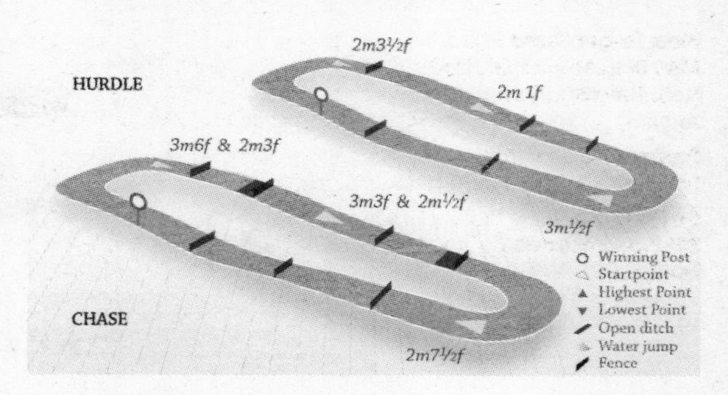

Trainers	Wins-Runs	%	Hurdles	Chases	£1 level stks
Paul Nicholls	50-153	33	34-101	12-37	+7.66
Philip Hobbs	21-106	20	12-69	6-23	-32.56
Harry Fry	20-73	27	14-58	1-3	-11.84
David Pipe	16-139	12	11-111	5-21	-64.38
Evan Williams	13-76	17	9-47	4-27	-1.92
Colin Tizzard	11-82	13	7-46	4-28	-18.75
Dan Skelton	10-43	23	8-32	1-7	-5.65
Venetia Williams	9-57	16	5-34	4-23	-7.43
Anthony Honeyball	9-48	19	9-38	0-5	+23.71
Tim Vaughan	8-72	11	4-53	4-15	-26.63
Alexandra Dunn	8-70	11	5-55	2-12	-1.75
Johnny Farrelly	8-58	14	8-52	0-5	-1.63
Nicky Henderson	8-28	29	6-22	0-1	-8.34

Jockeys	Wins-Rides	%	£1 level stks	Best Trainer	W-R
Sam Twiston-Davies	23-87	26	-20.95	Paul Nicholls	22-61
Nick Scholfield	16-100	16	-27.09	Paul Nicholls	11-36
Noel Fehily	16-67	24	-11.32	Harry Fry	10-29
Richard Johnson	14-85	16	-23.17	Philip Hobbs	7-45
Tom Scudamore	13-102	13	-54.68	David Pipe	8-65
James Best	10-106	9	-43.00	Philip Hobbs	3-9
Brendan Powell	10-69	14	+3.25	Johnny Farrelly	5-22
David Noonan	10-48	21	+2.08	Anthony Honeyball	4-12
Daryl Jacob	10-46	22	-5.08	Colin Tizzard	2-4
Paul Moloney	9-49	18	-3.42	Evan Williams	9-29
Micheal Nolan	9-47	19	+14.57	Jamie Snowden	3-7
Tom O'Brien	8-94	9	-50.31	Philip Hobbs	6-29
Aidan Coleman	8-69	12	-31.30	Anthony Honeyball	3-6

Favourites

Hurdle 40.1% -10.94 Chase 34.2% -12.97 TOTAL 38.1% -27.20

TOWCESTER

Easton Newston, Towcester NN12 7HS. Tel: 01327 353 414

How to get there Road: M1 Jctn 15a, A43 West. Rail: Northampton (8m) and bus service

Features Right-handed, 1m6f circuit, uphill from back straight

2017-18 Fixtures October 11, November 30, December 21, February 1, 14, March 15, 29, April 27

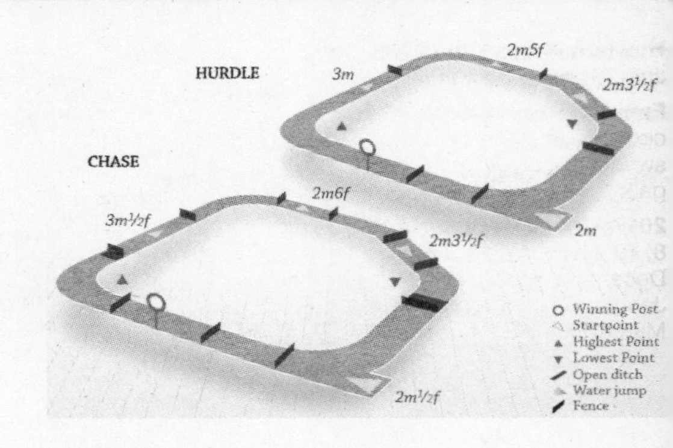

Trainers	Wins-Runs	%	Hurdles	Chases	£1 level stks
Kim Bailey	17-64	27	10-38	5-18	+10.59
Fergal O'Brien	14-64	22	11-34	1-19	+6.63
Ben Pauling	12-43	28	6-29	6-12	+47.38
Nicky Henderson	12-32	38	8-16	1-2	+1.97
Nigel Twiston-Davies	9-68	13	3-35	3-22	-14.13
Henry Daly	9-35	26	4-21	5-9	+29.60
Alan King	9-31	29	5-19	0-4	+3.70
Venetia Williams	8-47	17	3-23	5-23	-20.30
Neil Mulholland	8-21	38	4-10	3-8	+5.56
Jonjo O'Neill	7-52	13	4-39	3-11	-24.50
Oliver Sherwood	7-34	21	2-14	5-13	-3.73
Charlie Longsdon	6-45	13	3-26	3-15	-22.55
Henry Oliver	6-22	27	3-12	3-8	+10.55

Jockeys	Wins-Rides	%	£1 level stks	Best Trainer	W-R
David Bass	14-47	30	+15.18	Ben Pauling	6-16
Paddy Brennan	13-49	27	+16.77	Fergal O'Brien	10-29
A P McCoy	11-29	38	+2.59	Jonjo O'Neill	5-11
Liam Treadwell	10-48	21	+4.44	Venetia Williams	5-20
Leighton Aspell	8-59	14	-25.63	Oliver Sherwood	3-24
Sam Twiston-Davies	8-46	17	+26.25	Nigel Twiston-Davies	5-26
Jeremiah McGrath	8-21	38	+12.93	Nicky Henderson	4-9
Jason Maguire	8-21	38	+6.14	Kim Bailey	4-8
Noel Fehily	7-37	19	-9.00	Neil Mulholland	2-7
Jamie Moore	6-41	15	+28.00	Kerry Lee	2-5
Nico de Boinville	6-34	18	-5.25	Ben Pauling	3-11
Aidan Coleman	6-32	19	-20.77	Charlie Longsdon	2-4
Joshua Moore	6-29	21	+9.25	Gary Moore	3-10

Favourites

Hurdle 40.2% -4.79 Chase 34.4% -20.13 TOTAL 36.6% -38.95

Wood Lane, Uttoxeter, Staffs
ST14 8BD. Tel: 01889 562 561

UTTOXETER

How to get there Road: M6 Jctn 14. Rail: Uttoxeter

Features Left-handed, 1m2f circuit, undulating with sweeping curves, suits galloping types

2017-18 Fixtures October 8, 19, November 3, 18, 26, December 12, 22, 31, January 27, February 10, March 17, April 7

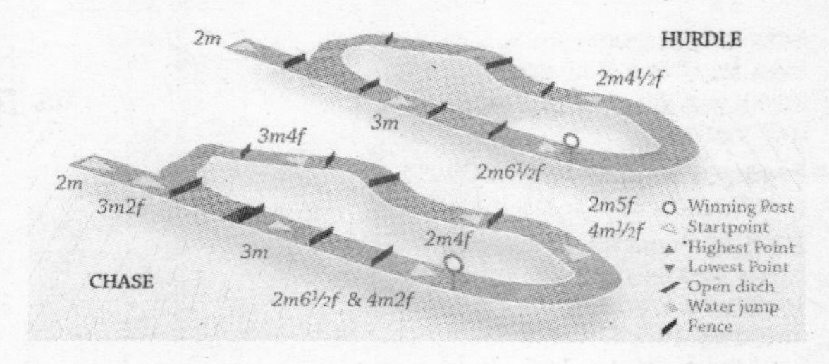

Trainers	*Wins-Runs*	*%*	*Hurdles*	*Chases*	*£1 level stks*
Jonjo O'Neill	25-223	11	13-128	10-80	-89.32
Nigel Twiston-Davies	23-128	18	12-66	10-50	+3.46
David Pipe	23-123	19	11-67	9-42	+13.47
Charlie Longsdon	21-101	21	11-55	10-39	-3.20
Tim Vaughan	18-140	13	14-105	3-29	-53.18
Sue Smith	18-96	19	10-44	8-52	+45.79
Philip Hobbs	17-93	18	11-51	3-35	-1.83
Warren Greatrex	16-45	36	7-26	3-7	+12.22
Nicky Henderson	15-57	26	11-38	2-13	-14.12
Neil King	14-78	18	12-56	0-14	-19.46
Fergal O'Brien	13-83	16	5-47	4-25	-7.84
Evan Williams	12-82	15	6-45	5-32	-0.15
Peter Bowen	12-75	16	7-43	3-21	-24.63

Jockeys	*Wins-Rides*	*%*	*£1 level stks*	*Best Trainer*	*W-R*
Richard Johnson	38-211	18	-13.55	Philip Hobbs	9-45
Noel Fehily	28-100	28	+16.50	Charlie Longsdon	11-27
Tom Scudamore	26-147	18	-32.39	David Pipe	17-76
A P McCoy	23-119	19	-50.13	Jonjo O'Neill	7-66
Aidan Coleman	22-131	17	-25.42	Jonjo O'Neill	5-22
Gavin Sheehan	21-84	25	+24.52	Warren Greatrex	11-29
Sam Twiston-Davies	20-128	16	-9.56	Nigel Twiston-Davies	10-52
Trevor Whelan	16-110	15	-26.79	Neil King	12-64
Paddy Brennan	15-97	15	-13.59	Fergal O'Brien	9-42
Paul Moloney	13-116	11	-20.15	Evan Williams	5-36
Harry Skelton	13-54	24	+18.31	Dan Skelton	10-40
Tom O'Brien	12-108	11	-25.25	Philip Hobbs	3-20
Wayne Hutchinson	11-70	16	+3.83	Alan King	6-34

Favourites

Hurdle 41.9% +38.05 Chase 36.6% +7.33 TOTAL 39.9% +40.23

WARWICK

Hampton Street, Warwick CV34 6HN. Tel: 01926 491 553

How to get there Road: M40 Jctn 15 on to A429 and follow signs to town centre. Rail: Warwick

Features Left-handed, 1m6f circuit, undulating

2017-18 Fixtures October 5, November 10, 22, December 14, 31, January 13, 25, February 10, 23, March 11, 28, April 5, 26

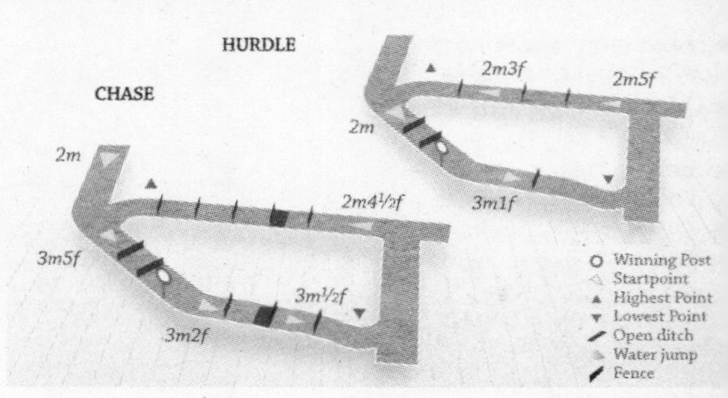

Trainers	Wins-Runs	%	Hurdles	Chases	£1 level stks
Alan King	23-100	23	17-65	5-20	-35.34
Philip Hobbs	22-86	26	10-38	6-28	-5.38
Dan Skelton	20-107	19	9-62	6-25	-36.26
Nigel Twiston-Davies	18-121	15	6-54	10-51	-45.75
Venetia Williams	16-82	20	6-31	9-46	-0.07
Jonjo O'Neill	15-111	14	10-74	4-27	+0.24
Charlie Longsdon	11-89	12	5-52	5-24	-40.01
Nicky Henderson	11-45	24	6-24	3-7	-8.51
Paul Nicholls	10-39	26	3-15	6-20	-4.87
Ben Pauling	10-31	32	3-14	0-6	+23.25
Warren Greatrex	7-46	15	2-29	1-5	-11.17
Neil Mulholland	7-34	21	2-16	4-16	-6.22
W P Mullins	7-11	64	6-9	1-2	+6.87

Jockeys	Wins-Rides	%	£1 level stks	Best Trainer	W-R
Richard Johnson	33-138	24	-6.39	Philip Hobbs	16-49
Aidan Coleman	21-108	19	-21.38	Venetia Williams	10-32
Noel Fehily	21-100	21	+4.60	Neil Mulholland	6-18
Sam Twiston-Davies	19-97	20	-20.25	Nigel Twiston-Davies	10-51
Harry Skelton	19-87	22	-19.76	Dan Skelton	18-82
Gavin Sheehan	10-54	19	+8.21	Warren Greatrex	5-23
Nico de Boinville	10-38	26	+3.09	Nicky Henderson	6-15
Leighton Aspell	9-89	10	-47.88	Oliver Sherwood	3-27
David Bass	9-53	17	-7.50	Ben Pauling	6-13
Jamie Moore	9-50	18	+66.75	Richard Lee	3-4
Daryl Jacob	9-47	19	+10.09	Ben Case	3-8
Sean Bowen	8-50	16	-19.93	Peter Bowen	3-30
Wayne Hutchinson	7-60	12	-38.44	Alan King	6-42

Favourites

Hurdle 41.7% -5.83 Chase 36.8% -11.44 TOTAL 39.3% -16.03

York Road, Wetherby, West Yorks
L22 5EJ. Tel: 01937 582 035

WETHERBY

How to get there Road: A1, A58 from Leeds, B1224 from York. Rail: Leeds, Harrogate, York

Features Long, left-handed circuit (1m4f chases, 1m2f hurdles), suits galloping types

2017-18 Fixtures October 18, November 3-4, 18, 29, December 9, 26-27, January 5, 13, 23, February 3, 20, March 20, 29, April 6

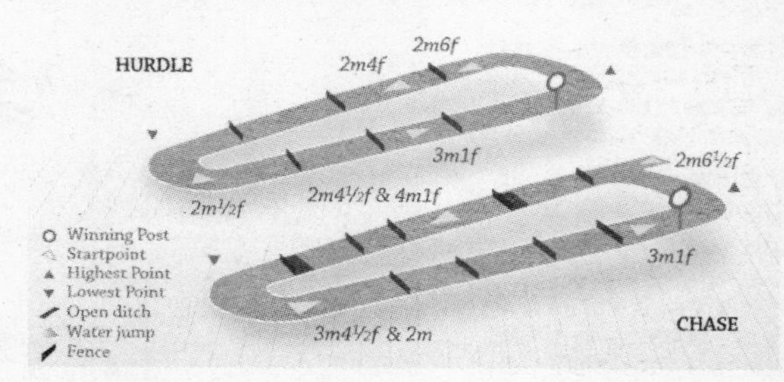

Trainers	Wins-Runs	%	Hurdles	Chases	£1 level stks
Sue Smith	28-189	15	8-88	19-95	-68.90
Micky Hammond	18-206	9	12-138	3-56	-67.67
Dan Skelton	18-57	32	9-31	6-18	+8.91
Warren Greatrex	16-51	31	9-32	4-9	+16.12
Brian Ellison	15-90	17	9-58	4-22	+8.37
Philip Kirby	14-102	14	9-83	2-8	-6.33
Jonjo O'Neill	14-75	19	10-45	4-28	-18.25
Donald McCain	13-113	12	9-74	4-34	-47.42
Lucinda Russell	11-95	12	3-36	8-53	-13.63
Kim Bailey	11-26	42	3-13	6-9	+35.38
Malcolm Jefferson	9-66	14	4-30	5-31	-15.42
Mark Walford	9-48	19	6-35	3-9	+18.75
Neil Mulholland	9-29	31	4-16	4-10	+2.32

Jockeys	Wins-Rides	%	£1 level stks	Best Trainer	W-R
Brian Hughes	25-222	11	-90.01	Malcolm Jefferson	9-60
Danny Cook	19-116	16	-16.77	Sue Smith	11-53
Harry Skelton	17-53	32	+6.33	Dan Skelton	15-43
Noel Fehily	17-52	33	+15.22	Donald McCain	3-6
A P McCoy	16-51	31	+7.13	Jonjo O'Neill	7-21
Adam Nicol	15-72	21	+53.51	Philip Kirby	8-39
Jason Maguire	14-71	20	-7.84	Kim Bailey	6-8
Dougie Costello	13-84	15	+10.48	Warren Greatrex	3-10
Gavin Sheehan	13-55	24	-14.66	Warren Greatrex	11-29
Joe Colliver	10-100	10	-23.42	Micky Hammond	10-77
Craig Nichol	10-57	18	+12.38	Lucinda Russell	4-14
Richard Johnson	10-55	18	-13.81	Philip Hobbs	6-16
Paddy Brennan	9-32	28	+27.35	Fergal O'Brien	3-5

Favourites

Hurdle 41.8% -1.59 Chase 37.9% -14.83 TOTAL 39.9% -21.92

WINCANTON

Wincanton, Somerset BA9 8BJ. Tel: 01963 323 44

How to get there Road: A303 to Wincanton, course on B3081, 1m from town centre. Rail: Gillingham

Features Right-handed, 1m4f circuit, dries fast

2017-18 Fixtures October 20, 29, November 11, 23, December 7, 26, January 6, 18, February 1, 17, 28, March 8, 28, April 3, 22

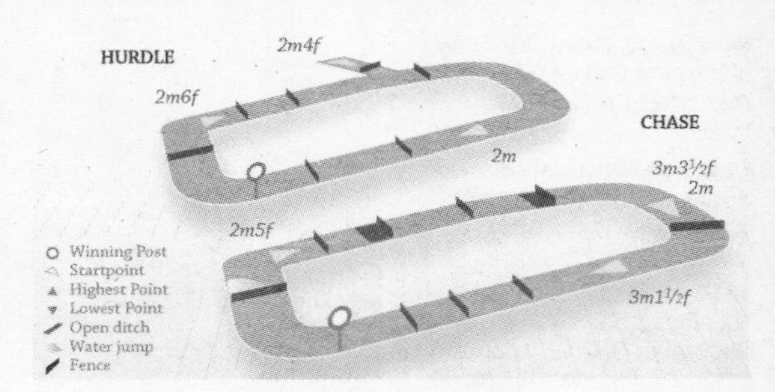

Trainers	Wins-Runs	%	Hurdles	Chases	£1 level stks
Paul Nicholls	74-211	35	50-123	17-66	-4.82
Colin Tizzard	21-182	12	9-94	11-63	-51.71
Philip Hobbs	21-133	16	11-69	7-47	-27.88
Harry Fry	17-78	22	9-55	2-10	-6.21
David Pipe	15-97	15	7-64	8-27	-24.81
Venetia Williams	12-75	16	5-26	7-49	-19.27
Neil Mulholland	11-122	9	6-76	4-35	-43.15
Alan King	11-66	17	6-45	3-15	-14.11
Emma Lavelle	11-56	20	5-22	3-23	+21.13
Tom George	10-51	20	1-10	9-37	-9.79
Jeremy Scott	8-89	9	6-55	2-26	-45.13
Seamus Mullins	8-75	11	3-43	5-25	-3.95
Tim Vaughan	8-38	21	7-30	1-7	+28.20

Jockeys	Wins-Rides	%	£1 level stks	Best Trainer	W-R
Sam Twiston-Davies	33-130	25	-29.38	Paul Nicholls	29-91
Daryl Jacob	24-102	24	+1.71	Paul Nicholls	8-23
Richard Johnson	22-120	18	-15.00	Philip Hobbs	10-62
Harry Cobden	21-50	42	+14.46	Paul Nicholls	17-26
Nick Scholfield	18-137	13	-35.15	Paul Nicholls	5-29
Noel Fehily	14-83	17	-31.58	Harry Fry	8-38
Aidan Coleman	14-77	18	+2.42	Emma Lavelle	4-15
Tom O'Brien	13-112	12	-37.20	Philip Hobbs	7-34
Tom Scudamore	11-88	13	-40.56	David Pipe	9-50
Brendan Powell	10-97	10	-16.40	Colin Tizzard	5-42
Paddy Brennan	10-73	14	-21.00	Tom George	3-28
Tom Bellamy	9-38	24	+15.38	Alan King	4-10
Gavin Sheehan	8-52	15	-7.50	Warren Greatrex	4-20

Favourites

Hurdle 43.7% -6.12 Chase 36% -24.79 TOTAL 40.4% -33.71

Pitchcroft, Worcester
WR1 3EJ. Tel: 01905 253 64

WORCESTER

How to get there Road: M5 Jctn 6 from north, M5 Jctn 7 or A38 from south. Rail: Worcester (Forgate Street)

Features Left-handed, 1m5f circuit, prone to flooding

2017-18 Fixtures October 12, 25

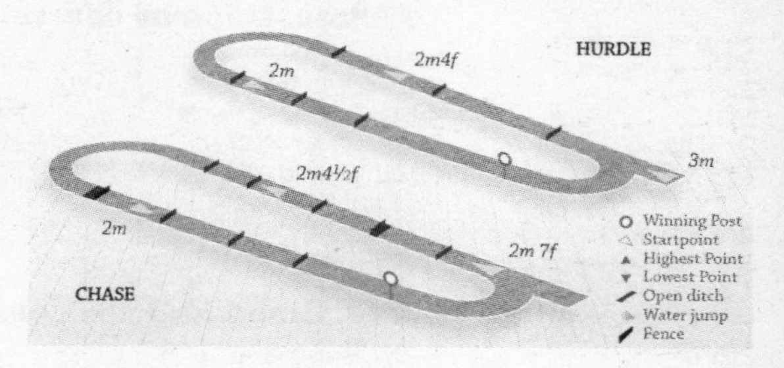

Trainers	*Wins-Runs*	*%*	*Hurdles*	*Chases*	*£1 level stks*
Jonjo O'Neill	46-234	20	19-127	25-97	-37.83
David Pipe	23-133	17	14-77	4-35	-34.77
Neil Mulholland	23-108	21	14-58	9-40	+8.18
Philip Hobbs	20-83	24	11-46	8-31	-3.65
Nicky Henderson	18-61	30	12-37	3-8	+10.40
Nigel Twiston-Davies	17-88	19	7-47	7-31	+16.28
Peter Bowen	17-76	22	4-29	7-34	+13.63
John Ferguson	16-42	38	10-29	1-6	-7.20
Tim Vaughan	15-109	14	7-60	8-41	-20.55
Dr Richard Newland	15-63	24	12-50	3-13	-27.54
Paul Nicholls	15-44	34	7-19	8-25	+0.31
Donald McCain	14-101	14	9-61	5-31	-24.10
Rebecca Curtis	14-52	27	7-29	4-11	+34.66

Jockeys	*Wins-Rides*	*%*	*£1 level stks*	*Best Trainer*	*W-R*
A P McCoy	56-183	31	-0.41	Jonjo O'Neill	23-87
Richard Johnson	38-229	17	-59.87	Philip Hobbs	16-53
Sam Twiston-Davies	35-188	19	-28.71	Nigel Twiston-Davies	13-61
Tom Scudamore	28-184	15	-25.90	David Pipe	17-86
Aidan Coleman	23-138	17	-53.71	Jonjo O'Neill	5-27
Noel Fehily	19-121	16	-50.55	Neil Mulholland	9-31
Paul Moloney	15-138	11	-30.18	Evan Williams	8-49
Brendan Powell	15-100	15	+135.13	Brendan Powell	6-32
Tom O'Brien	14-100	14	+11.00	Robert Stephens	5-20
Harry Skelton	13-75	17	-11.42	Dan Skelton	10-66
Nico de Boinville	12-77	16	-19.65	David Weston	4-6
Daryl Jacob	12-68	18	-14.34	Paul Nicholls	3-6
Gavin Sheehan	12-62	19	+25.15	Warren Greatrex	4-19

Favourites

Hurdle	41%	-8.76	Chase	37%	+2.79	TOTAL	40.3%	-3.41

Record and standard times

Aintree, Mildmay course

2m Ch	Nohalmdun (7 Apr 1990)	3m45.30s	3m49s
2m4f Ch	Wind Force (2 Apr 1993)	4m46.60s	4m48s
3m1f Ch	Cab On Target (2 Apr 1993)	6m03.40s	6m07s
2m½f Hdl	Spinning (3 Apr 1993)	3m44.80s	3m53s
2m1f Hdl	Gabrial The Great (16 May 2014)	4m04.30s	4m00s
	Hawk High (25 Oct 2014)		
2m4f Hdl	Gallateen (2 Apr 1993)	4m37.10s	4m43s
3m½f Hdl	Andrew's First (1 Apr 1993)	5m50.70s	5m54s

Aintree, Grand National course

2m5f Ch	Always Waining (8 Apr 2011)	5m19.30s	5m21s
3m2f Ch	Eurotrek (19 Nov 2006)	6m46.60s	6m38s
4m2½f Ch	One For Arthur (8 Apr 2017)	9m03.50s	9m04s

Ascot

2m1f Ch	Quite By Chance (29 Oct 2016)	3m55.90s	4m04s
2m3f Ch	Master Dee (29 Oct 2016)	4m29.50s	4m34s
2m5f Ch	Kew Jumper (11 Apr 2008)	5m12.60s	5m08s
3m Ch	Exmoor Ranger (29 Oct 2011)	5m49.60s	5m43s
1m7½f Hdl	Brampour (29 Oct 2011)	3m33.30s	3m41s
2m3½f Hdl	Overturn (19 Nov 2011)	4m30.80s	4m28s
2m5½f Hdl	Emmaslegend (19 Nov 2011)	5m10.90s	5m00s
2m7½f Hdl	Heronry (30 Mar 2014)	5m34.10s	5m29s
3m½f Hdl	Unowhatimeanharry (17 Dec 2016)	5m54.30s	5m46s

Ayr

1m7½f Ch	Clay County (12 Oct 1991)	3m38.60s	3m43s
2m4½f Ch	Cloudy Dream (22 Apr 2017)	5m02.00s	4m58s
2m5½f Ch	Star To The North (9 May 2001)	5m10.20s	5m10s
3m½f Ch	Top 'N' Tale (12 May 1982)	5m57.70s	5m54s
3m3f Ch	Joaaci (15 Apr 2005)	6m50.20s	6m35s
4m Ch	Hot Weld (21 Apr 2007)	7m55.10s	8m02s
2m Hdl	Chesterfield (22 Apr 2017)	3m43.20s	3m40s
2m4½f Hdl	Calivigny (26 Oct 2015)	4m54.00s	4m44s
2m5½f Hdl	Cucumber Run (21 Apr 2012)	5m04.70s	5m02s
3m½f Hdl	Nautical Lad (6 Apr 1964)	5m42.00s	5m43s
3m2½f Hdl	Meditator (18 Apr 1997)	6m26.90s	6m17s

Bangor

2m1½f Ch	Daulys Anthem (4 Aug 2017)	4m01.80s	4m05s
2m4½f Ch	The Disengager (24 Jul 2012)	4m49.70s	4m49s
3m Ch	He's The Gaffer (16 Aug 2008)	5m50.60s	5m45s
3m5½f Ch	Kaki Crazy (23 May 2001)	7m34.10s	7m10s
2m½f Hdl	Andy Rew (24 Apr 1982)	3m44.50s	3m48s
2m3½f Hdl	Smithy's Choice (25 Apr 1987)	4m34.10s	4m24s
2m7f Hdl	General Pershing (20 Apr 1991)	5m34.00s	5m20s

Carlisle

2m Ch	Germany Calling (15 Oct 2015)	3m53.70s	3m57s
2m4f Ch	New Alco (12 Nov 2007)	5m00.40s	4m57s

2m5f Ch	Amilliontimes (13 Oct 2016)	5m20.90s	5m13s
3m½f Ch	Ripalong Lad (9 Oct 2009)	6m00.70s	6m03s
3m2f Ch	Basford Ben (5 May 2016)	6m38.10s	6m27s
2m1f Hdl (Inner)	Idder (11 May 2017)	4m06.00s	4m02s
2m1f Hdl (Outer)	Supertop (25 Oct 1997)	4m02.60s	4m04s
2m3½f Hdl (Inner)	Officer Hoolihan (5 May 2016)	4m39.50s	4m39s
2m4f Hdl (Outer)	Gods Law (29 Sep 1990)	4m50.60s	4m45s
3m½f Hdl (Outer)	Maggie Blue (15 Oct 2015)	6m02.30s	5m48s
3m1f Hdl (Inner)	Takingrisks (26 Mar 2016)	6m17.90s	5m50s

Cartmel

2m1½f Ch	Altruism (28 May 2016)	4m05.80s	4m12s
2m5f Ch	Princeton Royale (24 Jun 2016)	5m04.40s	5m12s
3m1½f Ch	Better Times Ahead (28 Aug 1999)	6m13.40s	6m20s
3m5½f Ch	Chabrimal Minster (26 May 2007)	7m12.00s	7m20s
2m1f Hdl	Lisbon (25 May 2013)	3m56.20s	4m02s
2m6f Hdl	Shantou Tiger (19 Jul 2014)	5m10.40s	5m11s
3m1½f Hdl	Portonia (30 May 1994)	5m58.00s	6m03s

Catterick

1m7½f Ch	Preston Deal (18 Dec 1971)	3m44.60s	3m48s
2m3f Ch	Laissez Dire (30 Nov 2016)	4m47.70s	4m45s
3m1½f Ch	Clever General (7 Nov 1981)	6m14.00s	6m18s

CLOUDY DREAM: broke two course records last season, including at Ayr

3m6f Ch	Straidnahanna (12 Jan 2017)	7m46.00s	7m25s
1m7½f Hdl	Lunar Wind (22 Apr 1982)	3m36.50s	3m40s
2m3f Hdl	Smadynium (4 Dec 2013)	4m31.50s	4m32s
3m1½f Hdl	Seamus O'Flynn (8 Nov 1986)	6m03.80s	6m08s

Cheltenham, New Course

2m½f Ch	Samakaan (16 Mar 2000)	3m52.40s	3m56s
2m4f Ch	Black Hercules (17 Mar 2016)	4m55.20s	4m51s
2m5f Ch	Vautour (17 Mar 2016)	5m05.50s	5m03s
3m2f Ch	Theatre Guide (9 Dec 2016)	6m40.80s	6m26s
3m2½f Ch	Long Run (18 Mar 2011)	6m29.70s	6m37s
3m4f Ch	Gentle Ranger (16 Apr 2010)	7m14.50s	7m08s
4m½f Ch	Hot Weld (16 Mar 2006)	8m33.20s	8m22s
2m1f Hdl	Detroit City (17 Mar 2006)	3m51.20s	3m54s
2m4½f Hdl	William Henry (19 Apr 2017)	4m48.80s	4m47s
3m Hdl	Bacchanal (16 Mar 2000)	5m36.60s	5m41s

WILLIAM HENRY: Nicky Henderson's star storms home at Cheltenham in April

Cheltenham, Old Course

2m Ch	Edredon Bleu (15 Mar 2000)	3m44.70s	3m52s
2m4f Ch	Shantou Village (22 Oct 2016)	4m53.30s	4m45s
2m4½f Ch	Dark Stranger (15 Mar 2000)	4m49.60s	4m58s
3m½f Ch	Marlborough (14 Mar 2000)	5m59.70s	5m57s
3m1f Ch	Un Temps Pour Tout (15 Mar 2016)	6m17.80s	6m05s
3m3½f Ch	Shardam (15 Nov 2003)	7m01.00s	6m50s
4m Ch	Relaxation (15 Mar 2000)	8m00.60s	7m59s
2m½f Hdl	Annie Power (15 Mar 2016)	3m45.10s	3m51s
2m4f Hdl	Vroum Vroum Mag (15 Mar 2016)	4m45.00s	4m37s
2m5f Hdl	Monsignor (15 Mar 2000)	4m52.00s	4m57s
3m Hdl	Trackmate (18 Oct 2013)	5m46.96s	5m44s
3m1½f Hdl	Rubhahunish (14 Mar 2000)	6m03.40s	6m05s

Cheltenham, Cross-Country Course

3m6f Ch (32)	Balthazar King (13 Mar 2012)	7m51.70s	8m04s

Chepstow

2m Ch	Valseur Du Grenval (2 Nov 2016)	3m53.70s	3m58s
2m3½f Ch	Balder Succes (12 Oct 2013)	4m42.50s	4m45s
2m7½f Ch	Broadheath (4 Oct 1986)	5m47.90s	5m45s
3m2f Ch	Jaunty Jane (26 May 1975)	6m39.40s	6m34s
2m Hdl	Tingle Bell (4 Oct 1986)	3m43.20s	3m47s
2m3½f Hdl	Ballyoptic (8 Oct 2016)	4m37.20s	4m34s
2m7½f Hdl	Chucklestone (11 May 1993)	5m33.60s	5m36s

Doncaster

2m½f Ch	Clic Work (29 Dec 2016)	3m57.00s	3m57s
2m3f Ch	Gold Present (26 Nov 2016)	4m40.70s	4m36s
2m4½f Ch	Kalane (29 Dec 2016)	5m01.70s	4m54s
3m Ch	Killala Quay (22 Feb 2017)	5m55.80s	5m54s
3m2f Ch	Dancing Shadow (9 Dec 2016)	6m35.80s	6m24s
2m½f Hdl	All Set To Go (10 Dec 2016)	3m53.50s	3m50s
2m3½f Hdl	Just Milly (29 Dec 2016)	4m32.30s	4m33s
3m½f Hdl	Parish Business (29 Dec 2016)	5m47.50s	5m45s

Exeter

2m1½f Ch	Sir Valentino (1 Nov 2016)	3m57.50s	4m03s
2m3f Ch	West With The Wind (7 May 2013)	4m27.90s	4m30s
3m Ch	Dennis The Legend (13 May 2009)	5m42.80s	5m46s
3m6½f Ch	Thomas Wild (14 Apr 2015)	7m14.70s	7m24s
2m1f Hdl	Remind Me Later (21 Apr 2015)	3m49.20s	3m54s
2m2½f Hdl	Mr Brother Sylvest (18 Oct 2011)	4m14.70s	4m17s
2m5½f Hdl	I'm In Charge (6 Oct 2016)	5m05.20s	5m05s
2m7f Hdl	Very Cool (4 May 2010)	5m26.20s	5m29s

Fakenham

2m½f Ch	Cheekio Ora (23 Apr 1984)	3m44.90s	3m55s
2m5f Ch	Skipping Tim (25 May 1992)	5m10.30s	5m10s
3m Ch	Specialize (16 May 1999)	5m56.90s	5m52s
3m5f Ch	Rebeccas Choice (3 May 2016)	7m24.90s	7m10s
2m Hdl	Cobbet (9 May 2001)	3m45.70s	3m54s
2m4f Hdl	Ayem (16 May 1999)	4m41.20s	4m47s
2m7½f Hdl	Phare Isle (17 Apr 2017)	5m49.10s	5m40s

VIEUX LION ROUGE: we have standard times for the first time on Haydock's Lancashire chase course, where Vieux Lion Rouge won last season

Ffos Las

2m Ch	Get Rhythm (22 Jun 2017)	3m57.60s	3m48s
2m3½f Ch	Cold Harbour (31 May 2011)	4m37.34s	4m40s
2m5f Ch	Putney Bridge (17 Jun 2010)	5m09.70s	5m05s
3m Ch	Sea Wall (18 Jun 2009)	5m49.60s	5m50s
3m1½f Ch	Backstage (28 Aug 2009)	6m07.10s	6m10s
3m4f Ch	The Bay Oak (16 Apr 2017)	7m28.10s	6m49s
2m Hdl	Comanche Chieftain (9 May 2017)	3m37.00s	3m36s
2m4f Hdl	Positively Dylan (9 May 2017)	4m40.80s	4m32s
2m6f Hdl	Koultas King (22 Aug 2013)	5m15.40s	5m00s
3m Hdl	Chill Factor (21 Aug 2014)	5m39.00s	5m30s

Fontwell

2m1½f Ch	A Thousand Dreams (3 Jun 2002)	4m14.50s	4m20s
2m3f Ch	Chalcedony (3 Jun 2002)	4m38.10s	4m42s
2m5f Ch	Contes (3 Jun 2002)	5m13.90s	5m17s
3m1½f Ch	Il Capitano (6 May 2002)	6m24.30s	6m25s
3m3f Ch	Strolling Vagabond (18 Mar 2007)	7m11.10s	6m58s
2m1½f Hdl	Hyperion Du Moulin (3 Jun 2002)	4m06.80s	4m12s
2m3f Hdl	Hillswick (27 Aug 1999)	4m30.50s	4m33s
2m5½f Hdl	Mister Pickwick (3 Jun 2002)	5m06.70s	5m12s
3m1½f Hdl	Sir Mangan (2 Oct 2015)	6m14.00s	6m18s

Haydock

1m7½f Ch	Witness In Court (19 Apr 2014)	3m52.30s	4m00s

2m3f Ch	Purple 'N Gold (7 May 2016)	4m45.70s	4m50s
2m4½f Ch	Some Buckle (23 Mar 2016)	5m24.40s	5m11s
2m5½f Ch	Javert (7 May 2016)	5m20.20s	5m23s
2m7f Ch	No Planning (19 Apr 2014)	5m41.50s	5m51s
3m3½f Ch	Blenheim Brook (19 Apr 2014)	7m07.70s	6m55s
1m7½f Hdl	She's Our Mare (1 May 1999)	3m32.30s	3m40s
2m3f Hdl	Carlton Jack (19 Apr 2014)	4m33.00s	4m32s
2m3f F Brush Hdl	Horizontal Speed (19 Apr 2014)	4m32.10s	4m38s
2m7f Hdl	Whataknight (7 May 2016)	5m28.90s	5m22s
2m7f F Brush Hdl	Dynaste (19 Nov 2011)	5m37.60s	5m33s

Haydock, Lancashire course

2m½f Ch	Cloudy Dream (18 Nov 2016)	4m19.80s	4m05s
2m4f Ch	Ballybolley (15 Apr 2017)	5m02.40s	5m02s
2m5½f Ch	Politologue (18 Nov 2016)	5m50.40s	5m20s
2m6f Ch	Magic Money (15 Apr 2017)	5m47.50s	5m25s
3m Ch	Willoughby Hedge (15 Apr 2017)	6m13.40s	6m05s
3m4½f Ch	Vieux Lion Rouge (18 Feb 2017)	7m25.10s	7m20s

Hexham

1m7½f Ch	Imjoeking (22 Jun 2014)	3m52.80s	3m59s
2m4f Ch	Mr Laggan (14 Sep 2003)	4m55.40s	5m03s
3m Ch	Silent Snipe (1 Jun 2002)	6m07.60s	6m10s
4m Ch	Simply Smashing (18 Mar 2010)	8m34.00s	8m15s
2m Hdl	Francies Fancy (19 June 2005)	3m57.80s	3m55s
2m4f Hdl	Pappa Charlie (27 May 1997)	4m31.50s	4m52s
2m7½f Hdl	Fingers Crossed (29 Apr 1991)	5m45.50s	5m45s

Huntingdon

2m½f Ch	No Greater Love (23 May 2007)	3m53.30s	3m56s
2m4f Ch	Peccadillo (26 Dec 2004)	4m46.40s	4m48s
2m7½f Ch	Ozzie Jones (18 Sep 1998)	5m44.40s	5m45s
3m7f Ch	Kinnahalla (24 Nov 2001)	8m02.70s	7m40s
1m7½f Hdl	Weather Front (31 Aug 2009)	3m32.70s	3m38s
2m3½f Hdl	Sabre Hongrois (4 Oct 2009)	4m30.20s	4m36s
2m4½f Hdl	Sound Of Laughter (14 Apr 1984)	4m45.80s	4m48s
3m1f Hdl	Orchard King (31 Aug 2009)	5m50.20s	5m56s

Kelso

2m1f Ch	Simply Ned (4 Oct 2015)	3m57.80s	4m02s
2m5½f Ch	Romany Ryme (16 Sep 2015)	5m19.80s	5m01s
2m7½f Ch	Leanna Ban (24 May 2015)	5m40.30s	5m38s
3m2f Ch	Looking Well (29 May 2016)	6m33.20s	6m16s
4m½f Ch	Seven Towers (17 Jan 1997)	8m07.50s	7m56s
2m Hdl	Life And Soul (26 May 2013)	3m38.90s	3m43s
2m2f Hdl	Croco Bay (26 May 2013)	4m08.70s	4m13s
2m5f Hdl	Waterclock (16 Sept 2015)	4m49.50s	4m50s
2m6½f Hdl	Hit The Canvas (30 Sep 1995)	5m12.20s	5m18s
3m2f Hdl	Dook's Delight (19 May 1995)	6m10.10s	6m12s

Kempton

2m Ch	Special Tiara (27 Dec 2016)	3m46.25s	3m50s
2m2f Ch	Miss Tenacious (16 Oct 2016)	4m21.60s	4m19s
2m4½f Ch	Max Ward (18 Mar 2017)	4m58.90s	4m58s
3m Ch	Thistlecrack (26 Dec 2016)	5m53.50s	5m54s

2m Hdl	Yanworth (26 Dec 2016)	3m45.20s	3m42s
2m5f Hdl	Work In Progress (28 Oct 2015)	4m57.80s	4m50s
3m½f Hdl	Follow The Bear (1 May 2017)	6m05.20s	5m45s

Leicester

2m Ch	Thankyou Very Much (1 Dec 2016)	3m45.30s	3m51s
2m4f Ch	Oliver's Hill (28 Dec 2016)	4m54.20s	5m01s
2m6½f Ch	Forgotten Gold (27 Nov 2016)	5m37.40s	5m40s
1m7½f Hdl	Almantius (1 Dec 2016)	3m43.10s	3m35s
2m4½f Hdl	Ten Sixty (7 Dec 2016)	4m58.60s	4m45s

Lingfield

2m Ch	Authorized Too (8 Nov 2016)	3m57.80s	3m59s
2m4f Ch	Mr Medic (8 Nov 2016)	4m55.80s	4m59s
2m7½f Ch	Onderun (10 Dec 2016)	6m07.60s	5m48s
2m Hdl	Bobble Emerald (8 Nov 2016)	3m46.20s	3m50s
2m3½f Hdl	Phobiaphiliac (8 Nov 2016)	4m36.80s	4m40s

Ludlow

2m Ch	Pearl King (5 Apr 2007)	3m47.30s	3m53s
	Bullet Street (10 May 2015)	3m47.30s	
2m4f Ch	Handy Money (5 Apr 2007)	4m47.30s	4m54s
3m Ch	Alcala (18 Apr 2017)	5m57.00s	5m44s
3m1½f Ch	Moving Earth (12 May 2005)	6m17.30s	6m12s
2m Hdl	Frozen Over (10 May 2015)	3m35.70s	3m38s
2m5f Hdl	Templehills (5 Oct 2016)	4m55.80s	4m56s
3m Hdl	Dark Spirit (9 Oct 2013)	5m33.30s	5m38s

Market Rasen

2m1f Ch	Mister Wiseman (7 Jul 2013)	4m13.60s	4m14s
2m3f Ch	Bocciani (10 May 2013)	4m41.40s	4m45s
2m5½f Ch	Vintage Vinnie (24 Sep 2016)	5m17.40s	5m16s
3m Ch	Allerlea (1 May 1985)	6m01.00s	5m46s
3m3½f Ch	Carli King (26 Dec 2014)	7m26.10s	6m46s
2m½f Hdl	Australia Day (17 Jul 2010)	3m57.40s	3m55s
2m2½f Hdl	Attaglance (19 Feb 2012)	4m26.10s	4m25s
2m4½f Hdl	Fiulin (19 Feb 2012)	5m03.70s	4m55s
2m7f Hdl	Trustful (21 May 1977)	5m38.80s	5m39s

Musselburgh

2m1f Ch	Thankyou Very Much (14 Nov 2016)	4m16.60s	4m00s
2m3½f Ch	Klepht (17 Feb 2016)	5m06.50s	4m36s
3m Ch	Snowy (18 Dec 2005)	5m47.70s	5m40s
3m2½f Ch	Present Flight (6 Nov 2015)	6m47.10s	6m20s
4m1f Ch	Dancing Shadow (4 Feb 2017)	8m28.60s	7m50s
1m7½f Hdl	Superb Story (1 Jan 2017)	3m35.00s	3m35s
2m3½f Hdl	Strongpoint (9 Dec 2013)	4m34.70s	4m30s
2m6f Hdl	Mondlicht (24 Nov 2016)	5m27.60s	5m05s
3m Hdl	Monbeg Charmer (5 Feb 2017)	5m47.80s	5m32s
3m2f Hdl	El Bandit (5 Feb 2017)	6m26.90s	6m05s

Newbury

2m½f Ch	Valdez (30 Nov 2013)	3m57.34s	4m02s
2m2½f Ch	Highway Code (29 Nov 2013)	4m31.87s	4m22s

EL BANDIT: among the fast-time winners at Musselburgh in February

2m4f Ch	Espy (25 Oct 1991)	4m47.90s	4m48s
2m6½f Ch	Pepite Rose (24 Mar 2012)	5m28.93s	5m28s
2m7½f Ch	Long Run (17 Feb 2012)	5m42.53s	5m48s
3m2f Ch	Ikorodu Road (24 Mar 2012)	6m22.86s	6m31s
2m½f Hdl	Dhofar (25 Oct 1985)	3m45.20s	3m48s
2m3f Hdl	Songsmith (24 Mar 2012)	4m26.70s	4m28s
2m4½f Hdl	Argento Luna (21 Mar 2009)	4m48.63s	4m54s
3m Hdl	Lansdowne (25 Oct 1996)	5m45.40s	5m47s

Newcastle

2m½f Ch	Greenheart (7 May 1990)	3m56.70s	3m59s
2m4f Ch	Snow Blessed (19 May 1984)	4m46.70s	4m53s
2m7½f Ch	Even Swell (30 Oct 1975)	5m48.10s	5m44s
4m½f Ch	Domaine Du Pron (21 Feb 1998)	8m30.40s	8m21s
2m½f Hdl	Padre Mio (25 Nov 1995)	3m40.70s	3m41s
2m4½f Hdl	Mils Mij (13 May 1989)	4m42.00s	4m44s
2m6f Hdl	Bygones Of Brid (28 Nov 2009)	5m24.90s	5m13s
3m Hdl	Withy Bank (29 Nov 1986)	5m40.10s	5m37s

Newton Abbot

2m½f Ch	Bullet Street (13 Aug 2014)	3m49.80s	3m57s
2m5f Ch	Mhilu (13 Jul 2009)	5m02.10s	5m08s
3m2f Ch	No Loose Change (8 Jul 2013)	6m09.50s	6m24s
2m1f Hdl	Windbound Lass (1 Aug 1988)	3m45.00s	3m50s
2m2½f Hdl	Rum And Butter (22 Aug 2013)	4m15.20s	4m17s
2m5½f Hdl	Virbian (30 Jun 1983)	4m55.40s	5m00s
3m2½f Hdl	Veneaux Du Cochet (1 Jul 2016)	6m09.90s	6m20s

Perth

2m Ch	Robin's Command (7 Sep 2015)	3m48.00s	3m51s
2m4f Ch	Strobe (14 Jul 2013)	4m48.20s	4m52s
3m Ch	Problema Tic (9 Jun 2013)	5m46.20s	5m42s
3m6½f Ch	Laertes (24 Apr 2009)	7m43.70s	7m30s
2m Hdl	Court Minstrel (22 Aug 2015)	3m40.20s	3m42s
2m4f Hdl	Valiant Dash (19 May 1994)	4m41.20s	4m44s
3m Hdl	Imtihan (2 Jul 2009)	5m41.60s	5m35s
3m2½f Hdl	Noir Et Vert (28 Apr 2006)	6m37.20s	6m11s

Plumpton

2m1f Ch	Pearls Legend (17 Apr 2017)	4m04.40s	4m08s
2m3½f Ch	Dead Or Alive (10 May 2009)	4m42.80s	4m44s
3m1½f Ch	Sunday Habits (19 Apr 2003)	6m23.50s	6m15s
3m4½f Ch	Ecuyer Du Roi (15 Apr 2002)	7m19.80s	7m06s
2m Hdl	Royal Derbi (19 Sep 1988)	3m31.00s	3m38s
2m1½f Hdl	Baltic Storm (18 Sep 2016)	4m10.00s	4m05s
2m4½f Hdl	Urban Warrior (21 Sep 2008)	4m46.80s	4m48s
3m1f Hdl	Listen And Learn (18 Sep 2016)	5m49.80s	5m57s

Sandown

1m7½f Ch	Dempsey (28 Apr 2007)	3m43.40s	3m46s
2m4f Ch	Coulton (29 Apr 1995)	4m57.10s	4m57s
3m Ch	Arkle (6 Nov 1965)	5m59.00s	5m58s
3m5f Ch	Cache Fleur (29 Apr 1995)	7m09.10s	7m15s
2m Hdl	Olympian (13 Mar 1993)	3m42.00s	3m45s

PEARLS LEGEND: 2m chase stalwart set a new mark at Plumpton in April

2m4f Hdl	Oslot (28 Apr 2007)	4m35.70s	4m37s
2m5½f Hdl	L'Ami Serge (29 Apr 2017)	5m20.50s	5m00s
2m7½f Hdl	Rostropovich (26 Apr 2003)	5m39.10s	5m35s

Sedgefield

2m½f Ch	Mixboy (27 Sep 2016)	3m49.90s	3m50s
2m3½f Ch	The Backup Plan (27 Aug 2015)	4m38.80s	4m32s
2m5f Ch	Degooch (1 Sep 2016)	5m10.50s	4m58s
3m2½f Ch	The Gallopin' Major (14 Sep 1996)	6m29.30s	6m30s
3m5f Ch	Buachaill Alainn (27 Oct 2016)	7m20.40s	7m14s
2m1f Hdl	Country Orchid (5 Sep 1997)	3m45.70s	3m50s
2m4f Hdl	Grams And Ounces (27 Aug 2015)	4m32.80s	4m32s
2m5f Hdl	Palm House (4 Sep 1992)	4m46.30s	4m52s
3m3f Hdl	Pikestaff (25 Jul 2005)	6m19.70s	6m20s

Southwell

1m7½f Ch	Unify (27 Sep 2016)	3m53.70s	3m58s
2m4½f Ch	Gentleman Anshan (17 May 2011)	5m06.60s	5m04s
3m Ch	Best Boy Barney (22 Jul 2014)	6m10.10s	6m04s
3m1½f Ch	Midnight Jade (28 Feb 2016)	7m09.70s	6m26s
1m7½f Hdl	Dealing River (22 Jul 2014)	3m44.30s	3m42s
2m4f Hdl	Red Not Blue (17 May 2011)	4m57.30s	4m57s
3m Hdl	Jawaab (22 Jul 2014)	5m55.40s	5m50s

Stratford

2m1f Ch	Professeur Emery (1 Aug 2013)	3m56.70s	4m02s
2m3½f Ch	Gentleman Anshan (19 May 2013)	4m35.40s	4m40s
2m5f Ch	Spare Change (16 Sep 2007)	4m56.60s	5m01s
2m6½f Ch	Danandy (19 Jul 2015)	5m24.90s	5m25s
3m3½f Ch	Mossey Joe (7 Jun 2013)	6m38.30s	6m40s
2m½f Hdl	Chusan (7 May 1956)	3m40.40s	3m46s
2m2½f Hdl	Lostock Hall (24 Aug 2016)	4m17.30s	4m21s
2m6f Hdl	Broken Wing (31 May 1986)	5m06.80s	5m10s
3m2½f Hdl	Burren Moonshine (11 Jun 2006)	6m13.10s	6m17s

Taunton

2m Ch	I Have Him (28 Apr 1995)	3m49.50s	4m00s
2m2f Ch	Wait No More (28 Mar 2012)	4m24.90s	4m35s
2m5½f Ch	Howlongisafoot (12 Nov 2015)	5m31.80s	5m21s
2m7f Ch	Glacial Delight (24 Apr 2006)	5m39.80s	5m45s
3m2½f Ch	Jack Snipe (20 Dec 2016)	6m58.20s	6m30s
3m4½f Ch	No Buts (27 Apr 2017)	7m21.70s	7m09s
2m½f Hdl	Indian Jockey (3 Oct 1996)	3m39.40s	3m50s
2m3f Hdl	Prairie Spirit (2 Apr 2009)	4m19.70s	4m27s
3m Hdl	On My Toes (15 Oct 1998)	5m30.20s	5m33s

Towcester

2m Ch	Pinkie Brown (5 Oct 2016)	3m51.90s	3m52s
2m4f Ch	Rakaia Rosa (4 May 2017)	4m53.40s	4m49s
2m5½f Ch	Midnight Shot (4 May 2017)	5m14.30s	5m16s
3m½f Ch	Lucky Luk (29 May 2009)	5m52.60s	5m53s
1m7½f Hdl	Moonday Sun (5 Oct 2016)	3m42.60s	3m43s
2m3f Hdl	Ballygrooby Bertie (19 May 2014)	4m31.50s	4m36s
2m5f Hdl	Mailcom (3 May 1993)	5m00.90s	4m55s
3m Hdl	Dropshot (25 May 1984)	5m44.00s	5m40s

Uttoxeter

2m Ch	Festive Affair (2 Jul 2017)	3m45.70s	3m48s
2m4f Ch	Cut The Corner (19 Jul 2017)	4m55.10s	4m49s
2m6½f Ch	Brassick (26 Jul 2013)	5m35.60s	5m30s
3m Ch	Big Sound (9 Jun 2016)	6m00.10s	5m54s
3m2f Ch	Drop Out Joe (26 Jun 2016)	6m23.10s	6m25s
4m1½f Ch	Goulanes (15 Mar 2014)	8m41.30s	8m30s
2m Hdl	Mountainside (26 Jun 2016)	3m42.20s	3m39s
2m4f Hdl	Chicago's Best (11 Jun 1995)	4m39.10s	4m42s
2m5½f Hdl	Fealing Real (27 Jun 2010)	5m06.80s	5m05s
2m7½f Hdl	Princeton Royale (4 Oct 2015)	5m36.60s	5m32s

Warwick

2m Ch	Wells De Lune (20 Sep 2016)	3m51.00s	3m51s
2m4f Ch	Gone Too Far (22 Sep 2015)	4m55.60s	4m49s
3m Ch	Urcalin (1 Oct 2015)	5m52.60s	5m48s
3m1½f Ch	Kilfinichen Bay (20 Sep 2016)	6m27.50s	6m09s
3m5f Ch	Big Casino (24 Apr 2017)	7m37.10s	7m04s
2m Hdl (Outer)	High Knowl (17 Sep 1988)	3m30.80s	3m33s
2m Hdl (Inner)	Satanic Beat (1 Oct 2015)	3m38.60s	3m38s
2m3f Hdl (Outer)	Blairs Cove (13 May 2017)	4m32.50s	4m26s
2m3f Hdl (Inner)	Midnight Mint(22 Sep 2015)	4m25.60s	4m21s
2m5f Hdl (Outer)	Bendomingo (13 May 2017)	4m57.10s	4m50s
2m5f Hdl (Inner)	Atlantic Gold (1 Oct 2015)	4m54.10s	4m50s
3m1f Hdl (Inner)	The Tourard Man (24 Apr 2017)	5m56.40s	5m45s
3m2f Hdl (Outer)	Braventara (4 Nov 2016)	6m18.50s	6m03s
3m2f Hdl (Inner)	Mr Shantu (22 Sep 2015)	6m08.60s	5m57s

Wetherby

1m7f Ch	Oliver's Gold (14 Oct 2015)	3m41.60s	3m43s
2m3½f Ch	Village Vic (14 Oct 2015)	4m44.80s	4m45s
2m5½f Ch	Rosquero (4 May 2016)	5m17.60s	5m14s
3m Ch	Irish Cavalier (29 Oct 2016)	5m59.70s	5m57s
2m Hdl	Lightening Rod (31 Oct 2014)	3m43.20s	3m45s
2m3½f Hdl	Mustmeetalady (14 Oct 2015)	4m40.90s	4m34s
2m5½f Hdl	Kaysersberg (15 Oct 2014)	5m02.10s	5m09s
3m Hdl	Lilly's Legend (21 May 2015)	5m46.30s	6m04s
	Minella Hero (21 May 2015)	5m46.30s	

Wincanton

1m7½f Ch	Kie (13 Apr 2014)	3m37.90s	3m50s
2m4f Ch	Frodon (5 Nov 2016)	4m54.80s	4m56s
3m1f Ch	Swansea Bay (8 Nov 2003)	6m09.70s	6m15s
3m2½f Ch	Gullible Gordon (24 Oct 2010)	6m37.20s	6m44s
1m7½f Hdl	Cliffs Of Dover (14 Oct 2016)	3m22.60s	3m31s
2m4f Hdl	Deserter (14 Oct 2016)	4m28.30s	4m31s
2m5½f Hdl	San Satiro (23 Apr 2017)	4m53.10s	4m52s

Worcester

2m½f Ch	Owen Na View (30 Aug 2016)	3m51.60s	3m52s
2m4f Ch	Set List (8 Sep 2015)	4m47.80s	4m48s
2m7f Ch	Pawn Star (30 Aug 2016)	5m31.10s	5m35s
2m Hdl	Moonday Sun (30 Aug 2016)	3m37.30s	3m40s
2m4f Hdl	Mont Choisy (14 Oct 2015)	4m38.50s	4m44s
2m7f Hdl	Net Work Rouge (14 Oct 2015)	5m28.10s	5m22s

IRISH CAVALIER: Charlie Hall win was the best 3m time at Wetherby since the race two years earlier had led to the recent spate of remeasurements in Britain

Win - free form!

THIS YEAR'S QUIZ could hardly be more simple and the prize should prove invaluable to our lucky winner. We're offering a free subscription to The Jumps Form Book 2017-18, the BHA's official form book – every week up to April 2018, you could be getting the previous week's results in full, together with notebook comments highlighting future winners, adjusted Official Ratings and Racing Post ratings.

All you have to do is this: identify the three horses pictured on the following pages. And here's a clue – they all won at the Cheltenham Festival last season, doing so for the second year in a row.

Send your answers along with your details on the entry form below to:

2017-18 Jumps Annual Competition, Racing & Football Outlook, Floor 23, 1 Canada Square, London, E14 5AP.

Entries must reach us no later than first post on December 6. The winner's name and the right answers will be printed in the RFO's December 12 edition.

Six runners-up will each receive a copy of last year's form book.

Name..

Address..

....

Town..

Postcode..

In the event of more than one correct entry, the winner will be drawn at random from the correct entries. The Editor's decision is final and no correspondence will be entered into.

TSG
tsg.com

BETTING CHART

ON	ODDS	AGAINST
50	Evens	50
52.4	11-10	47.6
54.5	6-5	45.5
55.6	5-4	44.4
58	11-8	42
60	6-4	40
62	13-8	38
63.6	7-4	36.4
65.3	15-8	34.7
66.7	2-1	33.3
68	85-40	32
69.2	9-4	30.8
71.4	5-2	28.6
73.4	11-4	26.6
75	3-1	25
76.9	100-30	23.1
77.8	7-2	22.2
80	4-1	20
82	9-2	18
83.3	5-1	16.7
84.6	11-2	15.4
85.7	6-1	14.3
86.7	13-2	13.3
87.5	7-1	12.5
88.2	15-2	11.8
89	8-1	11
89.35	100-12	10.65
89.4	17-2	10.6
90	9-1	10
91	10-1	9
91.8	11-1	8.2
92.6	12-1	7.4
93.5	14-1	6.5
94.4	16-1	5.6
94.7	18-1	5.3
95.2	20-1	4.8
95.7	22-1	4.3
96.2	25-1	3.8
97.2	33-1	2.8
97.6	40-1	2.4
98.1	50-1	1.9
98.5	66-1	1.3
99.0	100-1	.0.99

The table above (often known as the 'Field Money Table') shows both bookmakers' margins and how much a backer needs to invest to win £100. To calculate a bookmaker's margin, simply add up the percentages of all the odds on offer. The sum by which the total exceeds 100% gives the 'over-round' on the book. To determine what stake is required to win £100 (includes returned stake) at a particular price, just look at the relevant row, either odds-against or odds-on.

RULE 4 DEDUCTIONS

When a horse is withdrawn before coming under starter's orders, but after a market has been formed, bookmakers are entitled to make the following deductions from win and place returns (excluding stakes) in accordance with Tattersalls' Rule 4(c).

	Odds of withdrawn horse	*Deduction from winnings*
(1)	3-10 or shorter	75p in the £
(2)	2-5 to 1-3	70p in the £
(3)	8-15 to 4-9	65p in the £
(4)	8-13 to 4-7	60p in the £
(5)	4-5 to 4-6	55p in the £
(6)	20-21 to 5-6	50p in the £
(7)	Evens to 6-5	45p in the £
(8)	5-4 to 6-4	40p in the £
(9)	13-8 to 7-4	35p in the £
(10)	15-8 to 9-4	30p in the £
(11)	5-2 to 3-1	25p in the £
(12)	100-30 to 4-1	20p in the £
(13)	9-2 to 11-2	15p in the £
(14)	6-1 to 9-1	10p in the £
(15)	10-1 to 14-1	5p in the £
(16)	longer than 14-1	no deductions

(17) .... When more than one horse is withdrawn without coming under starter's orders, total deductions shall not exceed 75p in the £.

**Starting-price bets are affected only when there was insufficient time to form a new market.*

Feedback!

If you have any comments or criticism about this book, or suggestions for future editions, please tell us.

Write

Nick Watts/Dylan Hill
2017-18 Jumps Annual
Racing & Football Outlook
Floor 23
1 Canada Square
London E14 5AP

email rfo@rfoutlook.com

Horse index

All horses discussed, with page numbers, except for references in the big-race form and novice sections (pages 83-120), which have their own indexes